In the
Shadow
of the
Pagoda

STERLING H. WHITENER

This book is dedicated

To the memory of
My missionary parents,
Sterling and Marie Whitener
and
Our daughter
Karen Marie

To my beloved wife,
Barbara

To our Children,
Chris
Kim
Bonnie
Dana
Katrina

Acknowledgements

It is impossible to write how important the role my wife, Barbara, accepted as editor. She helped me completely edit my story and add warmer touches to our family life. Her knowledge of our sixty-seven years together should identify her as a full partner in assuring some accuracy of many of my memories.

All of my children have been fully supportive and urged publication of these memories as a book instead of printing a few copies off the computer. They have generously contributed to inserting more pages of pictures.

Special thanks go to daughter, Kim, who has been a guide and a crucial helper in dealing with writing and publishing when I thought all I had to do was write a simple history-fable about my life.

Special thanks go to daughter, Bonnie, who completed a much appreciated copy edit of the manuscript as well as making invaluable suggestions.

Special thanks go to daughter, Dana, who has helped us in the final chapter edit process.

Natalie Mauceli helped with an early copy edit. Her suggestions on content led me to a clarification of style.

Bill and Lesley Barker have given many hours to scanning photographs to make them acceptable for prints in this book. All pictures from the 1920s to the present era were precious to us. What we are able to see is due to their dedicated help.

My good friend, Myles Walburn, has been a steady source of encouragement to get this manuscript completed and published.

I am most grateful to all for continuing interest and support.

Contents

Whitener Locations in China and Taiwan

- Lushan - Kuling American School 1930
- Yueyang - Mission Station - "Laujya" - Huping 1946
- Wuhan - "Liberation" 1948
- Hong Kong - Church and Refugee Work 1952 - 1967
- Taiwan - Teaching - Tainan Theological College 1984 - 1986

Foreword

I am attached to China. I was born in China and spent most of my formative years there. My aim always was to return to work in China, my "lau jia" (old home). Even my thought processes seem to maintain a connection. I find myself thinking through problems in a Chinese way. My family likes to joke that I am really half Chinese. Our friends laugh that my wife and I, in addition to many prior last trips, have made four "final" trips to China.

My parents went to Central China in 1919 and were assigned to mission work in the small town of Yochow in Hunan Province. Situated where the Dongting Lake flows into the mighty Changjiang, the Yangtze River, it was connected by rail in the early part of the 20th century to Hankow and Changsha. The name of the town changed as it grew; Yochow became Yoyang and then Yueyang, based on its population.

In 1928 when I was seven years old, my younger brother, Don and I shared a bedroom in an old Mission residence close to the hospital in our compound. Our room faced Yochow's famous Tang Dynasty (700 AD) pagoda, a tall sentinel overlooking the Dongting Lake. The view of this ancient stately pagoda, especially in the moonlight, was burned into my memory.

When I was ten, the first Christmas gift I received that year from America was a box camera from my favorite uncle. I proudly learned how to load the film and click. My greatest joy was finding interesting pagodas to photograph around Mt. Lushan where I was in boarding school. After I had bought my weekly supply of bakery cookies, my allowance was spent on film for my camera. Sadly, none of these early photo efforts have survived.

Because of my love for pagodas and, particularly, the Yochow pagoda, I felt its image belonged on the front cover of my story. This photograph was taken sometime in the 1930's by a member of our Mission, Edwin Beck, an outstanding photographer. It was given to us by another Mission colleague and dear friend, Gertrude Hoy, daughter of the founder of the Reformed Church Mission in Yochow.

A treasured gift, it is inscribed:

"To my "Lao peng-yu" (old/dear friends), Barbara and Sterling Whitener, with love and memories. – Gertrude" 3/3/76

The city Yochow probably had only a few thousand people in my earliest days, but now Yueyang must have a population of over half a million and has undergone tremendous physical changes as well. For me, the one constant remains – the Tang Dynasty pagoda. It continues to draw me to my "lau jia", my old family home!

Introduction

Throughout my life I have always wanted to record events and happenings important to me. As a result, at different times I have tried to write down my experiences with varying degrees of success. You will find that good intent was often sporadic and episodic. This has led me to struggle with the idea of assurance. Are my thoughts really fact or possibly fable? Napoleon once said, "What is history, but a fable agreed upon? By its very nature, history is always a one-sided account." (*The Da Vinci Code*, p 256)

Many years ago Barbara's and my first assignment as new missionaries was at Huping School outside Yueyang, central China. Teaching English to junior high, rural Chinese boys who had never heard many words of English, was severely trying. I decided that everyone ought to keep a log in order to remind one of life's difficulties and challenges. I located my effort a number of times over subsequent years but couldn't find it when I got started on this tome. In 1990, however, I uncovered the Sterling H. Whitener LOG, so flourishingly begun in September 1947. The entries show some interesting insights into our activities for only a few months. Sadly, it did not take long for the journal keeper in me to wind down, as I lacked both the discipline and the imagination to keep up a diary. I remember finding the small spiral notebook some ten years later when we were in HongKong and tried to begin again. The effort was quickly abandoned because I preferred analysis and thought pieces rather than mundane daily event recording.

In HongKong I got my start in analytical recording. A group of close missionary friends met every Saturday morning in the 1960s to share ideas and information and to study and analyze the current situation of that era. I was elected the task of writing the summaries that might eventually be helpful material for future scholars. These summaries can be located in my file of papers in the Day Missions China Archives Project at Yale Divinity School, New Haven, Connecticut.

During our 1984-1986 assignment to the Tainan Theological College and Seminary and Tunghai University in Taiwan, I was determined to keep a record of our work, life, and thinking. Nearly 100 computer pages later, I realized that it was not very readable, but had served its major purpose in helping me clarify what was taking place during some tense political days in that changing society.

A social work professor teaching human behavior at the University Of North Carolina Graduate School Of Social Work (1964) insisted that all of her students could remember something of one's birth experience. Otto Rank had convinced her that all class members should write up this memory. We managed to produce some interesting and varied stories. She was delighted and suggested that we now knew how history and life are interpreted and recorded. Our images and imagination were based on an actual experience buried deep in our subconscious.

This record may have a similar and yet quite different purpose. It is an effort to pull together memories; thoughts I may or may not have had, but wish I had; ideas that have come to me in later years, which have merged with dim concepts germinated years before. So let's agree that this is a record, part story and part fact, wishful thinking and memory, part fable and part history. My enduring aim, however, has been to give family members and friends a sense of Barbara's and my journey. I am indebted to my family members for pushing me in these later years to put the story together in the form of a book. I am very grateful for the part each has had in reading, correcting, editing and lending encouragement.

The fact that this history/fable was written in fits and starts accounts for its disjointed nature. A lapse of a year or so in getting to the task is not unusual. It follows a kind of time line, but at the same time I enjoy embellishing it with vague memories, facts, and feelings from other periods. Meandering came naturally. Readers may need to weave carefully through the maze thus created.

Chapter I

China – Birth, Growing Up, Schooling 1921 to 1938

Early Family History – Whitener

A winding staircase that seemed to be rolling from side to side, a big banister that I could just reach, some bars through which I could see a dining hall below – at age three these flashes are the very earliest memories I have. I was told the scene was on the SS "President Madison" when we were headed from China to the USA for furlough in the late spring of 1924. I was looking for Mom and Dad who were at dinner, though I cannot see how Dad could have been in the dining hall since he always took to his bed as soon as a ship reached the ocean swells. I had just escaped from the evening nursery and was quickly rescued by the children's nurse, much to my loud vocal displeasure....

Dad, Sterling Wilfong Whitener, was born August 12, 1894, in the Mountain View area outside of Hickory, North Carolina. When he was six, his father Daniel a schoolteacher died of pneumonia and "kidney poisoning." His mother Alice was left to raise six children, with the oldest, Gordon, only twelve. Dad, the fourth in line, helped with the two small ones. Remarkably, all children graduated from college. They lived on the old "home place" opposite Bethel Reformed Church.

In 1990, Aunt Suzie Uncle Gordon's widow, then in her 90s told me that the family had some very difficult days. A brother of Grandma Alice's, named Malcolm, was sent by their mother to help with the farming until the boys were old enough to do it all. She said that most often their suppers were cornbread and milk. The family was kept together but all had to work hard. Russell and Dad lived in a small boarding house in Startown so that they could go to high school, one of NC's farm community schools and then on to Catawba College in Newton. They worked for their room and board. Dad got some help from the church when he decided to go into the ministry.

Pictures of Dad during his college days at Catawba in Newton before it moved to Salisbury in 1925 show that he was thin. Aunt Suzie told me that he was a good student and that he wrote well. He was a track man, supposedly quite swift at the dashes. A classmate, Frank Fesperman, and Dad decided to enter the ministry. They were accepted by the Classis, a term for the organizational structure of the Reformed Church in NC, and enrolled in Central Seminary in Dayton, Ohio, in 1917.

When Dad decided to become a missionary is not clear, but in the war years (1917-1918) he was obviously influenced by the Student Volunteer Movement for Foreign Missions and the work of John R. Mott. Along with seminary classmates Frank Fesperman and George Snyder, he was accepted by the Foreign Mission Board of the Reformed Church to go overseas. Dad and George were assigned to go to China, Frank to Japan.

The scene shifts to the summer of 1918 when Dad was sent by the seminary as a student intern to the Prairie City Reformed Church, south of Kansas City and near Butler, MO. This experience in a charming farm community was very crucial to the future. He was paid only his expenses so lived with different farm families. They rode buggies to get around but social life revolved around the school/church. All services were held in the one-room rural school building which offered grades one through eight. In this community he met and stayed with the Christian and Anna Hegnauer family on their farm.

Hegnauer

Mom, Marie Anna Hegnauer, was the baby of the family of six children. She had completed the eight grades offered at the Prairie City School. Fable has it that Dad and Mom, age 18, conducted a very proper and sedate correspondence after the summer of church and group activities. Uncle Leonard, her brother, said that folks thought they were pretty "sweet" on each other. Sometime in the winter of '18-'19 Marie received a momentous letter indicating that Dad was prepared to accept official appointment by the Reformed Church Mission Board to go to China in the fall of 1919. He posed the big question: would Marie marry him and join the Mission enterprise? It was much to ask of an 18-year-old, but she was surely mature beyond her years.

This may not have come as a total surprise to Mom, but she said she had to consider this request very carefully because she felt she was not adequately educated to be a missionary. Her greatest support and encouragement came from Brother Leonard who as a young farmer with two children was her closest confidante along with her next elder sister Lizzie. As told by his children, it was several years later that Uncle Leonard felt called to serve the church. He uprooted his family from their farm to study for the ministry. He said it was the fact that his baby sister was serving on the Mission field, a world away in China that supported him and gave him his strongest motivation. He took his young family to the Moody Bible Institute in Illinois to prepare himself for a long lifetime of distinguished service as a pastor.

We have an official record of a contract that Dad signed with the Board of Foreign Missions of the Reformed Church in the US. Filled with legalese and signed by Dad, witnessed by Uncle Leonard and by President Good and Secretary Allen Bartholomew for the Board, the document stated and Dad agreed:

"to enter upon the work of Foreign Missions in behalf and in the service of the Board on his arrival in China, as an associate of the said Board's missionaries now in the field, and to remain in the active service of the Mission until providentially hindered or recalled by the Board."

For this the Board agreed, "To pay in US currency, or gold, a yearly salary of twelve hundred dollars." I often wonder if he ever got any gold! In China currency was called "Mex" for Mexican silver dollars, which were in common use. There were additional amounts guaranteed for each child, for travel for himself and his wife, and for expenses of outfit, etc. The date of the agreement was March 28, 1919. So we know that by age 19 Marie was engaged.

Mom and Dad were married in Rockville, Missouri on June 12, 1919, by the Rev. John C. Horning, West. Supt. H.M. (Western Superintendent of Home Missions?). The wedding certificate was witnessed by her sister Lizzie and fiancé, A. (Albert) J. Durst. For years I embarrassed my mother when in polite company I would proudly tell everyone "Mother and Dad were married on June 12th and I was born on the 27th!"

We can well imagine all the work the newlyweds had to undertake to get ready to travel by train, first to Hickory, North Carolina to visit the Whitener family; then to prepare to leave from Kansas City for San Francisco to sail via steamship to Shanghai, a sea journey of nearly a month. Aunt Suzie told me of the excitement of the family in going to the train station in Hickory to meet the new bride from Missouri. She said that Marie (Mom) was someone they were all curious about when Dad brought her to NC the first time in June 1919. She remembered how shy and red faced and lovely this 19-year-old farm girl was. She was "just like the rest of us and she sure could cook. She pitched right in and helped from the first. We all agreed that Sterling had picked a 'good one.'" She said it was a real special event as they gathered at the home place for a big celebration. Marie was so happy and jolly and made everyone love her.

In later years I remember that Mom always did seem "kinda special" to Grandmother, as we children were allowed the run of the house - even the parlor and porch. My cousin Alice tells me that they never got to go into those rooms except when we came home on furlough.

China: 1919 to 1925

Mom said that China was so strange and different she hardly had time to be homesick. They arrived in Shanghai and were sent immediately to Nanking for language school. They were traveling with George Snyder and his wife, so they did have some companionship. Study time was hard work. Pictures of language school days show them going together on some visits to temples and other famous landmarks. They spent nearly two years in study before they made their way to Yochow in Hunan Province, central China.

During this study time, they spent summers in Kuling, a unique, cool mountain oasis about 4,000 feet above the extremely hot plains. It was a summer resort established by foreigners back in 1900-1905. The Hoys and the Becks, members of our Mission, owned houses there as mission wives and children were sent to the mountains to escape the Yangtze valley heat.

I was born in Kuling at the Standard Oil Clinic Hospital on Sunset ridge just above the gap. A dimly typed half sheet of paper states that W. H. Venable, MD certified my birth date as June 27, 1921. My arrival definitely did not affect or slow down Mom's language study that year because she continued to have better spoken colloquial Chinese than Dad ever did.

They began their missionary work in Yochow in earnest in 1921. One job was the building of a new residence. With so many missionaries on the compound, living space had become very cramped; thus, my earliest memories are associated with the new home built for us some time in the mid-1920s.

Don was born on July 1, 1923, also in Kuling. This was a time of relative political calm in that period of "warlords." It would have been very difficult for Mom to have remained in the Yangtze valley for the summer with small children. Many missionary families lost young children to dysentery, cholera, and the usual childhood diseases. Life in the early days was for the hardy. Only a few pictures of early childhood days are reminders of what life was like.

Of those early years, Gertrude Hoy informed me that my parents were immediately thrust into the work of the Mission. Mom was even asked to help teach some of the women of the Women's Bible School who were training to become evangelists. Gertrude also said Mom really tried hard to help women learn how to knit gloves, sweaters and other garments for winter. She also organized for them a teacher of embroidery work which later was useful as an income producer.

Since wives of missionaries also had jobs, everyone hired helpers. We were always lucky to find healthy and strong servants. Our helpers were hired to buy our food on the street, cook, carry water, wash clothes and to keep the house clean. They became our friends.

An early memory is of my amah, Tata, who was my full time caretaker and teacher of Chinese. She was from the same village as our cook, Fu Qunyong, and his brother, Zhouyong, who had come to the city during hard times in the countryside. Our cook had learned from his own older brother, who had worked in the French consulate in Hankow how to cook for westerners. Zhouyong, who did all the other jobs, was our childhood favorite. He had such a pleasant disposition that we loved to be around him.

Early Memories: First Furlough – 1924

The clearest memories and impressions as we arrived in the USA after our voyage on the President Madison were of Missouri where we stopped first to visit Grandma and Grandpa "Chris" Hegnauer. Driving in the thick dust, he took me once with him on his rounds to collect eggs for the Rockville hatchery. Playing with my cousin Sterling Durst, named after

Dad by Mom's sister my Aunt Lizzie, was always a treat. It seemed we could do nothing but get in the way of the milking and the farm work. My cousin was also three.

Aunt Annie Laurie remembers that when Dad and family came home from China to North Carolina, about 1925, she and Uncle D.J. were living at the old Whitener home place opposite Bethel Church. She said she was scared to death to be there because she would have to do all the cooking for the whole crowd, so she got D.J. to find another place to live. He was teaching somewhere in a county school not too far away. She says that Grandma Whitener (Alice) was a very strong woman. She always took everyone in, but you did have to toe the line.

This strictness was something my cousin Alice also remembers, but her feeling was that Don and I got away with everything. We could even go into the parlor, which she and her sisters were never permitted to do. They lived a couple of miles away but visited the home place almost every Sunday. Still, they had to play outside or on the porch, NOT in the parlor. Parlor playing was permitted only when we came back from China on furlough.

Return to Yochow

We returned to Yochow uneventfully in the fall of 1925 to the new home that I remember so clearly. Don's and my chief activity was playing with our amah's son, "Luyi". His childhood name, pronounced correctly was, "lau yi" (oldest one). He was a year or so older than I was but considerably shorter and thinner. It was over 50 years later that I learned his name was Chen Lixian when he was a pharmacist in the Mission Hospital.

Don and I would get into sibling fights, but Lixian and Don together liked to jump on me. My mischievous nature often got me into trouble. Once, while running down the hall with a glass of water that I would not share with Don, I tripped and fell, cutting my arm near the wrist on the glass as it broke. The folks were at church so our faithful amah, TaTa, had to rush me to the hospital for stitches. The scar is still very visible.

Another common activity was for the three of us to wander around the compound to watch the carpenters or brick masons at work. The word we used for the walled-in area of the property owned by the Mission, including residences, girl's school, hospital and church was "compound" because it was the area completely surrounded by a six foot high brick wall. My favorite trick was to take a drink from the workmen's teapots. My folks never could break me of the habit of drinking as the workmen did – right from the spout because it tastes best that way. For years I preferred to make Chinese tea by adding fresh boiling water to the leaves, over and over again, and even chewing the leaves afterward. I no longer drink from the spout or chew up the leaves! Naturally, I flunk all Tuberculin skin tests, as I built up early immunity from my "teapot drinking" days.

Our cook arranged to make cookies available for me to "steal" for afternoon teas with my friend and playmate Yuan Mei, number two daughter of Pastor and Mrs. Tang. She was only a year or so older than me and would visit when Mrs. Tang came to visit Mom, her best friend. They lived next door to us in a small parsonage. Yuan Mei came to play in the afternoons after her kindergarten classes. She later would remind me that I was a superb thief. I reminded her that she was a real temptress who taught me everything I know about stealing cookies. Our wonderful cook always had an old cracked plate of them placed conveniently near the outside door so that she and I could carry them covertly into the shrubbery nearby to have our own tea party.

A very hazy picture comes to mind of an elderly, white-haired woman lying on a typical board bed piled high with satin covered, cotton batting-filled "pu gais" or comforters. The room was filled with many persons wearing white, the color of mourning. Small children were climbing up on the bed itself. About five years old myself, I wanted to climb with them, but Mother held my hand tightly. There were some women over at one side of the room moaning and crying. My mother had taken me with her to a dying. It was a family farewell or parting with a beloved mother, grandmother, and great grandmother. She never really opened her eyes, so I have no idea whether she was conscious. At some point, Pastor Tang asked the women to stop their crying because it was time for prayer and thanksgiving. The wailing stopped immediately. The pastor prayed for a long time. We all said our goodbyes to the old lady and to the family members. The funeral was held at the church several days later. It was my earliest experience with death, but it has left in me an understanding of the naturalness of this leave-taking of a loved one. It certainly was a cultural lesson that China has given me, one for which I am grateful.

The Revolution of 1927

This era was interrupted by the frequent battles and saber rattling of warlords. I can recall that we constantly heard threats of bandits nearby. Occasionally, we would hear gunfire in the hills outside of town, but in late 1926 and early 1927 things really got serious. The armies of Sun Yatsen's "Nationalist Party," led by General Chiang Kaishek, were on the march from Canton into Hunan. They were on their way to overthrow the corrupt warlords who had taken over many parts of the country after Yuan Shihkai had failed to maintain the Republic following the revolution of 1911. They also wanted to be sure to reach central China before the Communists, who had organized the Chinese Communist Party in 1921, took over. The Nationalist army was ready to come through our town.

Not only was the populace anxious about possible battles in Hunan province approaching Yochow, but the US Consulate sent an urgent warning that it would be important for all westerners to retreat to the larger cities. We were urged to evacuate to Hankow. Our own Mission Board asked us to leave China until the political situation was settled.

We left Yochow sometime in the spring of 1927 as refugees evacuating the interior. All I can remember of the trip to Shanghai was the small Japanese steamer on which we were given bunks in a large third-class cabin with about 50 other persons. I was on a top bunk, four high, but below me and around me many elderly Chinese gentlemen refugees were getting their last smoke of the evening. Unfortunately, the sickly sweet, yet pungent smell of opium, to this day, makes me feel queasy. This I know for sure. When traveling in the Golden Triangle of Thailand in 1985 with Bonnie and Tom, some of the tour group tried smoking a bit of opium in a remote mountain village. My nose and my memory made instant connection! I had to stay outside the bamboo smoking den to keep from getting sick.

A most vivid memory was the first talking movie that I ever saw, "Sunny Side Up," with singing, dancing and talking was quite a treat for a-six-year-old! I think we got to see several movies, but none was ever as exciting as that first one in the big city of Shanghai where we waited as refugees to secure reservations for passage home to the US.

My brother Don reminds me that we traveled with another MK (missionary kid) named Richard Winter, who kept needling us that the ship he was going to sail to America on was so much better and more important because it was a "President" while our ship was only the "Empress of Asia." We convincingly argued with that five-year-old that our ship had three funnels, proving superiority over the single-funneled President McKinley.

It was just at this time that the founder of the Mission, Dr. William Hoy, had a fatal heart attack as he was preparing to sail on the "President McKinley" for retirement in Greensboro, North Carolina. It was definitely the end of an era. The government of the first republic established in 1911 in Peking disintegrated and the new Nationalist Party established the New Republic of China with the capital in Nanking. Our destination that spring of 1927 was the USA, and we had no idea when we might return.

Extra Furlough, 1927 to 1928 – Thomasville, North Carolina

Visiting Mother's parents and her own brothers and sisters in Missouri so soon after we had left was especially exciting. Even though I was six in the summer of 1927 everything was new and very important. The things I seem to see most vividly, aside from the Missouri clay dust and the Ford Model Ts and Model As, are the wooden outhouses with old Montgomery Ward catalogues and sometimes corn cobs available in little wooden boxes. This was quite a change from our more civilized interior toilet facilities in China. Our wooden box seats with their tin containers always smelling of Lysol, and our local toilet paper, an improvement over Montgomery Ward catalogues, gave me an early sense of the historic superiority of culture in China.

After we reached Missouri in June, we visited all the relatives again for a few months. I asked Grandpa to take me out to the farms with him since the taste of pies, cookies and cakes were worth the dusty trips. We would go in his Model T Ford to the farms to collect the boxes of eggs which he would pile in the back. At the farmhouses we often had a chance to eat pieces of wonderful pies and cakes that had just come out of the oven. With a cool glass of milk, stored in a bucket cranked up out of the well, the refreshment was fantastic.

It seemed as though everything had to be cranked. Grandpa had to crank the truck. Since I was a little older, I loved to pull on the spark lever after he got the engine to turn over. After the morning's "helping" him, I never could eat any lunch. I do remember well the special event that transpired at the end of a day's run when Grandpa took me with him to a small store where he ordered a drink. I was given a glass of some kind of orange or grape pop. One time I insisted that I get a taste of his drink. He allowed me a sip. As the foam dripped down my chin, my face squinched up at the bitterness; so to this day, beer is NOT my favorite beverage.

Cousin Sterling knew many games which were fascinating and for the first time I was old enough to observe and understand farm life in America. Sterling Durst sure knew a lot about animal reproduction and assisted in my early sex education. He tells me that I was always a strange sort who seemed to know all kinds of useless facts about the world but nothing about real games and practical stuff! My older cousin Albert Stevenson was a lesson in relationships as I watched him kiss his girlfriend. They did get married. Life was definitely quite different in America!

Later in the summer, we headed to North Carolina where Dad was going to take up a charge of 3 churches in Thomasville. Again, we first visited the home farm house where Grandma Whitener lived. The home place itself was a two-storied frame farmhouse. The upstairs bedrooms where we stayed were reached by way of an exterior porch walkway. There was no central plumbing. The outhouse was out back. The well, with a crank-up bucket near the kitchen door, always had a big dipper hanging nearby so with some help one could crank up a bucket of cool water for a drink.

I recall playing with cousins Hazel, Alice, and sometimes Frances. The latter was too young to be much of a playmate. Our games took place out under the big trees or in the barn. One game that fascinated me was "Doctor." Hazel, who was several years older than Alice and me, always took charge. Alice, Don and I were alternating patient and nurse. Without any sisters of my own, it was my first lesson in female anatomy.

Dad clearly felt that he would need to serve some churches since we had just returned to China from furlough only a year earlier. Uncle Leonard, Uncle Albert and Aunt Lizzie decided to drive us the 800+ miles to NC. Back then we traveled for a number of days. I remember how very crowded we all were in two Model A Fords even with all baggage tied outside on the running boards. The interesting part of the trip was over the mountains. The roads had not changed since our earlier trip in 1924. They were mostly gravel and sometimes just mud, so we did get stuck at times and everyone had to get out to help push.

The three Reformed churches, Calvary, Zion, and Emanuel in Thomasville were small, wooden church structures. Only Emanuel had Sunday school rooms. Two were painted white, but Zion was unpainted inside and out and stood up on unenclosed short wood pilings. It was always fearfully cold in winter, so we crowded around the big pot-bellied stove. The people were friendly. We had a four-door "Whippet" car, which was always loaded down by the parishioners with fruits, vegetables, and home canned goods after almost every service. Many churches had "preaching" only twice a month because money was scarce. Emanuel, somewhat larger, met every Sunday. We lived in Thomasville in a small two-storied frame house that was not insulated. Our wood stove did not really heat very well, but we did have a new-fangled electric stove in the kitchen.

Several events left a lasting impression. A young man of about 17 in one of the church families had appendicitis and died. He was such a nice guy, that for many years afterward I felt that I would never live to be 18. It really was a relief to reach that age. Another incident, vivid in my memory happened as we were coming home from church one Sunday. An accident had occurred on a steep gravel road shortly before we came upon the scene where a car had skidded off the side and into some trees. Quite a crowd gathered. Dad went down the embankment to see what he could do. He came back with a very grim report that most of the family had been badly shaken up, several with cuts, but the father had gone through the windshield. In those days the glass was not shatterproof. His throat was cut and no one could stop the bleeding. Though we were not allowed to go see, the fear of an accident preyed on all of us for a long time.

School was about a mile or so away from our parsonage which was on the edge of town. I thought it was miles and miles, for as a six-year-old I walked each day to and from with a neighbor girl. On rainy days she got to ride in her father's Buick since he was the dealer. I was lucky because I got to ride, too. The first-grade teacher, Miss Eastly, was well known and I liked her very much. My mother had taught me to read, add, and write, so things went well at school.

Next door lived a boy who must have been over 12 years old. He seemed huge to me at the time. He did not have much to do with us little kids. One day, however, he saw us playing with the water hose out in our small front yard. We were squirting each other and having a great time. He came over and decided to squirt water in my face. I was holding the metal nozzle for dear life as he grabbed it and turned it into my face. It slipped, naturally, and took a chip off my front tooth. This really hurt! We were very careful not to play with that BIG guy after that. The dentist told us that the tooth should not be worked on for a few years until I was in my teens. Hot and cold food bothered my tooth, but like any Hunanese country boy, I learned to love red peppers instead.

The father of the bully next door remarried sometime during our year in Thomasville. The wife, much younger, did not dress as sedately as Mom did, as she was the preacher's wife. The neighbor wore the 1926-'27 flapper short dresses. Don and I used to love to go out into our backyard to watch her hang up the laundry or to look across at their kitchen window in the mornings, because the husband always kissed his wife goodbye before going to work. To the uninitiated this was SEX. This interesting performance was much more protracted than the kisses and pecks we were accustomed to seeing in our home. In this connection, however, we did welcome a baby brother, Robert Wilfong, born the 21st of November 1927 in Thomasville.

Return to China: 1928 to 1930

Before the end of the summer of 1928, we were packed up again and ready to return to Yochow. The revolutionary armies had ended up in Nanking and the warlords were back in business, though, nominally, they were a part of the central Kuomintang government. This return to the field was much more exciting than earlier trips because the activities aboard the President Lines passenger ship provided contests for children. We kept the deck stewards hopping just to keep an eye on us!

We landed once again in Shanghai. Don and I knew we were getting close when they closed the outdoor seawater swimming pool, and then a day later the toilets began to flush with muddy Yangtze delta water. Mom and Dad had a busy agenda to buy many supplies needed by schools, hospital, and fellow missionaries upriver in Yochow. All household items manufactured in China were usually from Shanghai, so purchasing and delivering necessities always proved to be a major task for travelers. We finally boarded one of the Butterfield & Swire or Jardine riverboats to begin a week-long trip back to our home.

Headed up the Yangtze River our cabins on the Tuckwo had windows so we could see what was going on, day or night. Often the small ship would slow down and whistle loudly, always waking us up. A large sampan would come alongside, with six men rowing. They would bring goods and passengers from small riverside communities. We also tied up at floating piers at all the larger towns and cities, Anjing, Wuhu, Nanjing, Jiujiang, and finally Wuhan, where we disembarked.

On shipboard, we loved to go to the open ventilator windows where we could peer down into the engine room. Marvels of steam propulsion machinery built in Scotland were lasting attractions. Of course we examined with care the large steel plate shields that could be lowered at the deck railing if any bandits on shore decided to take rifle shots at us. Only a couple times in my memory were there "pings" from the shots. These occasions were repeated later when I was going from home to school in Kuling or back.

Although Chiang Kaishek had organized a new government, there were still many soldiers/bandits who had their rifles and sought a livelihood through intimidation. In those days, British, American, and French gunboats on the river, ostensibly to protect their nationals, served to reassure us.

At age seven, I did not understand the idea of "Unequal Treaties," "Imperialism," or other terms assigned to foreign occupation. I did not realize that we were so privileged. I did not know that even missionaries had more money than most of our Chinese friends. We certainly did live in much better houses than they did, but I thought it was all right because our houses were just like the ones of our families in the US.

We disembarked in Hankow and made our way by train to Yochow. There had been some looting and destruction of property, so we were unable to return to our own home until repairs had been made. As mentioned earlier, we lived inside a large, wall-enclosed compound.

The property had once belonged to the London Missionary Society, but in 1900, Dr. William Hoy, a missionary of our Reformed Church in Japan, suffered so from asthma that he went to China to see if there would be some way to work there. He was led to visit Yochow in Hunan at the invitation of the London Missionary Society. This British Congregational Society, the earliest Protestant Mission group, had found the depression of the late 1890s a heavy burden on their resources and welcomed the interest of the Reformed Church of America.

The location of the property was convenient to a new railway station, yet only a few hundred yards from the Dongting Lake, which made this town a very strategic one. The mouth of the lake emptied into the Yangtze River only five miles away, so the town was a major transshipping and commercial port. Here many rafts of logs, cut in the forests of west Hunan, were combined, enlarged then floated or towed downstream to the major cities of China. The lake also provided large fish for drying and salting for shipment to the large cities.

Because of the importance of this center, the Mission compound became the focus for a major effort on the part of the Reformed Church to provide a small church, a girls' school, a hospital, and a women's Bible Training Institute. Expansion of the property encroached on a large burial ground. This was not really a cemetery, but presented a problem that remained with the church for some time, as alleged relatives tried to collect compensation for the moving of graves illegally placed on city property. Our wall was designed not necessarily to keep people out, but rather to delineate the boundaries as was customary in China. We could view the railway station from our house so could always tell when the express train arrived and then go get aboard, as schedules meant very little in pre-Communist China. Steam engines were switched or refueled and watered in Yochow.

Our own house which was at the back of the compound not far from the railroad station was being repaired after the ravages of the 1926-1927 revolution. We lived temporarily in the upstairs of a large home, named after Dr. Stukey, which was adjacent to the hospital. This was near the center of activities of the Mission, not far from the main gate to Mission property. As I wrote on the first page, in 1928 when I was seven years old, my younger brother Don and I shared a bedroom in this old Mission residence. Our room faced Yochow's famous Tang Dynasty (700 AD) pagoda, a tall sentinel overlooking the Dongting Lake. The view of this ancient stately pagoda, especially in the moonlight, was burned into my memory.

There was another family, the Yaukeys, whose two boys were several years younger also lived in a home adjacent to the hospital and church. The single ladies lived nearby. One was a very rotund nurse, Alice Traub; one, a schoolteacher at Ziemer Girls School, petite Gertrude Hoy, daughter of the Mission founder, Dr. and Mrs. Hoy.

While we were living in the Stukey house, the downstairs served as a kind of guest area for Chinese evangelists and friends who were passing through town. On one occasion, the principal of Huping school, which was four miles out of town, was the guest because he was going to the hospital in Hankow for some tests. It appears that no one quite knew the seriousness of his condition or he would have been admitted to our hospital next door. In any case, to the surprise of everyone, he died in his sleep. This was a real problem, as there was no embalming facility in Yochow. We children watched with great interest as the heavy, solid wood coffin was brought into the basement area. The inside of the coffin was nearly filled with lime and then covered with silk cloth. The body was brought all wrapped up and placed in the coffin. I am sure that the Mission kids were not expected to be such interested onlookers. It seems to me, however, that we stood on the back steps where a small window afforded a view of the room in which all the undertaking chores were being performed.

Another visitor was General Wang Yu. We liked him very much because he had some horses and would sometimes take us riding with him out beyond the train station near the lake. This area was always filled with backwater in the summer and early fall, but later when the waters receded, there was lush grass for the farmers' cattle and water buffalos. General Wang had a large white horse, not just the usual small Mongolian pony. I have a vivid memory of his holding Don on the horse with him. General Wang was a Christian who read his Bible every morning. A great favorite of the family, he served Generalissimo Chiang Kaishek to the best of his ability, but resigned from the army a few years later. He retired on his farm, not too far from Yueyang, to grow fruit trees and develop new ways for farmers to earn cash income. Years later, in 1946 when we returned to China as missionaries, he was in retirement a dedicated layman and the Church chairperson of the North Hunan District Association of the Church of Christ in China, Hunan Synod. At that time he reminded me of our rides out on the grassy plain. Tragically, he was martyred in the early Communist years because of his service in the Nationalist army and, in addition, was a landowner.

Not long after our return to Yochow, Dzau Lauban (contractor, Dzau) was able to complete renovations on our former home. We moved there gladly as Don and I could easily watch what was going on at the Ziemer Girls' School, and also over our back wall toward the railway station. Contractor Dzau was a grizzled carpenter who was always holding his fist over his mouth in the hope that we would then be unable to smell the fumes of his ever-present rice wine breath. He had a cadre of hard workers whom he set up at a work place to saw the logs into boards and two by fours. They made everything from scratch; all our parents had to do was to draw what they wanted and HOPE for the best. He was our builder in the 1920s and again in 1946 when Barbara and I returned.

It was a custom of all the ladies of the Mission to gather for late afternoon tea at one of the homes. Children were permitted to come by for a snack. For years, I was reminded that at one of these events, when we were visiting Miss Gertrude Hoy's home, I vowed that when I grew up I would marry her because she had such beautiful embroidered tea cloths. The fact was that Hunan was famous for its cross-stitched type of embroidery. Mom supplied many women with work making tablecloths, napkins, dresser scarves, and other pieces often sent back to the USA for sale.

It was a confusing era but Mother did begin teaching me the second-grade materials received from Baltimore, titled "Calvert Course for Elementary Study." Our days were pretty full. In the mornings I was placed at a little desk to begin my schoolwork. This was the CALVERT course, taught by Mom. I do not know the origin of "Calvert," but it was a fully accredited course of study with teacher's guides, student workbooks, and grade sheets, which were submitted back to Baltimore, MD, where the company was registered. The Board saw to it that the materials arrived in good time. It was always fun to help unpack the big boxes with Mom. Although she had not studied beyond the eighth grade in her little country school, she was an avid reader and had really educated herself. Mrs. Grace Yaukey, her good friend, was the sister of nationally famous Pearl Buck. Grace was herself an authoress (pen name, Cornelia Spencer). She once told me that she had never known a person who had educated herself as Mom did, who spoke such perfect colloquial Chinese and had such a pleasant, outgoing personality.

Schooling went well. As I had completed first grade in a "real school" I just knew it all, especially how lessons should be taught. I am sure I gave Mom a fit telling her how Miss Eastly (my first teacher in Thomasville) would have done it. Perhaps the reason I really learned was that Don, two years my junior, always bugged me to read to him what I had learned that day. As a result, I covered everything twice, once for Mom and then later for Don. I credit his shining success at Catawba College graduating Summa Cum Laude, and Johns Hopkins Medical School to his early education from a seven-year-old teacher. What I know for a fact is that I could never match his grades! It was just lucky I was older and bigger.

We managed to get into many differences of opinion with some of the local school kids. Boys from teachers' families lived inside the compound. Sometimes they had visitors from outside who seemed to take an acute dislike to foreigners. These were troubled times and there was much agitation by anti-Western groups who demonstrated against the unfair and unequal treaties that had been forced on China early in the century. As the Chinese developed a sense of national purpose and identity, the weakness of the central government was very obvious. Western learning was crucial to the development of the nation, but at the same time the idea of copying the West was galling to many intelligent persons. The schools run by Mission groups were the best in China. They caused resentment, however, since they produced an elitist group who became leaders in all walks of life because of their superior, scientific training. Thus, our own brushes with school kids usually resulted in some rock throwing and other face-offs. We were cautioned not to get into fights, but that did not always deter us. The Chinese boys with whom we played in the compound were looked upon by the outsiders as having "sold out" to foreigners so they often were right there with us protecting our turf.

The main street of Yochow was always fascinating to missionary children who were warned never to go out of the gate of our compound alone. Not much chance of that in any case during our younger years, as we always had an amah tagging along to make sure we did not get into trouble. The town had only one main street stretching along the top of the long embankment of the lake itself. All along the lakefront there were small alleyways, as well as a few wide commercial streets to accommodate the many men carrying their heavy loads from boat to shore and vice versa. The lake traffic also attracted us. We often asked to go down to view the busy boat life.

We regularly went to Huping boys' school four miles southwest of town. Usually we went by small wooden sampan rowed with double oars from a standing position in the rear by a strong boatman. Sometimes there would be another person in the bow of the 12 to 14 foot boat. If the wind was blowing a sail would be hoisted. We would make our way along the side of the Dongting Lake within view of Junsan, a large and famous island across the lake. We were never able to visit the island in my childhood, as it was always occupied by "bandits," whoever they were.

There were a few tugs and an occasional small river passenger steamer wending their way upstream to Changsha. Mostly, the lake was literally full of small sailboats and larger freight junks carrying cargo from upstream to the major cities along the river. The multicolored and many-times patched sails propelled both the sleek and newly tung-oiled boats, as well as older and decrepit looking craft. The sailors usually were able to sail both upstream and down so there was always plenty of activity.

With no others to organize any games, Don and I carried on the usual sibling rivalry, but once again I paid dearly for being larger, stronger, and more bullying. We had an aluminum pitcher of drinking water which we had carried with us as we went somewhere to climb trees. In my mind, I still see the flagstone walkway and small gate that led to our home at the back end of the compound. We were headed home and were drinking the water out of the side of the pitcher. It was nearly gone and Don insisted on his right to a share of the remaining supply. I grabbed the pitcher from him and immediately started to drink. The next thing I knew there was an explosion in my face as Don hit the bottom of the pitcher with his fist. I must admit that he has since been known as the "gentle, sweet" brother. At that time, though, he was definitely a determined little cuss! A cut lip wasn't so bad, nor the shattered dignity, but a second chip off my front tooth was damage indeed and that from a five-year-old! I lived with a very large hole between my two front teeth until I was sixteen.

One of our favorite pastimes over the years was associated with a group of very large trees near our home. These ancient trees must have been a part of an old temple courtyard, because large trees were a rare commodity in town. Even in the countryside all the trees were cut for firewood as soon as they grew an inch thick. These trees held ancient wisteria vines, which were three or four inches thick. They could hardly have grown so big in the time the Mission had held the property (perhaps 35 years).

Our play consisted of using the trees as "Yankee Clippers," with the wisteria vines the rigging for the sails. We would climb up to the top of the trees, some 50 or 60 feet in the air to serve as lookouts, as captain, or whatever. I suppose by age nine I was quite daring, though I do not remember ever hearing our parents complain about our climbing. It may be that they did not know how high we could get.

Once, a missionary family in Changsha gave us a beautiful dog, a white setter with black spots. Peggy was a wonderful companion. One difficulty was that we wanted to take her upstairs to bed with us. This just was not allowed. She became subject to the diseases that Chinese "wonks," mixed breed dogs, seemed immune to. She died one summer while we were in Kuling. We decided that western domestic animals were not acclimatized to China conditions.

We often went to Huping for Mission or prayer meetings and to visit Nana Hoy. My memories of her husband, Dr. William Hoy, who founded the Mission in 1900, are less clear. Nana was a very strong woman and a real matriarch. In 1910 she had founded Ziemer Girls School, the first school for girls in North Hunan. She was noted for her flower gardens.

Another missionary, Edwin Beck, lived next door to the Hoys. He was an excellent photographer who had a large collection of beautiful photos of the sailboat traffic on the lake. He also took the picture of the pagoda which is featured on the cover of this book. He was noted for his use of a "belly band" (a wide wrapping of flannel cloth) because he always had stomach trouble. I can still see him sitting in an easy chair or at the table with a blanket around him. How he taught the boys English I don't know, because he hardly dared leave his house for fear his bowels would move unexpectedly. They were always in an "uproar." His favorite food was the beef extract "Bovril." I always have liked it, partly because he really did not want us to take any of his — we always had to sneak a taste. His wife, Irene, was of the famous Ohio Poling family who never let us forget it. In later years, I learned to appreciate his son Bob who was in seminary at Yale when I was. Though several years older than I, he and his twin sister Mary both attended Kuling American School. We saw them in the summer as the Becks owned bungalow #160 next to the KAS campus on Kuling.

A Special Note: In 1947 Barbara & I bought the bungalow from the Becks for the princely sum of $750, a half of our yearly salary. We spent only one summer there, as it was taken over by the Communist government in 1949. During the 1970s after the "war claims" settlement, to our complete surprise, we received payment plus 6% interest. With 30 years' interest, we received the tidy sum of $2,500.

Christmas in Yochow

I have a mental picture of going out to Huping Boys' School to look for a Christmas tree. The only ones around were scraggly pines growing on the hillsides, both inside the campus walls and outside. We usually went out to the nearby hills in order to avoid cutting trees within the campus. We took the tree back to town in a sampan; Dad would nail a board to the bottom, and we proudly gathered around the beautiful pine Christmas tree in our living room.

Don and I got busy with flour paste and cut strips of colored paper to make long chains to hang on the tree. Some tinsel from the USA was carefully hoarded and handed out to us to decorate with the final touches. We had small candle holders to clip to the ends of the boughs for colored candles in a few carefully chosen spots. In the evening Mom lit them for only a short while as we sang Christmas carols. Luckily, we did not light them often, because I now realize how dangerous the candle flames really were.

We always opened our presents on Christmas Eve because there were so many church activities on Christmas day. In any case, the presents were given out, one by one, until all were distributed. Then each person opened one at a time, beginning with the youngest.

We had an open coal fire in the grate of our living room. By the light of the kerosene lamps and the fire, the room was cheery and spirits were high. Mother had a good voice and could play hymns pretty well on the little pump organ, so we learned at a young age to sing carols as well as most of the hymns in the hymn book.

Learning the Hard Way

A very keen memory of early days in Yochow was the anti-foreign feeling among the youth. Students were always stirred into revolutionary fervor and, of course, this was often attributed to the Communists. Just prior to the revolution of 1926 - '27, when I was about six years of age, I can remember being cautioned often about going out of the main front gate of the compound which was on the main street. We were told that gangs might try to beat us up. This did not mean that we never sneaked out of the gate. In fact, we became quite adept at frustrating the gatekeeper. He often scolded us soundly when we finally made our way back in.

Our favorite excursion was to the "yo tyau" shop near the big, ancient pagoda just down the street. We would find a few coppers and then go out to buy these delicacies. Just plain twisted dough, about a foot long and quickly deep-fried in peanut oil, they tasted much better than anything we could find at home – like cookies. We did know enough to insist that the vendor use chopsticks to hand us the deep fried dough stick directly from the hot smoking oil in the wok. Ones that were standing around had many flies on them and of course had been handled many times. Funny thing, we learned at a very young age the essentials of hand washing and elementary hygiene. Kids who did not learn, often had dysentery and many died. Little

Herbie Beck, son of the Karl Becks at Huping, was a case in point in our own Mission, so we knew firsthand what would happen. He contracted dysentery in the early 1930s and died.

We frequently found ourselves in shouting matches within the compound with boys our age who were attending the Mission primary school, but outside was much, much worse. Even when we were walking down the main street with our parents we would often be followed by a ragged and shouting band of children shouting "yang gwei dz" (foreign devil) or "gau bi dz" (big, high-bridged nose) to annoy us. We had learned a number of choice swear words and phrases that our parents did not use or really understand so we managed to give as well as take.

On one occasion I vividly remember walking toward the railroad station on the dirt street with Dad when the taunts got worse and worse. Finally, one boy my age threw a small rock at us. This was the last straw. I quickly reached down, picked up the rock, and had drawn back my arm to throw it when I was immobilized by Dad's hand over my wrist. Shaking the rock out of my hand, he said, "No matter what they do, you cannot throw rocks or shout bad language at them." It was clear that missionary kids were expected to behave quite differently from normal folk. It was a lesson, however, that I never forgot.

Summers on Kuling (Early Days)

Kuling, the mountain summer resort on Lushan in Jiangxi province was established by Westerners in 1902. The Chinese term "Lushan", means Mount Lu. The mountain is roughly 3,500 to 4,000 ft. in elevation in a very small range next to the Poyang lake. Kuling was originally organized by E. S. Little, a British missionary who lived in Jiujiang on the Yangtze River at the foot of the then very sparsely occupied mountain. Little resigned from the Mission and became a business man. He purchased the land (illegally, I understand) from a Manchu official in Jiujiang in order to make it possible for families to escape the summer heat. . It was not easy to get permission to develop the top of Lushan Mountain even though, at that time, it was home only to small temples and firewood cutters who denuded this small mountain range by cutting brush to make charcoal and firewood. A century earlier the mountain had been home to a large number of temples and monasteries, which had fallen into complete disrepair. In the modern era there were only three or four left.

A summer resort for missionaries and Westerners was urgently needed because the lowland of the Yangtze valley was so full of summer pestilence and deadly diseases that many foreigners succumbed to dysentery, cholera, typhoid, and numerous other endemic diseases. Our Mission Board did not have houses there, as some did, but several of our early missionaries did buy small stone bungalows so that they could get away in retreat for a vacation. Little was the grandfather of a New Zealand missionary friend, Peggy Hawkings, who served the London Missionary Society in Wuhan when we were there in the 1950s, and who also loved to go to their mission cottage in Kuling.

Summers spent in Kuling were very special. We once lived in Grace Yaukey and Pearl Buck's house on Highland Ave. We managed to rent other missionary cottages when the owners went to the US on furlough. I learned to swim at age 3 in a pool called "Russian Pool" and another named "Duck Pond" in the main stream in Kuling. In my early days, probably when I was about five, it was increasingly troublesome for Mother to take us to the Russian Pool every day. It had lifeguards but it did cost an admission price. After all, what do active children do but "bug" parents to go swimming or go somewhere? I recall that Mom eventually let us go down to a pool that had been dammed up in the main stream. In those days pollution was not as great, I believe, even though the runoff from the whole valley found its way into this main stream. This pool was public property so anyone could come to swim there but there were no lifeguards. We would get a bunch of kids together to go to the pool, Duck Pond.

Since this pool was a small one with a deep end next to the dam, it was not exactly a wading and children's pool. All of us had learned to swim and really were quite adept. Sometimes an amah was sent with us so that someone would be aware of what was going on and was charged to get assistance if it appeared any child was in trouble. Usually there were a number of older youth present who would help pull us out.

Most vivid for me was learning the crawl stroke from a Norwegian Olympic swimmer, Nicolai Shaier, the Norwegian husband of Mabel, one of the daughters of the founders of our Mission, Dr. & Mrs. William Hoy. My first instructor, he was a superb swimmer and diver, a marvelous athlete. He spent many hours with us little ones. I have always been grateful for his careful instruction, which I tried over the years, sometimes successfully, to pass on to my children and grandchildren.

Memories of those early years in Kuling consistently revolve around community social activities and group play. This was an important part of growing up in China, acculturation to other Western kids mostly American. Though we had many summer church-related activities, such as Bible School and Sunday services, we also learned how to visit in homes. My mom took special care to indoctrinate us in being polite when we visited Bishop and Mrs. Tyng's Sunday afternoon tea and music sessions. Ann, a year older than I was, always played the piano or an instrument. We learned to sit quietly to "appreciate" the sometimes painfully rendered pieces.

My earliest clear Kuling summer memories, however, center on a house up near Methodist valley where we lived with the Hilgemans, also of our Mission. He was a teacher at the seminary in Wuchang. A younger couple, they stayed with us in order to share costs. He was always on the wide porch reading. I slept on the porch on a cot and I remember the moon shining in my face at night. Our chief activities were hiking, swimming, and later gang fighting up on the ridge. I also remember joining a boys' brigade type of pre-scouting troop where we did some tent camping. The leader was a Mr. Kolness, a Norwegian missionary. I felt rather left out because he never invited me to sleep in his bed with him and his two or three favorite boys. His wife had a new baby so we sometimes helped carry the child around because the amah was busy washing clothes. It was quite a few years later that I learned he had been packed off back to Norway for molesting young Chinese students at the school where he taught.

As we grew older and more independent, probably aged 8 or 9, we were increasingly involved with the missionary kids of the neighborhood. We all went together to the Kuling community auditorium for several weeks of summer Bible study. Here the most dedicated teachers were Pentecostal (so-called "faith") missionaries who stressed that they were doing the work of the Lord without pay because they relied on gifts from prayer partners at home. It never did cease to amaze me that they seemed to have more money and things than we did and liked to brag about their success. They spent most of their days writing letters to their supporters back home! Years later, when Don and I operated a summer printing press, we helped churn out many an urgent appeal for more money.

It was in the Bible study class we learned the gospel songs and ditties such as "wide, wide as the ocean, deep as the deepest sea." Some of the more enlightened parents began to take some exception to the very narrow theological interpretation that we were getting. They eventually organized a Sunday school class for us, which gave us alternative versions of the Creation and less literal interpretation of the scriptures. I think that this may have been the beginning of my own search for a clearer understanding of my place in the order of things.

We often hopped rocks in the streams, went skinny dipping, and swam in the dammed-up area "Duck Pond" mentioned earlier. We did a great deal of running around the mountain trails and roadways which were mere widened paths as there were no vehicles for transportation. To ascend from the plains at the bottom of the mountain, one was required to hike up one major trail or three very steep and rough trails. I remember hiking up all three during my high school years.

When younger, I do remember riding a chair up the mountain. Four local men would swing the chair that was mounted on two long bamboo poles up on their shoulders and then off we would go swaying in grand fashion as they kept in step. The trail up the mountain from the plains was a good four miles. Most famous on this main trail was the 1000 steps which had to be carved out of the side of a cliff. We always tried to count the steps but as they were poorly put together, each count was always suspect as we never could reach consensus on the actual number of the famous "Thousand Steps." It seemed to us that it must have been nearly impossible to build the villas and houses on Kuling and especially our Kuling American School. It was not until 1960 when a motor road was finally constructed. Most of my Kuling memories come from the years after I started boarding school at the Kuling American School in 1931 when I was 10 years old and in sixth grade. The early years are hazier and memories tend to be intertwined with the later times.

Vignettes: Yochow

Though Mom took us to Kuling to get away from the heat for the entire summer, Dad got away for three or four weeks only. At the end of September the family would return to Yochow and until I was 10, it was to resume my schoolwork at home. There were always interesting and memorable events, such as the occasional visits of American gunboats, one being the "Monocacy". These visits were appreciated because the sailors seemed to enjoy the contact with American kids and we surely did enjoy the trip out to the little gunboat in the captain's gig. Life on these gunboats of the Yangtze River Patrol was made famous by the book and movie "Sand Pebbles." Of course, the chance to see some movies and get all the ice cream we could eat was the very BEST!

The saddest day of my young life came, therefore, when an American gunboat arrived and I could not go out to party with the rest of the Mission kids. I was sick in bed. A day earlier we had gone out to Huping by sampan/sailboat. It was a great fall day. There was a wind blowing and the sail made the trip easy for the boatmen. We all sat around enjoying a big bag of raw peanuts. Typical to my nature, I overate so that by nightfall I was throwing up and miserable. The next day I did not get to go to the Panay for ice cream. To this day, I do not like raw peanuts, as I vividly remember the disappointment.

The Panay was the gunboat sunk, a few years later; by Japanese planes bombing Nanking in 1937 during the serious invasion of China that led to all out war. It created quite an incident at the time, leading to more active American intervention and support of the Chinese cause.

Sentence of the Court

In those days of warlords and severe unrest in the countryside in the late 1920s, there were always bandits. On top of that, the conflict between the Kuomintang (Nationalist Party) and the Kungchantang (Communist Party) meant that the latter were also classed as bandits. Times were difficult because warring factions always lived off the land. Soldiers of all kinds robbed the ordinary people of the farming villages and towns leaving many unable to earn a livelihood and literally facing starvation. The hills were unsafe for foreigners to travel far from the towns and cities. For instance, we never could take a boat across the lake to the famous island of Junsan, where the concubines of a 10th-century Ching Dynasty emperor had lived and committed suicide. Bandits in the 20th century had made the island a hideout. We finally were able to visit the island when we returned to China after the Cultural Revolution in 1981 and on subsequent trips.

A number of American and British missionaries in other parts of China in the late 1920s and 1930s were captured in small out of the way places. The Mission Boards never paid ransom as such, but we did learn that some churches supplied medicines through the Red Cross to smooth release.

One result of the unrest was the frequent sound of bugles calling the populace of Yochow to an execution. The calls were a shrill, special series of trills that ended in three high notes, which were always followed by a loud, raucous shout, "shaaaa" (kill)! When we heard this parade approach the Mission, we children would run to the front gate to peer out at the criminals. They always looked thin and disheveled, walking in line surrounded by soldiers with guns at the ready. Their hands were tied behind their backs. A large, flat wooden sword was also tied to their backs with the Chinese characters describing their crimes. As the criminals were paraded around the city the crowds swelled and the shouts became ever louder. They marched around our compound on the way to the railroad station where a large, flat, open parade ground served as the execution spot. From our first view at the front gate, we would excitedly rush to the back of the compound. Unknown to our parents we could climb to the top of the wall that surrounded the Mission property. We were only three or four hundred yards from the railroad station and could see the line of march reach the open space. The crowds ran around the area to find a vantage point for a good view. Between our wall and the rail station was an old graveyard and some small truck farms. People climbed up on the graves to get a better view.

The criminal was always made to kneel. We could dimly make out the figures as the execution came to a climax. A large soldier with a red sash came forward. We could see the flashing of a wide and shiny blade as it was swung around his head. The conclusion was difficult to see, but the roar of the crowd told us that the sentence had been carried out. On only one occasion can I remember thinking that I actually saw the head fully severed.

Winter

Cold weather was a time of suffering on the part of most people in Yochow because they had no heat in their homes other than a charcoal brazier. The school kids wore knit half-gloves with their fingers exposed so they could write. Most small children were layered very thoroughly. In fact, their arms usually stuck out straight. The only thing that never changed for the little ones was the "easy-peeses." The slit in their pants meant their little bottoms were always red with chilblains. People often carried little brass pots with a lid full of holes because live charcoal coals were placed in these pots to keep hands warm enough to function. We were lucky because we did have coal fire grates in several rooms and even a metal stove to take the chill off the room. At night, a brick was heated in the kitchen coal stove oven to be placed in our beds so our feet could be warmed up. The smell of a hot brick wrapped in newspaper has a very unique odor, which is still comforting and makes me feel sleepy. I am, however, still sensitive to the fumes of charcoal. They make me somewhat nauseated. I find that my sense of the need for oxygen also makes me wish to open the windows of any crowded room. In fact, the modern Japanese kerosene heaters used by many persons today give off enough carbon monoxide to make me feel almost sick.

Snow was not frequent, nor did it last very long. It was always special, however, because we got ice cream! There being no electricity and no ice available, we naturally had great sport in the snow. Fox and geese games, making snow trails, and other games fascinated us. Then there was always the packing of the ice/snow house. This small building was constructed with two brick walls with sawdust between for insulation. The whole Mission group turned out with servants and helpers to roll large snowballs. These were carried into the icehouse to be stored for later use. If there was ice on the ponds, men were hired to break it up and carry ice to store in the icehouse. It was amazing that this method worked so well. We often were able to have ice cream even into May! The supply of snow and ice was carefully rationed. It seems to me, it almost took an official vote by the Mission to use it. Naturally, we younger ones felt that the elders were much too conservative.

In later years, we were always home for Christmas from Kuling School. School vacation lasted about six weeks because of the cold weather on the mountain, as well as the time it took to get home and back. Some kids had to travel nearly a week. We were usually met in Hankow to spend a few days shopping for Christmas, as there was really very little available in our small country town.

When we had a real snow storm, we loved to go out to roll big balls of the wet snow to make forts or Santa figures. Snow fights were serious. We had a few Chinese friends who would help us defend against the Ziemer school kids. Usually these were boys who went to different schools in town but were sons of Ziemer teachers. We were pretty good at throwing snowballs, as we had practice with baseball. The Chinese kids were soccer and basketball players. Interestingly, we had to teach them how to throw accurately.

One event in my younger days was the arrival of the box from Uncle Leonard. He and his big family always sent us a Christmas box. Often it arrived in January or later because the Chinese customs department always took its time deciding how much duty we should pay. One year, when money was tight during the Depression, our parents had a tough time deciding whether they could afford to go pick up the package. The reason was that they had to pay duty on each item imported, even if it was a gift. They did not disappoint us! This box was not the usual "missionary barrel" of used & outgrown clothes and castoffs. We really got NEW stuff. My biggest and most welcome gift was a trombone that Dad and Mom ordered for me. I must have been in the seventh grade. Kuling American School was starting an orchestra. I had watched Don Mead, a roommate, blow his trombone and knew I wanted one, too. A good roomie, he had let me try to learn on his, so when I got mine, I drove the family nuts trying to make tunes. But we did have a good orchestra at school.

One year, the lake froze. We walked out on thick ice to see people chopping at the ice to get at large fish that had been trapped in the ice. It was so cold that many refugees, living in straw shacks, actually froze that winter.

Winter was also the time we could get delicious Siberian geese to eat. Hunters would bring in the geese they had shot, as the lake was one of the flyways and overwintering spots for the large geese that would come over in large flying Vs, honking loudly. It is a great wonder we did not all get lead poisoning.

Footbinding

Technically, the binding of girls' feet was banned after the Republic was established in 1911. Styles, however, were difficult to change. Most of the mature women I knew in my childhood had bound feet. Our amah would soak her feet in a wooden tub of hot water every night. She showed us that her toes had been turned under her foot at a very early age, the bones either broken or not developed. She actually walked on her heels because she really had no feet at all. She unwrapped the bandages and then rewrapped her feet with new bandages each night. She told us that her feet always hurt, but her classic Chinese reply to questions was "mei you ban fa," "there is nothing to be done."

Sometimes, when we were walking down the street in town, we would hear unearthly screams coming from behind the shutters of houses. I could not imagine that any child was getting such a fearsome beating. Mother told me that it was a little girl having her daily footbinding. In order for the foot to be a beautiful "lily" the small toes were turned under and bound, a most cruel and inhuman practice. Only the Hakka women of south China and a few women of mountain tribes were never forced to bind their feet. This was because they were the farmers of the family and did all of the heaviest work. I should note that in 1981 we saw women on the streets of Beijing who, though they may have been in their 60s, definitely still had bound feet.

Our Amah: Tata

I never knew very much about our amah's background, not even her surname. It must have been Chen, as she gave that name to her son. Mother told me that her husband was a soldier and never came back from some war. I do know that our earliest pictures, when I was age three or four, show that Tata was our constant guardian. She certainly plays a very prominent role in my earliest memories. Mother also told me that I learned to speak Chinese from her even before I spoke my first words in English. That I do not remember. In any case, my facility in the use of Chinese, both colloquial dialect and the good swear words of my youth, must have been learned very early, as Tata took me with her on her daily rounds of the Mission compound, encountering all kinds of workers who shared her vocabulary.

Tata was a cheerful woman who mothered us along with her own son, nicknamed Lu Yi, our childhood playmate. His real name was Chen Lixian, who later worked in the hospital lab. Many a night when our parents were at a late meeting or were at church, Don and I went downstairs to the small room she shared with her son. I marvel at the patience and the acceptance of servants when they saw us living upstairs in the BIG house with a bedroom for Don and me and another for Dad and Mom. Tata was responsible for us, washing our clothes and us, and carrying us around when Mom was busy with church women or attending meetings. I often think that our love for the Chinese people and their wonderful food was born of the very simple way she cared for us and from the fare she cooked for her son and herself. Just rice and a little salt fish or pickle and perhaps a little vegetable, and always fried red peppers, was her staple. But any time we came down and were hungry, she happily shared her meal with us. I know not how many times I was scolded for taking her food. Yet, I was sure that she wanted me to eat whatever I wanted, as we were as much her children as her own. She taught me how to eat and enjoy very red and extremely hot, spicy Hunan peppers. That lesson has stood me in good stead for many years.

She even went with us to Kuling. I remember that she would painfully attend us as we raced off to go to the swimming pools. She could have done nothing to save us if we had gotten in trouble, but she would stomp along on her tiny bound feet trying to keep up with us as we impatiently urged her to speed up so we could get into the water. She always wore the working woman's long shirt buttoned with the cloth buttons down the right side. Her black or very dark blue trousers were always spotless. Her little pointed shoes were made of cloth. She spent most of her time, while supervising us, endlessly sewing the soles of the shoes. They must have lasted about a month, so she was unendingly busy. Her long hair was brought back into a bun at the back of her head. She always had a smile and a pleasant word for us. We learned in 1946 that Tata did not survive World War II.

On our 1989 trip to our Kuling American School Reunion, her son, Lixian, asked me if I had any pictures of his mother as he had lost all of his during the various wars and disruptions. I sent him four or five, which we located in our old family albums. One showed the two of us carrying a bench with a pole (aged about 4) and others showed Tata with Don and me. He wrote that when he received the pictures he could not help but weep.

Church

We always went to church on Sundays, attending the Chinese service. It was here that we enjoyed learning to sing the hymns in Chinese. Some of the Chinese ministers were very long-winded. After all, if a member had walked for several hours into town from miles away, this was the event of the week or month. So an hour of exhortation was quite common. People came and went all the time. In the back of the church there was usually a continuing "hubbub," because the Bible woman would be showing tracts and picture storybooks to new visitors who just happened to drop into the service from the street. It was a fact that only stores and temples in China kept their doors open to anyone. Thus, there was always a constant stream of curiosity seekers. These persons often were the next converts, so there was no real attempt to keep down the noise level. Occasionally, a mother would come in and give a great shout for a child to come "chi fan" (eat rice). Everyone would turn, the preacher would stop for a moment, but after the child had been located up front and headed home, the sermon went on. These interruptions were always welcomed by us kids. We thought we would like to arrange for someone to send us a message like that. The most successful ministers used the storytelling methods of the street storytellers. We certainly learned our colloquial Chinese in this fashion.

The story of Pastor Tang's conversion and ministry is one that should be the subject of a book. He was a good friend to my father, and his wife was a joy to my mother. He supported his young family as a tailor. They lived near the foreigners' entry gate. Once, when his very assertive wife was ill, she told him that he must purchase some incense, take it to the temple and pray to Kuan Yin, the Goddess of Mercy, to heal her. Tailor Tang was a frugal man and had learned well from his wife, who was a superb manager. He decided not to spend the money. A few days later, when Mrs. Tang was still unwell, she berated him, suspecting that he had not followed through on her wishes. After a severe tongue lashing one evening, he left their small shop/home to get away from his wife's complaints that he was insensitive to her. He was about to capitulate and was on his way to the store to buy the incense when he passed the open doorway leading to the small chapel of the Mission. There was singing so he stopped to listen. After he had spent some hours there, he found the message of healing and salvation so compelling that he decided his wife did not need to bow down to a piece of wood. He was convinced that idols could do nothing anyway. All I know about his conversion is that he went home, told his wife he knew she would get well, and that he had learned that the God of the "Good News Hall" would heal her. He then undertook instruction and was baptized. Later he participated in the Bible school/seminary training led by missionaries, Paul Keller and others. My earliest memories are of the church services held in the same "Fu Yin Tang" (Gospel Hall) with Pastor Tang as the minister and preacher.

Disruptions and Major Flood – 1930

Those days were turbulent politically. The nationalist government was not very competent; warlords cooperated in name only; foreign governments were taking all they could out of a weak and disunited China; and corruption was rampant. Dad used to say that the "salt gabelle," a tax on the transporting of salt around the country, was staffed by the British; kerosene was sold by both British and Americans, cigarettes also by both. The Germans had some other monopoly. It is small wonder that there was almost always anti-foreign and anti-Western unrest, which was evident in strikes and turmoil. This was usually blamed on the Communists, who were adept at fomenting dissatisfaction. It was also quite true that Western navies and marines had historically assured the division of China into spheres of influence, which also meant economic imperialism in an era of widely rampant imperialistic actions.

This political turbulence was increased by the efforts of the Chinese Communists to consolidate their many bands of fighters and sympathizers. We never really knew the political inclinations of the so-called "bandits" who were ever present on the borders of Hunan in the mountainous areas. That summer of 1930 a large band decided to cross the lake to reach Hubei to join another large group. They chose Yochow as a likely town to loot on their way. Dad and another missionary were in town when they learned that a small army was approaching. The local gendarmerie and other troops were insufficient to meet the challenge and were planning to leave town. Dad was told to get out of town fast so the two of them walked to Huping School four miles away. When they heard rifles firing in town, they decided to take a sampan out toward some launches anchored in the lake that appeared to have government troops aboard. About halfway there, a Japanese steamer approached. Dad was able to wave the small steamer to a stop. Once aboard they informed the captain of the situation. He immediately had the steel shields which were always carried by river steamers, lowered against the exterior railings and sailed by town as far from the shore as possible. This was to secure the interior from rifle bullets. Dad said that they were close enough, however, for some bullets to reach the ship and ping loudly on the shields. Fortunately, no large guns were available to the rebel group. When Dad returned to Yochow a week later after the invaders' departure, he learned that a reward had been offered for the foreigners. It was just part of the hazards of missionary duty.

In addition to the constant "bandit scares" during the spring of 1930, there was rain, rain, & rain. The warm weather did not slow down the planting of rice in Hunan, but it did help to melt the Himalayan snows to add to the swollen streams and rivers. By summer, large sections of the Yangtze Valley were inundated. Dad was pressed into being a planner and provider for refugees who had fled lowland areas. The International Red Cross and other relief agencies turned to missionaries to help set up feeding stations and relief centers, as the government itself had no relief system infrastructure. Daily, Dad worked with many others to see what could be done to alleviate the suffering. Our hospital staff worked overtime.

Mom took the family, as customary, to Kuling. One continuing visual memory is of the view from the Cave of the Immortals that was located on the western escarpment of the mountain. It overlooked Jiujiang and the winding Yangtze. That summer, the entire valley off into the dim distance, probably 30 or 40 miles, was one gigantic lake. Because of the flooding and the desperate conditions of the people all the way back to our area of Hunan, the families in Kuling were asked to go to Shanghai. The sheer instability of the country was a concern to our consulates. We were refugees a second time to Shanghai, on a special river boat sent to move all foreigners. Mother was able to get space in the Blackstone apartments in the French concession, not far from the Shanghai American School. We shared an apartment with the Paul Taylor family, of our Mission. Dr. Taylor taught at Huachung University in Wuchang while Mrs. Taylor taught music at the University. Ed was older than I was; Jane was just my age. I think that we ate our meals together, though we only had one big bedroom for each family. During the fall of the year we continued to study our Calvert system schooling with some added activities and studies held at the community church. One thing we liked was the swimming pool at the apartment house. Unfortunately, the pool was not properly cared for so we all came down with ear infections. In a few months the floods had receded, having done great damage. Transportation was restored and we were able to return to Yochow by Christmas.

Boarding School Days – Kuling American School 1931 to 1934

During the Yangtze River floods of 1930, when we evacuated to Shanghai, Mother and Mrs. Taylor took turns teaching the four of us. When we reached home Mother decided that teaching two of us at home was not her calling. During a hot, frustrating fall day in 1930, Don and I had managed to be in constant disagreement. We fought, we tripped each other, we threw spitballs, and we did just about everything we could think of to disrupt the other. I suspect that much of the time I managed to initiate the turmoil. My mild, sweet, and loving mother finally reached the very end of her patience. She yelled at us, "You two are driving me crazy," and burst into tears. I can't remember that we really straightened out for very long, but we certainly were cowed at the time. Shortly afterwards, following long discussions between Mom and Dad, it was decided that I should go in the coming fall to Kuling American School, the boarding school sponsored by our Mission and five other Church Mission groups. It was about two and a half day's travel by train, river steamer, car, and a walk up to about 3,500 ft. elevation above the plains near Jiujiang in Jiangxi Province, where we had enjoyed our summer vacations.

Leaving the mission station in Yochow at the beginning of the summer of 1931 was a very special event, as I would be staying on the mountain to become a boarding student at Kuling American School until the long Christmas vacation. All spring, Mom and Tata had been sewing name tags to all my clothes, sheets, towels, and socks. At ten years of age, I was impressed with my importance, what with my name everywhere and Don not having his name on anything. We made our way to Hankow, 120 miles away but an eight-hour train ride. We stayed several days at the Lutheran Home, a hostel/hotel run for missionaries of all denominations, while we bought still more school clothes and summer supplies. The overnight steamer ride down the Yangtze river was always exciting. Don and I had a cabin to ourselves. A number of times on trips we would be cautioned to be sure to stay inside our cabin area. Sometimes we were told that we had been fired on from shore, but I do not recall ever hearing a hit. All night long the ship seemed to be slowing down to permit a large sampan from some small town to come alongside to take on and discharge passengers and some special baggage. We always had to get up to see that everything was being attended to properly. As a result we got very little sleep. Arriving in Kiukiang (Jiujiang) at mid-morning, we disembarked to the shouts of people pushing to get on the ship with their big carrying poles and bags at the same time as those on board were struggling to get off. The chaos and confusion was a part of the charm of travel in China. It never ceased to amaze me that even fifty years later, the same chaos existed.

We usually took rickshaws to the China Travel Service where we would gather with other foreigners to negotiate a bus or private car to take us all across the plains some 20 miles to the foot of the mountain. Our cook would always stay with the heavier baggage, which would come later by truck. I recall that one year, the road was so bad, the trucks and buses couldn't get through, and so we all rode by rickshaw an entire day across the plains. At a place called Lien Hua Dong, we transferred to sedan chair or just got ready to hike up the mountain trail.

The trail up Lushan mountain wound for a mile through the foothills, past small villages with rice fields and bamboo groves and along a stream.

As the climb began, one soon learned that taking a step at a time without rushing was the way to manage. I was never a fast hiker, but I could keep going. About halfway up the steep mountain trail, a series of steps was called the "thousand steps." We used to count them, but I know we never came out in agreement as to the actual number because the way the rocks were placed made it difficult to assess the definition of a step. In any case, it usually took us several hours to make the top of the mountain, or the "gap," as the little store and shopping area were called.

Life at Kuling American School really began for me after a typically wonderful summer in the cool mists of the mountaintop. Mother went to Kuling when the weather in the central valley of China started to reach the 90s F and the humidity even higher. This was usually by the end of May. The summer of 1931 was no exception. In early June, we were firmly settled in the Edwin Beck family house because they were on furlough. Days for a ten-year-old settled into the summer routine of swimming, visiting friends' homes, or having them visit, especially on stormy days when we couldn't meet at the pool. We were also into a pre-scouting club that met at a large community hall where we also went for Sunday school and Bible school. Some of my friends were living in Methodist Valley. They had their own small pool, so it was always a treat to be invited up to join them on occasion. Each summer there were at least two or three swimming meets. I was a pretty tubby 10-year-old but had plenty of endurance, so tended to finish respectably in the longer distance races and in the underwater swims. We took many hikes to "Three Trees," "Lion's Leap," "Incense Mills," "Emerald Pool," and even "Paradise Pools."

All homes were made of cut stone quarried on the hillside. Every day one could hear the chants of the stone cutters carrying the heavy blocks to some site or other. Blasting was at noon and at five, so the hill shook with the blasting of the granite slabs.

The cooking fuel of choice in all Kuling kitchens was wood, cut from the hillsides by an army of local woodcutters into 12 – 14-inch lengths. The saplings were never much over an inch thick. The hillsides thus were constantly denuded. Any thicker wood was made into charcoal, a much more desired fuel. Often the valley held a pall of smoke from the green wood burning in the cook stoves, especially if there was no breeze. The wood and charcoal were sold by weight, so there was no incentive built into selling "dry" wood—we often had to buy it wet.

Sunday teas were a common form of social life in the summer. At one home or another, friends were asked to drop in for afternoon tea. Children were invited to come, but were usually sent to another room to play "quiet" games. The fact that one had to "dress up" did not add to the children's' eagerness to participate in this community social life. The only exception was tea at Mrs. Tyng's home. I knew three of the four children: Billy, Ann, and Franklin. Ann was a year older than I was; Franklin was three years younger. Mrs. T., an Episcopal bishop's wife, had come from a wealthy Boston family so had built a large house near the school with a spacious living room/music room. Her teas were always accompanied by a "sing." Hymns and songs of choice were special to us all. I believe we learned our first lessons in harmony from Mrs. Tyng.

One of Mom's favorite activities was to view all the "goodies" that the roving peddlers carried from house to house in large bamboo baskets, a pastime her daughter-in-law, Barbara, shared enthusiastically years later. If an entrepreneur was rich enough not to carry his own baskets and had several hired carriers, then an entire afternoon could profitably be spent viewing silks from Shanghai, brocade from Hangzhou, cloisonné from Beijing, and many artifacts unearthed from the graves of all parts of China. That these items were very reasonably priced did not mean that Mom ever bought anything. She was the world's best viewer and though the merchants knew she spent little, they loved to come by because she was a master at local banter, in Chinese of course. They enjoyed their visits as much as she did. She once even served a wily and effective salesman some Chinese tea!

Kuling American School – September 1930 to 1932

When the family left for Yochow early in the fall, I was already in my dorm room on the fourth floor of the school, a large multipurpose building. It housed kitchen and dining room and some classrooms on the ground floor; administrative offices, classrooms, and several apartments on the second; an assembly room, classrooms, and some music rooms on the third; and dorms for girls as well as the younger boys on the fourth floor. This top floor was well divided and access was by stairways at each end of the building. In fact, the boys were required to use one set of stairs and girls another. This had the effect of often offering some challenges to all young, independently minded American children. Older boys were housed in a separate small cottage with a tough-minded house parent to try to keep them in line. The very young children of Principal Roy Allgood and several other married faculty members were taught in a one-room school bungalow nearby.

Memories of that first year are sketchy. I found the study hard but rewarding. After all, with only eight or ten students in a class, the teachers gave us individualized attention. There was always morning chapel for 15 minutes. Classes extended pretty well to mid afternoon when we got out for sports and recreation. A large "rec" field just in front of the school was the proper size for a soccer field and also held a baseball backstop at one end. Thus, we learned early to play both. In later years we were able to try some gymnastics, but I just wasn't built for it. Winters were special because the field was used for a game of "Fox and Geese." The deep snow was packed down on the hills so that we could sled. Many a scrape from hitting a stone wall and even a broken leg or two did not deter the intrepid sledders of KAS. The school day ended after supper with required study hall and evening prayers. On Friday nights, those who wished to could go to the little Episcopal chapel for "preparation," a service to prepare for Sunday. It was a kind of study program for church membership that was enlarged for all of us even though we were not Episcopalians. It was also a time for the choir to practice, so many of us non-Episcopal types were involved anyway.

As a sixth grader, I lived with eight other junior highs on the very top floor. Our rooms were small. We were required to make our beds properly, keep them neat and clean for daily inspection, and be sure to change our socks and underwear regularly. We were assigned bath days when water would be carried up to a large communal bath room where galvanized tin tubs would be assigned. After bathing, usually once or twice a week, we would dump the water into a drain trough and clean up the tub. Trouble came when someone did not do a good job and the next in line set up a loud complaint!

Behavior was modified through a system of demerits. Student government proctors and officers had the power to give these demerits. Faculty also had the privilege but usually limited their assessments to classroom-related activities such as late homework, tardiness, etc. My memory is not clear as to the exact number of demerits that, when accrued in one week, created the condition known as "OFF PASS," but I cannot forget the penalties. For some reason, that remains unclear to me, my nature seemed inclined to an inability to follow every rule. I sometimes ran in the halls, real "no, nos."

I managed to fail room inspection on a fairly regular basis – dirty hands or dirty shoes? – anyway, the result was the same – too many demerits. The list was posted every day on the student bulletin board. One could always see the increasing debit, but I seemed powerless. In retrospect the system was quite unfair. If one was caught out of line, there was a built-in prejudice that you would be expected to be there again. In fact, demerits accumulated from week to week, but only if you went over the magic number of 12; otherwise, you started with a clean slate.

Being off pass had its penalties. One could not attend the Sunday night banquet. Instead, the offenders had milk and bread for supper in a separate dreary location and could not attend the evening concert or special event. For chronic offenders, there was another way to come to grips with too many demerits. After you got to the place where one was hopelessly in debt and likely to be off pass for weeks ahead, it was possible to appeal for a new start. I think I was in the 7th grade when this situation came to a head for me. Three of us were chronics. We appealed for relief. The relief came when we went to the principal's office and there agreed to accept a certain number of lashes to get a clean slate. Mr. Allgood was a determined man and he did his duty. He had prepared a small bamboo switch. I remember that I was first, leaning over and getting the prescribed number of switches on my butt and legs. It hurt! Though I do not remember crying out, I had tears in my eyes. Eddie Fitzsimmons was next. He did not stand still after the first lick, but started to move ahead. Mr. Allgood reached out and caught his hand to hold him in place. The comedy continued as Eddie danced and jumped around the principal who, all the while, vainly tried to hold him in place as he swung the bamboo. Eddie cried out as he danced, but kept going. Don Mead, our ringleader, took his punishment like a man. The red-faced principal finally completed the task by warning us that next time he would bend us over the desk and ask Boyd Russell, a very strong young man who helped with athletics and the generator room, to wield the switch. The lesson did stick with me, as I don't think I was ever in that predicament again.

Each year we were given a few days off at Thanksgiving, most of the time spent going on a Boy Scout hike or a camping trip. In the 8th grade, Don Mead invited me to join him for the few days' holiday down at the foot of the mountain in Jiujiang. He had been invited to bring a friend to the Standard Oil Company quarters where his father's friend was in charge. What was unique about that vacation was the opportunity to shoot at ducks on the river. Don, who was taller and larger than I was, very easily demonstrated his skill. I keep telling him he missed them as badly as I did, but he claims to have bagged one. This first experience as a hunter has really helped me become more of an environmentalist, though in later years I have taken a dim view of the expanding population of Canada geese on our lawns and ponds!

Christmas vacations usually lasted about six weeks. This was to enable all of us to get back home, often a trip of three to four days or more for those whose parents were in the far west of China. The long winter vacation also alleviated the cost of heating the school over the very coldest part of the winter. The very first vacation must have been the most traumatic for me. My homesickness seemed to hit me when we got to Hankow, a trip of a day and night down the mountain and then by boat. Faculty delivered me to my parents at the Lutheran Home. For some reason I was quite distressed but I didn't know why. I was, undoubtedly, reacting to homesickness but decided my unhappiness was because one of my friends had a man's hat and I had none. A ten-year-old weeping really confused Mom and Dad, who immediately took me to the local department store to remedy the situation. You know, I never did like that hat! It helped me understand that one's feelings of inferiority and pain are not necessarily helped by merely adding possessions, as we often tend to do.

Back at school, socialization with girls began by weekly assignment at a dining room table for the three meals of the day. At first, the boys always sat shyly on one side of the round table seating 8. As we grew older we managed to sit next to someone we liked if we were lucky enough to get a good draw. The teachers who made up the lists each week were often helpful if they got little messages. With only 60 to 80 students in the entire school, we were really one large family. Everyone knew everyone else's business. Saturday afternoons we could get our allowance. We first had to do our weekly cleaning up and make sure that we would be ready for the new week. After getting our allowance from Mr. Tao, the office manager, we would walk to the gap to shop for eats for parties. If one was off pass going to the gap was not allowed. When older students went to the gap, they often invited someone to walk along with them. This did not mean a "date" but rather that a group of fellows would accompany a group of girls, and each fellow got to walk beside the one he had invited. Some of the kids of the business families of Shanghai were much more aggressive and experienced in this process than those of us from the boondocks upriver. They did not unduly influence us. That can be inferred from the fact that only on May Day did we kiss the girls. We gave them a rose or some flower and then quickly with embarrassment kissed them, mostly on the cheek, but occasionally some couples really showed the rest of us HOW. It worked both ways because the girls got to reciprocate.

The treat of signing out to go to the gap or to go on a short hike was granted to the younger boys as a group privilege. Later, as we grew older we were permitted out on our own. Those were the days of the box camera, so we often took our films up to the shop to get developed and printed. My concern, however, was to be sure to go to the bakery to buy some delicious S-shaped sugar cookies. These were heavy and sweet. By the time we got back to school we had usually finished the entire bag, the paper of which was always transparent with the residual oil or grease. We usually couldn't eat much supper either.

Our fourth-floor dormitory looked out over a lower section of the roof. The walls under the windows were made of wooden paneling. We discovered some time in my second year that we could gently (?) loosen and remove a panel or two to gain access to a crawl space under the roof eaves. The space had been covered with rough flooring, so we proceeded to set up a secret club meeting place. We managed to procure some dry cell batteries and some copper wire. We set up a lighting system, using flashlight bulbs. Ingenuity and planning, some would say natural devilment, came easily. We thought we were pretty clever, but years later we learned that the girls who lived on the fourth floor also had found out the same thing and had managed to sneak outside our other dorm room to spy on us through the panels.

Mr. Roy Allgood was principal. With his wife and five children, he brought a sense of keen insight into youth of all ages and such patience with staff and students that would have tried Job. He was from Alabama originally but did not have a heavy accent. Besides my "demerit whipping" I remember his lectures to the boys on sex.

At least once a month, Principal Allgood brought all boys (eighth grade through high school) together for a talk. We learned that this was supposed to be sex education. But he had such a hard time with his "talk" that sometimes we were left in doubt. Our library was pretty good so we had a fair understanding of female anatomy. We also had reading resources on pregnancy and birthing. We didn't have nearly as good an understanding of sexual intercourse, though we got the picture explained to us by the older boys. This was a follow up, of course, to the early reading about "birds and bees," which we had been given at home.

One lecture, which stuck with us, was on the nature of sexually transmitted diseases; on this, Allgood waxed eloquent. The poor principal was so red in the face that he had a hard time telling us; most of us had an even harder time understanding what he was trying to tell us. The fact that one could get "clap" in college almost turned us eighth graders into drop-outs. At least we did learn that body lice did not necessarily come from sexual contact. At that age, we weren't quite certain what that kind of contact was, but didn't dare ask, We were told that all you needed to do was go to the doctor for some kind of blue ointment. We definitely learned about the horrors of disease and went back to our dorm room to conduct minute examinations to reassure ourselves that we were still safe!

Teachers

A number of our teachers were real characters. Most of them had joined the faculty, not merely for the sake of adventure, but with a sense of "mission" in going to teach missionary children in the wilds of central China.

Mrs. Rhode from Alsace Lorraine spoke with a heavy German accent. Quite elderly, it seemed to us, she taught us French. Years later we learned that her pronunciation of French, with a German accent, was as faulty as her English. She was renowned for her feet. She wore soft shoes because she had enormous bunions that must have made for very painful walking. We managed to play many pranks on her. She did not last too many years.

Frank Lauridsen was our scoutmaster and physical education teacher. He also taught other subjects but his favorite activity was hunting. He would go out with groups of local farmers to try to hunt down the small Asian tigers that were molesting the farm animals down on the plains. Great was the shouting when they returned once, carrying a fearsome beast. He was more successful in hunting wild boar and pheasant. He was a real favorite of the school's students.

Mr. Underwood was an Episcopal priest, a roly-poly, short man who later married our piano teacher. "Undy" was an excellent instructor and directed the choir. Many of us were fond of him, but he turned out to have a fondness for boys. Long after the scandal of his dismissal and disgrace, I learned that he had told the principal that there were a number of us younger boys he had not "befriended." It was reported to my mother that, because of her friendship and out of respect for her management of the summer hotel, he had not included me in his circle of special boys. I had an inferiority complex because I knew he liked some of my other classmates much more than he liked me. I do remember the shock of learning what "homosexuality" meant.

Mr. Chapman was an Englishman who taught for a year or so at his own expense. He brought his two nephews who had been at the Canadian Academy in Japan. They were often, rather obnoxiously, comparing their education in Japan with KAS, making statements to which we took strong objection.

Grace Ekvall was our favorite 7th-/8th- grade teacher. With a sweet disposition and a gift for being a mothering caregiver, she won our hearts. A missionary kid herself, she knew what we were facing in being away from our own families, so she helped build the family spirit in the school. She later married John Beck, son of Edwin Beck of our Mission, who had returned to China to teach at Huachung College in Wuchang.

Miss Shelley, an accomplished violinist, was a patient teacher and we received really excellent training. Her good work made an impact on all of us as we now appreciate classical music and fine orchestras.

Jean Keller, another missionary kid from our Reformed Church Mission, was teacher of lower grades, later our Scoutmaster and helper with athletics. He had a real ability to organize the overnight hikes and to tell stories. His ghost stories around a campfire were famous.

The Furst family, Philip and Mama, were the only faculty to produce offspring. The little daughter, Duna, was our baby, as all the girls vied to hold and spoil her. A Presbyterian minister, Phil Furst was an excellent preacher. We really enjoyed church when he was in charge. He was also a very good French teacher. My three years of high school French paid off when I tested out of French in college and later passed a French reading exam for an MA in General Studies at Yale in 1952.

Rev. William Leete and Rev. Clarence Day had both been sent to China as missionaries for their respective churches. Due to bandit unrest in Central China in the 1930s, they were reassigned to Kuling American School. My first acquaintance with Kenneth Scott Latourette was through his text, *Short History of China*, which Rev. Leete taught when I was a junior in high school.

Paul Maslin and wife, Mary, were young and came in time to leave after only one year. He taught sciences and I was looking forward to studying under him. The Japanese invasion and our evacuation cancelled that expectation.

We often had the mothers of some of our classmates as teachers. This occurred mostly when conditions up country were such that bandits (almost always called Communists) were rampant. Due to the unsettled conditions, many missionary families were separated, with the father staying near the work, the mother caring for the children. Mrs. Storrs came with her children and helped teach the lower grades. Mrs. Thompson taught upper classes English. Her husband was a faculty member at Nanking University.

Scouting

Scouting was an integral part of life in Kuling American School, an activity that took much time and effort on the part of the faculty and students. We spent several days a week at it, with excellent supervision and instruction. I was 11 when I began to study scouting in preparation for becoming a member of the KAS Troop. Most of my classmates were 12 so I was permitted to join and prepare to take my "Tenderfoot" tests alongside them. I started as a member of the Eagle patrol. Of the four patrols, we always managed to win the fire building and water boiling contest. I had learned this skill from our Chinese servants while very young, but they always provided nice dry wood. I had to learn all over again, however, as my memory of my early attempts to boil water in a large can formerly containing tomatoes with wood gathered in the springtime in Kuling, using no more than two matches, was one of complete frustration. First of all, there is no dry wood in Kuling in the spring. There may not be many places in the world where fog, mist, drizzle, and good heavy rain keep the trees, and in Kuling, the famous Lushan "Yun Wu" (Cloud and Fog) tea, growing gloriously! The moisture was not helpful to us would-be pyromaniacs. We would chip many small slivers of wood and try each week to retake the test. I know I was one of the last ones to get that particular Tenderfoot test behind me. As a result of subsequent long effort and training, when the patrols held contests, I was the firebug who was able to get our pot boiling first. The skill has stood me in good stead. Not quite a pyromaniac, I did love to set fires for our camping trips, creating beautiful and fast-burning fires, teepee style, log cabin style, or just carefully criss-crossed. My children can attest to the fact that I still like to light up the Blowing Rock cabin fireplace every chance I get.

My short, chunky size those early years made it very difficult for me to carry the packs that we took on our long hikes twice a year. We would construct our packs by putting down an oil cloth, then blankets, and then clothing that we thought we would need. When flashlight, soap, and all the other necessary gear was added, my pack always seemed to come out about 10 pounds heavier than anyone else's. I usually managed to struggle down the mountain trails, but I could never make it back up. Many a time our patrol leader or one of the coolies had to relieve me (the Chinese carriers were called "ku li," bitter strength, for doing ordinary hard labor). In fact, it was not until my sophomore year that I finally grew and stretched up even taller than my Dad. I still marvel when I meet old classmates from KAS because my memory had them towering over me; now I stand a head taller than most of them.

My Chinese language ability was one of the few things in which I could really say I excelled. I felt fat, shy, shorter than most of my peers, not capable athletically, and had a feeling of inferiority. Things changed, however, when we were on our hikes. Whenever anyone wanted to find out where we were or how to get where we wanted to go, the leaders always sent for me. I also was a good purchasing agent. When the Scouts needed to buy something to eat, Sterling could always get the best price. Thus, I was always the person sent ahead to negotiate and arrange for food and shelter. I never did stop to wonder why. It seemed so natural.

Some of us knew the little trails and byways all over the mountain. I remember picking up woodcutter's trails and trying them all. With a good sense of direction, I could always lead us home. Our scout map contests were always planned to puzzle us, but I could intuit which fork of the trail to take and usually was the one put at the front to get us there and to find our way back home.

My roommate Merwin was the one scout we would always follow when we were tested to recognize bird calls. He knew every bird personally we were sure. His sense of their calls and knowledge of their names made him the expert we sought.

During my high school years, I worked my way up from Assistant Patrol Leader to Patrol Leader to Senior Patrol Leader/Assistant Scout Master in my senior year. When I left China for college, I lacked only one merit badge for my Eagle Scout award. Scouting was important to all of us, so much so, that sometime before my sophomore year a large hall, which we named Scout Hall, was built near the school. We met there each week to have contests among the four patrols, to complete our merit badges, and to practice various scouting skills. Almost every week there would be a "first aid" drill of some sort, so each patrol always had the least skilled tenderfoot as the patient. I can remember being really happy when I had graduated to the upper class level and left that chore behind.

As referred to earlier, the spring and fall hikes were the highlight of our scout year. We also enjoyed the Court of Honor festivities because we could invite the girls to come as guests to see the awarding of merit badges and prizes. Paul Sherertz has captured the enthusiasm of the hikes in the pictures he has enlarged from the *Lushan Lantern*, our annual yearbook, published by a specially selected staff of students. (The last volume was published in 1937, my junior year.) Paul was responsible for the publication of "Lushan Memories," the collection of stories and essays written 50 years after the happenings. Though some aspects of the truth may have been stretched a bit, these stories really bring back many highlights and events that occurred. This collection is available to any of you who wish to read how we lived in an American School in central China over 60 years ago.

The fall and spring hikes of about a week are also well documented in "Lushan Memories." You will find pictures of naked boys frolicking in the sand dunes along Poyang Lake, absorbing plenty of vitamin D from the sun which has now led to annual trips to the dermatologist. We camped on islands of the lake, in temples, such as the famous one at "Goddess of Mercy Bridge." We also camped at the ancient academy at "White Deer Grotto" and at "Incense Mills." Here very active water-wheel-powered stone pounders pulverized leaves and chips of aromatic wood to make incense. One island in the lake is actually a famous Chinese meteorite, "Xingzi," which also housed a small temple used during spring or fall hikes. This was especially reserved for the girl scouts. Today it has become famous for Chinese tourist visitation.

In my eighth-grade year, 1933–34, we were moved downstairs to a suite on the second floor. John Wahl, Tom Helde, Jimmy Libby, Merwin Haskell, Leland Holland, and I roomed together. When Tom brought a new Royal typewriter to school as a Christmas gift from his folks, I was green with envy. I kept after him to teach me to type. After long negotiation, Tom taught me to touch type on his typewriter, a skill for which I have ever been grateful. Of course it was necessary for me to undertake some special cleaning of our room when Tom's regular turn came up—a small price to pay for the wonderful privilege of learning to type.

The summers in those years, 1932–1934, had been pretty hard on our parents, as the Mission had to make a decision about what to do with shrinking budgets. The Depression in the USA had really hit the church hard, so the missionary group in each country had to decide whether to cut the budget by taking a salary cut or by sending some of the missionaries back home. The Japan Mission had decided to cut the missionary staff by 25%. The China Mission decided to cut their own salaries by 30%. In order to provide a summer vacation, Mom accepted the job of managing the summer hotel/guest house at the Kuling American School, which included planning all meals, arranging work schedules for staff, and assuring neatness and cleanliness. Don and I helped her some. I remember carrying sheets and towels to rooms for her and acting as messenger boy for the guests. Usually, some families, single missionaries or business persons would seek relief from the heat by taking a vacation on the mountain. For her work, we lived in one of the small bungalows and received board in the dining hall for the family.

Furlough Year in Tiffin, Ohio – 1934 to 1935

Early in the summer of '34, about the time of my 13th birthday, we sailed from Shanghai on one of the President Lines ships to arrive in San Francisco ready to trek across the USA. Dad had arranged an order to pick up a new 1934 Ford V8 Tudor sedan, one of the early V-8s with plenty of power. We excitedly began our odyssey to find that Dad had driven a car so seldom that he was learning as we went along. Stopping at night at small rest homes or motels in the '30s left much to be desired. With no air conditioning at that time, it was hot! The rooms weren't especially neat and clean, and sometimes did not even have inside toilets. We suffered through the first 500 and then 1000 miles as we "broke in" our engine. Don and I were really mortified that even old Chevrolets were going around us. When we got into the mountains the touring was wonderful, even if the roads were not. We stopped by Estes Park, Colorado, where the Stukeys (former missionary doctor in Yochow) lived. It was cool like Kuling, so we finally realized the US wasn't such a bad place after all.

Our first long stop was to be in Missouri with our Hegnauer grandparents and all our aunts and cousins. Don and I quickly decided we liked to visit Aunt Rosa and Uncle Louis Steiner best because they always let us ride the tractors. They had a dairy farm so taught us to milk, though I took so long that even the placid cow they picked for me got tired of waiting. She scared me by restlessly stomping her feet and switching me with her tail.

After a few weeks, we headed on to North Carolina to visit another set of relatives. This time we stayed at Grandmother Whitener's farm. Before long, however, we were back on the road because Dad was to go on deputation, speaking in many churches while we stayed in a furnished missionary home in Tiffin, Ohio.

The year passed quickly while I completed my freshman year of high school. I learned that I could study and earn good grades because I had received a better foundation in Kuling American School than that offered by the Tiffin school system. My best subjects, Latin and algebra, were the ones that most of the kids did not like. Guess who was the "odd-ball - "that Chink." It was not an unhappy year, but I had to accept the fact that American kids thought of me as different (maybe odd?). I was asked often to speak "China talk," which I did reluctantly as it occasioned great amusement. Being different was only a temporary phenomenon as we did make friends at the church. I biked to school each day except in the heavy snow.

One special event during the year was the Chicago World's Fair. Mom's brother Rev. Leonard Hegnauer, Aunt Anna and their five children were living in a large parsonage in Chicago. You may remember that Uncle Leonard was Mom's brother who left farming to become a preacher because his younger sister went to China as a missionary. Several of the cousins were just about my age. They were very knowledgeable and socially way ahead of us, but were willing teachers. They took us to the fair several times. Our eyes bugged out, especially at the scientific exhibits.

It was soon time to catch the passenger liner back to China so that we would get back in time to begin school at KAS in early September. It always took a month or so to travel from North Carolina, via Missouri and then San Francisco to Honolulu, Japan, and Shanghai. Then we had to travel by river steamer to Jiujiang.

Final High School Years – 1935 to 1938

My sophomore, junior, and senior years at Kuling American School bring back the strongest memories. Because of a perforated eardrum that resulted from an infection contracted from the use of a poorly chlorinated swimming pool at the Blackstone apartments in 1930, Don had to remain in Shanghai for medical treatment and attend Shanghai American School. It seemed that Dr. Dunlap, in Shanghai, was the only specialist in China. A bluff Scotsman, he certainly did a good job because Don rejoined us in Kuling the following year.

In KAS, all sophomore boys were housed in a suite on the first floor. Leland Holland, Jimmy Libby, Merwin Haskell, Don Mead, and several others were my roommates. As we have gathered together in recent years in reunions and mini-reunions, we have retold many times the kind of family life we enjoyed during these years. Many tales are recorded in the booklet "Lushan Memories," which has been mentioned earlier. I will try not to repeat any of these experiences but will record only those that were not told by others.

Developing Some Skills – Milking, Trombone, Printing

Principal Allgood had returned from his year of furlough convinced that KAS students really needed to have experience in the workplace. He had visited Berea College and other institutions where everyone helped with the chores and were given work assignments. This meant that we, too, were to be taught how to wait tables, sweep halls as well as clean our own rooms, and help in the new dairy where five new Holstein cows had been imported to provide milk. I was assigned to be assistant milker and "clean-up boy" for a couple of the cows. This involved arriving earlier than the milkers did in order to secure hot wet towels to clean the udders and teats before milking. We also used some special disinfectant even though all milk was thoroughly boiled before serving to faculty and students. From the second and third years and until we left, I was head milkman and cow-boy. Grass was cut on the hillsides by paid grass cutters and brought to the cows, as there was no pasture available. The milk was strained and brought to the kitchen where it was boiled or pasteurized before being served to us.

It took most of us a long time to get accustomed to "real" milk since we had all grown up on "tinned" (evaporated) milk. My cow care experience was good training, as we had to rise early in the morning before everyone else so that we would be on time for breakfast and classes.

The school orchestra was another very good development for all of us. My classmate Don Mead played the trombone. I thoroughly disliked practicing the piano so I decided to play the trombone which Uncle Leonard had sent me. I found that the only way to learn to play it was to PRACTICE, PRACTICE, and PRACTICE. As it must have cost a bit to get it to me, I buckled down and finally did a creditable job.

We had a respectable orchestra with good strings, woodwinds, double bass, cellos, cornets, and three trombones. A small tyke, Elsa Allgood, who could hardly hold her instrument and whose feet were at least six inches from the floor, was quite an accomplished trombonist. We could hardly believe it yet we gave regular concerts for school events. A highlight for us was the opportunity to play a concert for Generalissimo Chiang Kaishek in the spring of 1936, when he was recuperating from his experience of being captured and released by Marshal Chang Hsuehliang in Xian. The big soft comfortable chair reserved for the Generalissimo was hard on his back, so he stood up and made a large, heavy chief of police take it while he sat on a straight wooden chair.

The Generalissimo's Trail

At that time Generalissimo Chiang was busy providing Kuling with multiple trails to get up to the mountain top and escape to the plains as well. The following experience describes our use of one of these trails.

The destination of our Scout Troop's three-day spring hike in 1936 was Incense Mills, a favorite camping place at the foot of the mountain. There were about 20 boys in the group and several adults, including the Scoutmaster, Frank Lauridsen. This hike turned into quite an adventure for me.

While we were hiking down on a very steep woodcutter's trail, the Rev. Phillip Furst twisted his ankle and cut his leg. He made it to the camp, but after the second day it was decided that he needed more than first aid for his injuries so should return to the school. As an assistant patrol leader and because I knew the language as well as the trails, I was asked to accompany him. Another student, Hector Sherertz, who was having stomach problems, went along.

The plan was to return by way of the main Lien Hua Tung trail, the usual route up the mountain, in order to find a sedan chair and carriers to take Mr. Furst up the mountain. This main trail was a long distance away, however, so we decided that the quickest way to get back to school was to cut over to a new, more direct trail that had been built by the Army, later called the Generalissimo's Trail. Part way up the mountain we sighted a large army camp, surrounded by a fence, but we could not find an entrance gate. It was noon and we were getting very tired so we decided to go under the fence and make our way through the camp. All went well until we came upon a guard who ordered us to halt, questioned us, and then led us to headquarters. There we faced a completely nonplussed captain who did not know how he would explain the presence of three foreigners who had reached the center of his camp without detection. He kept protesting that we should not be there. I kept begging his pardon and asking his gracious help for our revered teacher who was unable to speak the language, but who needed to get to the school at the top of the mountain. He let us know that this was a military trail that only the army used. We pointed out that it would take many hours to find another trail and it was urgent to get medical attention for two of us. He finally telephoned someone who gave permission to use the trail.

After we were served tea, two very pleasant soldiers accompanied us to the Gap, having saved us hours of climbing. We were very grateful for the gracious help we did receive, as I feared much harsher treatment for having trespassed on military property. We were exhausted campers when we finally made it to the school.

Sophomore Year

During the school year '35-'36, a job as assistant production worker for the KAS Echo, our weekly school paper, became available. It was really a rather "hack" job of just running off the paper. The hard part was that the school had a rather cranky AB Dick Mimeograph. I learned that if I took it apart regularly and cleaned the whole thing in kerosene, it would act appropriately grateful and not ruin too many pages. Bill Mitchell was my boss and teacher, but he did not have as technical a bent as I did. Where this came from, I don't know. It certainly was not from my skill as a carpenter, because I shall never forget what happened to that 10"x16" board in

8th grade manual training class. It ended up 3"x5" because it took sawing that much wood to get square corners!

In the summer of 1936 to earn money, I applied to the school to continue the summer community printing service that had been started by Walter and Harry Allen in 1936. This meant that if I produced all of the notices and mimeographed reports needed by the school, I could use the machine to print for the community. This experience as an entrepreneur served me well. Don joined me as we decided it was a definite improvement over the job of running all over the valley trying to sell candy bars, as we had done in previous summers for Eugene and Frank Turner. We also discovered the benefits of seeking out the best wholesale prices we could find for paper, ink, and other supplies that we needed. In several summers' work, Don and I were able to share over $500 to bring with us back to college in the States. The work was hard. We solicited business by printing and then hiring a gang of smaller kids to deliver a business solicitation, with prices, to every foreign home on the mountain. The investment paid off. We were asked to print programs for many community events, church meeting minutes, memoranda, notices, and personal letters to folks back home, and the list went on. Though it was impossible to type Norwegian or other language characters on our typewriters, the Scandinavian missionaries were happy to type up their own stencils.

Junior Year

In the fall of 1936 the school was almost overflowing. During the year a new boys' dormitory had been built to take care of the increasing demand for space. We moved into this beautiful dorm in my junior year. I roomed with Merwin Haskell, the famous bird man.

With the large student body, there were also some very creative young people always trying out new ideas. Our study hall was adjacent to the library. One year the boys decided we would study in the library and each seek an anatomy book. The discoveries led to a big "two/three argument." Where ever they could they would hold up two fingers or three to separate into groups. One faction insisted that the female anatomy had three orifices and the other faction just as strongly argued for two. This silent argument went on for some weeks before dying out, but as far as we know the girls never did figure out what we argued about. I guess they never caught us poring over the library books. It was a time when some guys finally used the library, and then clearly defined the activity as sex education.

Our year was a busy one with activities and study. For the first time, I began to take real interest in both English literature and a marvelous course on Chinese history. English was taught by Mrs. Thompson, whose twins, John and Sydney, were a year behind me. The Rev. Leete introduced us to the book on Chinese history written by Kenneth Scott Latourette and also introduced us to Chinese art and drama. The highlight of the year was a trip to Jingdezhen, the famous site of the imperial ceramic kilns. It has a history from the Han dynasty and was the center of beautiful porcelain making for over 1000 years from the Sung dynasty.

We hiked down to Jiujiang to catch a rather rickety bus to Jingdezhen. All baggage was piled high on top of a locally made bus body mounted on a truck chassis and filled with small wooden seats. In 1936, the road was packed earth pocked with large holes. We crossed the mouth of the Poyang Lake by a small ferry that could handle several trucks at one time. It was motorized but the ferrymen still used sweeps to steer.

The trip took an entire day. As we approached the pottery center, we saw hundreds of smokestacks belching black coal smoke. Our few days in Jingdezhen were spent visiting the pottery kilns and watching the potters who sat close to the ground on small stools. They turned their wheels, which were sunk into the ground, with a small stick. After the wheel was turning rapidly, they threw their clay and fashioned the beautiful vases and chinaware for which the city was famous. The making of rice pattern bowls was most interesting, as grains of rice were actually pressed into the clay. As they were burned out, the glaze covered the hole that was left to leave the pattern of rice in the bowl or dish.

I was particularly enamored of a small rice bowl that was paper thin and was decorated in the imperial yellow. It is called "egg shell" ceramics. As it was very difficult to make, there were very few examples available. I kept pestering a kiln owner for two days to sell me the bowl. He did not really want to and only later did I find out that it really is an antique because it was probably made many years before we visited. In any case, I was finally able to buy the piece even though it took all the money I had. I proudly carried it back to school in the tin box that was provided to protect it, but many years later it was broken in shipping back to the USA. Barbara mended it and we still proudly display it.

In sports my rather short stature proved to be a disadvantage. I did manage to do a respectable job as a halfback or fullback on the soccer team. I bemoaned the fact that I was not tall enough to jump over any stick that was over 3 feet high and not swift enough to do more than keep running in long distance races. In swimming, however, I was pretty good at underwater distances, as well as fairly speedy in the longer events.

The *Lushan Lantern* of 1937 had some interesting comments about Sterling. I was quoted for a favorite expression: "Who's been fooling with this machine again?" It came from my time as publisher of the KAS Echo. Other characteristics attributed to me:

Often said:	"Don't get tough"
Weakness:	Annabelle, the Holstein cow I milked twice a day
Frequently seen:	trying to lose weight
Pet aversion:	being "off pass"
Noted for:	flippancy and riding water buffaloes on our hikes
Ambition:	Charles Atlas II
Activities:	choir, orchestra, *Echo*, *Lushan Lantern*, photography club, French club, Assistant Patrol Leader of Eagle Patrol

One year, a classmate and I bought a small wild boar from a passing farmer. We managed to erect a small enclosure at the edge of campus and bring the pig some food each day from the dining room leftovers. The trouble was that it grew out of its cute stage when it enjoyed handling and petting. It then grew bigger and less friendly. Sometimes we couldn't really get very near to it as it ran from us unless it was very hungry. Though disappointed, we were not too surprised when one day it jumped the fence and made off. We were surprised it was not stolen long before because the Chinese like boar meat, especially tender young pig.

Senior Politics

Events during the last three months of school in Kuling center on the fact that it was most difficult to be the only senior. I had had no experience at being the head of the student council, the chief prefect of the boys, the Scout Senior Patrol Leader, and a number of other task assignments usually shared among members of the senior class.

When school started, the administration appointed a student council, pending elections. Don, a junior, was nominated in due course. A female classmate was also nominated. A week before elections, when he asked her to go to the weekly dance with him, she declined. She said she was "taller" than he was, so refused to go with him. This angered us, but upset me much more than my "easygoing" younger brother, Don. I decided to put her in her place, so organized a political movement against her. I campaigned loud and clear for other candidates and privately organized a grassroots campaign for them, very obviously excluding the "culprit." The election was close, but we defeated the girl. This distressed her greatly. We had our revenge, but it was really a hollow victory. I learned two things. One, that politics really isn't my "thing" and secondly, that I knew I had treated her badly. When the principal had a long heart-to-heart talk with me, I was made aware that others also felt she had been victimized by persons in power, which pointed at only one senior!

Religious Life and Influences

David Beck, Don, and I had been confirmed in Yochow as members of the Reformed Church at a Christmas Mission meeting by Rev. Keller, who was a teacher at the Central Theological Seminary in Wuchang. He gave each of us a verse of the Beatitudes to remember. Mine was "Blessed are the peacemakers for they shall be called the sons of God" (Matthew 5:9). We had studied the Heidelberg Catechism while at school, but I cannot really remember that we did too well memorizing the answers to all those questions.

Kuling School was founded by missionaries. There was a concerted effort on the part of the School Board to see that all youth were given moral, ethical, and religious instruction. This was undertaken by Mr. Underwood, an Episcopal priest, one of our teachers. Though the Episcopal Church had a more regular instructional pattern, there was no attempt to make us all into little Episcopalians. In fact, after growing up under that influence, I was convinced that the hierarchy of that Church and its risings and kneeling were mostly for show rather than producing any real deep spiritual benefit, at least for me. The mass comings and goings during a communion service always turned me off.

I did participate in Friday night preparation service because I was a choir member and the choir often sang special songs. I first joined the choir at the age of 11 as a soprano. Alto section was skipped when my voice suddenly changed over our furlough in 1934 – 35. When we got back, I was placed in the baritone section, singing bass. In a year's time, my voice went up a few notes, so I ended up singing tenor which I sang in the Catawba College choir and ever since.

We processed in robes every Sunday service. Preaching was usually by faculty members, some of whom were excellent preachers. We particularly liked a Princeton Seminary graduate, Rev. Phillip Furst, who could keep us entranced with his visions and stories. The school service was always held in the Anglican Chapel which accommodated the hundred or so students, faculty, and winter residents on the mountain. We were taught to pledge from our weekly allowances. Good instruction on tithing and serving others was a part of both the church life, as well as the very meaningful scouting life at school.

Once, in the fall of my senior year, I decided to take a long walk by myself. Details of the circumstances leading to my unrest and general dissatisfaction with life are unclear to me, but it must have been that at sixteen, I was finally trying to determine just what I would be doing with my life. Things were not easy for me as the only senior student in KAS and suddenly having been thrust into a leadership role that had been shared widely in my junior year with many others. It had taken some years for me to gain confidence in myself and overcome the sense of inferiority I felt as a nine-year-old and even later. I was not sure where I would go to college, as I was corresponding with several. I got permission to leave campus to walk and think.

My wanderings led me to the three sacred ancient trees that were held in reverence by the local Chinese community and even were famous throughout the province. Two redwoods and one ginko were at least 20 feet in circumference. To get to the trees I hiked down a steep hillside path and through a thick grove of bamboo trees. The grove was of the ancient 40-foot tall, 3 to 5 inch diameter, bamboo variety. I had a sense of being in a cave. After reaching the three ancient trees, I sat meditating a long time on my future. As I started back to school, I remember emerging from the bamboo forest and feeling that perhaps my way was clear, moving out of darkness into light. It was during this time of contemplation that I felt that I would like to return to China; that I wanted to prepare myself in college to go on to seminary. I wanted to become a missionary. It was not like a bolt out of the blue; it seemed that this is what I was born to be. I do not think I ever felt I had some dramatic CALL, but this experience gave me a sense of well-being and assurance that this was to be my direction.

The Beginning of the End – The Japanese Invasion of China

The political situation in China was fast deteriorating as Japan began to increase pressure begun in 1931 when the three northeastern provinces (called Manchuria) were taken over and effectively annexed. In 1936 and 1937 it became increasingly clear that hostilities would break out. The Chinese Communists in North China were insisting that the weak central government of Chiang stand up to the Japanese.

During those difficult days, our parents were finding the cost of sending Don and me to Kuling and the prospects of including a third, Bob, was almost overwhelming. We did not learn of these problems until many years later when I was searching the archives of the Board and came across this letter written by my father to Dr. Casselman, Executive Secretary of the Board of International Missions:

"February 25, 1937

Mrs. Whitener has just received a request from the Kuling American School authorities to help out again this coming summer in the Summer Hotel. We had hoped that it would not be necessary for her to do this again. But our hope that the Board might see its way open to help out in school fees has not been realized. So she has agreed to go there for the summer. As Robert, our youngest son will be ready for sixth year next autumn, and, since he has been here at Yochow without any foreign playmates for the past two years, we feel it is imperative that he too shall go to Kuling. We can't possibly put the three boys in boarding school without using more than one half of our total salary, including children's allowances, for school fees alone. Thus the only alternative to working is borrowing. This situation is serious enough to us now but will be worse in 1938 when Sterling should enter college. I confess that this has made me wonder if I should not resign from the Mission and attempt to find some work that would open a way for us to send the children at least to high school."

The three Whitener boys were in school in Kuling in the fall of 1937 after Mother worked all summer. We were never told what arrangements were forthcoming from the Board. The situation changed dramatically when the Japanese began their invasion. Missionaries in the interior of China were advised to leave. Many did depart. Mother went back to Yochow. We continued in Kuling studying, hiking, and playing as though nothing in the world could interfere.

This was the year that Bob, the youngest Whitener, came to boarding school. Don and I roomed together and were charged with looking after him. In fact, Bob was very capable of taking care of himself. I don't think he got into near the amount of trouble I did when I first came to school.

Political events early in 1937 in North China, which included the Japanese army's move below the Great Wall and their attacks on civilians in North China, had a very sobering effect on all Westerners. Some of our classmates either did not start the year with us, having returned to the USA with their families, or were kept in schools near their homes in order to be able to evacuate more easily. In the fall of 1937 the Japanese army finally entered Shanghai and took all of the Chinese suburbs. They did not enter the French Concession and the International Settlement because the world community had condemned this aggression.

Although Kuling was really out of the way and not as fully "in touch" with world events as the larger cities of China, we did have some radios and we received city newspapers. Even though the news was somewhat late in getting to us, the local grapevine was really excellent. We learned of the fall of the cities along the Yangtze when they happened. We learned much of the rape of Nanking. It was obvious that the Japanese army would soon be in our vicinity. The school authorities during the fall of 1937 kept an anxious eye on both the war and international reactions. They had at least 80 children in their direct care. Communications with parents were sometimes very difficult because the postal service was slow and unreliable, transportation was cumbersome and intermittent as trains, busses and even small ships were not keeping their original schedules. The Japanese air force was beginning to bomb indiscriminately.

Departure from Kuling – December 1937

There are several accounts of the Kuling American School evacuation from Lushan to HongKong in Lushan Memories. My own recollection is of much chaos - a very confused situation. I know I was always being asked to help this person or that to help with translation. It was a big task to transfer so many persons down the mountain at once, so the school was divided into groups. There were not enough carriers to get all the baggage down to the boat in one day, so we actually traveled in three different groups to make our way to Hankow via river steamer. It was in Hankow that we joined a large group of westerners from central China to take an International Red Cross train from Wuchang to HongKong.

The train, itself, was draped with the flags of many nations, as well as painted with large Red Cross markings on the roofs of the cars. It was a true international train. Families of business persons, missionaries, and teachers of a large number of nationalities from all over central China were transported on the train. Much was made of the fact that it was cleared with the Japanese government at the highest levels. We students considered it a part of our Christmas vacation, as it was just prior to Christmas 1937. We missed going home. In fact, the train passed through Yochow, our home, in the early evening of the first night after departure from Hankow.

Meals were served in the dining car and were good Chinese food. Unfortunately, some of the more adventurous students decided to purchase local goodies when we stopped at stations to change engines, take on coal or water, or whatever. In any case, a number of them came down with gastric upsets and diarrhea, adding to the problems of overcrowding and lack of facilities.

Two events provided some excitement. One day we came to a bridge that had been destroyed a day or two previously and we had to change trains to one on the other side of the small river. We carried our packs and belongings down to the river and across a pontoon bridge made by placing large boards across sampans. We then climbed back up on the other side to board and find places on the replacement train. We organized a group of boy scouts to help smaller kids and girls who needed assistance. At that point, there was a paint crew back on top of our new train carriages to paint on the required Red Cross symbols. The accommodations on the second train were not as good as those prepared for us on the train we had just left.

Near the Hunan/Gwangdong border, the mountainous area contained a number of tunnels as we wound through lush valleys and ranges. On one occasion, we stopped in a tunnel, staying in the dark for several hours. The word came back to us quickly that there was a Japanese air raid on a small town not far ahead of us. This news was unsettling to some and full of excitement for others. Some of us got out of the cars to walk in the tunnel to see what we could, and find out what news was available. There really wasn't anything consistent. After several hours, the engine whistle sounded and we continued our journey to learn that the planes merely had been flying over on a mission far interior. It was not long, however, before we arrived in Canton where we changed at last to a train to go to HongKong.

In Kowloon we were put up in a variety of places. Most of us were housed in a British school adjacent to St. Andrew's Anglican Church in Kowloon. The few weeks in HongKong were new and exciting to all of us. Some of us older boys rented bicycles to ride out to the countryside. A number of Christmas events were arranged for those of us who were without families. In fact, the city was so exciting that we did not have time to be homesick.

In early January we boarded an Italian ship, the Conte Biancomano to go to Shanghai to continue our studies. The boys were assigned to the very front end of that ship. It was exciting as we plowed through heavy seas for a few days. Unfortunately, a few with weaker stomachs did not appreciate the violent ups and downs of the bow. Breakfast of *cafe au lait* and hard crust buns was a real treat. It was only a few days later that we landed in Shanghai. We went immediately to #10 Avenue Petain in the French Concession to the Shanghai American School, where we were accepted as students in good standing.

Shanghai American School – Final Semester Senior Year, 1938

My time in Shanghai lasted only six months. It was quite a shock and also a relief to be a more normal senior with a total of eleven other senior classmates. The entire KAS contingent of students was welcomed. Because so many students had already evacuated Shanghai, there was plenty of dorm space. The school had not run a boarding department since the beginning of the school year when so many students had left to go back to the USA. We Kulingites moved right in as our faculty took responsibility for the dormitory life. Although Shanghai American School was operated on a more sophisticated basis than Kuling American School, the basic curriculum was much the same. We fit in easily to the classes and adapted well. In fact, the KAS dorm structure and even roommate selection was continued in the SAS dorm as it had been in Kuling. With the large influx of students, many of our KAS teachers, who had accompanied us, were put right to work as though we had merely changed locations. Many years later I learned that some of the younger SAS students resented the "takeover" by KAS. This was not true of the upper-class students, but younger students felt they were cheated out of some leadership opportunities by stronger and more capable KASites. This attitude is reflected in the book Fair is the Name, a history compiled by Angie Mills in 1997.

Mother wrote to Dr. Casselman, our Mission board secretary, February 12, 1938:

"The children have entered school here and are having no difficulty at all that I can see. Donald was here two years ago so that he had quite a number of friends, and Sterling never has any difficulty making friends. And of course quite a number of the Kuling group came here. In fact, nearly all of them came here. Since the Shanghai school is not running a boarding department this year, the parents and refugees have taken over the dormitories and we pay room rent and run our own dining room. That makes the parents responsible for the children and in that way we can live here, too. I do not care especially for this kind of life but then I must remember that I am the kind of refugee that refuses to leave my husband out here alone while I run home to the comforts of our dear homeland. And I just want to say now that to go home to the US and homefolks is much the easiest thing to do now - with one child graduating in June and the second one ready to graduate in another year. Sometimes I am tempted to send all three of the boys back home to my family and go back to Yochow. But that takes some careful consideration, too."

My coursework was not quite as difficult as in KAS, but still plenty of studying to do. As a senior in Kuling, I was taking some courses alone, which meant that I had to study and get my work done. In SAS the sharing of reports and homework made life easier. When I now return to the China Schools Reunions, I fit into both groups, but my loyalties really lie with Kuling. The six months passed very rapidly. One reason was that I was interested in the drama club. With a small student body, it was easy to get a part in the senior play. We put on Shaw's "Arms and the Man." I drew the lead part which was quite a boost for me and increased my confidence. The leading lady, Carly, became my girlfriend at our weekly dances on Saturday nights. Preparing the play kept me so busy I was excused from the track contests. Although I had by now trimmed down quite a bit, I still was no speedster or weight lifter.

Saturday night dances were a highlight of the social life of the campus. I developed into quite a dancer. Cannot remember when they taught me the "box step," but it must have been long before while still in Kuling, because by my senior year my dancing was much better. Carly and I were light on our feet, whisking rapidly from one end of the dance hall to the other.

On weekends we boarders had free time to visit downtown. This was accomplished by tram. At that time, Shanghai was an island in a sea of war. The Japanese had taken the entire Chinese city by assault, destroying much of the industrial area and the outlying areas where bitter battles had taken place between "crack" Japanese troops and rather poorly equipped Chinese armies. In the International Settlement and the French Concession, foreign governments were in control. Sikh policemen kept the traffic in order. British soldiers were particularly evident in the business area. As students we were aware of the political overtones, but not really involved in the sometimes violent events that took place on Soochow creek, for instance, when thousands of Chinese were slaughtered by the Japanese army when they tried to escape "into" the refuge of the foreign enclave.

On several occasions a group of us rented bicycles to ride out into the countryside, ostensibly to get "exercise." What we actually were after was to collect some war booty. We had been told that the battlefields were literally "gold mines" of bayonets, gas masks, trinkets, and bullets. I went on two of these excursions during that spring of 1938. The first time was quite uneventful. We crossed the border between the French Concession and the Japanese-held countryside without a problem. The Japanese guards smiled at us. We found the farms devastated and there were trenches beside the road. Large blackened areas showed us that something had been burned. When we went up to these we saw some bones that had not been fully turned to ash. We later learned that these were the cremation pyres of Japanese soldiers. Their ashes were sent back for sacred burial in Japan. In the trenches, however, we found the decaying bodies of Chinese soldiers. The stench was terrible! We were really scared, the bodies were frightening, but we were determined to get some souvenirs. It was hard to remove a belt buckle, or a gas mask holder. I found a gas mask and a small compass and was anxious to get away. Large fat dogs were gnawing at bodies that had not yet disintegrated. You should realize that in the early spring of 1938 it was only a few winter months after the battles and the bodies had not yet been buried because the entire population had fled. Even though it was nerve-wracking the first trip was counted a success by us schoolboys. About ten of us raced back to school with our trophies tucked inside our shirts. At the Japanese guard post, the traffic was thick with Chinese vegetable carts and baskets. The gendarmes waved us through; after all, we were just a few kids out for a ride.

Our second visit to the battlefield was quite different. The death scene was being cleared up with conscript labor. We had to travel farther out to find a few items of interest. When we had collected them, we headed back to the border post expecting to sail through. Unfortunately for us, there were no farmers trying to get their produce to market. The guards did not have much to divert them so when we got there, the officer-in-charge decided to see what we were up to. He started asking questions in passable English. We tried to say we were out for a joy ride. One boy's bayonet seemed to be sticking out of his shirt, so the officer began to go around to all of us. He ordered us to line up in a row. Then he made us take our little items out of our shirts. You can imagine how frightened we were. In fact, we began to realize that we had actually been "caught" and that we might cause some kind of international incident. He spoke briefly to the seriousness of our stealing war materials, to the effect that he was being very lenient not to make this a major crime. Then he went down the line slapping each of us in the face. Needless to say, we were both humiliated and determined to get out of there. He sent us on our way, telling us not to come into the war zone again. We were half-afraid that the information would become public knowledge and we would suffer at school. Thankfully, that did not happen, but we had learned a lesson. The slap has probably contributed to my life-long anti-Japanese feelings.

Choosing a college had been a bit troublesome. During my senior year, Uncle Leonard had written from Canton, Ohio, that he would like to see me enrolled in our Reformed Church College, Heidelberg, in Tiffin. In due course, the catalogues and applications came. I had always wanted to go to Dad's college, Catawba, in Salisbury, North Carolina, also a Reformed Church college. I pored over the literature from both for many hours, debating all the finer points with those other seniors who were applying to Stanford, Williams, Oberlin, etc. In the end, after sending in my applications and being accepted at both institutions, I enrolled at Catawba College in the fall of 1938 because they had offered me $50 more in scholarship funds. In those days such a scholarship was really important. Funny, how we make our decisions! My dad had graduated from the old Catawba in Newton. We had visited the new Catawba in 1925 when we came back from China on furlough. I remember a big muddy field with planks for walkways to the only building—Hedrick Administration.

Graduation was a big event! We were most happy that Mother had come out of central China to be with Don and Bob and me. The only senior from Kuling, I was sixteen, the youngest in my class of twelve and had been accorded full standing in Shanghai American School. I graduated with the fourth highest honors. What a boost to me since I had always considered myself a mediocre student. Don always excelled with superior grades.

The 1938 Shanghai American School annual, The Columbian, spoke of a few of my accomplishments. I had starred in the senior play. I was the Senior Patrol leader in Scouts, played in the orchestra, sang in the glee club, and played chess. It said I was noted for "fresh, trombone, curly locks, KAS, and gals." I had grown out of my shyness.

Departure from Shanghai and Culture Shock in the USA

After graduation, on June 26, the day before my 17th birthday, I sailed on the "Empress of Asia" to Vancouver. I was on my way to college! Getting to North Carolina from Shanghai was a long, epic journey in itself. It involved crossing the continent all by myself, learning all about ordering food, visiting grandparents and cousins in Missouri I had not seen for five years, and arranging to make my way alone to college in North Carolina.

On the Pacific crossing, Marjorie Moore Gus, the senior class clown, was my tablemate. We walked the promenade deck together and enrolled in all the deck sports and tournaments, either singly or as a team. We actually won some of the prizes. We always had the stewards draw our baths at the same time in the evening. The fun part was the singing. On shipboard, the baths were all in a row across the middle of the ship. We enjoyed harmonizing and singing in the bath, she in her room and I in mine, but since there was a three-inch space at the top of the room for air circulation, we could talk and sing together without difficulty. Hey, it was too high and too narrow for viewing, we know — we tried!

We parted in Victoria, British Columbia. I made my way to Seattle before catching a train to Kansas City. The pullman ride across country was exciting as the vistas unfolded, but after the excitement of graduation and the ship activity across the Pacific, I really felt alone. I missed my companions of the past semester and I felt sad as I faced the fact that I might never see China again. A man and his wife took me under their wings and helped me with the dining car system. Later, they tried to talk me into agreeing to join the Masons when I got settled.

In Missouri, life exploded with new experiences for me once again in that summer of 1938. Although I stayed with Grandpa and Grandma Hegnauer for awhile, I actually spent the summer working with my cousin, Sterling Durst, on their family farm. It must have been comical for them to see a young man without any farm muscles, not knowing how to use a milking machine, operate a tractor, drive a car, or really know his way around modern "Prairie City" society. Prairie City, in this case, was the big metropolis with one small store/drugstore, a few houses, and a small schoolhouse/church.

Cousin Sterling Durst quickly taught me how to do the chores and to milk. He and his father had a new milking machine, but there was still a lot of hand work to do in those days. Working in the fields was a bit harder. They let me operate the smaller tractors if there were no hillsides or dangerous curves. When I visited my Aunt Rosa's farm, an older cousin Willard took over my neglected education, remarking that I was getting along "pretty well."

The biggest shocks were the ice cream parties at someone's big farm-house. The first one must have had at least 30 young men and ladies of high school age. We all had worked hard in the fields, come home and washed up behind the well house, and dressed up to get to the party. Sterling and I did not have dates; though he did have a "sweetie" he wanted to see. I was properly introduced to all as the "China boy" cousin. I got tired saying "something" in Chinese, or teaching a swear word. I spent the night helping crank the ice cream churns and then eating that wonderful, farm-fresh, homemade ice cream. We gathered around on the large porch to sing and tell stories. It was soon time to get on our way home. The crowd had thinned considerably, so Sterling and I made our way toward his 1931 Ford Model A. On the way to the car we passed another car where there was some giggling and activity going on in the back seat. I wanted to stop to look, but my cousin grabbed me and steered me to our Ford. I asked quite loudly why he was hustling me off; then, what was going on in that back seat, anyway? He told me that it was one of the biggest jokes of his life that I did not know what "necking" was. My education, which had been seriously neglected, was quickly brought up to date. At least he filled me in though it was a whole year before I got up the courage to try it myself!

Early China Years

1. My newlywed parents, Sterling and Marie Whitener, 1919
2. My baby brother Donald with me and our beloved amah Tata
3. Yochow, as Yueyang was called in the 1920s.
4. My family in 1933 - L to R: Don, Sterling and Bob

Kuling American School Years

5. The Kuling American School (KAS) erected in 1916
6. A segment of the Lushan 1000 steps, part of the trail to Kuling
7. Sterling, the intrepid cowboy
8. Sterling on left in back row, assistant Scout patrol leader, Eagle patrol

Chapter II

College, Courtship and Seminary 1938 to 1946

It was late August 1938 when I headed for North Carolina. I hated to leave Missouri and what had now become a comfortable life there, hard work at times, but so much to learn from fellows who knew all about life. Catawba College in Salisbury was to begin on September 12.

Arrival in North Carolina was somewhat anticlimactic after all the learning experiences in Missouri. I would have preferred to stay with Uncle Gordon and family outside Hickory. There was just no room as Cousin Hazel was home from Lenoir Rhyne College, Alice was getting ready to go there, and the three younger children at home meant a real crowd. I did get to stay a night or two on a cot in Harry Lee's small cubicle. As the only son, he rated a small space of his own. Uncle Gordon was a schoolteacher, and Aunt Suzie had always been the best cook in the world.

My first stop was Newton, where my Uncle Russell, a lawyer, took me under his wing. He had promised my parents he would see that I was outfitted properly for college. We went to men's stores for shirts and stuff, but the best thing I got was a watch at a real jewelry store. Aunt Harriet tolerated me, but she was very much wrapped up in her two young daughters, Cousins Jean and Joan, who were 6 & 8 years younger than I was.

Uncle Russell drove me to Salisbury in his Ford. My trunk was sent separately, but otherwise all my worldly possessions were in the car. We unloaded at the main college building, Hedrick Administration. Classrooms and men's dorm were all in one. A new dining hall was just being completed. I learned my first job was to work in the dining hall, helping serve and clean up.

My room was large because three of us were assigned to it: John Henry and Robert Sargent, "Sarge" to us. I was the only one to last beyond the freshman year. Henry decided he wanted to go to school closer to his Pocono Mt. home at a teachers' college in Pennsylvania. Sarge just disappeared. No one really knew what happened to him.

Catawba College – Freshman Year, 1938-39

When I arrived on the Catawba campus in September 1938 I won the distinction of being the freshman from the greatest distance — Yoyang, China. As is surely the experience of all college freshmen, initial adjustments are difficult. Added to my stress was the tragic death of my cousin, Charles Abernethy, aged 12, who lived at Dad's old home place near Hickory, NC. He was killed during a rough horseback ride across the fields when he slipped off the saddle and caught his foot in a stirrup causing his head to hit a large rock. Though I hardly knew the young boy, I wrote my Aunt Maye that I was very sorry to learn of the tragic accident. I didn't get to the funeral in Hickory due to illness and getting behind in my work.

I was also very worried about my finances. It was helpful to write to the Reformed Church Board Secretary, Dr. A. V. Casselman, a kindly man who always reassured me. A few excerpts from letters I wrote shed some light on a 17-year-old freshman living in a strange land. I reported that I had spent $8.00 more than my travel allowance and that I also needed to see the dentist. I "wondered just what I ought to do; send for some money from my Dad or get some direct from you. The $200 you sent for School ought to carry me until February or March as I have some work and the missionary children's allowance, which amounts to $150...College starts Monday, and I am very anxious to begin work." He made it easy and said just send him reports and receipts.

A letter dated September 26, 1938, included a full report of my travel account but also reported spending two days in bed with a cold and missing study and work.

I really was conscientious in those days. I also wrote to Dr. Casselman:

"I am having a fine time...The initiation was not very much. They made us wear our clothes backwards for three days, and then parade around the campus in our pajamas. Shining shoes and cleaning rooms once in a while are just little jobs we get. Classes are not much of a joke, for the teachers really know how to make one

study. There are many friends of my father's down here, and they have been very nice to me."

On October 5, I wrote to ask how my allowances work, so the fact that money was tight was evident from the first. We traveled by hitchhiking the two miles from the campus to the center of town. Several locations, one near the college and one in town, were known as the "bumming" corners. We would line up and get in willing cars for the ride. I went to town with the guys to see a movie, but not very often. I learned how to get a bank checking account. This came in handy as I had some medical expenses that were refundable. I had neglected to get receipts, but my cancelled checks sufficed. My report:

Dr. F.B. Marsh, 1 call	$ 2.00
Innes St. Drug, medicines	2.00
Dr. E Carr Choate, 2 times	3.00
Dr. McCutchan, glasses	12.36
	$19.36

The dentist was a brother-in-law of my uncle's so he put a crown on my tooth for only $3. The same job was done in 1935 in Ohio for $14.50. Awesome, wasn't it, especially as I had a crown placed in 1998 for $667.00?

I continued my pattern from Kuling American School of writing a letter home each Sunday, at least for about a year. In late September four of us missionary kids from overseas were featured in a short article in the *Salisbury Post*, the daily newspaper in town. On the front page Joe Fesperman, his older sister, cousin Jim Fesperman who was in my class, and I were pictured on the front page, titled "Across the seas to Catawba." The Fespermans were from Japan. The next month I was in the paper again, only this time with many from our marching band. As a trombone player I managed to be in the front row.

Socialization was not easy. High school in China had been in a relatively protected environment; our dates were for Sunday night suppers and public events. At Catawba I did not feel comfortable asking a girl for a date my entire freshman year. Social life? Catawba had to teach me! I had never had a date with a girl all alone until I got to Catawba. Can you believe it took me a whole year to learn the ropes and get up the courage? A group of us loved to go to Martha Trotter's home which was big enough for the gang. Her mother always welcomed us and served great snacks and we had lots of fun! Dancing was difficult for me even with a rug rolled to the side.

Whenever I saw Rufus Agnew or Scoop McCrary jitterbugging I knew I had grown up in the wrong part of the world.

I wonder now what the mothers thought of all the college boys coming on Saturday night to eat the family out of "house and home." Martha Trotter and Adele Swaim were always game to have a group of five or six of us invade their homes, as they had extra girlfriends who seemed to enjoy boisterous male company.

College years tend to blend into each other but I was sure that I wanted to return to China as a missionary, and I elected to major in English I clearly remember my professor, Dr. Raymond Jenkins, who taught composition and English. Dr. Jenkins remained a lifelong friend.

I respected the religion professor, Dr. D. E. Faust, who later assisted me in applying to enter Yale Divinity School. I was not a consistent student at Catawba, although I did make the Dean's List sporadically.

I tried to be friendly... but Tony, a big football player, said that someone with a "dink," the blue and white sailor cap with a large C which freshmen wore for three months, could hardly be called Sterling, so he named me WANG PU. I never could get away from that sobriquet for all four years at Catawba. In graduate school in New Haven, it took me months before I readily responded to my real name.

During the fall semester, I had learned that I knew nothing about American football, as I had grown up playing what the world called football, i.e. soccer. With my "gentler oriental nature" I was quite unprepared for a course called "Phys Ed" under Coach Tom Brown (we called him bully and brute). We crossed the road to the field where the library now stands to practice a sport called "touch football" but actually it turned out to be an American game called "maim 'em or mayhem." I learned all about being knocked around by something called a "rolling block" after a ministerial student named Detwiler had given me multiple bruises and a few black eyes. He was constantly using his experience "mean style" to whip us with his legs as he rolled against our knees. Without any pads we often ended up black and blue. Big joke for him, but left me puzzled, as we were both in the pre-ministerial group called the Adelphians. I wasn't even sure I was cut out to join the Adelphians so I spent my time playing trombone in the football marching band for three years.

I did enjoy being in the band. My trombone came in handy, as we always got to sit in the front row at any concerts and march up front on the football field. We traveled with the team several times to cheer them on. Actually, during the years I was in college the team was pretty good, mostly made up of older guys from the coal fields of western Pennsylvania. Only in my senior year, after spending a summer toughening up by working as a laborer in an Ohio steel mill did I volunteer my services to "Chubby" Kirkland, the football coach, but more on that later.

My roommate, Robert Sargent, wrote an erudite essay that was printed in the *TOTEM*, the school literary magazine. I helped him with some "high falutin" names of famous educators: Leslie Whitehead, Dewey etc. He did say that a college education was worth $25,000. That would go over big these days, since it takes that much to get through one year in most schools. He and Helen Snyder were asked to write about what they expected as entering freshmen. I think Helen did the best job: she said she expected to "wear saddle shoes and go to football games."

One great event for me occurred when the International Relations Club won the contest for the best presentation of what their club proposed to accomplish. We demonstrated a debate on the state of the world in 1939 all dressed up as different world leaders. My specialty was a brocade bathrobe and a small Chinese hat, which no respectable Chinese gentleman would have been caught dead wearing, since 1920. I was Chiang Kaishek but no one could understand my Chinese dialect anyway.

In December I was cast in the play "Craig's Wife." The comment of the college critic in our weekly *Pioneer* was, "Sterling Whitener as Harry, a detective's assistant although only a short time on stage, added some rare humor." I never thought of myself as funny!

Christmas in 1938 was spent with relatives in Newton and Hickory. Once again, I found that my Aunt Harriet was only tolerating me. I could not wait to get to Uncle Gordon's and Aunt Suzie's, but they had such a full house that my home away from home was in Newton.

Having a "so-so" tenor voice, I had high school ambitions to be a soloist in the college choir. I did make it, though I sang solo only when they needed a bit part. My years in the choir also led me to take some music studies in addition to the required music appreciation, a course that helped me listen more carefully and with understanding. This resulted in my continued enjoyment of classical music ever since. With the voice professor I studied at least a year to learn how to breathe and project. One year I took a course in music reading and I prided myself in getting better grades than a musician student who served as organist for the Salisbury First Reformed Church and its successor, First UCC, for over 40 years.

Highlight of our freshman year in choir was a two-week concert tour to Pennsylvania in the fall and then an opportunity to join the Westminster Choir College and about 40 other choirs to sing several days at the 1939 New York World's Fair in the spring. This took place after school exams, so we had a fantastic time. Our director, Mr. Dickensheets was a graduate of the Westminster Choir College and a friend of the director Dr. Williamson. I think all the choirs invited to participate were led by former students so it was like old home week. We traveled by bus, spending time in Princeton, NJ, to practice several days, then going on to the fair out on Long Island, the site of the present J. F. Kennedy Airport. We got to spend only the day at the fair, leaving about the time it closed up at midnight to bus back to the choir school dorms. What an experience for a China boy! I was sure I really should have gone to the choir college. Our huge joint choir, at the World's Fair for some special celebration, really did sound good.

Prior to the above event, I began to get uneasy about how I was going to finance a college education since my brother, Don, was to graduate from Shanghai American School in June. I had been attending a club called Adelphians, formed of men who were planning to enter the ministry. I found that most of the guys had some special funds they were receiving from the church. They weren't exactly helpful on how this was done because it was always their local church pastor who helped get things rolling. I wrote my mentor, Dr. Casselman, at the Board on March 29 asking him if he could tell me how to apply. He wasn't too helpful as he suggested I talk to the local pastor. I did attend church pretty regularly, but the local Reformed pastor was pretty dull and the church folk did not exactly welcome students, so I usually managed to visit other churches because they provided transportation.

I worked as part of the National Youth Corps. I couldn't get over the fact that I could get 25 cents an hour just for waiting on tables. We had to do that in China for nothing as a part of going to school. Spring semester 1939, was an active time. I had joined the Blue Masque acting club. After my debut as a budding actor in my senior year in HS, I thought I should see how plays were directed in college.

In May, just before the end of school, I wrote the Board secretary once again. He really was a long-suffering man, trying to keep up with missionary children. I had learned earlier that Jimmy Fesperman never did write Dr. Casselman. All their communications were through the Dean's office. This time, I was concerned that I had refunded too much to the Board on my travel account. It turned out I did, but it took a letter some eight months after I had sent in my report to get my refund. The money came in really handy for my New York trip. I tried to write Dr. Casselman some interesting news. One especially, that I had found a summer job as a waiter at my roommate family's small hotel in the Pocono Mountains. I also informed him of some interesting talks with a visiting missionary.

I returned from the New York World's Fair to North Carolina eager to get to my new summer job. Since several of my college friends, Bill Dovey, Park Loy, and Bob Hoke were also going to work at the hotel, we decided to get there together by meeting in Hagerstown, MD, to tackle the journey to the mountain resort. Bus was my only feasible means of transport, so with my duffel bag, I set off. I reached Hagerstown after a night on the bus, and fortunately Park Loy's father took us on through Lancaster, PA, to pick up Bob Hoke.

To say that I was disappointed in the small Brewer Hotel in the Poconos would be putting it mildly. It was exciting to be shown the tiny attic where all of us were housed, but the dining hall seemed so small that it appeared impossible to serve more than a few families at once. Roommate Bob Henry, who had recruited us, was helpful and informative, promising us that on our day off we would find all kinds of girls who would just "die for a date." We later found that this extravagant claim was not necessarily true. What was true, however, was that his very pregnant stepmother was a good, though harsh, teacher of proper wait service manners. Her strictness made us respect her highly.

For a few days we learned the ropes. The process of taking an order, writing it clearly, and then taking it to the window where "BIG JOHN" produced the meal which should have been simple but somehow managed to keep at least a few of us confused. My brilliant future scientist friend, Bob Hoke, seemed to have the most trouble. He managed regularly to drop food and mix up his orders. Our occasional slips and drops of silver or glasses caused consternation but no injuries. I remember being very embarrassed when I spilled soup on a small child, which turned out to be only a small splash on her big thick bib. There were only two others who served the tables, a girl of great experience and a fellow from some unknown college who had seniority, as well as a sense of superiority because he had been at the hotel the summer before. We were so happy when he once dropped a full tray of food and drink that we actually clapped!

The summer was a learning experience. I did not know what to do on my staggered day off. We could not get off at the same time so we each had a different day. As all waiters took our days off sequentially, we never had anyone with whom to pal. Bob Henry, the owner's son, tried to get me dates with a variety of his girl friends, but I found this difficult and awkward, as I did not know what to do except pay for a movie. They always seemed to expect more and were disappointed, but I did not know why.

I guess I learned the hard way. Late in the summer I saw a Model A Ford for sale at a nearby auto company. The price was equal to my bus ticket to North Carolina. Model A Fords seemed to be selling quite inexpensively. Don, my brother, had written that he would be spending some time in Canton, Ohio, and then coming to Pennsylvania to travel with me to Catawba for the fall semester. I figured our finances closely and bought the Model A for $35. Then I got it all ready to run like a clock. I was the proud possessor of transportation.

One of our guests had a daughter. She must have weighed nearly what I did; she was "husky" to say the least. She asked if I would take her out to Pocono Manor for a snack and a coke. After several discreet demurrals, I agreed to drive up to that incredibly ritzy place, as she was inviting me as a guest even to buying a tankful of gas which clinched the deal.

The Manor was the "in" place for all the rich people. We parked the old Model A, ourselves, quite out of view to the chagrin of the doorman, I should add. The large and ornate entryway was bigger even than the Peninsula Hotel in HongKong, my only other experience of high-class hostelry. We found a small club room area where we found snacks and Coca Cola, nice and friendly-like. Problems developed on the way home when she decided she wanted to go to a movie. Easy enough, only the huge amount of crunching on popcorn distracted from the show. After the show ended, about ten PM, I said we had to get back so I could be ready to serve early breakfast. We were in the very dark, town parking lot. Before I could start the Model A, she launched her heftiness at me and started kissing me right there in that limited front seat space. That really scared me! I got the car started and we noisily drove back to Brewer House. No more dates for me until much later in the fall semester of 1939.

Summer work was productive in that I saved most of my paychecks to buy clothes and books, etc., and even some help with tuition. Summer over, Don arrived at our Inn so we headed back to Newton, NC, to visit a few days before the semester started. The first night south we stopped to visit the Yaukey family in Silver Spring, Maryland. We had telephoned ahead and were welcomed. Grace Yaukey was our mother's best friend in Yochow. We had grown up with their sons. Raymond later entered the State Department and David became a college professor.

We arrived in Newton in a couple of days, driving all of 40 miles an hour, with a huge bag of dirty laundry. Our Aunt Hatt nearly flipped! She had been coached by Uncle Russell obviously, as she turned over the washing machine to us with detailed instructions that we followed with great care. We each must have had a dozen shirts so she was sure the clothesline would break. When the wash was dry, she handed us the iron and pointed to the ironing board. Luckily, our mother had taught us well. We went back to college with neat-looking shirts. We managed to visit Uncle Russell several times during the semester, every time we ran out of shirts. Getting the 50 miles to Newton was easy with the Model A. I suspect Aunt Hatt figured we visited only to use her washing machine—and she may have been right.

Sophomore Year, 1939-40

As a high and mighty sophomore, it was my chance to have fun getting back at the poor freshmen. Don and I, however, were rooming together in a suite with Bob Hoke and his brother called Odie. Since both younger brothers were "frosh", we really didn't have the heart to be hard on them. We wanted our younger brothers to fit right in.

This year's work-study job was a step up from the dining room wait staff. Don and I had the assignment to clean the entire basement area of Broadbeck Music building. In 1939 we still earned 25 cents an hour, but we thought it a great privilege to work to earn the funds for school and spending money. The basement held three classrooms: a large one used by accounting classes and two smaller ones where Dr. Rice taught a variety of languages. Our nightly cleanup job offered us the requisite number of hours, and since we had learned good work habits in Kuling American School we were commended by the faculty who taught there, as maintaining the neatest rooms in many a year.

I joined the International Relations Club and the Writers' Club. The latter always met at Dr. Jenkins's home. I do not recall writing anything very special, though I did try my hand at a short play. Unfortunately, I borrowed Shakespeare's idea of mixed identity in a setting in China. My effort at "pigeon English" was not understandable to the sophisticated readers of North Carolina. It just did not mix with the accepted southern dialect. I won no prizes, only the comment "needs work!" Needless to say, I took this as a clear sign I was no playwright.

During the fall, I was emboldened to talk "one-on-one" with a shy girl, Mary Jane. At least I thought she was as shy as I was. We sat in the student lounge and finally I asked her for a date to a movie. We started dating more often in the lounge of Zartman Hall where all freshman girls lived with the elderly Dean of Women Miss Augusta Lantz. Plenty of boys and girls were around so I didn't panic. Miss Lantz was famous for keeping an extra close eye on male visitors. She also insisted that girls smooth down their "hair dos," because boys became too excited by flowing and blowing hair.

By late fall Mary Jane and I were on pretty good speaking terms and even held hands some. Don and I decided that we didn't want to impose on Uncle Russell again for Christmas vacation and we knew Uncle Gordon did not have room for both of us. I was invited to go to Chambersburg, PA, to visit Mary Jane. It was a real "learning curve" experience as we double dated with her sister in the Chamberlain living room. Listening to records and the radio was fine. Problems developed when Mary Jane's precocious younger sister, whom we were "baby-sitting," decided she and her boyfriend would take over the couch for their "necking." Their behavior was way beyond my limited experience. It was so hot and heavy that we were both embarrassed. When I returned to school a few days later, I wasn't at all sure what might be expected of me. Though we dated sporadically during the spring semester, we really did not go "steady." In fact, Mary Jane did not return the following fall semester, as she transferred to a college near her home. I learned that she married her high school boyfriend a year later.

In December, I was in Shaw's play "Arms and the Man." The only comment I have found in the *Pioneer* was:

> "...Praise must go to Sterling Whitener who, along with the leads, showed he could go places on the stage were he given the chance. The smooth way he handled Major Petkoff ranks him with the leads in making the performance a success..."

WOW! I did manage to perform in another play that spring, "Monomee," written by our class playwright and intellectual, Franklin Marsh.

Again I went out for the track team. To this day I cannot reason why. In any case it was always a matter of being listed as "also ran."

In the spring, I wrote a friend from Kuling American School who was attending the University of North Carolina in Chapel Hill to inquire about some kind of summer job. Eugene Turner said he was recruiting counselors for a YMCA camp and offered me a job helping youth at Camp Wawayanda in New Jersey. I felt this was an experience that would be helpful for the future. Don had a friend who successfully suggested they work at Silver Bay in New York.

My Model A had been sold to help pay tuition so I had quite a challenging trip with a number of bus changes to get to the camp at Lake Hopatcong in western New Jersey. My assignment was a tent platform with cots for eight seventh graders, a high school junior, and this rising college junior. Gene gave me a rapid course in supervision and continued that process all summer. It was good training as we met as counseling staff every day at the rest hour. Our high school counselors were to keep campers quiet and orderly. They were successful part of the time.

My daytime activity position was to help the swimming instructor, who doubled as sailing instructor. Having passed the Red Cross Lifesaving course, I took my section of the beach each day. Only once during the entire summer did any of the 200 or so boys need to be pulled from the water by all of us life guards. On my days off, it was too expensive to travel into town since I was saving funds for school, so I learned to sail and to canoe. The lake was quite large, so several of us with the same day off could pack sandwiches and spend a leisurely day away from camp.

One extended weekend was offered during the summer. A whole three days away from the little kids was truly astounding. Lucky for me, a fellow counselor and canoe/sailing partner took pity on me and invited me to his home in Montclair. What we did that weekend is vague, but his family lived in a big home and the food was good.

So it was soon September and time to return to school. Eugene Turner and I hitched a ride back to North Carolina with a senior counselor who had a car. I caught the bus from Chapel Hill back to Salisbury to start my junior year little realizing that it would be quite a turning point in my life.

Report on the Whitener family

Dad and Mom had been in Yueyang during our Kuling American School evacuation to HongKong. That same spring in 1938, they finally had to evacuate 300 miles west because of the Japanese air raids and advances. In that summer Mom made it to Shanghai in time for my graduation and then spent the summer with Don and Bob in an apartment. She went back to West Hunan during the school year to return the following summer of 1939 when Don graduated. While Dad remained at work in Yuanling, she stayed in Shanghai for the summer with Bob, leaving again for Hunan when school started. That year the Japanese army took Changsha and Canton so the folks were finally cut off from an easy exit via HongKong. Thus Bob was in the dorm at Shanghai American School for his 7th grade, '39–'40; Don had joined me at Catawba.

Then in the summer of 1940, Mom and Dad came out of China for their regular furlough via a portion of the Burma Road to Hanoi, French Indo China now Vietnam. The situation in West China had deteriorated with increased Japanese bombing of cities and transportation hubs. Dad and Mom were forced to use sections of the Burma Road to get around the Japanese advances. Their bus rides over parts of the Burma Road and connecting roads in Kweichow were harrowing. Allowed only a bag each, they often had to hold their bags on their laps as the truck/buses were so overcrowded. One time they had the front seat next to the door. On a steep hairpin turn, which the truck could not accomplish in one turn, Dad hopped out and found a rock to place under the rear wheel when the brakes could not hold the overloaded bus as it crept slowly backward toward the precipitous ravine. From Hanoi they made their way by ship to Shanghai to pick up Bob for the trip back to the States for furlough.

It was much later that the folks told us about the hazardous travel from Yuanling to Kunming down to Indochina to reach Hanoi for a ship to Shanghai to pick up Bob.

I found some references to this trip in a Presbyterian Missionary's diary/ narrative written many years later by Gertrude Bayless.

"…On May 30, 1940 there were two Red Cross trucks leaving for the west and I was able to get a ride with them…I rode in one truck and Mr. & Mrs. Whitener rode in the other truck. There were breakdowns and stops. At one place we saw three opium smokers being marched out to be shot.…We reached Pu An in the next evening where Marie Whitener and I slept in a carpenter's room. The trucks were breaking down at various places...When about 20 kilometers from Pin I, we met dense fog and stopped for the night. Two walked the 15 miles into town in the rain. The Whiteners and I spent the night in the truck, and it continued to rain.

We started again at dawn, slithering in deep mud from one side of the road to the other along the mountainside, with a 300 foot drop on our right. It was nerve racking and when finally the truck turned over on its side, toward the mountain, it was a relief. The cargo in the truck was tung oil. Mixed with alcohol, tung oil was being used in place of gasoline. The drums broke and the oil began flowing down the gutter. From seemingly nowhere, some women appeared with buckets and began dipping up the oil. Marie and I walked the 6 or 7 miles into town in a drizzle. Later Sterling Whitener brought our baggage in two bullock carts...."

While the folks were traveling I was oblivious to their whereabouts. Only at the end of the summer did their letters finally catch up with me.

In the summer of 1940 I was at Wawayanda working. Don was invited to Canton, Ohio, to travel with Uncle Leonard to the West Coast to meet Mom, Dad, and Bob who were returning from China on furlough. Arriving in Seattle, they were met by Mother's brother, Uncle Leonard, and Aunt Anna, who had decided to drive to the west coast for a vacation taking Don and daughters, Naomi and Delores. With youngest cousin, Bob, they headed back to meet at the old home place in Missouri while Mom and Dad traveled by train with all the baggage. Bob says that the biggest arguments were about who had the softest shoulder to sleep against.

The Hegnauer family headed back to Canton, Ohio, while the Whitener three made it back to North Carolina for a visit before settling down for the school year in Lancaster, PA, at one of the missionary apartments. The first time our whole family had really been together in four years was during the 1940 Christmas vacation when Don and I made it to Lancaster.

Life at Catawba College – Junior Year, 1940-41

With great expectations, I returned from the Y camp in New Jersey to my junior year at Catawba. Calvin Stein, a senior, had asked me to room with him in a small duplex dormitory called Foil House. Eight men shared an enlarged bathroom but the dorm rooms were a bit larger than the old dorm. Cal was a tennis player, as well as a disciplined student. We got along well. My summer as an assistant in canoeing and counselor to very active junior high boys had helped me to get in shape physically. I had shed quite a few pounds. That fall I enjoyed playing my trombone in the band. We didn't get to travel with the football team everywhere but did get to a few out-of-town games.

The increasing closeness of US entry into the war lent urgency to decisions that had to be made by all college students. Some signed up with various programs of the armed services; many of us kept our fingers crossed as it became clear that there would be a national draft. The decision to prepare for missionary work in China, made during my first year at Catawba, seemed to be the right one for me. At the appropriate time, I applied to the Newton, NC, draft board for a 4D classification to prepare for the ministry. Later they transferred me to the Salisbury board. I still have my draft cards marked 4D. Our club, the Adelphians, was hosted and advised by Dr. David E. Faust, a Yale Divinity graduate. He encouraged everyone to consider that when young men were sent to war, there would be a great need for many chaplains. Most of us declared that we would be ready for that call. Upperclassmen were signing up for Officers' Candidate Schools. I had applied to Yale Divinity School and received acceptance so was encouraged to remain steadfast in this decision by professors at college and seminary.

That spring I went out for track. Never noted as a speedster, I did manage to learn the low hurdles. The physical training, however, prepared me for my next summer job in a steel mill.

Usual activities of choir, Writers' Club, Adelphians, and several others kept me busy. I was elected "Campus Day Chairman" and then Junior Marshall for graduation exercises. One more play for the Blue Masque in the spring was "Dick of the Woods." I got to be Roaring Ralph Stackpole, a really fitting role.

Summer Labor in Ohio, 1941

Uncle Leonard and Aunt Anna invited me to Ohio to find a summer job. Young Leonard, my cousin, was working in the Timken Roller Bearing Company office. He said he would share his room in the attic with me if I wanted to come up to get a good-paying job as a laborer. Sounded great to me, though Mom felt it was too much to put on Aunt Anna's shoulders, as she would need to cook for an extra big eater. In any case, I was soon in Canton, OH, applying for a job. At the time, steel mills were working 24-hour shifts and there seemed to be a shortage of strong backs. In no time at all I was assigned to a work gang. Our first job was to work fifteen-minute shifts with jackhammers cutting slag out of blast furnaces that had cooled down only somewhat. There was a real rush to get them back into production, so we wore asbestos boots over our work shoes and had heavy gloves to hold the air hammers. We drank gallons of water and swallowed salt tablets during our fifteen-minute rest periods and then back onto the hot slag heap. I tried to work out a payment plan with Aunt Anna for my meals, but she wouldn't hear of it. Said I didn't eat that much, but actually I was a big eater. Even so, I lost quite a bit of weight, so she was worried that my folks would think she hadn't fed me properly.

I was offered a transfer from my laboring job to learn to be a crane operator. They suggested that I seemed to have enough intelligence. What a compliment coming from a hardheaded foreman. I decided that such a change, though helpful by offering better pay, was too much of an imposition on Aunt Anna since it would mean changing shifts every other week. As a laborer we laid railroad tracks, dug ditches, cleaned up a variety of spills, and kept working pretty hard. By the end of the summer, my muscles were really tight and I was in good shape when I got back to school. In fact, I thought I was tough and strong.

During the summer we did get a few days off from work. Most of the time on days off I "hung around" with friend Chuck a Youth Group member of my Uncle's Church. Once we took the back seat out of Chuck's car and opened it up to the trunk so we could camp in a state park nearby. And of course we also took a flying drive down to Salisbury!

Senior Year – Fall Semester 1941 to Summer 1942

Mom, Dad, and Bob moved to Ithaca, New York, where they were all in school. Mom and Dad studied in a special rural Missions course at Cornell while Bob was in 8th grade. I went back to Salisbury ready to try out for football proudly wearing # 24.

Football practice showed me very quickly that a great variety of skills are required to be proficient and successful. Needless to say, my contribution was limited entirely to being "cannon fodder." I was regularly a live practice dummy. My good friend of later years, Chub Richards, who became registrar at Catawba before retirement, trampled me on many plays until I learned enough to grab him, surreptitiously, and pull him down on top of me. About mid-season I sprained my ankle so was excused from practice for a few weeks of blessed relief. The coach paid me a compliment by saying he could have used me if I had only come out my freshman year. I'm sure he was talking about being good "cannon fodder" material. My final shot of glory was in the last game of the season when we were playing arch-rival Lenoir Rhyne. My friends on the sidelines kept shouting "Sterling, Sterling" when we got ahead sufficiently to make sure we could not lose the game. Coach Kirkland sent me in as right guard with the explicit, simple instruction to "run straight ahead and keep out of the way." My friend Park Loy put it this way in his weekly Pioneer column: "Put in for the last few minutes for one play, Wang Poo Whitener did his part in the victory. When asked what he did, he said he blocked the tackle. But after going to his room and restudying the play book, he found out he was supposed to get the line-backer. What price glory!"

My scholarship job for the year was to continue to be an assistant to Miss Price, as well as to teach a class in English grammar to freshman students who were having difficulty writing their themes. Having learned in Kuling American School how to diagram sentences, I worked somewhat haltingly to transmit the skill to several football players and others who, fortunately for me, knew a lot less than I did. Don and I roomed together in Foil House, a small dorm, duplex style of four rooms.

Graduation was a special time because our whole family was together for the event and my parents met Barbara. I think my mother fell in love with her then!

The summer of 1942 was spent with the Whitener family. We lived in a rented house while the parsonage at Mt. Hope Church was being remodeled and renovated. There was a tennis court in back of the house where Don and I played many games. We also found a summer job making popsicles on the second shift of an ice-cream factory. This lasted for a month or so until the Popsicle business declined with cooler weather. At that time the family moved out to the church parsonage in the country at Mt. Hope Church, not far from Whitsett where I helped Dad with Bible School. I did have a chance to go visit Barbara some during the summer.

Yale Divinity School – September 1942 to June 1943

Yale Divinity School was located on a hilltop above New Haven, a beautiful location with an outstanding architectural design funded by Rockefeller money and low-cost construction during the depression years. I was excited to be there, challenged by my courses and professors.

Bacon House was to be my dormitory in the beautiful classic campus "on the hill." It was one of a series of dormitories lined up in columns approaching the chapel at the highest point. That fall in New England was a heady experience. Dick Hutcheson, my roommate Hutch, was a tall, lanky Presbyterian minister's son who had graduated from Emory and Henry. His interest was preaching; mine missions. He excelled in the former; I sure covered missions, taking every course Professor Kenneth Scott Latourette offered. Hutch was an avid bridge player, so we enjoyed many a game with Mark Baker and Bob Yoh, our fellow hall mates.

Yale had many distinguished professors. It was difficult to enroll in all the courses offered, so we would often go to lectures offered by Roland Bainton and others when the word was out that a favorite topic about Martin Luther was coming up. Daily chapel services were led by a professor each week except for the Friday special when one of the seniors was in charge. There was usually good attendance but the place was always crowded when Halford Luccock, our Homiletics professor, or another of the better faculty preachers was speaking. Then there was the elderly Old Testament professor Dahl who, to our dismay, was a dismal instructor, boring and very unclear in his instructions. Our term paper was to buy a small section of the OT, select a book or a long episode, and write a commentary. In our elementary knowledge all we could do was copy what the experts said, so he received a large box full of cut-up Bibles pasted opposite to whatever commentary we could find or make up. Even major schools have their problems with faculty! It was almost ten years later that I had the opportunity to take a really challenging and stimulating course in "Genesis" under Davie Napier, an outstanding scholar.

As most of us had to work our way in order to pay for seminary studies, my job was with the YMCA youth program. Called Gra-Y, about thirty seminary men worked with seventh and eighth graders all over New Haven and surrounding communities. Some of the married students were able to find assignments in small churches where a parsonage was usually attached. My Y club was in East Haven so I rode the trolley car to get there. It was a residential area for blue collar workers and during the war they were doing very well indeed. We met in the family homes once a week. This was a wonderful way to relate to the junior high boys and to provide a role model. I was particularly fond of Ben Newton, a rather chubby son of a single parent. He tended to be overbearing and not too popular. He probably reminded me of my own growing pains during my junior high years. I took special pains to relate to him and his very personable but worried mother. We related so well that Barbara and I visited Mrs. Newton's home in ensuing years always enjoying a huge, steaming cup of good coffee. We became corresponding friends for years, finally visiting her at a nursing/retirement home in Maine in the 1980s.

Our Gra-Y clubs also met weekly at the YMCA for basketball or other games, as well as a swimming session. I planned the weekly program, took them on outings such as hikes and picnics and really worked on their swimming skills. Our club managed to get a pretty good record in the competitions.

New Haven, Connecticut, was a busy war-time city making munitions and all kinds of weaponry. The factories were humming three shifts a day. There certainly was full employment. At the time, the draft had not seriously affected college students, as draft boards encouraged youth to get ahead. Many were accepted into the various navy, army, and coast guard officer candidate programs in order to prepare leaders for the future. Though gasoline was rationed, there was a very good street car system running, as well as bus lines, so we could get almost anywhere we wanted to. Our favorite hike was to walk to East Rock Park, a four-or-five-hundred-foot high area with a rock cliff overlooking the harbor itself. An obelisk monument was visible from many parts of the city. Not too far away was a ridge of low-lying hills called "Sleeping Giant." All the boys' clubs from the Y paid regular visits to the park and to the Giant for picnics, hikes, and fun.

Our course work was demanding. There wasn't much time for social life. Much of our free time was spent in "bull sessions," theological, of course in the common room of the Divinity School or in student rooms. These sessions were usually conducted by the older students of the second and third years, as they were much more deeply involved in advanced studies. I kept particularly quiet because the first semester New Testament course was a challenge for me. I had serious questions about my own calling, my sense of purpose, and my inadequacies as a future missionary. I was not alone in my feelings and doubts in the confidence of my sense of call to be a Christian minister, but I did have a sense of wanting to go back to China to serve the Church as my father had. It was over sixty years later that Barbara helped me identify that a strong part of my "call" was directly related to a desire to serve the Chinese people with whom I felt a close affinity. I never considered playing a role in the institutional church in the US or even looking for some other professional job.

Dr. Richard Niebuhr was our Evangelical and Reformed mentor and polity teacher. He was most helpful to me when I got the courage to go to him with my doubts and concerns. He spent hours with me going over how I might resolve some of the issues by rereading the Gospel of Mark, which, for him, had helped give perspective on the most important issues of theology. I shall ever be grateful that over the years of my theological study, he sought me out for regular sessions to go over what I was thinking and understanding. I learned that I was not the only student who had such doubts.

I had selected Yale Divinity School because of Dr. Kenneth Scott Latourette, Professor of Missions. He proved to be a constant inspiration. He regularly attended the Missions Group. His secretary at the time was Creighton Lacy (Corky), a "Missionary Kid" from China, a few years older than I, who became a lifelong friend. He and his wife, Fran, later served in China with the Methodist Mission in Foochow. Corky then completed his doctoral studies and taught Missions at Duke Divinity School.

Our group met on a weekly basis at the Disciples of Christ Mission House. Brief worship, a talk by a visiting missionary or church leader, much discussion, and then refreshments always made for lively sessions. It is amazing how many YDS men and women were involved in preparation for overseas Missions. Many of our friends come from this era.

We managed to exercise in the small gym. We had some rough and rowdy basketball games because we never really had a referee. Bacon House had a small college "all-American" player, Rex Knowles. Brainerd House had a huge guy, Coleman, who had played football on Yale's second team. When the two of them mixed it up, we usually stood back and watched or at least got out of the way. On one occasion in the spring, I managed to break the bone behind my little finger of my left hand when a hard thrown ball hit the tip end. That cut down on my basketball days for the time it was in a splint.

Because this was war time, the apple orchards of Connecticut were hurting for field hands. We were able to go out to the apple orchards not too far from town any time we had free hours and could earn a few very valuable dollars picking apples. I also got to bring a batch back to the dorm for friends. Of course we were in demand to help sell programs, etc., at the Yale football games. Although the team wasn't very good, the enthusiasm of the young Yalies was as great as ever.

I have a letter that I wrote on February 27, 1943, to the Evangelical and Reformed Church Mission Board secretary, Dr. A.V. Casselman, in Philadelphia:

> *"Upon entering Yale Divinity School last fall, I came with the express purpose of preparing for foreign missionary work in China. It is my hope that I will be able to go out to China under our own Mission Board. It is certainly a privilege to be able to work under Dr. Latourette, who is also my adviser.*
>
> *The Missions group on campus is one of the most active groups here. There is always someone from the field or closely associated with missions who can speak to us. Dr. Bates from Nanking has been especially interesting.*
>
> *The E. & R. group, of which there are about eight of us, has met with Dr. Niebuhr and has decided to study our church polity together. We are also very interested in the proposed merger with the Congregational Church.*
>
> *When you are up in New York sometime, you might take a day off and come up to New Haven. There are about three others in our church that need only a little guidance who are interested in missions."*

I think I received a polite reply, which puzzled me because Dr. Casselman was a good friend of my parents. It was only a few months later that I learned of his illness and early death. That left the question of my possible mission service up in the air to be settled two years later.

Memories of spring semester activity focus on frequent letters to and from Barbara! The letters were my lifeline. Several of us started a quartet for our Bacon House. We organized it over many bridge games to decide what kind of songs we would practice and for whom we might sing. Of the four bridge players, three were basses and I was the only tenor (2nd). We needed a first tenor so recruited Bob Clark, next door neighbor. We began by singing for some church youth groups and actually kept the group singing for a couple of years. Another activity I undertook was the Water Safety Instructor's course at the Yale gym and earning my Waterfront Safety Director's Certification from Coach Bob Kiphuth, Yale's famous Olympic swimming coach. This took quite a block of time and effort. I had hopes of securing a summer job at a camp.

Late in the spring of 1943, just before exams, I woke one night with acute abdominal pain. The guys rushed me to the Yale hospital, where a young physician removed my appendix. He was ahead of his time and was applying new principles of immediate recovery. He made a very small incision and had me up the next day blowing into a huge bottle of water to improve lung action. It was a real pain but a surefire cure! I was able to take my exams in my dorm room on schedule.

On the second day Hutch came into the hospital room to find Professor Latourette in my room chatting with me. His jaw fell. I think he never expected a professor to take time to visit any student in the hospital. It was really the first time Hutch had had a chance to talk with Dr. Latourette. After quite a long visit, Hutch later told me how impressed he was and would never ridicule mission work again! That chance meeting was very significant because my roommate had often been somewhat respectfully critical of missions as a topic for study. Any pastor would be a good missionary. He was a good pastor and eventually Navy Chief of Chaplains.

Camp Sequoia Summer Job – 1943

It was urgent that I get back on my feet, recover my strength, and get back to North Carolina before too long, as I had secured a summer job at Camp Sequoia, a private camp not far from Asheville to be the Waterfront Director, swimming and canoeing instructor.

I was very excited as I took the train to Asheville and then the bus into Weaverville to be picked up by the camp transport. Camp Sequoia was an expensive private camp tucked into the mountains near the crest of the Blue Ridge and the Parkway in the Black Mountain range between Craggy Gardens and Mt. Mitchell. A curmudgeonly owner, Mr. Robert Johnson, was experienced, mean, quite miserly, and a hard disciplinarian. He wanted all of us to carry a proper pocketknife so he purchased a rather expensive brand and deducted the price from our first paycheck. I did not see that as reasonable since I had no part in the decision and didn't really want that knife to begin with. To say the least, I managed to get off to a rather rough start. Our weekly staff sessions were full of directions on what to do and how to keep all the forms and reports filled out, with very little discussion from those of us who were doing the work. The program was varied so there were all kinds of sports: hiking, campouts, and even special backpacking trips in the mountains. I was kept at camp for the home program, which always included swimming in the very cold mountain pool.

Fortunately, I knew my job and did it well by organizing the swimming classes, training the lifeguards, and instructing canoeing so campers could qualify for canoe trips. I enjoyed teaching swimming best. In fact, I was good at it. Many years later, Stahle Linn, a successful Salisbury lawyer, who was very handicapped with a crippling condition that may have been the result of polio, complimented me for teaching him to swim. The summer's responsibility also included being the head counselor for eight boys of junior high age in a small cabin. My assistant counselor was a very likeable high school rising senior. One of the campers for the eight weeks was a Cuban boy, Carlos Lopez-Ona, who was somewhat less robust than the other boys, but a good swimmer. I ran a very tight lifesaving drill and water safety program. At the end of the summer "Chief" (Johnson) was complimentary and even asked if I would come back the next year but I declined because I had in mind beginning an entirely new life!

Yale Divinity School – September 1943 to June 1944

"409 Prospect Street, New Haven CT, and here I come." My second year at Yale Divinity was busy. Still living at Bacon House and rooming with Dick Hutcheson again, a good set of dorm mates made life full and interesting. I found the courses just as difficult. This year, however, with greater motivation I managed to get better grades. My job for the year was to be a Gra-Y supervisor. I met with the first year divinity school students who organized the junior high Gra-Y clubs and regularly visited each of them. Wherever there was a club I was busy traveling in the afternoons all over the city and nearby small towns for a visit.

At one point early in the year, many of us discovered that a good way to get a free education was to sign up for the Navy's V-12 program to train officers. We would be trained as Navy chaplains. The offer of free tuition, uniforms, and board and room was enticing since we would also be serving our country. My roommate was immediately successful and was soon wearing a blue uniform and destined to become a Chief of Chaplains in the future. I took the physical exam and flunked it. My red-green colorblind condition read the wrong numbers on the Ishihara test. How ironic that I was flunked by a test prepared by a Japanese scientist when we were engaged in a major campaign against Japan in the Pacific. It was increasingly ironic that the officer in charge asked me to step into his office. He offered me the opportunity to sign up for a special officer's standing as an "observer." He then explained that I would contribute greatly by flying in a small plane looking for major enemy weapons which were camouflaged by green tree branches. I smiled and said I was more interested in mission service as I had been born in China. Shortly afterward, I wrote to the Board of International Missions of the Evangelical and Reformed Church to ask about procedures for applying for Mission work after graduation.

Our preaching class was more serious the second year as Dr. Halford Luccock, a world-famous preacher, taught the course. He was able to take our feeble practice efforts and turn them into something that sounded like a sermon. Many a seminarian was able to overcome palpitations, fright, nervousness, and timidity. He regularly enabled those of us who were hesitant to present our ideas to state our thoughts boldly. He could turn the most pedantic and simple idea into a masterpiece. This style of encouragement was at first dismaying, but gradually we were enabled to reach out. The fact that I felt I was never going to be a preacher in the United States led me to volunteer at the Yale Hope Mission, a respite and overnight sleeping space for homeless men. Seminarians were regularly scheduled to lead evening prayers with singing, Bible reading, and a short meditation. Even in those days, many persons with mental problems were not being regularly employed and needed supper and a place to sleep. It was good experience to try to say something that would make the weary and disheartened wake up and listen.

To get home for Christmas vacation, I traveled by train to Baltimore where Don was at Johns Hopkins Medical School. We had a ride south with a friend of his to save expenses. Mom and Dad let me hurry on to Salisbury for Barbara and my long anticipated time to celebrate our official engagement.

It really was a busy spring. I had to find an apartment for the summer and a final year at the Divinity School. Many places were available, but I was looking for one that could be paid for with my labor. One place was the funeral home apartment that Bob and Mimi Beck served by answering the phone at night. Bob was from our Mission family in Yueyang. Though he tried to help me, my classmate, Charlie Heuser, beat me to it. I was finally able to locate an apartment that included cleaning an old three-story building owned by a physician as an office. The job was simple enough and could be performed in the evenings, but it included the stoking and care of a cranky steam furnace system. The apartment was quite spacious, as it included a large bedroom, living room, small kitchen, and bath on the third floor with an extra room up in the peak of the building that could double as a study room. It was a great relief to have that problem solved.

Some time during the spring break I was able to hitch a ride to Baltimore to visit my brother Don at Johns Hopkins. It was certainly an eye-opener for me. On one occasion, he took me to the operating theaters and told me to don the proper outfit of robes, hats, etc., and just go on in to see what was happening. I did so, joining the other white-robed gallery, probably first-year medical students. A surgeon droned on and on about what he was doing. All I could see was a mass of blood, bloody hands, and strange instruments. After a bell rang and everyone else left for class, the surgeon looked up at me and told me to come down closer so I could see. Though I hesitated, a nurse told me to come closer, which I did, and then she spoke rather harshly, "Don't touch me." I hadn't realized that in craning to see a patient's internal organs, which I could not identify, I had brushed against her sleeve. The combination of feeling I did not belong and the close-up view was enough to start my head reeling. I thanked the nurse and said, "I really ought to go." She nodded, "You do look a bit pale, go sit down awhile." I got out of there fast, found fresh air, and later recounted my experience to Don, who agreed that the first time was not always easy. He showed me his research dogs, as he was the keeper of their kennels. He was helping Dr. Blalock, who pioneered the technique of operating on "blue babies" after practicing on her dogs.

The Divinity School semester ended but my job of cleaning the doctor's building just started. I had to be sure that all the wastebaskets were emptied, the rooms swept, and floors mopped. The hardest jobs were the two stairways, a larger main one and a narrow back stairwell that was dark and hard to keep really clean. Fortunately, the summer did not require the furnace. That was a special treat in store for me to learn, as the weather got cold in October.

This summer before my last year in Seminary was to be my introduction to married life. I felt I was ready and at the same time, I had that job to earn the apartment on Whitney Ave. I had asked the Mission Board to provide a small grant for Chinese study in the Language Institute at Yale. Army officers were to be trained to become interpreters for the army and air force. I was put in a class of eight or nine beginners. These officers were being prepared to fly to West China to work with various units stationed to help in the war effort against Japan. It was interesting that none of them appeared to have very much language ability and certainly never had entertained the idea of studying Chinese. No one could figure out why I wanted to study with the army interpreters, but the Yale director was sympathetic to my plea to prepare for Mission work in China. He was working to set up a Chinese language study program for persons wishing to work in China after the war. I think he wondered if I were committed enough to pursue the rigors of constant study and repetition that was to be demanded of army personnel. He might then determine just what curriculum he could follow for his planned institute for missionaries.

The classes were very intense and concentrated. The officers really were on duty all the time. We learned how to parachute into friendly territory and seek the Chinese resistance fighters. When we got to the study of everyday life, I was in my element. We all spent much time listening to lessons-on-disks. The six-inch green plastic recordings made by our instructors and tutors were not of good sound quality, but it was easy to learn the tones that were vital to understanding Chinese.

I got into the swing of study very quickly in June before our wedding. At the same time, I had already gotten into our apartment and had reluctantly begun "batching" it.

* * *

Please go back in time with me. I ended Chapter 1 on the note of a "turning point" in my life. I often referred to Barbara throughout but have always felt moved to put my love story all together. It seems to fit best here.

A Tale of Courtship – 1940 to 1944

In the fall of 1940, I met a young woman named Barbara Louise Brown. Life for me was very different after that. In retrospect, it really became clear to me during that winter of 1940 and spring of 1941 I wanted Barbara to join me in life's great adventure. That it took three years of discussion and struggle to accomplish this will not surprise her children, who know that she is strong-minded and a very careful planner. This is how it came about.

My summer earnings in 1940 went toward clothes and other expenses. My allowance from the Mission Board was $350 a year, but it was ever necessary to find additional income for tuition, books, and spending money. An offer to become the assistant to Miss Frances Price, who taught freshman English and history was a real blessing. The 10 to 15 hours a week grading and correcting papers was much better than sweeping out the basement of the music building. The stipend rather than an hourly rate was also much more lucrative! It was in this assistant's job that I began to understand and know Barbara Brown. I found Barbara's European history and English papers so carefully crafted and interestingly written they caught my attention.

We first met, officially, early in the semester when Collin Choate, a "kissing cousin," niece of Aunt Annie Laurie's, the wife of Dad's brother Jay, was entertaining a group of day students in the student lounge. Her "gang" of very attractive "frosh" girls was taking a break. As I walked through the Student Union lounge with Don, now a sophomore, we were invited to meet this comely group. We were introduced as cousins to Pat, Fannie, Barbara, and others. Collin had already bragged to Barbara that Don and I were "the smartest guys at Catawba." Factual or not, this caught Barbara's attention. A few days later, Collin asked me to go on a double date with Barbara. I have never heard the end of the fact that I broke the date because I wanted to see the "hell drivers" at the county fairgrounds, only later to be unable to go at all. The program I was looking for was postponed for a few days. All the girls of the group took the opportunity to remind me of that gaffe! Naturally, the offer to double date was never repeated. I did, however, often chat with that day-student group in the Student Union. More and more during September and October I found time to be sure to visit when Barbara was available. I felt I was getting to know her.

To a question posed by our Pioneer reporter, "What do you think of Catawba boys?" Barbara stated, "Don't quote me please." I never did find out what she meant, nor does she remember. I think I felt she was attracted to me so I continued to find occasions to meet her.

The semester proceeded smoothly. Of great interest in my schedule was a projected November choir tour to Pennsylvania churches. We really did have a good choir. Traveling by bus we sang every night in churches for at least a week. Church members put us up in their homes but we usually ate dinners in "Pennsylvania Dutch" abundance at the church. Choir members became quite chummy, with couples sitting together as we drove from town to town. The tour ended with a late night trip back to Salisbury. This long tale is to let you know that I found a seatmate, Nell, a day student. After our return to school, in the ensuing weeks, my weekend free November nights were spent visiting her. I thought I was getting along pretty well until one night she asked, "Wouldn't you rather be in the arms of Barbara Brown?" Can't remember how the topic came up, but I do remember how difficult a time I had making a stumbling reply. The question obviously struck a chord because I never went back to visit Nell. I realized that I wanted seriously to cultivate Barbara's friendship. For three or four weeks, I remember concentrating on visiting the "girls of the student lounge."

It was in December 1940, however, before I bravely called the Lutheran parsonage to ask Barbara for a date. Since I never had any money, I am sure we sat in the Brown living room and then went into the den to listen to records. It was not long before I tried to visit as often as I could.

Back in school for the spring semester of 1941 our college choir director asked me if I would like to sing in a church choir for $4.00 per month, a princely sum. It involved a practice during the week and getting up early on Sunday mornings, but an added attraction was that it was St. John's Lutheran Church, where Barbara's father was the pastor. P.D. Brown was a very good preacher; he and I really got along well. Once when I rushed in at the last minute for the Sunday service, he welcomed me with a twinkle in his eye, "I thought you must have gotten tired of my sermons – I'll try to do better!" Tenors sang on the side of the chancel where the pastor sat, so I was often placed next to him. I must say that P. D.'s voice was made for preaching and definitely not for singing. Another advantage of my seating was that I could see Barbara in the congregation from my perch, a most rewarding view.

During that spring semester, Barbara and I spent quite a bit of time together, seeing each other between classes in the Student Union. I sent her roses when cramps put her to bed and that meant a lot to her. I know she began to care for me and I was ready to devote much time and energy to furthering our relationship. Her view, however, was her college years were for meeting many and being friends to all. After all, she was only seventeen, but I highly resented her dates with Malcolm and a few others. Jealousy was not easy to overcome. We attended some of the church youth activities such as Luther League, went to college dances together, and on weekends dated at the parsonage on what I soon learned was the "torture seat." That sobriquet was given by her sister, Janice, to a plastic covered hard couch located in the den. It must have originated many years earlier in the experimental era of couches that folded out into beds. With heavy straight springs, the seat was really hard, not at all conducive to a relaxing date.

The two strongest pulls/interests for me during the year were: (1) my need to prepare for seminary study, and (2) to seek a commitment to "go steady" from Barbara. The first was much easier than the second was. You can see why, as Barbara was a first year, day-student freshman, and I a junior. I was very persistent in trying to persuade her. My preparation for study was easier because, as a junior, I began to apply myself more seriously to my classes, earning better grades and receiving support from faculty members. This was probably good for my psyche because I had always considered myself only a mediocre student. Don found study simple; I envied that easy learning ability. I felt I lacked discipline but found that when it was applied I really could do well, especially in the area so close to my heart — China. Barbara, of course, knew about my love of China, my early life there and my determination to return as a missionary some day.

The *Pioneer* reported that Catawba had registered nearly 500 students that spring semester. It was also reported that in the Writers' Club, Whitener's play, "Jap Jitters," was read. Barbara's offering was "A Penny for His Thoughts." Three were admitted to the club: Barbara Brown, Sterling, and Bob Hand. The latter's article was entitled "Tragedy." Was it a prediction of the future? The annual listed Barbara and Sterling as "friends indeed" and a personal note in my '41 annual *The Sayakini* had this wonderful comment by Barbara, "You made the year perfect."

A major event of the summer was a drive from Canton, Ohio, to Salisbury to visit Barbara. I was working that summer at Timken Roller Bearing Co., living with Uncle Leonard and family. Barbara and I corresponded regularly. My cousin Leonard, a friend, and I drove to Salisbury one Friday afternoon and night. I had a date with Barbara on Saturday and then we started back on Sunday. The roads in the 1940s were narrow, winding, and steep. Going through West Virginia was harrowing, but the thousand-mile trip was worth it for a date. No promises made, but I felt I had made some progress in assuring Barbara of my seriousness. The summer ended and it was time for school again.

Most important, my greatest challenge during that senior school year remained my inability to receive assurance from Barbara Brown, now a sophomore, that I was the one for her.

Once during the fall, as we walked from the Church Senior Youth League meeting, Barbara suddenly posed a question, serious or not I never could determine, "What would you say if I said I would not go to China with you?" I thought a short moment and said, "It's been nice knowing you," as I waved my hand in a farewell gesture. I surprised myself with this response, but Barbara really knew that this plan for my life was foremost, and she respected it.

I continued with vigor to pursue this beautiful girl, and my pressure finally got to her. She decided during the fall semester that we needed a period of separation or respite. Courting is difficult. When compounded by conflicting agendas it becomes impossible. Her concept of "just dating" was quite different from my own, so we went through a difficult period of nearly six months when I tried to avoid her completely. This caused unhappiness but I persisted. In her new freedom, she dated my dorm mate, Bob Hand. Completely in sympathy with me, my other dorm mates would dramatically rush up to me "to pull the knife out of my back" whenever they saw Bob and Barbara walk by. Needless to say that did not make it any easier in the dorm itself or on campus when I unexpectedly could not avoid her. I did try to date other girls, but it was obvious that my heart wasn't in it. It wasn't too hard as a senior to find someone who would attend an event or a dance with me. A small, cute freshman girl, Judy, did enjoy dancing, but our dates were really quite casual. My prevailing memory that final semester of my senior year was of a painful time.

It was also very awkward to be in the same Spanish class. I managed pretty well to stay out of sight, but inevitably we would at times bump into each other. At Sunday services, Barbara's father always spoke kindly to me, wondering what my plans were for graduate school and sensitive to what was transpiring between us. Many "bull sessions" in the dorm during the spring did help put some perspective on my personal problems, especially those concerning Barbara. Rooming with brother Don was always helpful because he had opportunities to report to me what he learned from her and her friends, as he was friends with everyone. When the 1942 Annual came out with a picture of Barbara walking in front of the administration building with Bob Hand, it was tough days!

Then there was an awakening! The final graduation choir concert was held in the auditorium/chapel and Barbara was there. As the choir recessed down the aisle I kept looking at her and saw that she was looking directly at me. Something sparked! It was as though all the feelings we had had for each other were there again. Very tentatively we reached out to each other, first exchanging friendly greetings, then dating again.

My graduation was a really joyful time. My whole family was in attendance. It was especially gratifying to my mother who was able on that occasion to meet Barbara.

During that summer while I was living in Greensboro Barbara and I saw each other occasionally. I do not recall getting over to Salisbury very often, but I do remember that she told of dates with Malcolm. I dated a girl several times who was a member of the Greensboro church, but she was definitely way out of my "intimacy" league, expecting more than I was willing to give. The summer of 1942 ended and a new chapter began.

Going to New Haven

A Yale Divinity Senior Student who lived in Newport News, Bob Cole, called me to ask if I needed a ride to New Haven. I was grateful and happy to share expenses. I arrived at Yale Divinity School to find that my roommate and I lived across the hall from my benefactor who helped guide us through all the preliminary registration process.

Barbara and I had a pretty good system of correspondence going. I must hand it to her because she was extremely busy as a junior taking two majors. Almost every week we exchanged letters, which meant a great deal to me. Dick Hutcheson, my roommate familiarly known as Hutch, was corresponding with a college girlfriend in Virginia. This gave us quite a bit in common. For both of us it seemed like a long time until Christmas vacation when we could get back home to see them. When it arrived we both headed south. I hopped a bus to Greensboro, where the folks were living not far out of town. Dad let me use the car to drive over to Salisbury, a real privilege to use some of his gas ration to visit Barbara.

Her father and I had always had a good relationship so on this first return from Yale, he was anxious to know what my course work was teaching me. I realized that my theological background did not necessarily fit his, so I tried to tread carefully through this mine field. He was a Lutheran minister, educated in the tradition of Luther. I grew up in the Reformed Church with Zwingli and Calvin our guides. I did not want to raise doubts in his mind as to my fitness for his daughter. I need not have feared. He never questioned my beliefs. He had always done his reading in theological journals and knew of Richard Niebuhr, a Reformed Church theologian at Yale. He respected my New Testament professor, a Lutheran, so we had some very thoughtful and lively discussions. He always showed appreciation for my goal of returning to China.

That summer of 1943 was most significant. I needed money for school and was fortunate to land a job as waterfront director at Camp Sequoia in the mountains near Weaverville and Asheville. At the end of July or very early August, Barbara came by train for a weekend visit. Staff "days off" were usually spent in Asheville so I knew my way around. She was registered to stay in our camp's guest house, a nice cabin on the rise above the mess hall. It was a wonderful time for me: the moon was full and bright, the setting beautiful, the breezes gentle.... Memory gets fuzzy, but I know how exciting it was to feel that she really loved me as I loved her. We had become very close during that year and had discussed marriage at various times. That special weekend seemed to bring it all together. On the porch of the cabin in the lovely North Carolina Mountains I asked her to marry me. She readily consented and I knew her consent included her commitment to go to China with me. When she said, "Yes," I really was on cloud nine! She must have been right there beside me on that cloud as she later reported that she had anticipated that her ride back to Salisbury would give her time to savor this special experience. Unfortunately, a talkative friend of the family was also on the train and sat with her, destroying her reverie.

We arranged that at the conclusion of my summer job we would go to Newton to look for an engagement ring. The jeweler, Mr. Waggoner, a friend of the family, had told me years before that he would help me out when I needed a diamond ring. Barbara and I embarked on this daunting task when we learned that Dad would lend me the money. To our delight we found a ring that was beautiful to our eyes. Being of a very practical nature, she suggested that she save it to wear at Christmas and we would announce our engagement then. This would make the year until our wedding seem shorter.

In case you are wondering, I managed to pay Dad off quite quickly. At the end of the summer we also had a chance to go with Mom and Dad to Morehead City for a few days of vacation. The folks had invited Barbara to come with us to the rented cottage. It was a great time for all of us. I think that Mom was very happy that she had a wonderful daughter-in-law to be and that she learned to know her. She wanted to make sure that I treated Barbara right. Barbara was also very fond of Mom.

In our day, hormones raged as much as they do in young people today. It seems to me that in the dorm bull sessions we talked about sex as much as any generation. Perhaps this was not as common for day students, as Barbara says the girls she was with were more reticent. Certainly the subject has been covered in the many war stories of that era almost *ad infinitum*. We certainly did our share of "petting, necking," etc., and wrestled constantly with refraining from what we called "going the limit." The upbringing of our generation imposed restraints that were in great contrast to the sexual freedom practiced by young people in ensuing generations.

The fall term got under way at the Divinity School. In spite of a heavy study and work load, my mind quite obviously was also looking ahead to Christmas and the summer of 1944. Barbara and I carried on a pretty consistent correspondence on plans for our wedding. She was busy with being class president and taking heavy duty majors with the usual occupation of being a senior during difficult days. That she wrote me so faithfully was a measure of her love as well as her ability to plan. I know she often wrote late at night. I always looked forward to her good letters.

The army was beginning a class at Yale for interpreters in Chinese to start right after the 4th of July for which I learned I would be eligible due to my background. The new class was to begin in early June. Because of this, I was insistent that an early June wedding date right after Barbara's graduation was ideal. Quite a few serious discussions resulted. My *magna cum laude graduate* was the practical realist who knew that some lead time was needed to get organized for a wedding and to enjoy prenuptial festivities. By spring, it was decided that July 1st was a good date!

Christmas finally arrived. I couldn't wait to get to North Carolina. My memories are of a whirlwind visit home and time in Salisbury with Barbara. I traveled by train to Baltimore where Don was at Johns Hopkins

Medical School. We had a ride south with a friend of his to save expenses. Mom and Dad let me hurry on to Salisbury. Then everything blurs except for the wonderful moment when I put Barbara's diamond ring on her finger. Our engagement was official!

One big event in the spring was Barbara's visit to New Haven on her spring break. I found a place for her at the Divinity Women's Hostel, where she met some of the "Divinity Dames," as well as some of the wives of students. She attended some classes with me and I think we even visited several apartment options at that time. She had a chance to meet our Missions Group to get a sense of what lay ahead for her in a few months. We had a wonderful picnic in the East Rock Park with my roommate, Dick (Hutch) and a friend.

The biggest event of the spring, however, was a trip for me that had not been planned and was a total surprise to Barbara. I was moaning around the dorm that she was going to be crowned May Queen at Catawba on the next weekend and I would not be there to see her in her court. The guys all got together and raised a few dollars and told me I should try to make it. After grave deliberation and their urgings I decided to head south. One guy took me out to the Merritt Parkway so I could try to hitch a ride to North Carolina. No superhighways in those days, but I was lucky and got a good series of rides on Friday into the night. Near Washington a slow driver said he was going to Winston-Salem, so I hopped in and helped him drive through the night. By early the next morning, he dropped me beside the bus station. I found a bus going to Salisbury, but it wandered through the countryside, poked through a number of small towns, dragging its ancient tires all the way. Finally, in a panic I descended from the bus at the front lawn of Catawba. I had missed the coronation ceremony but I got to witness my Queen departing her throne. After the court had recessed to the strains of the stately music, I found her and really surprised her. It was awkward for her to tell her escort for the May Day dance that night that her fiancé had arrived unexpectedly and she was going to the dance with him. It was a momentous occasion and I was so proud of Catawba's new Queen of the May, Barbara Brown. The festival dance that night was a constant succession of men wanting to dance with the May Queen. I did manage to have my share.

Of course, the next day I had to start on my return journey, this time by bus all the way. I slept most of the trip, arriving exhausted in time for

Monday morning classes. Who cared that I probably got nothing from the lectures that day!

July 1ˢᵗ the long awaited day arrived. Of course, many things led up to the wedding itself. I arrived in Salisbury in time to take part in all the obligatory functions. The night before there was the rehearsal at the church with Janice, Barbara's older sister, as our program guide. Following the rehearsal, the wedding party went back to the parsonage for the cake-cutting. This was a small reception for family and friends. Barbara wore her May Day dress and I wore my one and only suit. We cut the beautiful 3-tiered cake and saved the top tier to be frozen for celebrating our first anniversary. I was greatly amazed that one room was filled with wedding gifts. We had sent out only a few invitations, but St. John's members were very generous with gifts to the daughter of their much-loved pastor.

The wedding was at four o'clock on Saturday afternoon. The pastor's daughter was being married so the congregation had responded to fill the church. Bob was one of the ushers. During the music before the ceremony, Barbara's longtime and childhood friend Millie Carroll Hart sang favorites: "Through the Years" and "The Lord's Prayer." Barbara's father and mine both officiated and Don was my best man. The four of us waited at the foot of the steps of the foot of the chancel. The "Wedding March" began and Lois, Barbara's sister and maid of honor, entered wearing her May Court dress. Then I saw Barbara in Janice's wedding gown starting down the aisle of St. John's Church on her brother-in-law Doug's arm. She was beautiful!

After the first part of the ceremony, we proceeded to the altar for our vows. These were very hard on Barbara's father, for the weddings of his daughters always made him choke up. The hymn "O Perfect Love" was played while we knelt. What a joy it was to turn around to the congregation and march proudly out of the church with my new bride.

As our cake-cutting the night before had served as a reception, we went back to the parsonage for more pictures in the living room. Our suitcases were already packed as we had to leave that afternoon to head back to New Haven.

Dad and Mom drove us to Greensboro with tin cans tied to the bumper and a big "Just Married" sign on the car itself. The two-lane main road, which went right through the square at Salisbury, led us to Spencer, where we untied the cans and tried to erase the sign. Arriving in Greensboro after dark, Mom and Dad let us out at the railroad depot. I had tried to make a reservation for a Pullman berth to New York, but they could only put me on the "waiting list" because during wartime, all accommodations went to military personnel as a priority. The rest of the population stood in line. It grew later and later and finally they called me over to the counter to say they had two upper berths available. I said, "Two! I only need one!" Thus we spent our wedding night in one upper berth on a bumpy train ride to New York.

We were headed for a few days at the "Farm on the Hill," a honeymoon retreat center in the mountains north of New York City. We took a bus to the town where the owners of the farm, the Van Hoevenburgs, met us. We had saved up for many months for this special getaway. We arrived to find four or five other couples already there. We were shown our room in the lodge and given instructions to come down and meet everyone. It was a very friendly atmosphere, but you can guess how nervous we were when one by one the couples reported how long they had been married – a year, two years, and one couple three weeks before. Barbara, whose turn was next, turned beet red and murmured, "Yesterday." Didn't matter, for we teamed up with the other most recently married couple to hike and talk. Paul and Jane Peak have remained close friends throughout the years. The days at the farm were far too few as we had to get back to New Haven to begin our life together, my dream for so long now a wonderful reality.

New Haven – July 1944 to June 1945

It surely was wonderful to have my partner through the summer as Barbara made the apartment beautiful and homey using our wedding gifts. We painted the whole apartment with bright and cheery colors. We have never forgotten the first meal she cooked. Taking all day, she produced mashed potatoes, cauliflower, and pork chops fit for a king!

My routine for the summer months was study. Barbara also helped me with some of the weekday caretaker work for the apartment building. Collecting the trash and cleaning took an hour or more a day. Weekends we visited different churches on Sunday, visited some other Divinity couples, and enjoyed listening to Andre Kostelanez's Sunday afternoon classical concerts on the radio. I remember the shock of hearing the announcement that F.D.R. had died.

The three-month intensive army course was completed in early September. I was an "add on" so a simple graduation ceremony was really for the officers. They complimented me on my accomplishments but admitted that I had an unfair advantage, having been practically "born Chinese."

Near the end of the summer Marguerite Petrini, the administrator of the doctor's office in the house where we lived, asked Barbara if she would work as a part-time lab assistant. Having worked in the Salisbury Hospital laboratory two summers, she had some skills but was very reluctant to assume such a responsible position. Ms. Petrini was quite persuasive, suggesting that she could do the routine work. Barbara finally reluctantly agreed to try this first part-time job. Except for the machine for testing basal metabolism, the lab was poorly equipped. After a few months she did not really want to continue so asked the administrator to find a replacement.

We should note that we learned to know the Petrini family. Living in West Haven in a community largely composed of Italian immigrants who worked in the industries, they continued to cling to their cultural ways. Mr. Petrini, the father, loved to buy grapes in the fall to make the most delicious wine. They invited us several times to their home and we enjoyed their warm hospitality and really authentic Italian food!

By fall, Barbara agreed to teach Sunday School at the nearby Trinity Lutheran Church and greatly enjoyed her relationship with a class of eight-year-old girls. Phyllis Kallert has remained a friend with whom we still correspond and have visited over the years. We also have kept in touch with a teacher, Lillie Lundby, who with her husband were missionaries in Taiwan.

We often attended Battell Chapel at Yale University where some of the nation's outstanding preachers spoke. Dr. Howard Thurman, an African-American minister and professor with such authority, dignity, and ability, preached one powerful sermon that sticks in my memory, "You have searched me and known me, O God." There was absolute silence in the Chapel as the immense congregation listened in awe to this profound messenger.

Having secured a part-time job in the Divinity School Library, Barbara was entitled to audit the New Testament course taught by a Lutheran professor, Dr. Kraeling. This study was eye-opening and challenging for her. As I had discovered several years before, some of our student assumptions of just how biblical events might have occurred do not hold up under critical, scholarly examination.

A special event was a tour of the Catskill Mountains during the fall leaf coloring time. The daylong bus trip through golden and deep red hardwood trees was almost too much of a feast for the eyes. We came home appreciative of the New England fall splendor. Barbara also went with me to the Mission Group meetings, making friends with many whom we have kept in contact. We traveled around New Haven mostly by bus, walking, or biking. Most students had bikes to get around even though some of the hills seemed very high. Sometimes we would take an evening off to go play bridge with the Queeners, enjoying a glass of Sauterne or Mogan David wine together. Our tastes were not discriminating. Then on rare occasions we would buy tickets high in the "peanut gallery" of the Schubert Theater. New York plays used the venue as a "tryout" or "shakedown." We were able to see several shows that later had long runs on Broadway.

In addition to earning our apartment, my paying job at the YMCA was a continuation of the supervisor's job in the Gra-Y program. Another source of income was a job I had started the year before. Once a week I collected the suits, coats, and shirts from the men at Divinity School to be taken to the cleaners. As many were preaching on Sundays, the need was great. It was always quite lucrative. I made a deal with one of the students to get all his cleaning done free for the use of his car twice a week to take and then pick up the garments. My cash income with Barbara's earnings fed us. My school scholarship and a grant from the North Carolina Reformed Church Synod paid my tuition.

Christmas back in North Carolina was a long-awaited event, and there was great rejoicing in reunion and reconnection. "Family" for Barbara meant parents and siblings. My life at KAS and away from parents so long gave me a different perspective, an attachment to an "extended family." Not that I think Barbara was necessarily homesick, but this first homecoming was really very special.

Barbara's sister, Janice, with small daughter Charme, was living with the Browns while husband, Doug, was in the Air Force overseas. We spent time in both Salisbury and in the country at Mt. Hope Church where my folks were. The little parsonage was pretty crowded with Don bunking in Bob's room. We stayed in Dad's study. In Salisbury, we participated in the various Christmas services. One sidelight was the very meaningful discussion Barbara had with her father on her New Testament studies. He was concerned about Barbara's questioning the Virgin birth of Jesus. Though he had kept up his reading, he was not as convinced as the scholars in the interpretations that resulted. I always respected his view and especially that he granted us the right to seek our own understanding of the scriptures and faith, guided by the Holy Spirit. This support was very helpful to us both as we prepared to go to China.

Some time after the beginning of the new semester, I learned that my major professor and adviser, Dr. Kenneth Scott Latourette, Professor of Missions, had sent a hand-written letter to our new Mission Board Secretary, Dr. Goetsch, on December 7, 1944:

"My dear Dr. Goetsch:

May I write you about one of our students here, a Mr. Sterling Whitener? As you know he is the son of one of your Chinese (sic) missionaries and is graduating this June from Yale Divinity School. In due course he will get in touch with you, indeed, you may be already in correspondence with him. I simply want to say that during his years at Yale I have come to have a high opinion of him. He has shown enterprise and industry. For example, last summer he remained in New Haven and gave the entire time to the study of Chinese. He married a few months ago a most attractive girl whose father is a minister of the United Lutheran Church. My impression is that they will make excellent missionaries. It will, I suppose, be two years or more before they can go to China. They are wondering what their course should be in the meantime. They could continue on at Yale for part of that time studying Chinese as several appointees of other Boards are doing. I suppose that you will also wish them to have some practical experience.

It is questions of this kind of which Mr. Whitener has written you or will be writing you, but I wanted to have this letter on your desk in case you have not had much contact with him.

Faithfully yours,

signed,

K. S. Latourette"

Back in New Haven, Barbara was able to audit Dr. Latourette's course on the History of Missions in the spring semester. We did not have much money, but we seemed to have enough. Barbara walked from our apartment some five or six blocks to State Street where shopping for food was less expensive. She was a genius at balanced meals and provided them by walking to the Italian market stalls on State Street with a little wooden wheeled shopping cart to wheel home her bargains using war food coupons. Her frugality was exemplary; I never could match her.

Once I bought an ancient revolving tub washing machine for $25. I thought we would be able to save megabucks by not taking our laundry out. There were no self-service machines available in those days. Alas, my bargain machine soon gave up the ghost. It was so old it couldn't be repaired. I never lived down the fiasco as I have continued to be joshed through the years that I always contended, "It had a good motor," which I was able to sell for $5.00. It is a useful phrase subsequently often used to remind me not to get too rash with purchases of somewhat questionable utility.

The caretaking job at the doctor's building was much more difficult in winter than during summer and fall. The ancient oil furnace provided steam heat but was at times quite balky. The worst problem was the constant need to monitor the water level. Whenever I paid too little attention to the addition of water to the system, I flooded the basement through the overflow valve. Several hours of mopping did not improve my disposition when I needed to get a paper written, nor did the furnace cooperate by quickly making steam. Barbara and I had to wrap up to keep warm until steam was restored by morning for everyone else!

At some time during the spring, while Barbara was hanging clothes out on the roof outside our apartment, she spied a small pigeon, which had fallen or flown from its nest in the surrounding trees into the roof gutter. It was abandoned, for no mother came searching. After a reasonable period Barbara carefully nurtured our new family member and named it Beedoo, Her niece Charme's word for "bird." Tender loving care bonded foster mother and feathered child. In fact, as it grew older and flew from the window, Beedoo always came back home for food, which was good and plentiful. We both enjoyed our first "baby."

My mother had been having health problems. Nausea was constant, making her feel weak. Finally, the physicians at Bowman Gray Hospital in Winston-Salem diagnosed her condition as Boeck's Sarcoid, a rather rare lymphatic auto-immune condition of unknown origin and with no known cure. Though not in itself a life-threatening disease, it was a miserable one that caused heart damage and pernicious anemia. It went through a variety of phases. Her arms and legs developed splotches where there was subcutaneous bleeding. She lost weight and felt very tired. How she kept up her good spirits and positive attitude, we could not understand. Though Dad tried to help with housekeeping, she insisted on cooking and cleaning to keep busy knowing that he had much on his plate with two small churches.

I felt that school was rapidly drawing to a close with many papers to be completed, as well as decisions to be made. We were getting rather nervous about what kind of work or employment we would seek if we could not prepare for mission work in China. I had continued my correspondence with the Mission Board. By March we had been asked to come to a Board meeting to be considered for candidacy.

I learned only years later what an advocate Dr. Kenneth Latourette (often called Uncle Ken by his students) had been, as these letters show:

"My Dear Dr. Goetsch:

At the risk of seeming to be presumptuous, may I inquire what progress is being made on the appointment of Sterling and Barbara Whitener? You will recall that I wrote to you about them some weeks ago and had a very courteous reply from you. I am much interested in them, for, as I wrote you and as you well know, they are an extremely promising couple. Of course they are wondering what their plans should be for next year. I gather that Sterling and Barbara have talked it over and have agreed that if it were the wish of the Board, he could go to China without her and that they would be prepared to stand separation until such time as war conditions permitted her to join him. So far as I can see they are the temperament of those who can stand being separated without endangering the happiness or efficiency of either or placing in jeopardy their future home when they are reunited. Naturally, they are not eager for the separation, but they feel that since so many of the chaplains are having to have a similar experience, they ought not to seek exemption from it in case, in the judgment of the Board, Sterling is needed in China. I shall be grateful for any information or counsel you would care to give me as I advise the two of them.

"March 1, 1945

Dear Dr. Goetsch:

   Thank you very much for your kind letter of February 20 with its copy of the one to the Whiteners. They are writing you directly. Sterling has talked with me about some of the questions which he feels it wise to have answered before meeting your Board, and I have suggested that he raise them directly with you. I am delighted with both Sterling and Barbara. You have in them a quite unusual couple, a soundly Christian one, poised nervously, and with the physical basis, the good sense, and the devotion to make excellent missionaries.

   With every good wish, cordially yours,

K. S. Latourette"

At the meeting in Cleveland, we met three other couples appointed to China. We were assigned to Yoyang which I had considered my "lau jia." We all celebrated our appointment to the China Mission. You won't believe this, but Barbara had always wanted to see a burlesque show. This appeared to her to be "one last chance to sin." She easily persuaded us and led us around the corner from the hotel where we really had a hilarious time. Later, in China, our mission colleagues reminded her how she had led us all astray. I bet it would have brought a chuckle from Dr. Latourette!

Preparing for China

   I was now a Yale Divinity School graduate and proud of the fact. Strangely, however practically no students were staying until mid-June for the all Yale Graduation ceremony. A few of the doctoral candidates represented us. Most of us were too anxious to get to summer work assignments.

   As official appointees of the Board of International Missions, we were placed on a small salary/stipend for the summer to begin preparations for language study in the fall of 1945. We did not require any housing allowance until we started our study in New Haven in September. Staying at the parsonages in Salisbury and near Whitsett was a considerable advantage and wonderful to be with our families. The Board alerted the Synod that Barbara and I would be available to serve as Mission teachers at John's River Valley Camp in the mountains of North Carolina, particularly for the Senior Camp. We had plenty of time to get to North Carolina. We could store our few boxes in New Haven with friends over the summer.

We left New Haven in early June, having turned over the caretaking chores and apartment to another Divinity student. We decided to hitch-hike back home with a suitcase and a box for Beedoo. Standing on the edge of the access road to the Merritt Parkway, we must have presented an interesting sight. It was not long before a nice car with a single driver stopped. The man said he was going to Atlanta for an army appointment but would take us to Washington since he was making a stop there. We were in luck. It was nearly dark by the time we reached Washington. By then he knew we were going on to Greensboro and Salisbury. He said that if we wanted to wait while he took his date to dinner, he would be glad to have help driving on during the night. So that is what we did. We spelled him with the driving and arrived in Greensboro in mid-morning. He came in and after a shower some lunch and a rest, he drove on his way. We had made it home.

Beedoo was slowly becoming accustomed to the new location, as we first kept him in his box. He then flew around happily after we freed him from imprisonment. We thought things were going just fine until he flew up, circled a few times, then headed away from us, never to return. We kept looking for him to come back but never knew if he was headed for New Haven or had become the prey of a hungry hawk. We were sad to lose him.

Summer of 1945

The first item of business for me was to seek ordination. It was not very difficult to meet in June with the Ministry Committee of the Synod. They interviewed a group of us, the others from Lancaster Seminary. I recall that each person came out of the meeting room very relieved with a huge smile saying something like "it really is a piece of cake." I wasn't sure but that they were saving up ammunition to fire at the maverick from Yale. I was fortunate, however, because another interviewee was Dr. David Faust, a Yale Divinity grad, who had taught me in the religion department at Catawba. After our successful interviews, which did not discuss theology at all, much to my relief, the date of July 1st was set for our ordination service in the chapel at Catawba College.

The event was significant for a number of reasons. It was Barbara's and my first anniversary. Both my dad and my father-in-law were participants in my ordination. Dr. Faust and I were ordained in the same service. Another item of significance was the program of music, sung by my college music teacher, Mrs. Faust. A member of the First Church choir and with quite a good voice, she had a mannerism of facial contortions that one needed to see to believe. Little Charme whispered loudly to her mother, Janice, in the middle of the solo, "Will she get better?" Perhaps that is the clearest memory of that very solemn service. Barbara and Janice kept their cool with greatest difficulty.

During the summer, while we were at Whitsett, Grandpa Hegnauer came from Missouri to stay for a while. I will always remember his smile and his pipe. We loved to play Pinochle with him. I was asked by a small church near Winston-Salem to serve as a full-time pastor for the summer but agreed instead to supply the pulpit several Sundays before we were due at John's River Valley Camp to help campers study missions. The service was a learning experience because I had never been coached on the serving of Holy Communion. Why seminarians are assumed to know automatically just how to conduct a smooth service, I can't figure. I do recall that the elder who was assisting me had to whisper to me to dismiss the communicants after the serving (before the altar) with the brief blessing, "Depart in Peace." It served to remind me not to take anything for granted.

Summer at John's River Valley Camp

The summer camp program was not a new experience for me because I had been a counselor for camps and had also helped for a week of Senior High Camp at John's River several summers previously. Barbara had a cabin of girls while I had a cabin of boys for the month we served. I helped with swimming instruction, but basically we held sessions on Mission work overseas and the plans and hopes we had for China. I cannot remember what we said, but we did have some artifacts to show, some stories to tell of the work of other missionaries, and certainly shared our enthusiasm for our study of Chinese in the coming year. Barbara also helped with the craft program. The friendships developed at that time have kept coming back to us, as we have visited our NC churches in subsequent years. Even in the year 2000, fifty-five years later, we continued to meet people who remembered us from their experience as young campers. We were young, energetic, eager hikers, and glad to be with young people, enjoying the hikes, camaraderie, the campfires, the evening worship high up Vesper hill, and the wonderful evening programs of square dancing and games. Barbara's hair was semi-long, and with a new permanent it often stuck out at many angles. Her picture is one of health and beauty. She also qualified as having the most chigger bites. And so on to the future.

Language Study – September 1945 to June 1946

We left North Carolina with enthusiasm for our next step, Chinese language study. We headed back to New Haven to find an apartment not too far from the Language Institute, yet one we could afford on our missionary salary. It was gratifying that we would be able to devote our entire energies to study and not be required to worry about another job. We tramped the streets looking for rental signs which were abundant as students flocked to New Haven to return to Yale. We studied the newspaper ads. I don't remember how we found Mrs. Ilg on Dwight Street, but it was a fortuitous meeting. Our one-room apartment on the second floor of a row house faced the street. There was a small kitchen alcove and some space where we could sit comfortably or at the table to study. Another apartment was vacant in back, with which we would share the toilet and bathtub. We met other prospective students, missionaries all, who were arriving daily to find accommodations. Fortunately, we met David and Virginia Stowe, whom we introduced to Mrs. Ilg and they rented the apartment behind ours. The four of us formed a firm and lasting friendship as we lived in such close proximity for the year. We enjoyed some of the cultural events of New Haven together when we could take some time off. The Stowes were under the Congregational Board and headed for North China. David later became the Executive Secretary of our United Church of Christ Mission Board. We also learned to know Dick and Dorothy Jackson, Congregational; Loren and Ruth Noren, Northern Baptist; Mac and Jessie McCoy, Methodist; Dick and Addie Bryant, Presbyterian; and many others.

The language study in preparation for China was for two semesters, an excellent program. Several hundred prospective missionaries from a number of denominations were devoted students and friends. Because of my study the previous summer with the Army officers, I was placed with an advanced class whose members had started the previous semester. Barbara began her studies with a wonderful, talented teacher and former missionary, Gardiner Tewksbury. He introduced Chinese through "Mr. Ju", a boar head mounted on the wall in the classroom from the days the building had been taken over from a former Yale society club. Mr. Tewksbury, born in China, conversed with Mr. Ju daily, using all the usual colloquial expressions of everyday life we would be using.

Each day we met with Chinese tutors, who helped us by correcting our pronunciation and tones. Each word has a specific tonal sound. A change in the tone meant a change in the meaning. You can imagine what a difficult task our instructors had with all of us especially a South Georgia boy who spoke Chinese with a distinct southern drawl. Although he never really mastered Chinese, his pleasant personality clearly overcame his lack of skill in the language.

Each afternoon and evening we listened to recordings on small lesson discs of plastic that were made by our Chinese tutors speaking slowly and clearly. We labored over the sounds to make our tones the same. Some of us were relatively successful, others less so. The grammar itself was not as difficult as English grammar and certainly the tenses were simpler. It was always the "TONES" that were hard to master.

Each week we also had the privilege of learning Chinese songs. The National Anthem of the Kuomingtang government was a must. We also learned several songs popular during the war. One of them, "Chi Lai," became the National Anthem of the Communist government in 1950. Lily Tong also taught us Chinese folk songs that came in handy after we got to Huping School. Our teachers, Henry Fenn, Bob Tharp, and Prof Kennedy, were an interesting group of experts. The School Director, Kennedy, a missionary kid, had grown up in China and even went to Chinese schools before returning to the USA. He got his doctorate in Chinese Classics; he had learned them so well by rote as a child. Unfortunately, though brilliant, he was also an alcoholic.

Early in the fall, we purchased a Model A Ford very cheaply. It definitely needed work on the engine. The first task was to find a garage where I could work on it. Fortunately, we noticed a sign across Dwight Street at the Frank X. Hald Moving & Storage Co. that they had a space for rent. We made lifelong friends when we met Walter Hald and his sister, Pauline. Walter was a great mechanic, took us under his wing, and helped rebuild our Model A engine in time to drive to North Carolina for Christmas vacation. We will never forget that ride. Jesse & Mac McCoy rode with us to NC, as she had family in Randleman not far from my parents' home. It was cold and the car had only a minimal heater. Though blankets helped, we nearly froze. In addition, we had the misfortune of a flat tire. It blew out, and the $10 for a new tire blew our budget. We stopped overnight in a cheap motel on our way south, as the trip took nearly two days of driving.

That winter of 1945 Mom and Dad were preparing to leave for China. They had decided to return to China because they both felt compelled to help their Chinese friends and colleagues rebuild the churches destroyed by the Japanese army. Though Mom was definitely not strong, they both felt she would be able to get excellent household assistance. There certainly was none available in NC. She could not believe she would feel worse back home in China where Dad was greatly needed. We had reservations about her health condition being able to tolerate the very challenging rebuilding of mission work but were glad that we would soon be working with them in Hunan.

The Mt. Hope and Brick churches were sorry to see them leave but supported them with loving gifts and prayers. Getting to China for them was more difficult in January because of the lack of ocean transport. They were able to secure accommodations on a freighter leaving from Brownsville, Texas, with a load of foodstuffs and building supplies for Shanghai. After a trip through the Panama Canal and up the west coast, they made their way to Shanghai nearly a month and a half later. They then traveled by river steamer up the Yangtze to Wuhan and thence to Yueyang by train. The two-month trip and the task of settling into a war torn compound definitely took a toll on Mom's health.

Not Long Now

During the final months of language school, much attention was given by all of us prospective missionaries to items that would be needed to carry out our Mission work. Elder missionaries and reports from China spoke of the lack of basic supplies, clothing, health items, and furniture, including stoves. The devastation of the war and the Japanese removal of anything of value was the main topic of conversation as all of us began to plan for the fall of 1946 when we would finally be able to "get to work." One school friend was a veritable fountain of information. Dick Jackson had an ability to search out all kinds of unique and vital supplies. His favorite source was Mickey Finn's Army Navy Surplus Store. Daily he had a new find. Money belts, special flashlights, sleeping bags, and even belly bands were on his endless list of necessities. As all

Mission residences needed to be refitted we realized the need for planning. Very few items could be purchased in China except at exorbitant cost. So we began to collect what we anticipated would be required. Barbara and I had the advantage that my parents had already arrived in China in the spring of 1946, so could tell us exactly what was needed. Their reports identified the items that we should bring, an endless list that seemed impossible to fill. A special outfit allowance from the Board assisted in paying for the purchases.

As mentioned earlier Walter Hald and his sister, Pauline, of new Haven were wonderful friends. When we related our list of items, we learned that Walter had contacts where we could secure, at almost no cost, a kitchen stove, as well as a "Warm Morning" heating stove, both of which burned coal or wood. Because there was no electricity in Yueyang, we were urged to bring a generator. True to form, we found two. One we bought, one was given to us. Our accumulation of what we had bought and what Walter had found for us in his warehouse soon filled much of the little garage space we had rented. The next big question was how to pack and ship these items. Walter solved the problem by locating five huge wooden boxes. His expertise in packing was a marvel to behold. We have been forever grateful for his immeasurable help in getting us to China. No trouble shipping these huge, heavy boxes and baggage from New Haven, but we feared the problem would come on the other end. There the boxes had to be handled by dockworkers that would need to lash bamboo poles to carry them! Our freight was shipped by rail to San Francisco where we would join it in September to sail on a converted troopship to Shanghai. Because we had been told, "take what you want to live with, it is to be your home," we packed many of our wedding gifts, including sets of china and crystal. We later found this was not good advice. Many things we never did use because we found no occasions to do so in our rural assignment.

My language study year ended with a special paper to write on Chinese culture and a language exam in French. Fortunately, the exam was to be a reading translation. The passage I received had to do with Chinese history and culture so I managed to pass that hurdle and thus be eligible for my Masters Degree in General Studies from Yale Graduate School in 1946. The only reason I was able to complete the degree work was due to my Chinese study with the army the summer before. We finished our spring semester with fitting ceremonies. Barbara and I bundled up our remaining belongings, loaded our Model A Ford, and headed for North Carolina.

The summer months were to be spent with the Browns in Salisbury and visiting other members of the family. As it turned out these plans were interrupted. While Walter Hald was visiting Salisbury in July, I was hit with some kind of bug. I felt terrible, nauseated, weak, and listless. The doctor did not know what had hit me, but Walter said I looked "yellow" to him. Sure enough, acute infectious hepatitis was finally diagnosed and I went to bed for three weeks. That was the treatment of the 1940s. Summertime on the top floor of the parsonage in Salisbury, North Carolina, was no picnic. It was a miserable time in nearly 100-degree weather. For a while, it appeared we would not be able to make our ship's departure date. Recovery, though slow, was complete.

Always fully supportive, it was difficult for the Browns to see their daughter going so far away into uncharted experiences in a war-ravaged land. It was hard for Barbara, too. We have always been grateful for the way they took us in during our homeless summer months. Though their hearts must have been heavy, they never said anything to dampen our enthusiasm for our new mission in life. Our bags packed and farewells complete, Barbara's sister, Janice, with daughter, Charme, drove us to Barber Junction to board the Southern Rail Road West at the end of August 1946. A stopover with Barbara's brother Robert and wife, Hermine, in St. Louis was a chance to prepare for our transcontinental Pullman ride to San Francisco. Having purchased a used Leica camera to take slides, it was amazing how many I wasted on empty stretches of prairie landscape and high Rocky Mountains.

Expecting to sail for China in a week, September 7, we arrived in time to be greeted by a longshoremen's strike. Most of the missionaries were staying at the St. Francis Hotel. The end of the war saw longshoremen ready to see their contracts reflect the new day of prosperity in the country and not revert to prewar depressed wages and time conditions. The troopship, "Marine Lynx," was prepared, two hundred Chinese students were ready to return home, and four hundred missionaries were eager, ready, and willing to get started in mission work! With no strike settlement, Mission Boards rapidly tried to find churches willing to take in boarders. Turmoil, confusion, and false expectations of a quick settlement of the strike were rumors each day. September ended with no sailing date in sight. We were most fortunate that Barbara's uncle, Jack Brown who was working with the customs service in San Francisco invited us into his home. Our new Mission Board executive, Dr. Ehlman, who was also going to China on a familiarization trip, found help from a church member. Lucile Hartman stayed with a Wheaton College friend.

A sailing date was set many times for our "Marine Lynx" troopship! Excitement was high among the network of eager young missionaries anticipating the departure date. Much excitement kept occurring during the month of September as we heard that the strike was "about to be settled" and subsequently that negotiation had been broken off. It was a time of constant uncertainty; we were kept on tenterhooks!

During this time, the churches of San Francisco and the Foreign Missions Conference of North America had organized a huge worship service to dedicate the group of over 400 missionaries who were going to China. This was really kind of a mass movement, as only a trickle of personnel had been able to return earlier in the year because transportation was so limited for civilians. You remember that Dad and Mom were able to embark on a freighter from Texas in January. The big farewell worship event was held in the San Francisco Opera House where the United Nations had been founded in 1945. It was one of the most thrilling moments of our lives as four hundred young missionaries processed to the stage and filled the bleachers to the strains of "Lead on O King Eternal." The service of commitment was inspiring and uplifting. We were ready to go; we were confident; we felt fully supported.

Unfortunately, our three-week delay was about to begin. Uncle Jack was exuberant and he and Aunt Hazel treated us royally. He helped us buy some last minute items. They took us to the huge San Francisco Park, to swim in the frigid Pacific, and for a short weekend trip to Yosemite Park. We were immensely grateful for all their generosity. We did see high school son Philip on occasion and college sophomore daughter Marge once.

We were kept busy checking our big boxes that had been damaged in transit and in making some last-minute purchases. We also telegraphed Dad in Yueyang to find out if the Canton to Hankow Railway was operating.

We knew that with so many missionaries trying to reach the interior from Shanghai on the limited number of riverboats operating in China, there would be a crowd vying for the same spaces. Dad reassured us that the trains were running, though they were not very comfortable. We wired back that we were heading for HongKong, the last stop of the "Marine Lynx," where we would arrange to take the train from Canton.

The date for sailing was finally announced - September 29 was departure day. Our benefactors Uncle Jack and Aunt Hazel drove us to the dock. We sailed on a Sunday afternoon after holding a large farewell song service in the upper area of the dockside warehouse. Hundreds of paper streamers were handed out to us as we gathered at the ship's rail. Songs and hymns were sung as the ship sounded its deep horn and pulled away from the dock. There were mixed emotions as the ship to shore streamers broke and all ties severed. We were leaving our homeland for a new and challenging future.

What fun to sail under the Golden Gate Bridge toward the sunset with the long slow Pacific swells reminding us that this 12,000-ton troopship was no large cruise liner. Though it could accommodate as many as 3,500 troops, the bunks were arranged for us so that only two persons slept in each stack; a third bunk at top was used for storing our bags. Men were in one section, women and children were in a different section of the ship. It was a difficult voyage for families with children. Food was served on aluminum trays cafeteria style in a large mess hall. We really had quite adequate and good food.

Unfortunately, Barbara was quite seasick for a few days. I was luckier in that I did not get seasick. I remember Dad always hit his bunk when the ship left dock but Mother and I always got out into the fresh air and walked vigorously to get used to the rising and falling motion of the ship. If I could see where it was going, my internal gyroscope seemed to take over effectively. I did manage to get Barbara out on deck and tended to her lovingly. A sulfurous stench from below deck did not help her misery. The "Marine Lynx" was dubbed the "Marine Stinks."

The few weeks on the water passed quickly. Barbara got her sea legs and really enjoyed the fresh air on deck and sightings of porpoises and flying fish. We had many sessions with our fellow missionaries sharing what we knew and did not know about the challenges ahead. The Chinese students were also very friendly and helpful by speaking Chinese to help us practice and in telling us about their homes. Games such as chess were organized. At last we began to see a few islands as we drew near Japan.

As we approached Shanghai our excitement grew as most of the missionaries and all of the Chinese students were to disembark. Our first signs of land were the muddy waters of the Yangtze delta with low-lying mud flats. Our next sign was the inevitable dirty water in the toilets! We then entered the Huangpu River, a large tributary of the Changjiang (Yangtze), finally anchoring in midstream near the famous "Shanghai Bund."

U.S.A.: 1938 to 1946

9. With Mother at my graduation from Catawba College, 1942
10. Barbara's parents, Florence and P.D. Brown
11. My family: L to R – Sterling, Bob, Mother, Don and Dad
12. Our Wedding Day – July 1, 1944 Lois,
Barbara's sister, Maid of Honor, Don, Best Man

China – 1946 to 1950

13. Farnhams and Whiteners ride the rails into Changsha and Yueyang.

14. Our "cozy" home (a la Pennsylvania houses) on Huping campus

15. Liu Yunchu (Jyusheng) our house helper, and still a good friend

16. Dasifu, our faithful and talented cook

17. The Campus of Huping Boys School viewed from the Dongting Lake.

18. 1947: My parents in Yueyang - Mother died a few months later.

Chapter III

China – Four Unforgettable Years! 1946 to 1950

Disembarking Shanghai and HongKong

We finally touched Asian soil on Tuesday, October 15, 1946. Our troopship had landed the troops. As the 200 Chinese students stood watching the ship tie up, they broke out cheering, as did at least three hundred of us missionary shipmates. Immigration had processed all persons who were landing in Shanghai while we were anchored in midstream so we did not get to dock until late afternoon. Those of us who were going on to HongKong were last in line to get approval to leave ship. It was just as well, too. The scenes on the dock were hard to believe because all baggage in the hold had to be unloaded to go through customs before anyone could leave the dock area. We watched, horrified, as refrigerators were tumbled end-over-end to move them to the customs shed. What would have happened to our big boxes being dropped and rolled if we had disembarked? As baggage came out of the hold in big nets, one end was loosened with the result that huge piles were dumped out unceremoniously on the concrete dock, often from a great height. Workers then piled it in disorder off to one side as owners sought their bags to take through the customs process. We began to be very grateful that we were not leaving the "Marine Lynx" in Shanghai, but were going on to HongKong along with several dozen others who were assigned to South China. Chaos reigned for several days before our four hundred colleagues in mission were able to get all their papers, bags, and freight straightened out.

Lucile Hartman and Dr. Dobbs Ehlman were going up the Yangtze River with some supplies for the hospital. The latter was on a visit as the new Executive Secretary for the Mission Board of our Church. As he had never been to China before, Lucile was going along to help him on the river journey to Hankow and then on to Yueyang. Returning to teach at Ziemer Girls School, Lucile was an experienced missionary teacher. She was in the intermediate age range, between the "old timers" and the youngsters who were arriving for their first assignment. We often went to her for counsel.

While all this was going on, Barbara and I took the opportunity to do some looking around. I wanted to get to the Associated Mission Treasurers to make sure that our salary funds would be coming through. Dad had asked that I check several Mission accounts as well. In fact, I was to secure cash to bring him, as well as funds to pay expenses in HongKong. We were amazed that it took almost a suitcase for the Chinese currency we got in exchange for a few hundred US dollars. Inflation was already evident in late 1946. The printing presses had started rolling. On our way to the treasurer's office Barbara got her first rickshaw ride. She still resents that I took her picture as she was looking back into the sun; my reading of her sour expression suggests that she was reacting to the acrid new smells of China—always a shock to newcomers.

We got in a bit of sightseeing, but our days were limited since the "Marine Lynx" sailed on after a few days in port. Barbara managed to get in some shopping for Christmas presents to send back home because she could mail them on the "Marine Lynx" to take back to the States. We were also able to visit Don Mead, my high school classmate and roommate from Kuling American School days. He was associated with his father's firm, Standard Oil Co. A dinner in a penthouse apartment with Don and his Russian-born wife was fancy after the "chow line" of the "Marine Lynx."

A few days later we arrived in HongKong which showed great changes from my previous visit in 1938. It was now a bustling metropolis compared to a rather sleepy pre-war seaport. We noted that in the very busy business areas almost anything could be bought "for a price." I knew my way around and there was much to do to get everything ready to travel to Hunan, a thousand miles to the north.

We were able to find a room at the Basel Mission hostel: no luxury hotel, bathrooms at the end of the hall. It was located on Taipo Road and was quite a distance from town. Fields still surrounded the area. In an old

19th-century building with high ceiling fans for the summer heat, we felt fortunate to have arrived at the end of October, because these were the days before air conditioning. Simple European style meals were served in a communal dining hall. It was simple food, European style cooking, along with plenty of Chinese vegetables. I know I began to feel at home again since rice was a staple.

My time was spent running about town checking on our five huge boxes of freight that required transshipment to Canton. The time passed in a frenzy of activity because we had been asked to purchase a variety of food products and daily use items for my parents, as well as for the Hartmans of our Yoyang mission. We arranged to travel with the Presbyterian missionaries who were returning to their station in Canton after having departed six years earlier. Several of them had been interned in HongKong under the Japanese and were well known.

Barbara did have one task given her by Zula, who had traveled with us on the "Marine Lynx." She had come to marry Vernon Farnham, a Changsha missionary with the Evangelical United Brethren. Their Mission was also a partner of the Church of Christ in China. Vernon's wife, Zula's sister, had died a few years earlier. Barbara's challenge was to press Zula's wedding outfit, a white wool suit. With an open iron heated by burning charcoal, it was really a hazardous task. Barbara was so nervous that a live coal might fall out of the iron onto that white wool as she was working, she was sure it took years off her life! We all attended the happy wedding in St. Andrew's Episcopal Church.

Departure on the "SS Fatshan," an ancient river steamer that plied the Pearl River to Canton, was always a major event for missionaries. Barbara and I went to the "godown," the storage shed where our five huge boxes were stored during transit to make sure they were placed on a junk to transport them across the harbor to the ferry. We nearly panicked as we watched the freight junk move away from the wharf just as the first, and largest, box was being loaded. There was much shouting. The men held the box on shore as ropes were tightened and the junk secured to the dock. Our stoves and nearly a ton of goods almost went into HongKong Harbor. The resulting relief reconfirmed for us that our calling to Hunan was definitely on track. We most certainly were "predestined" to get there in one piece with everything. Hindsight told us again we should have packed in smaller boxes.

This Calvinist perception persisted as we all found our places on the "SS Fatshan" itself. It appeared that all of us were included in the Presbyterian fold. Friends of the Presbyterian missionaries in HongKong gave them a fond farewell as we sailed forth. It should probably be noted that we were, in fact, all in the same united Chinese church. This union had occurred in 1935 when my father had participated in the decisions. Over twenty-five denominations from all over the world had joined to form a single Chinese denomination, The Church of Christ in China. The notable exceptions to this exciting union were USA groups: Methodist, Lutheran, Episcopal, and Baptist denominations. (It took the Communist Revolution to force union of all Protestant churches in China into one Church.)

We arrived in Canton in early evening, met by a huge crowd of Chinese Christians and the few missionaries who had arrived in China earlier in the year. We saw immediately that most of the Chinese had been students of Rev. Merrill Ady, as we heard them calling to him as the riverboat docked, identifying themselves and their schools. Others knew Vernon Farnham through the widespread missionary network. He had made arrangements for accommodations for himself and his bride on his way through to Hunan. Fortunately, he also had telegraphed ahead to find us a place to stay at the Evangelical-United Brethren Mission with his colleagues, the Shoops. We had agreed in HongKong that the newlyweds and the youthful Whiteners would travel together from Canton to Changsha by freight train to attend to and protect the baggage of five new families going to Hunan.

The first potential hurdle on our way was entry customs. We had anticipated a long wait and endless haggling over the proper papers, etc., for our bags and our hold boxes, including the usual heavy customs import charges. We could hardly believe that as we walked off the ferry following in the wake of Rev. Ady and friends, we were all waved through. Our pages and pages of inventories of each bag and box were looked at but merely stamped with approval. Though we were prepared to pay duty on all kinds of things, it appeared that customs was welcoming anyone who had come back to China to help in the tremendous task of rehabilitation and reconstruction. We did pay "token" duty on a ream of paper and a bag of flour. We gave our customs-approved papers to Rev. Ady's friend who had a transport company, with full confidence that the five huge boxes would be properly cared for.

We went with the Shoops who lived in a school compound on a nearby island across the river, for Canton is a city on the Pearl River delta. Bridges were built later so, at that time, the only way to travel from one part of the city to another was by small sampan, rowed usually by a woman with a long, stern-sculling oar.

Our introduction to their home was a delight. Spotless tile floors, slippers at the door where one sat to remove outside shoes, and a very home-like atmosphere, all combined to make us feel comfortable. The women who served the Shoops had been well trained and were so neat and efficient they captivated Barbara immediately. She knew that she would need much assistance when she set up our home in Yoyang, so her aim was to have an amah in Hunan just like Mrs. Shoop's. She spent time with Mrs. Shoop to learn what she could during our stay.

Arranging Transportation to Hunan

Vernon Farnham and I were involved immediately the day after arrival searching for the proper officials of the Canton-Hankow Railway in order to see how we might ship our household boxes to Changsha and Yoyang. Vernon needed to get tickets on the express train for three families so he was pretty tied up. I camped out at the railway offices each day, negotiating with one official after another to rent a box (freight) car for our massive supply of baggage for five families.

Fortunately, I had learned in HongKong that though one could not offer money to any official in China, it was acceptable to leave packs of cigarettes on a desk as a "token of appreciation." This process was so widely practiced that had I not been alerted and bought a supply, I'm sure we would have been delayed many days in getting where we wanted to go. It worked this way. On entering an office, very polite expressions were used to greet the first man at the desk. Upon being invited to sit down, I would bring out a pack of cigarettes, open it, and offer one to him. I had observed this was the proper protocol. We would then exchange pleasantries while he inhaled his first puff of NC and Virginia's finest. At that point it was proper to bring up our hope to find a way to lease a freight car and settle all the details quickly. This really was an unusual request because foreigners seldom negotiated this kind of deal themselves. They sent brokers or office helpers to negotiate. I am sure that this disappointed the officials since they could more easily set rates where kickbacks were expected. Usually, the first man then left his desk to enter a closed office. Of course, the cigarette pack was left conveniently on his desk.

When we were invited into the next stage, the process was repeated, but now that we were getting close to decisions, a couple of packs were left conveniently behind. The rolling stock of the railway was very limited. It would have cost a princely sum to hire a reasonably new freight car in addition to waiting until the military would release one. We finally ended up with an old boxcar that, like most of the ones available, had over 250 shell holes on sides and top. We decided we would take the chance on rain and see what we could do to find sufficient dry space inside for the Farnhams and the Whiteners to camp out for the trip. What this process involving cigarettes did to increase the risk of cancer in Chinese railway officials is a thought I would rather skip over! Needless to say, with the long negotiations for the shell-shocked car, my supply of American cigarette cartons was going fast.

It was interesting to me that though I was brand new to work in China, I had a feel for what was expected from my long experience as a Boy Scout and as a student in Kuling American School. Vernon was a wonderful man, but he didn't really have a clue as to this kind of negotiating. I am quite sure that his experiences were limited to church situations rather than to the business world.

With the wonderful assistance from Rev. Ady's efficient friend we finally had a freight car and had negotiated a date when it would be attached to a train headed north. We saw the freight car loaded, directing placement of the many large boxes so that we had space at the doorway to move around and be somewhat comfortable. We spread our bed packs on easily purchased straw on top of all the boxes which were piled high, but left room to sit up without hitting the roof. We really slept surprisingly well. We were attached to the train near the old steam locomotive, which was noisy but convenient.

We were on our way to Hunan, a thousand miles to the north. The first order of business in the mornings was for one of us to go to the engine to get hot water in a basin or bucket so we could wash. There were typical Chinese toilets at stations. Otherwise, we ducked behind bushes like everyone else when the train stopped in the countryside. The old steam engines seemed to need regular rests to build up steam for any hill climbs ahead.

We had thermos jugs that we filled with boiling water from the vendors' kettles at each station stop. We could buy Chinese tea and we could make our own English tea with tinned milk and sugar. These items, along with canned foods, crackers, and bread, we brought with us. The vendors at each station stop sold steamed bread, "baudz," fruit, and a variety of other dishes. In fact, one could purchase a meal of rice, vegetables, and soup by sitting on a stool right beside the train in front of the vendor's stand. The man or woman carried a charcoal stove in a clay pot or kerosene tin with clay firewall, kitchen pots, and a bucket to wash up the bowls and chopsticks after they were used. We were old timers enough to know that a traveler always carried one's own chopsticks and rice bowl! We were careful to sterilize everything we used and to make sure that edibles were either peeled or carefully boiled, so we escaped any illness. It also helped to have a bottle of alcohol handy.

It was not until later that we found out that freight trains were not "through" trains like passenger trains. They were made up for travel in about 100 to 150 mile segments. This meant that by traveling about 15 miles an hour and taking our turn waiting for priority passenger trains to pass at stations spaced every ten miles or so, we had many long waiting periods. The single track system was managed pretty well, but it was slow.

Taking about 12 hours for the first segment, we reached a junction town where we learned that a train was being made up for the next segment and was due to leave in several hours. To make sure our car was hitched on that train, we made a foray into the station master's office. This again, was one of slow protocol with good results. This time we traveled onward overnight.

Arriving at a station near the mountains between Guangdong and Hunan, we learned that rain was expected ahead. On our first day without ongoing transport, we went in search of a carpenter. When we found one he brought along his whole crew to try to figure out what these crazy Westerners wanted. We showed him all two hundred plus shell holes on the roof of our boxcar, asked him to make wooden wedges, wrap them with cotton waste, soak them with the best oil in the world, "tungyou," and then pound them into the holes. The carpenter lit up with understanding and in short order our roof was repaired to our great satisfaction. Tested by rain the next day, our rolling home stayed completely dry. (Tung oil was extracted from the tung nut, forming the base for most paints until more recent years when synthetics took over. I had known of tung oil since childhood, as all the boats on Dongting Lake were constantly painted and repainted with it.)

As hoped, we finally got on our way but not before some excitement. Before Vernon and I went to seek a lazy station master in order to get hitched to the next freight train, we told Zula and Barbara to make sure no one came aboard our private boxcar. Careful instructions were given them to tell everyone that the freight car was a leased car, "bauche," and was not available for passengers. We returned to see a crowd gathered around the door and feared something had happened. Zula and Barbara were blocking the entryway. Curious onlookers were watching, but a few were seeking a place to hitch a ride. As we approached, we saw that most were enjoying a good joke. We learned that Zula had loudly and emphatically warned those who were trying to climb aboard by shouting, "This car is a 'baudz,' (a steamed bun)!" Oh, the difficulties of language and similarities of words.

Some nights we rocked along the single rough track, swaying from side to side. One day we enjoyed the beautiful mountain scenery as our ancient engine puffed its way up the hills and around the curves. Small villages, nestled in the valleys, were really the "old China" I remembered. It was more and more exciting as we felt the reality of getting to Hunan.

After five days we arrived in Changsha early in the morning. Baggage and freight of four missionary couples were promptly unloaded. We said goodbye to Vernon and Zula who had been great fellow travelers. The adventure was quite an exciting introduction to China for both Barbara and Zula, but hardly an ideal honeymoon for the newlyweds.

We traveled on to Yoyang, arriving there by evening. We could not believe that we had arrived at my "old" home and our future assignment together. How wonderful it was to see my parents waiting at the station! It had been ten months since they sailed from Texas. Mother had found the hot summer weather hard, but she was full of spirit as she welcomed us.

We were to stay with my folks in Yoyang in their large two-story house until we could get our freight moved to our new home. It was a good thing that Mother and Dad insisted that we should take plenty of time to get our home organized. Our five boxes had to be left at the station overnight and then moved to the Mission compound the next day. It was decided that we would unpack the large boxes in town even though a residence had been prepared for us at Huping Boys School four miles west of town.

We had been assigned by the Mission to teach English and study language half time. The school was situated right on the Dongting Lake. When the summer sun melted the Himalayan snows, the lake rose about

40 feet, so a heavy stone wall had been built at the foot of the long hill where the school had been built back in the early 1900s. In the fall the lake water receded, leaving great expanses of grassy plain. Dormitories, faculty housing, and missionary housing were all within a large and beautiful compound at the top of the flattened hilltop. To access Huping School from town, one had to walk along the single track railway more than three miles before taking a path to the school. To go by lake, one hired a sampan or a small sailboat to reach the gate facing the lake. This trip took about an hour.

As anxious as we were to get our own home out at Huping prepared before school reopened in the new year, it was quite clear that we needed to unpack and get basic furnishings in before we actually moved out to Lakeside (Huping). A further complication was the necessity to hire servants, as helpers were called in those days. We needed someone to do the marketing and purchasing of daily vegetables and also cook. When there is no refrigeration, a daily trip to the food vendors in the village is required. We had no running water, so a person to carry water from the well would also be needed. Without washing machines, someone would be hired to wash clothes. Finding good workers with whom we could communicate was not easy.

It really was fortunate that we had a good place to stay in Yoyang until all these necessary steps had been worked out, and it was a real blessing to have this learning and planning time with my parents. Many suggestions were offered to smooth the way for us newcomers. Barbara says she was so envious of Mom's fluency in the Hunan dialect which sounded so very different from her studied Beijing "hwa," the national language as spoken in Beijing thousands of miles north of us. Hunanese is a provincial form of "Mandarin Chinese" which has extra sounds and tones. I was most fortunate, as I understood what people were saying even though I preferred to use the national language.

One thing we learned very quickly back at my parents' home was that all the seats and boxes holding the toilet cans had been freshly painted with Ningpo varnish. It had a base looking something like mortar, with black varnish painted over it. Noted for its long-lasting dark beauty, it was made of the sumac bush berries. Like poison ivy it was highly allergenic. Quite quickly we had beautiful, fiery, red rashes on our posteriors that itched and burned. It took quite a while to get over the discomfort, especially when we had to go places where we sat on hard chairs! We took great care, thereafter, to assure ourselves of Ningpo-free toilet seats.

Prior to our move, we did go out to Huping School to meet with Principal Liu who introduced us to the faculty. He wanted us to take full charge of the English teaching program. It was not our idea to take over, as we had not really been trained to teach English as a second language. Furthermore, as part-time language students we did not think we could handle more than a few classes at first. In this we found great support from Miss Hoy, a veteran English teacher at the Ziemer Girls School in town. Principal Liu acceded to our request so we worked with Mr. Hsiang, Head of the English Department, to decide what we should be teaching in the new semester, which began in January. Our assignment to Huping was to be for only two years, as I had always hoped to work with the Chinese churches in evangelistic work. I must admit that I felt we would be marking time teaching English; I wanted to get to the "real work."

Getting Settled at Huping School

The lake waters had receded so that junks and sampans had difficulty getting close to the school because of the mud. Nevertheless, local school and farm workers were able to transfer all our possessions from the junk to our home.

With many helpers and with great support from faculty at Huping, the other missionaries, and my parents in town, we got our first home in order and moved out to the school. We soon learned that we did need an orientation period which the students and faculty at the Boy's School provided. We appreciated their tolerant acceptance of our beginning efforts at communication in their language and their friendly helpfulness as we adjusted to our new life.

The residence assigned to us was a large two-story house of red brick located at one end of the campus next to the principal's residence. This was one of seven original houses built in the early 1900s much like the solid Pennsylvania Dutch residences in the USA. High ceilings and large windows were needed because of the heat in summer. Outside, facing the lake was a covered porch both upstairs and downstairs. That design, however, did not make it easier to warm up the rooms in winter with fireplaces and small stoves. Several residences had been destroyed by bombing during the war. Ours had been repaired after the Japanese occupation by replacing many of the doors and windows and completely repainting the house.

Downstairs was a very large sitting room connected by sliding doors to a large dining room, so that one whole side of the home could be enlarged to make a room for meetings and student gatherings. In the winter we closed off the living room and used the dining room as our all-purpose room. The weather was getting quite cold by the time we moved, so we installed the good-sized "Warm Morning" coal stove downstairs in the dining room. As this room was also our study, we used a Coleman Aladdin lamp, an excellent pressure lamp which we had brought with us. It had two mantles, was easy to light and provided a bright light. We were very fortunate to have been able to buy in Canton a drum of unleaded gasoline which the lamp required.

The pipe of the Warm Morning stove was placed directly through the floor of our bedroom upstairs and into a large drum with a water bucket inside to heat the water. This took the chill off our bedroom, an ingenious system. It also provided warm water for the washbasin in the bathroom.

The bathroom had a porta-potty which we had made sure did not have Ningpo varnish. The pot was dumped and cleaned daily. The contents, no doubt, were used to nourish a nearby farmer's vegetables but not ours - we hoped! The bathtub was an oval-shaped tin tub large enough to sit in. Hot and cold water had to be carried upstairs for a bath. In the winter we used a kerosene heater to take the chill off the room, but it wasn't very effective.

Our kitchen stove, which we had also brought with us, was an efficient coal-burning stove with dampers, good draft control, an oven, and a tank to heat water. Kerosene, lamps, and coal were readily available in the market.

Crucial – A Good Cook

Mom and Dad had a wonderful cook, the same man who had cooked for our family before the war. He had located a young man, about 18 years old, from his village eager to work for us as general helper to do anything: cleaning the house, carrying the water, washing the clothes. His name was Jyusheng. We found out many years later that this really was his childhood nickname meaning "orange seed." In any case, we were quite willing to hire him right away, as he could also help oversee getting our freight and baggage out to Huping School.

Finding a cook was a different matter. Barbara continued to be adamant that a young woman on the order of those working for the Shoops in Canton was what she would like to find. My mother undertook to see what could be done, even though the traditional role of a cook serving Westerners was a male role in central China. My mother's cook said it was not appropriate for him to bring a woman from his village, so negotiations with various Mission personnel ensued. Mother's good friend, Miss Yang, our Mission Bible woman and evangelist, always had a way to solve problems. She found a young woman who had helped a teacher at the Girls School and persuaded her to try to cook for foreigners.

The problem was that this young woman helper that Barbara had insisted on had been brought up in a country village. There, a Chinese stove was an open space underneath a large circular iron pan called a "gwo" where straw, twigs, or brush was burned. They also used a smaller stove in which charcoal was burned. Kitchens were usually separated from the house or placed so that the smoke could exit the room easily and so the house would not be destroyed by fire. Farmhouse kitchens, as well as city kitchens, were sights to behold, almost universally real "black holes." In any case, this poor young woman did not have a clue as to how to light or use our stove, how to prepare food for Westerners, or really how to begin to learn. To her, Barbara's "Beijing" dialect was a foreign tongue, almost as unknown as English. The woman's country dialect was an equally huge problem for Barbara. It was understood by our young male helper, Jyusheng, as well as by me, so we became interpreters for Barbara. Without electricity and refrigeration, our fresh meat, fish, eggs or vegetables needed to be purchased on a daily basis. Survival became an urgent daily task of necessary communication. Barbara and her protégé struggled valiantly for several weeks but both were inexperienced in the process. The end was near.

One day a kind faculty member, wishing to welcome us to campus, brought around a lovely live goose. I noticed that the goose was tied near the back door and carefully fed, but no move was made to prepare that goose for our table. Barbara had no idea what to do with it and neither did our trainee. When Barbara mentioned to her that it was time to do something about the goose, they both burst into tears. Our country lass then tearfully asked if she could go home. Greatly relieved, we made the appropriate payments through Miss Yang, assuring the family that we had no hard feelings. Barbara reflects that one of many first lessons she learned was, "When in Hunan do as the Hunanese do."

We then were able to secure a wonderful cook who had been a chef for the French consulate in Hankow before the war. He was the older brother of my parent's cook, also named Fu. He came to us known as "Dasifu", which means head servant, as was the common practice. We really never called him by his full name, a fact, in hindsight, I regret. He was a marvelous cook who could make an angel food cake with very coarse Chinese granulated sugar and heavy flour, which we could buy locally. He could decorate the cake beautifully but never would let Barbara watch, for her presence made him too nervous. He was a gentle man and we were very fond of him. He had trachoma, a painful disease of the eyelid that formed small granulations which scratched the eyeball and could eventually cause blindness. Barbara treated his eyes every evening with swabs of silver nitrate which we got from the hospital in town.

In addition to securing the cook "Dasifu" and our "jack of all trades," Jyusheng, we also hired another young man from the same village who carried water from the well for our use and did other outside work. I privately called him "Dumb-dumb," a name not used outside the house, but descriptive of Li Dz-Ming, who was very good-natured but never did get over his country ways. He had grown up always smiling and could make you love him even though he drove you to distraction with an inability to understand clearly the instructions of our cook or anyone else. Years later on our first return to China (1981), he came to our hotel in Yueyang to greet us, an act requiring much courage at that time. On several of our subsequent visits he always found out our time of arrival and with his ever-present smile, warmly and wholeheartedly welcomed us. At that time he was a faithful worker at the local rice mill.

Spring 1947

Finally, we were really ready to start part-time language study and also begin teaching English classes in the new semester. The weather was gloomy and the school classrooms were unheated. The woolies we wore helped, but beginning English, particularly the "This is a book...a desk...a chair..." variety was uninspiring for teachers and students in the bitter, damp chill of a Hunan winter. Gradually, however, we began to feel more at home with students and faculty. One of the first requirements was to give our students English names, trying to find easily pronounced names. Forgetting the difficulty of "r" and "l" for Orientals, Barbara, unfortunately, named one student "Ralph". In spite of much practice, he always called himself "Arf".

We had our students in our home for meetings, games, and for instruction on Western customs. We were particularly interested in working with our senior classes so had them come to our home for a Western dinner. Such occasions were learning experiences for us as they ate at our table just as they would at their own, with boarding house reaches, standing up to spear a piece of bread with their fork, or emitting loud belches of satisfaction at the end of the meal to let the hostess know how much they had enjoyed it. Sometimes it was hard to keep a straight face!

We had divided duties in that we also spent time studying Chinese language. My study was with Mr. Hsiang, English Department chair, most of the time reading the Bible. Barbara studied Bible reading with Mrs. Hsiang and also worked on colloquialisms and some Hunan phrases. In this study we both learned enough Chinese characters to read the Gospels.

Mr. and Mrs. Hsiang had a handsome little year old son, David, born after the war ended. She told Barbara about the tragic loss of their other small children as the family fled on foot from Yoyang westward to escape the Japanese army. One by one the children died along the way from the terrible conditions of their flight. This heartbreaking account brought home very deeply the suffering the Chinese endured during the war.

Of great help to me was an opportunity to meet regularly with Principal Liu, as he was anxious to be assured that his representative to the Mission had full information on the rehabilitation needs of Huping School. It was an education in internal pressure, building and creating mutual interest groups. Though my own priority was to begin working with the ministers and workers of the Chinese Churches, I quickly learned that it was appropriate to create support networks among the Christian leaders in the Mission schools.

We were very pleased to learn to know Leonard Liu, the son of Principal Liu, who had graduated from Yali High School where he had been taught excellent English. Yali was in Changsha and regularly had graduates of Yale University in New Haven as English teachers. Leonard helped teach beginning English, worked very hard, and always sought advice. He was a great blessing and help to us by translating and explaining many of the local

customs, polite and proper etiquette, as well as interpreting the expectations of students. We had good discussions about the future of China and
what kind of careers young people might be able to find. He became a life-
long, close friend.

The spring of 1947 proceeded smoothly for us with weekly trips to
town to stay overnight with Mom and Dad. We usually biked the four and
a half miles into town along the railroad tracks. Crossing the large railroad
bridge was often really scary, as we had to listen carefully to make sure a
train was not approaching. As we were pretty isolated at Huping these trips
provided a welcome break from our routine. It was nice to get to the "city"
and be with other Westerners.

It was especially meaningful to be with my parents. Neither Dad nor
Mom was really physically well. Dad's high blood pressure was difficult to
manage. Mom's condition had not improved with the heat of the previous
(1946) summer, but she never complained. She was so delighted to have
us in China and Yoyang, and she and Barbara were very fond of each other.
Mom's help and support to Barbara were immeasurable as Barbara struggled with her immersion in a new culture. Mom repeatedly said Barbara
was a "hau xifu" (wonderful daughter-in-law). The weekly break was also to
attend a regular mission gathering for news sharing, a special dinner, and
a meaningful prayer meeting. Mom's worries were about youngest brother,
Bob, who was in Japan in the US Occupation Army.

Barbara and I had been married nearly three years and were anxious
to start our family. In those days of new beginnings for us, and in light
of the unstable political conditions and the spiraling inflation, we sought
my parents' advice on the best timing to have a baby. They felt that China
was about as stable as it had ever been and encouraged us. That spring,
Barbara thought she was pregnant and she and Mom rejoiced together. The
prospect of a grandchild delighted my mother. Unfortunately, it was a false
pregnancy and those hopes were dashed.

In the spring, I was delegated by the Mission to travel to HongKong
to welcome two new missionary couples, Paul and Kit Gregory, and Bill
and Jane Daniels, who were assigned to Yuanling. It was a city where our
Mission had a hospital, schools, and a large church. It was located in the
western part of Hunan Province, at least three or four days travel from
Yoyang. We had advised these new families to follow our example to travel
by boat to HongKong and then by train to Changsha to avoid the transfers

required in coming via Shanghai. They arrived on the same troop transport on which we had traveled, the now famous (or infamous) "Marine Lynx." I was charged to purchase in HongKong a long list of supplies for individuals, the hospital, and the schools in Yueyang. China's supplies of paint, hardware, and foodstuffs were still strictly limited. In HongKong I rushed around for several days getting the long list filled and packed.

Jane and Bill Daniels were newly married. In fact, they had first met at the meeting where they were being interviewed for missionary service. Kit and Paul Gregory had 2-year-old, Nancy. On the train we had two comfortable roomettes, four bunks to a room. Arriving in Changsha, they stayed with missionary friends until they could get their baggage sent ahead to Yuanling. Rev. Snider took the Gregorys on by bus a few days later. Travel was difficult but possible with careful arrangement. The Daniels came on with me to Yoyang to visit with us at Huping for a few days, a real treat for Barbara. I was glad to get home with my load of supplies.

Our First Evangelistic Excursion to the Country

We took a break in the spring of 1947 to go with Dad to Taolin for a few days of evangelistic services at a church and school operated by a very strong and independent preacher, Rev. Mei Hauran. When I was 9 years old, he had visited Dad about going to seminary. He had a frightening look because as a young man he had lost one eye and his glass eye was always askew. He was also a fiery preacher. At meetings in 1947, his viewpoint was consistent that the Mission should turn over a big budget to the Chinese Church for five years and then not send any more money. The church would be independent and would thrive. All that was needed was a good financial start. He insisted that he had proved his point when, during the Japanese war, he had led his congregation into the hills and then brought them back after the war. He was prophetic in this vision as the Hunan Church did thrive after the Cultural Revolution thirty years later (1966–1976).

Taolin was only twenty-five miles from Yoyang, but to get there we took a train three stations distant (30 miles) to Linhsiang and then hiked ten or twelve miles to Taolin. As mentioned earlier, Dad was not feeling too well so we made him hire a small donkey to ride. He had wanted to make the trip, as he always enjoyed sparring with Rev. Mei. That the donkey required a small boy to lead it and was so small Dad's feet nearly touched the ground did not dampen our enthusiasm.

The church and school buildings in Taolin were to be rededicated following reconstruction after being destroyed by the Japanese army, 1938–1945. It was said that the destruction was in part due to Rev. Mei's outspoken opposition to the Japanese plan for a "New Order" in China, which was their watchword to the world. Unfortunately, their concept required the complete submission of the Chinese people. Rev. Mei had led most of the capable townspeople to the hills. Of course, the fact that his son was a ranking officer in the Nationalist Police system meant that Mei was also merely taking precautions. He was able to make his way out of Hunan and finally joined his son in Taiwan.

In any case, we walked along a road that had been constructed by the Japanese military for their three-wheeled motorcycles which could tow gun trailers. The road had fallen into disrepair but was clearly capable of being used by jeeps. We passed through fertile fields that showed good care. The people had no trucks or cars to use on an almost passable road. That required nearly another thirty years and a Communist revolution.

I had offered to bring a small generator and slides of the Life of Christ to be shown on Saturday evening. The generator and our bags were placed on a wheelbarrow, which made remarkably good time because "the load is very light," according to the barrow owner. This surely beat hiring three or four people to carry everything on their shoulders. The Hunan wheelbarrow had two wheels in line. In front was a small one used to cross ditches or to go up a few steps as the big central wheel was moved forward and upward. It should be noted that there was no need to call to people to get out of the way as the loud, squeaky noises from the wheel alerted everyone.

We were warmly welcomed by pastor and family, as well as a number of church members. Dad had visited many times so he had old friends. Barbara was the only woman who had ever made the trip except for Miss Mary Myers, our Mission itinerant nurse whose gospel lessons went along with sanitation sermons on cleanliness (obviously "next to Godliness"). The curious school kids gathered around and were just as curious about what that generator was going to do, as most of them had been too young under Japanese occupation to have much appreciation for electrical equipment. When they found out I could really understand them and speak their language they had all kinds of questions.

Our trip was memorable also for the morning tea that Mrs. Mei brought us before we got up in the morning. I wonder if that was the motivation, nearly 15 years later, for our own morning tea ritual that has persisted to this day. Mrs. Mei said that her husband could not get going until she had brought him his tea. It was a Chinese green tea with small chips of some kind of pepper-wood, liberally laced with honey, and a fresh egg stirred into it. My, it was good!

The weekend services went well. The generator did its duty and was not too noisy as I had a very long cable to carry the current to the projector. We projected the slides on a newly whitewashed wall of the church to the great enjoyment of most of the small town that had turned out to see what was going on. Dad accomplished his objective of getting a final accounting of all monies spent on renovation; I got to experience what I had thought I was supposed to be doing in China. We returned home to our English teaching knowing that we would soon be reassigned to evangelistic work.

Mission Reporting Begins Early

After our Taolin trip, Barbara and I wrote a report and news article for the "Southern Standard", the monthly newsletter of the Southern Synod of the Evangelical and Reformed Church, detailing how difficult it was to transport the equipment by donkey and wheelbarrow. We spoke longingly of having a jeep to travel over the rough roads built by the Japanese during World War II.

Imagine our surprise when we received a letter later in the year dated on Catawba College Homecoming Day written by the college president's wife, Mrs. Frances Omwake:

"Dear Barbara and Sterling:

Instead of going to a horse show and other things this morning, I want to spend a little time with you. Dr. Faust gave me your last letter to read and I am just as interested in your life and your work as I can be. This letter really has a purpose and I hope the mails will not be too slow as having an answer to my questions – and any additional thought, information or suggestion you may make – (is important). Remember last spring when in one of your letters you expressed the hope that someone would send you a jeep. Perhaps it was a joke at the time, but some of us took you seriously and have talked a good bit about the possibility. At our Catawba Regional meeting in Conover last Wednesday the matter was brought before the house –

Your hearts would have rejoiced if you could have been there and seen the enthusiastic response, at least mentally, the pocket-book response remains to be seen — but our hopes are high.

You would also be surprised at the questions a bunch of women can ask, and it seemed each question presented a new problem to be worked out. We do feel a little handicapped because of our lack of knowledge about the markets here and there, the type best suited to your work, the customs to be paid, the best place to buy, here or China where we can get the best price. And how we will raise the money — how much will it cost? The last two items will be our headache not yours. Could you send me a reassuring letter that the Catawba Regional is really thinking of doing a worthwhile thing and try to clear up a few of these purchasing problems? ... We are sure both of you will fully appreciate the situation way back here in NC and will write us frankly and fully just what you think is the very best line of procedure which will eventually land a four-wheeled something at your door — we hope!...

I have no idea how long it will take to have an answer to this appeal but be assured I will be watching the mails very anxiously for the next month. With every good wish to you in your work and much happiness in your chosen field,

Most sincerely,

Frances G. Omwake

PS — Catawba won... Miss Lantz has been here with me since Friday and looks like she will stay a few days longer. She is just the same with an interest in everything and everybody — still telling boys and girls the proper decorum for a college campus. You must know she gave me five dollars yesterday, the first contribution toward your jeep, car or station-wagon. Tho' a little hard to impress folks until I know definitely what I am talking about, I am counting strong on you. Frances Omwake"

Of course we were overwhelmed by the North Carolina women's support and generosity and wrote her right away, doing our best to answer her questions. It was sometime in January that we had a letter from our Board Secretary that a group of church women in NC were undertaking a project to purchase a Jeep for the Whiteners. We were told to correspond with Mrs. Hal Hoyle about our needs. The response was such that in a very short time the Jeep fund was assured. Procuring a Jeep in China, however, became increasingly problematic. The political situation in North China had begun to change dramatically with Communist victories in the northeast provinces and even a threat to Peking. But that is getting ahead of what we were thinking about at that time.

Mission Meeting in West Hunan, 1947

In the late spring our annual Mission meeting was held in Yuanling, located in the high hills near Kweichow Province. We traveled by train to Changsha where we visited the Farnhams, our boxcar companions, before heading on to Yuanling by bus. In those days the roads were mud or gravel, so the bus trip took two days crowded together on hard wooden benches. The first night we stopped in Changde where we stayed at a Chinese inn near the bus station. We had time to cross the river to visit the McCullough family, Presbyterian missionaries whom we had met in language school. They invited us to stay for supper. We enjoyed the visit returning to the inn rather late. In the middle of the night we both were violently nauseated and had to run to the bathroom. Unfortunately, the inn had only an outdoor Chinese toilet. It was quite a strenuous experience for both of us but especially for Barbara to have to use a Chinese "outhouse" (two boards over an open drain) for an hour or so with diarrhea as well as vomiting. She had just recently discovered she really was pregnant so was very fearful that she would miscarry. We never figured out what made us so sick since our hosts remained well. Though weary and worn in the morning, we were over the illness and able to travel. We arrived at the Yuanling bus station and crossed the river on a small sampan ferry to the other side. A rather steep walk up to the Mission compound ended the trip, which was soon forgotten in the warmth of the welcome given us by the Gregorys and Daniels.

At the meeting we found our Yuanling Mission quite clearly divided between younger and older missionaries. The three younger couples considered that we were called to evangelistic work, while strong emphasis on schoolwork seemed to be paramount for most of the older persons. With our coming, the tide appeared to be turning. Our concern was the rebuilding of the church infrastructure, personnel as well as buildings that had been destroyed. We were really quite unprepared for the kind of political infighting that took place as the large Eastview Boys School in Yuanling sought to have the hospital closed so they could take over the buildings. Built inside the city and on a hillside, space was very limited for any expansion; thus, the terrain contributed to the kind of cat and mouse game that ensued. The hospital was definitely outclassed with no foreign missionary on the staff. Though we younger ones were thoroughly lobbied, we determined to have some time, at least a year in those uncertain times, to learn the ropes before being called on to make huge changes. We relieved our frustration by jokingly establishing the CCC –"Committee on Crapper Construction," a missionary indoor toilet construction planning project! We clearly were disgusted with the idea that hospital work was no longer a vital part of service to the people.

The young upstarts found one common goal in a strong determination to initiate correspondence on issues. This regular sharing of concepts, hopes, and dreams did result in an almost monthly exchange of letters between us that offered encouragement to us all. One result of the meeting itself was that the two new couples who had arrived in the spring and were taking language study at a Lutheran Language Institute in Hankow would be available in the fall. They were assigned, Herbert and Dottie Beecken to Huping School to take our places in teaching English and Reynold and Anna Mae Ziegler to Yoyang to take one of the two counties of the area as missionary pastor. Barbara and I looked forward to beginning work in Linhsiang County.

Mother had not undertaken the difficult trip to Yuanling. Shortly after we left for Mission meeting, she became very ill and was sent by the Yoyang physician to Hankow for treatment. We corresponded regularly, but because it was nearing the end of the school term we visited her in Hankow only once.

Mother wrote Bob on June 6, 1947, from Hankow:

"Dearest Bob,

Another week and all our mail waits at Yoyang for Dad to return. He should be back now in a day or two and then I will get your letters. It just seems ages. No letter from Sterling & Barbara either for, of course, they are busy in Mission Meeting.

Dad writes that they had a time in their meetings up there - a fight between the boys' school at Yuanling and the hospital. The school people wanted to give the hospital building to the boys' school and of course stop or close down the hospital. So that caused some trouble. The school lost out in the end I believe.

We have had a nice cool spell. The very hot weather did not last long. It has rained a good bit lately and that usually keeps it cooler.

Bobby Hansen the youngest Hansen in the family is home from Kikung School. He is twelve years old and looks like the other boys. He is cute and bright - reminds me of my boys.

I have been feeling pretty good but still could be much better. I seem to have stiffness in my knees and ankles and I don't walk as freely as I would like.

The two new couples here in Language school belonging to our Mission have just been appointed to their work by the Mission group. Mr. & Mrs. Reynold Ziegler to Yoyang, Mr. & Mrs. Herbert Beecken to Huping. But I do not know where Sterling and Barbara are to be appointed. Probably to the evangelistic work in the Yoyang district and live at Yoyang too. Dad is not to do Evangelist's work but is to spend his time on the Treas. job and we may live here in Hankow or in Wuchang across the river from here. That has not been settled.

These two new couples are very nice. The Zieglers are expecting a baby any day now. Hope it comes before the weather gets too hot. And I should be knitting a baby sweater or something for the expected baby but yarns are so very expensive I just can't afford to buy. But of course if we should ever have any hopes of a baby in our family I will afford some yarn some way. Somehow, I'm getting anxious - you know how I like to love and cuddle a baby. Wish mine were here - I'd hug them up good even though they are bigger than I am. Maybe Dad will help me catch and hold them for me. Ha.

You are a grand three and I love you with all my heart. Yes, I'll make it four for Barbara is almost like my own and I love her too!

And again - Bye Bye. Hope to hear soon.

Lots of Love,

Mother"

My Mother's Death

On June 22, we received devastating news. Lucile Hartman came out to Huping to bring a telegram that had just come from Dad saying that Mother had died in the International Hospital of congestive heart failure.

Even though we recognized how frail she had been, her death was a terrible shock to us. She was just too young to die at age 47.

We had not shared the news of Barbara's pregnancy with Mom and Dad because we wanted to be sure this time. We have always regretted that decision. We were making plans to spend the summer together with them in Kuling so planned to tell them our good news then. We knew how happy she would be. Barbara was a tremendous comfort to me as we tried to look ahead.

We went immediately to Hankow to be with Dad at the Lutheran Home. He was heartbroken with the loss, in part because he blamed himself for bringing her to China when she was not really healthy. It was hard to convince him that he held no blame, for that was really what she herself had wanted and had insisted upon. She had seen how happy Dad was in his work with the Church in Yoyang and the connection with leaders of the Church of Christ in China in Changsha. She voiced her optimism that the work they had given their lives to was going to go well in the future. Her last months in Yoyang with her Chinese friends, especially Miss Yang, were very satisfying to her. Added to her great satisfaction of being in the China she loved was the fact that we were at Huping and that she learned to know and love Barbara. The feeling was fully mutual. Barbara and I grieved that our future children and we had lost her.

There were no funeral parlors in China at that time for embalming the deceased. The Chinese have different ways of burying the dead. Mom's coffin was a wooden box lined with lime on which her body was placed, clothed in one of her dresses. Barbara combed her hair and put a bit of rouge on her face for Dad and me to see her before the box was nailed closed. She also removed Mom's wedding ring which Bob gave to Marion when they were married.

A graveside service was quietly held at the International Cemetery in Hankow where she was buried. We went back to Yoyang to pack Dad's clothing to go to Kuling for the summer. In Yoyang, church members and Pastor Tang held a memorial service for Mother. It was a tribute to the many years of work of my parents that the church was overflowing. They rejoiced and praised God for her life among them, her lively spirit, her openness and loving concern for all. It was an inspiring service.

We rented Miss Hoy's summer house on Kuling and spent about two months with Dad on the mountain. We were able to locate the son of the pastor of the Chinese congregation on Lushan who agreed to be our part-time teacher to read the Chinese Bible with us individually.

We also corresponded with the Edwin Beck family to negotiate the purchase of their little house next to Miss Hoy's. Before the end of the summer, we had bought the Beck house for $750 and started repairing it for our future use. One day up at the Gap, our small shopping area, I located two gallons of good yellow paint of US origin. I bought them and proudly started home. The paint was heavy so I stacked one gallon on top of the other and placed them on my shoulder. Walking happily, while whistling, along the main stream road, I noticed across the stream an official group of soldiers and an empty sedan chair. Walking right in front of the chair was Generalissimo Chiang Kaishek, the President of China. As I turned to view this extraordinary sight, alas, my paint buckets toppled to the sandy road. One bucket opened and my valuable paint started pouring out. I forgot my vision of the high and mighty and immediately righted the bucket and started scooping sandy paint back into it with my cupped hands. Amazingly, I was really quite successful. The sequel came when I had to explain to Barbara my misadventure. My clever wife found a suitable piece of cloth and sieved the sand out of the paint. Our walls didn't even appear too grainy after we finished the paint job!

We enjoyed the evenings with Dad, talking about old times and memories he had of his earlier days. It was a healing time for all of us. Barbara and I really relished the hikes around the mountain, the hills lush with many wild lilies and fresh growth. This was possible because the government ordered that the Lushan Mountain would be planted in Chinese firs as a preserve. They established a forestry station to begin the process. We also loved to go to remote mountain streams where we skinny dipped in the pools. The long walks around the mountain gave us plenty of exercise. We often went up to the Gap to look at the great variety of Chinese art objects for sale. Kuling was becoming a favorite spot for foreigners to take vacations so the tourist trade was picking up rapidly after the war.

We all returned to Yoyang in early September—Dad to his place in town and we went on to Huping School. We asked him to come out to Lakeside to stay with us but he felt he had to be in town to take care of all the Mission business since he was Mission treasurer. Barbara helped with clearing out Mother's clothing and other items, but it was a lonely time for Dad who was not too well himself. The doctor found that he had elevated blood pressure, as well as some prostate problems. His hypertension was serious enough that he was encouraged to limit his work or even to consider returning to the USA for treatment. At that time, the president of the Mission, Ward Hartman, and his wife, Frieda, moved back to Yoyang to live in the same large house. Ward started to take over some of the duties that had fallen to Dad.

We were able to continue some language study each day with the teacher we had located that summer in Kuling. Mr. Donald Cheng agreed to come with us to Huping to be our instructor and Chinese secretary. No Westerner of our acquaintance could undertake to write Chinese coworkers except in English. Most of us had the calligraphy expertise of a second grader so a secretary was essential.

A Deteriorating Political Situation

Dad, as treasurer, was much sought after for advice by Chinese and other Americans. He often carried on correspondence with mission treasurers whom he knew in North and Central China. His advice was often sought to help Americans decide whether or not to leave China because of the unrest. A great complication was the deteriorating political situation in China. It is difficult to summarize the failed efforts of the US government to mediate the conflicts between the Guomindang (Nationalists) and the Gongchandang (Communists). The United States government kept sending mediators of renown to China, such as General of the Army George Marshall, who was ill prepared for the job because Washington was deeply convinced that Chiang Kaishek was a stalwart bulwark against the Communists and Russian influence. Post war understanding of the needs and desires of the Chinese people could not be met by pouring American dollars into the government in Nanking. Many missionaries were thoroughly indoctrinated in the US viewpoint, so it was not too difficult to understand how some of our Chinese friends felt that the poor peasants of China needed to share in some of the largess flowing from America. Yes, there was wide distribution of foodstuffs through the United Nations Relief Programs, but at times inappropriate items for the Chinese diet were sent. The rural Chinese did not drink milk or eat dairy products. Their yellow cows were used for plowing. When blocks of American cheese were distributed, the people complained — "What terrible soap you Americans have."

As more and more money came off the printing presses, inflation soared. It was an endless task for the treasurer to exchange US funds into Chinese paper currency. No longer could we rely on bank transfers, as even telegraphic exchange often took at least a week. During the interim it was possible to lose as much as 10% or more of the value of the exchange. Bookkeeping was a nightmare. Mission books eventually had to be kept in US$ amounts with an insert showing what the exchange really was. All schools, the hospital, and all church workers wanted to convert their salaries and funds as quickly as possible into rice or some staple commodity such as kerosene and preferably old silver dollars. The paper currency would soon be worthless.

When Dad could go to Hankow, he would hurry back and immediately send for those persons responsible for dispensing funds. He always had a harrowing few days because all teachers, preachers, doctors, miscellaneous staff, and servants would spend the next few hours or days off their jobs purchasing goods or silver dollars to preserve the value of their salaries. On several occasions when there was a precipitous drop in exchange value, even the city merchants demanded payment in silver or rice. We also were affected. Barbara and I often had our salary held in the USA or sent directly to our Salisbury bank to try to preserve its value. This meant that we had to spend carefully and to plan ways to conserve whatever cash we received in paper. During the period from 1947 to May 1949, the Chinese dollar dropped twice in value from Y5 for 1$ US to over 12 million Yuan for one US dollar. At that point we were carrying suitcases and duffel bags of paper money around. An amazing fact was quite apparent: the ancient silver dollars came out of hiding and became the currency of choice. Supposedly illegal, it was the only way the economy could operate. Before a transaction was completed, one would hear the clink of the silver coins as they were always tested by sound. A dollar that tapped with a "clunk" or dull note was immediately rejected. Unfortunately, foreigners were often considered inept at such detection, so I learned quickly to listen carefully. Dad said it was cheaper to have his Chinese secretary or other helpers do the testing for him as he had responsibility for too many thousands of silver dollars.

Herbert and Dot Beecken, who had been assigned to Huping, quickly got settled into language study and began teaching English which was what they had hoped to do. They were great company for us and joined us on our weekly trek to town for our Mission gathering.

Representing the Mission in Shanghai

In November Barbara and I flew to Shanghai to represent our Mission at a meeting of the Missions associated with the Church of Christ in China. Over six months pregnant, Barbara was glad to get away and do some shopping in the big city. I don't remember that we made many purchases, but we did enjoy a movie, good food, and visits with friends. We flew from Hankow to Nanking and took the train from there. I remember that the planes were the old standby DC3s left over from the war. Even the seats were canvas bucket seats along the sides of a very noisy plane. In Nanking we got to visit Yale classmates and our long-time friends the Allens. We also visited a famous park which had a row of huge stone animals along the road. We were told that a pregnant woman could determine the gender of her baby by tossing a pebble up on the elephant's back. If it stayed there her baby was a boy; if it fell back off it was a girl. Of course we tried it, and —————— (to be continued).

In Shanghai I learned much from the leaders of our Church of Christ in China and was invited to seek affiliation as a registered ordained minister. You can be sure that I followed through on that invitation as soon as I returned to Hunan.

Of interest too was the opportunity to visit Don Mead for the second time. His work with Standard Oil was clearly very profitable. We enjoyed an evening with him to catch up with all the Kuling American School friends with whom we had lost contact.

On our return, we celebrated Christmas with the Mission folks in Yoyang. It was also a good chance to have Dad come out to visit us. Our school had special Christmas programs and it was a bit jarring to see one of our male students in the role of Mary looking quite unfeminine. Without heat in the little church, we sat around charcoal braziers to keep our feet warm while the program went on for hours! Our little Huping church was gaily decorated with paper chains. During the Christmas season I was asked to baptize the small baby and four-year-old son of the Hu family. Mr. Hu was a teacher of Chinese. This occasion was very special because it was really the very first baptism I had ever performed. I studied hard with Donald Cheng, my teacher, to learn all the proper phrases and, being the son of a minister, he also helped with the local protocols. The service was appreciated and a joyous occasion for the small congregation.

Usually about once a month, the school provided the faculty a special meal. This gave us a good opportunity to have fellowship with all the other Chinese faculty members and their wives. We also loved the menu because it always included, in addition to wonderful fresh stir-fried vegetables, a dish of fatty pork laid over sour cabbage (almost like sauerkraut) with black beans, cooked to perfection. They also had several other dishes that we loved.

1948

In early January on one of my many trips to Changsha to help Dad by meeting with the Church of Christ in China Hunan Synod, I learned to know the Synod executive secretary, the Rev. Li Yungwu. I felt we related to each other well and looked forward to his direction of the work I was anticipating in Linhsiang County. Our conversations reflected my own perceptions of the need for missionaries to work themselves out of a job, called "devolution." That we were guests in China to serve as the Chinese church directed was a new concept to Rev. Li. It very obviously refuted the Communist ideology that we were all imperialists.

In Changsha I also spent a night with the Farnhams. I learned that one of their Mission couples had an American bike with large tires and a small gas motor, called a "Whizzer." This motor was mounted on the bike so that a belt could turn the rear wheel. The bike could still be pedaled to get the motor started. It was light enough to use in the countryside where small trails wound through the rice paddy fields and were often cut with open drainage ditches so that water could flow freely from one field to another. I was able to buy the bike and motor, take it home to Huping, and put it together. I learned to be quite proficient so that in time I could even hop the small drainage ditches between paddies without getting off the bike. The best fun was racing the slow freight trains from bridge to bridge, as I would get off the bike to roll it on the track across any railroad bridge ahead of the train. The engineers always greeted me with waves of their arms and whistles. "Crazy foreigner," I'm sure they thought.

Barbara had been urged by the Chinese physician at our hospital to go to Hankow for her delivery in case of complications. At the end of December there were rumors of bandits becoming active along the Jiangxi border not too many miles to the east. Our baby was due in early February and plans had been for Barbara to go to Hankow at the end of January. Anxiety about the bandit threat pushed her to Hankow much earlier.

Karen Marie – February 4, 1948

We arranged for Barbara to stay with Dr. Paul Taylor of our Mission who had a home at Huachung University in Wuchang where he taught philosophy. Her obstetrician, Dr. Mabel Gao, trained in the USA, was in Hankow across the river, but there was good emergency care available in Wuchang if needed. We appreciated Dr. Taylor's warm hospitality. He was a congenial host and Barbara enjoyed leisurely days of knitting and taking long walks. We agreed that at a convenient time, I would come down to Hankow and we would move to the Lutheran Home, near her doctor and the International Hospital. We managed to do that before our daughter decided to put in an early appearance on February 4, 1948. When labor pains started midday, we went to the nearby International Hospital by rickshaw. The Catholic nuns there got Barbara all settled. Of course, in those days, they kept us quite separated. In the evening a nun frantically came running to me and said, "Go get the doctor, the baby is coming" or something on that order. Dr. Gao lived only several blocks away, so I started running. In my haste on the rather ill-lit sidewalk, I fell in a gutter and tore my trouser knee. When the doctor arrived at the hospital, she let me go with her into the delivery room. It was not very long before Karen arrived, six lbs., four ounces. What an outstanding treat to be present at Barbara's side. I was so proud of her and of the beautiful little girl we named Karen Marie, after my mother.

The nuns were excellent caregivers, but they insisted that Barbara stay in bed for a week. She was anxious to get up, get moving, and get back home. We did stay in Hankow for a short period before returning to Huping. Of course, telegrams were sent and received from Salisbury.

Homecoming was really a festive occasion. We took a sampan from Yoyang to Huping. Firecrackers were necessary to welcome our first-born back home. It was still winter weather and quite cold in the unheated bedrooms. Getting up for night feedings was quite an operation to put on heavy clothing and still nurse Karen. Barbara managed so smoothly one would have thought that we lived in the lap of luxury with central heating. We did run into one problem, however. Karen was rather small and wiry and did not seem to gain weight to worried Barbara's satisfaction. We did not have baby scales, so I weighed her with Chinese scales—a hook into a hanging diaper serving as a tray with weight balances to indicate the number of Chinese catties she weighed. Translating catties "jin" to pounds became a constant imprecise and imponderable calculation. All we could really tell was whether she gained or lost weight.

Without a pediatrician, all Barbara had was a copy of Dr. Spock's Baby and Child Care book, which served as an "at her elbow" consultant. Karen had her crying time, particularly at bedtime. Later, she loved to sit in the middle of the large dining room table and suck the local "gandz", an incredibly sour lemon-like orange. Barbara confesses to having been a real "worry-wart." She sorely missed my mother whom she had been counting for guidance and support. We were indeed blessed that we had no serious medical problems to deal with.

We particularly welcomed Dad when he visited, because he loved to hold Karen and sing to her all the family bedtime songs. We have enjoyed singing them ever since to all of our kids: "Go to sleep, go to sleep, when you wake you'll get a cake and a whole lot of little horsies," "I'm so sleepy...," and "Go down, Moses."

Looking Ahead

That winter, Gertrude Hoy, fellow missionary and daughter of the founder of our Mission, Dr. William Hoy, returned from furlough in the US and bringing me a photo enlarger which had been purchased for us. I was a neophyte but quickly learned to process negatives and enlarge them. I set up a rather primitive dark room so I was able to send pictures back to our family and to our Board headquarters for their publicity purposes.

There were many opportunities to take pictures during Chinese New Year. More important than our own Christmas and other combined vacations, this was the one time the entire nation had a week-long or extended holiday. The celebrations included lion dances, much drumming, singing, music on shrill snakeskin covered bamboo stringed instruments, and dancing in the city streets and in rural villages. Celebration events included visiting extended families and enjoying very special treats and feasts. There were always red packets of "lucky money" for the children.

During the Chinese New Year's vacation, the students went home if they lived reasonably near. Some, however, stayed on campus, so we organized some special slide shows on the life of Christ in the nearby villages.

We hung a white sheet, the students sang hymns to attract a crowd, and I cranked up the generator. Students then talked about the pictures and explained what they were depicting: parables, Sermon on the Mount, and other stories from the Bible. The program was usually received with wonderment, curiosity, and in some cases real interest in this new religion.

In this New Year, 1948, our thoughts began to turn toward our assignment to Linhsiang county. Having studied under Dr. Latourette, it seemed only natural to consider changing the lifestyle of the missionary living in a compound to one of moving nearer the members of the Chinese Churches in this rural county to which we had been assigned. I wanted to be an advisory pastor, helping the four men and one woman who were working for the Church of Christ in China. They had lived through years of war and destruction. I planned to bike around the county weekly to support them in ways they determined might be helpful.

After discussion and prayerful consideration, we sought permission to build a small home in the town of Linhsiang, the county seat. Linhsiang was a new town with only a few thousand or so inhabitants, but it was the center hub for reaching all the little towns in the county where we had small chapels: Yanglausz, Niehjyasz, Yunchi, and Taolin. Linhsiang was 30 miles by train but several hours away from Yoyang if we encountered any emergency, as there was no medical care any nearer, and there were no Westerners in the village, but our faith was great.

A small chapel and parsonage had been completed that spring. There was no church worker at that time, so my Huping colleague, Mr. Mei Shouchun had been appointed to help with personnel matters and self support. He and Mrs. Mei were living in the parsonage. The Mission appointed Mr. Mei to be my associate in Linhsiang County. He had taught at Huping for a number of years and was highly respected in the church. At first he was not so sure that there was a meaningful position for him, but I assured him that his time would be spent working on self-support for the churches, as we fully subscribed to the Three-Self Movement first initiated in 1935 by the Church of Christ in China. It should be noted that the motives of self-support, self-governing, and self-propagation were also objectives of the Chinese Communists for all agencies and programs of the country. The fact that the churches of China were in tune with this goal greatly helped in later dealings with the next government.

As it was a fairly large residence, arrangements were made for us to share the parsonage with the Meis. We asked to move in the fall to Linhsiang to oversee the construction of a simple home for us. We found great support from Dad and others in our Mission group as we continued to plan for this new venture. In the meantime our life continued at Huping.

The United Nations Relief and Rehabilitation Services continued to bring surplus food supplies to China. In the market place we could purchase large 5 gallon tins filled with dried apples, dried potatoes, and all kinds of other foodstuffs that had been used by the US army and navy, and very useful to us. Often the Chinese who received the food would empty the tin in order to use the can itself, as the contents were not adaptable to their rice diet.

The saddest situation was the case of some large American milk cows. No farmers wanted milk cows because they used cows only to plow the fields. Their little yellow cows were strong and well trained, as well as immune to many bovine diseases. The bigger foreign cow was a huge grass eater that required protection because of the many local diseases. We got involved in helping with the Heifer Project cows. Huping School, which had been at one time an agricultural academy to help educate farmers' sons, decided to take some cows and a bull. Holstein and Guernsey varieties were ill suited to the diseases of Hunan, so we were forced to cut all the fresh grass for them, as hoof-and-mouth disease was rampant. In addition, even Western experts did not fully understand the local unsanitary conditions. The person who had accompanied the cows all the way from the US decided to dehorn the young bull for safety reasons. It was an unfortunate decision. Though we tried to treat the sites with sulfa powder, they became infected and sadly caused the death of the bull.

We finally decided, personally, we would try to care for one cow so purchased a beautiful Guernsey from the school. We had an old empty storeroom near our Huping home that we turned into a barn. We got our good water-carrier to cut grass and buy extra grass from the farmers to bring to the cow. We could use rice bran and other grains for feed. The big job was to teach someone to milk. I had to do the milking twice a day, but soon Jyusheng caught on and enjoyed his milkman job. Even Barbara learned to milk! We had to boil the milk at first because pasteurization was difficult until we learned to rig up a good system. We soon became very attached to the milk and even tried making butter. We shared the milk with other families but though most of them found they preferred soy milk to real cow's milk, quite a few asked to buy cow's milk for their children because the price was low.

Dot and Herb Beecken had taken up our English teaching at Huping but in April, Herb had some severe back pain. He was sent to Hankow to get expert medical tests and opinions. The result was a diagnosis that he had tuberculosis of the spine. The doctors recommended immediate repatriation for specialist consultation in the USA. This was a most difficult time for Dot, as she had to pack up all of their belongings to be shipped home. There was no reason to expect that they would be returning in a few months, as the political situation was not improving. We were so sorry to see them leave since it meant our own fellowship was growing smaller. US doctors subsequently found that his condition was not TB and did respond to treatment; the Beeckens were sent to Japan for a lifelong service to the Japanese church in Annaka.

Dad's health had been a continual concern for the doctors in Yoyang. After consultation with the Board in Philadelphia and Don in Winston-Salem, it was decided that he should return to Winston to seek medical evaluation and care. I went with him to HongKong by train to help arrange his passage to the States by ship. We did not know that it would be the last time we would be together. He left on May 28, 1948. While in HongKong, I had the opportunity again to purchase needed supplies for all the missionaries in Yoyang. I had to leave for home before Dad's departure, so we both spoke of his need to recover his health and we would see him in a few years when we came back on furlough.

The Mission had agreed that the younger couples should take the summer of 1948 to study Chinese in order to become more language proficient, as we were all expected to begin full-time service in September. Together we decided to undertake our study in Kuling where we could avoid the terrible summer heat of the Yangtze plains. We had just bought the Beck cabin, Miss Hoy's was available for the Gregory family of three (Nancy was 3), and the Zieglers (with their new daughter) were able to rent a cabin that was being renovated. The Daniels would live with us. The Daniels and Gregorys left Yuanling on June 12 but the travel situation was so bad, they had to take a bus trip to Nanchang and Kiukiang to get to us. It was better, I think, than traveling down from Hankow by junk for four days since all river steamers had been commandeered by the Chinese army.

Summer Study in Kuling

It turned out to be a wonderful summer of study, sharing, refreshing hikes, and renewing spirits. We often gathered at one place or another for hymn singing, storytelling, and dreaming of what we might be called on to do. The only down part was the trouble with money. In June we received about one-half the value of our US$200 per month salary because the bank in Jiujiang did not cash our check for over five days. The money was deteriorating very rapidly. One US dollar brought in over one million in Chinese paper.

Karen, now five months old, was growing fast. We held her baptismal service in the church where our Kuling American School worshipped during my years at school. Reyn Ziegler baptized her in a private afternoon service attended by friends. It was in Kuling that summer that Mary Lou Allen and Barbara first became fast friends. She had Louise and Netta and often came by our cabin on her walk to town. Mary Lou was the wife of Harry Allen, who had preceded me at Kuling American School by two years. You may remember that Don and I took over his summer mimeographing business in 1936 and 1937.

The summer ended more quickly than we expected. There were so many young missionaries from all up and down the Yangtze valley that there was always something to enliven the days and evenings, such as special events at the community auditorium. It is interesting to note that many of those we learned to know were later appointed to responsible positions in various Mission and ecumenical bodies.

Many discussions centered on the political developments in China and the lack of success of the various USA truce teams who sought to negotiate a peaceful settlement of the Communist–Nationalist conflict. At the time it appeared that the country might actually be divided into two parts. The Chinese economy was fast falling into chaos. In retrospect, we appeared to think that this process was a normal transition, Chinese style, which would be settled by negotiation in the manner many differences had been resolved in the past. The intensity, however, of the Communist movement, and the extreme disgust of the common peasant with the corruption of the Nationalist regime made this revolution a serious one. In correspondence with the Stowes in North China, we began to realize that all of us might need to consider the option of staying on under a new government or putting on hold our hopes to serve the Church in China.

As a final planning effort, the younger missionaries decided to hold a "work camp" as a part of our Mission meeting early in the fall. It would be held at Huping where we would create an outdoor worship center. At this October meeting, we had a wonderful gathering, working together outdoors carrying rock and creating the worship area under the trees near our house. The men were challenged to participate in a soccer match with the senior Huping boys. It was in that losing effort that Paul Wu and I became entangled. He rolled neatly, unhurt; I tore a ligament in my knee, an injury from which I suffered until I received knee replacement many years later. At the business session, Barbara and I received authorization from the Mission meeting to proceed with our move to Linhsiang and I was appointed Mission treasurer.

As we considered the kind of house we would build in Linhsiang, we found that a corrugated tin Quonset hut, a surplus from the US Army that had been donated to the Yoyang Hospital, was available. No Chinese person was willing to consider using such a monstrosity to live in. The hospital was glad to sell it to us for erection in Linhsiang.

Donald Cheng, our teacher/secretary, was a very talented and ingenious person. He arranged to secure a flat railcar to transport the Quonset hut to Linhsiang and to get it moved from the RR station to the town where we purchased a lot on which to erect it. Mr. Mei was the key person who negotiated the official permission to purchase the small plot of land and to contract the erection of the usual Chinese brick wall to delineate the boundary. The site was conveniently located beside a very small stream, next to the bridge on the road leading to the RR station. It was also adjacent to the army guard post of the contingent guarding bridge and town.

During the fall semester, I was on the go to Linhsiang to see to the erection of our home. The villagers watched curiously with expectations and discussions as the Quonset hut took form. We were delighted with our design of the interior. Of course, there were no windows on the metal sides, but a large picture window in the front end looked out on distant hills. Behind the living room were our bedroom, a bathroom, a little room for Karen, and a large storage room. On the rear of the hut was attached a brick extension for a kitchen and rooms for our helpers and storage. Importantly, we had to build a shelter for Dolly, the cow.

As we came to grips with what was really happening in China, we realized that we might not have many years or even many months before each family would need to make a decision whether to stay under a new Communist government or return to the USA. Three of the young wives, including Barbara, were pregnant, a further complicating factor. Uncertainty was the order of the day, and a decision made one week often was altered the next. The exchange rate for one US dollar reached twelve million paper dollars before Chiang Kaishek printed a new currency at the rate of four dollars to one US. He had his picture on the bank note, which was to symbolize that now the money was really worth something. Unfortunately, the new paper was not backed by real reserves and the common people did not trust it very long.

The Joys of Life in Huping

Our year and a half at Huping was a pleasant and very useful time of adjustment, preparing us for the tumultuous years ahead.

The location of the school, overlooking the Dongting Lake, was quite beautiful and serene. The sinking sun beyond the lake highlighted the graceful line of Chinese junks. Often in the line were blue sails, mended sails, new sails and even tattered ones majestically permitting the Hsiang River current to carry them past Junsan Island's small white temple still visible in the evening glow. In the fall there was constant motion on log rafts, floated from the western mountains to be made into giant rafts for delivery to the major cities down the Yangtze River. As the men rolled the logs into larger configurations, their chants and songs with haunting melody kept the timing of the workmen together, often saving them from falling into the dangerous currents. Multiple long sweeps were usually the only guidance the rafts possessed, though at times they were tied together and towed by a powerful launch. Small huts on the rafts housed the workmen and a few families.

Though the Japanese army had cut down all of the trees on the Huping campus, they had been respectful of the valuable bamboo groves. We loved to walk through them, but most of all we enjoyed eating the spring sprouts prepared for us by "Dasifu" in the Chinese style.

Birds returned to the trees and hillsides of Huping after the war. Long-tailed magpies swept gracefully from tree to tree. The rare Golden Oreole was a spectacular sight on its migration to its summer home. Many smaller varieties we couldn't identify had lovely songs and interesting calls.

Our house was comfortable, our living situation quite adequate and we were very appreciative of our servants with whom we were compatible.

Our young helper, Jyusheng, was very bright so we asked him if he would like to study English with us in the evening when we lit up our pressure lantern. We had brought with us a copy of the famous Laubach method of teaching English so anticipated great success. He was very eager at first but the project proved to be too much for student and teachers. It was fun while it lasted. He did in later years educate himself and was successful in being the manager of the yearly collection of tons of lakeside reeds for paper mills down river.

Though we could not call it a joy, it should be noted that I did come down with a case of mumps. I thought I had managed to get them when a child, but I sure had a clear resurgence. Then Jyusheng, our wonderful helper, came down with a very healthy case. If you are wondering, both of us fathered large families!

Mail from the USA meant contact with HOME. I was already home, but Barbara's hunger for mail from her family was insatiable. Her parents wrote faithfully, her siblings somewhat less regularly, but all letters were read many times. Barbara wrote letters home every few weeks, a total of about 140 letters over our four years in China. Her mother saved these letters, giving us an invaluable informal record of that immensely eventful period in our lives. Mail also meant reading material. We had several magazine subscriptions which Barbara's parents mailed to us: *Saturday Evening Post*, *Reader's Digest*, and even the *Salisbury Post*. Books were a real treasure.

We were sad to leave Huping, but very eager to begin our next venture in Linhsiang.

Move to Linhsiang

In spite of the very uncertain political situation we proceeded with the move in November to the church parsonage in Linhsiang village, sharing it temporarily with Mr. and Mrs. Mei. We had two small rooms and they also had two. We shared a central living room area though we ate separately. Our cook and house helper, Jyusheng, lived in the servants' quarters in the back near a kitchen area. Though cramped, we felt that we had finally been able to achieve a goal of moving nearer the people. During the winter, we often sat in the evenings with the Meis in the living room sitting around a charcoal brazier to keep our feet warm. As we sat in the bright light of our Coleman lantern we had rewarding discussions about the future of the church and what the role of a missionary might be. Karen had a crib in our small front room. When she went to bed she often cried awhile. This was hard on Mrs. Mei because Chinese babies are never allowed to cry themselves to sleep.

Mr. Mei performed invaluable work with the evangelists and pastors of the county. He handled all of the personnel issues and paid out all the salaries. When I was not off on Mission treasurer's business, I visited the chapels and workers, Bible women, evangelists, and ordained men on a regular basis. As an example, one Saturday I rode my "Whizzer" to Niehjyasz to conduct an evening session with the local consistory of the little church to examine six young people and a few older adults for membership. After a simple meal together, several elders, the evangelist, and I met with the students individually, to question them as to their understanding of the meaning of church membership. They really had been prepared pretty well: reciting the creed, speaking to why they wanted to join the church. Several adults also had learned their lessons well. The baptismal service the next day was a celebration.

Christmas was a busy time. Barbara was the one who was doing all the real missionary work in Linhsiang, as I was often on the road. We should have called her the "flannel graph lady," as she worked up a number of Bible stories to share with the village children. She helped arrange the decorations for the little chapel and a Christmas tree as we were planning a party for the children. Fortunately, Donald Cheng was available and was a great help. His experience as a minister's son enhanced his ability to work with the children of the town. Karen made a big hit with the women of the community, and since Barbara was pregnant, many local women offered all kinds of suggestions.

We were hurrying the workers to complete our Quonset home and were able to move in the first of the year. Hanging over us was the fact that there were no medical doctors or facilities nearer than several hours away. Without telephone connections it was always a worry. We have since described ourselves as crazy, naïve, or having great faith. It was probably a combination of the three, but we have been most grateful that there were no emergencies.

Spring of 1949 – A Ford for West Hunan

Sometime around the first of the year it was decided that those in West Hunan urgently needed a car for fast communication and possibly for evacuation westward should the need arise. I was commissioned to find a vehicle that was not too expensive, could be maintained and repaired fairly easily, and could take the very rough road from Wuhan to Changsha where I would deliver it to Bill Daniels. I located a 1946 Ford station wagon in Hankow, which was available because an American company executive had decided that it was time to cut his company's losses and clear out. Most American businesses had heeded the analysis of the US Consulate that the situation was deteriorating and that central China could expect to be a battleground. I can't remember just what we paid for the Ford, but it was not given away. They threw in a 55-gallon tank of gasoline, which was placed in the back with the rear seat folded down. I bought many hospital supplies and other items needed in Yuanling. I also decided to take a payroll of 2000 silver dollars in a bag that I could place directly under the front driver's seat. It took some work to find out just where the road for Hunan started in Wuchang. I had bought the car in Hankow, so had to get it across the river on a pontoon car ferry.

Donald Cheng had found a hand sketched map with a series of towns where the road was supposed to pass through. The two of us had loaded the car with all kinds of Ford spare parts: several tires & tubes, a generator, all kinds of belts, and just about all the bulbs and fuses that might need replacement. We carried a sleeping roll for each of us in case we had to sleep out in the wilds. We also bought some tinned goods in case we could find little to eat. We need not have worried, for strangers and travelers are usually treated as guests and provided with a meal. We started out on one road, which we found was not heading in the right direction. Stopping often to seek advice and directions, we finally got out of Wuchang on a highway built by the Japanese that carried us close to the Jiangxi border near some mountains.

Being the only driver, I thought it would be impossible to drive all day. I found, however, that at the speed we were going, it was a breeze. We could hardly travel more than 25 mph most of the time. The roads were all of clay with little gravel. Fortunately, we did not have rainy weather so all we had to worry about was the rutted and pot-holed road. We were making good time and hoping to arrive at a fairly large city near the Hunan border by nightfall when the old Ford got the hiccups. What a worry! We were at least one hundred and fifty miles from Wuchang and perhaps two hundred from Changsha. There was no choice but to limp along. As it was getting dusk, we turned on the lights and proceeded very slowly. Suddenly, we faced three fully armed soldiers standing right in the middle of the road with their guns at the ready. The signal was obvious. My first thought was of the silver under my seat. What would keep them from searching and then making off with more money than they could earn in a lifetime! Further insight was really scary as I realized what a bullet into the gas tank might produce.

With a big flashlight on my face a non-com came to my window and was surprised to find a foreigner. I greeted him and asked what I could do for him. His reply was, "I am sorry, but I must take your car as my colonel needs this car to get to town." I replied that I too wanted to get there but the car was not operating properly. He then told me that he had a squad of 15 men and that they all needed to go along in order to get to town. I explained that this car belonged to the church Mission and that it was due in Changsha tomorrow. He backed off a bit and said he was not taking it away from us, but needed it tonight. I asked if it would be possible to speak to his commanding officer. This was obviously what he wanted also, as he asked if we would kindly wait until his officer came.

It was not long before a very good looking officer approached and was briefed by the non-com. The soldiers were still holding us hostage so we could not make a break, not that I even considered the idea. Those old advertisements about "faster than a speeding bullet" did not entice me to run. Anyway, the man in charge was no older than I was. He asked if he could take his squad to the next town since he would have transport from there. I immediately invited him to replace me in the front seat, as that was the only space available. I offered then to walk if he would give me a receipt for the car, the gasoline, the spare parts, and other supplies, as I would need to collect the dollar value from my friend General Wang Jienbo who was waiting for me in Yoyang. It became clear that he really did not want to get involved in that manner. He also pointedly said that he had no driver with him and that it would be pointless for me to give up the car.

The next negotiating point was the number of his squad who could be accommodated in the car. The final adjustment was that we had four in the front seat: Donald Cheng, the officer, his aide, and me. We then agreed to two bodyguards on the front fenders, as we were only able to "hiccup" along at about 10 miles per hour. We reached the little town in about an hour. The officer and I had a long discussion about what missionaries were trying to do in China, particularly in the hospitals and schools that were trying to help the common people.

In town he directed me to the large city administration complex. Exhausted, we really looked forward to some rest and also to find someone to fix our ailing Ford V-8. Our friendly colonel invited us to share his supper that was being prepared. It was really a treat to have a good dinner. He also asked his adjutant to go find a mechanic to fix our Ford. There were a number of army trucks parked in the schoolyard next door, so it was not long before a mechanic came to talk with me about just what I thought was the trouble. "Not getting the gas properly," I insisted. It was not an hour later that he came back to show me the fuel pump with its torn diaphragm. I was sure we were stuck for the duration, but he smilingly said, "Yo ban fa" (have a solution), and sure enough, he did. He cut a circle out of an old inner tube and in a few minutes had our V-8 running better than it had since we bought it.

Our night's sleep was really heavy. The only trouble was that my pillow was terrible, as two thousand silver dollars do not make a soft pillow. The next morning after a breakfast of rice gruel and "100-year-old eggs," we left for Changsha. The ferry across the Yungjiawan River was nothing after the excitement of the night before. With three sampans lashed together with some heavy boards for tracks, we were poled across the river, hoping that the lashings stayed in place. By afternoon we had arrived in Changsha to find the Presbyterian Mission compound, where I turned the whole problem of the V-8 over to Bill Daniels. The sequel was that he did drive the car to Yuanling and they used it for awhile, but found it took too much time and money to maintain. They finally sold it, relieved that they did not have that added responsibility especially in the light of the expected coming regime change.

Money, Money, Money

My job as Mission treasurer was taking more and more time. Keeping accounts in US dollars was the easiest part. Trying to make sense of the daily change in exchange rate was a nightmare for the folk who had to audit the books. I regularly traveled from Linhsiang to Hankow each month to cash the US checks for the Mission grants to hospitals, schools, churches, and individual salaries. We sent the Yuanling monies by telegraphic transfer, but for Yoyang I often carried large sums of money back by train.

One experience I will never forget. Carrying the equivalent in the new Chinese currency of four thousand dollars (US) for the various payrolls in Yoyang, I expected to go there directly. I arrived at Linhsiang station shortly after midnight, so I then decided to go home for the night since it was on the way and an arrival in Yoyang at 2 A.M. would disturb everyone there.

It was a dark and chilly night. There was no moon, but the stars shone brightly. The two-mile road from the railroad station to town was very familiar so I started out alone with my money in a small suitcase and my flashlight full of new batteries. Whistling a tune, I could easily make out the roadway as I became accustomed to the dark, so walked cheerily along without using the flashlight. Suddenly, not too far from the roadway, a rifle shot sounded in the hills. After a second shot, I considered what to do. The shots were not very close, but I had no idea whether some bandits were attacking a farmhouse, or perhaps hunters might just head my way. Looking carefully for a place to hide my suitcase, I found a spot behind a bush beside the road on the hillside. I then walked about a hundred yards away, sat down, and waited. There was one more shot fired but it sounded even farther away, so I determined to wait for fifteen or even thirty minutes before venturing on. Without any further disturbance in the hills or sounds of anyone approaching, I retrieved my hidden treasure and silently made my way toward Linhsiang town.

A further possible complication came to mind as I neared the dark town itself. Without electricity in China, there were no streetlights. The hour was late so no shops had any kerosene lanterns hanging over their wares. In fact, the whole place was shuttered up. I knew that an army patrol was stationed just across the bridge from our house. When I got within several hundred yards of that patrol hut, I decided that I had better let them know who was coming. I started singing hymns, in English, of course. Can't remember whether I stuck with the Titanic favorite "Nearer My God to Thee," but I do know that I had moments of wondering if some trigger-happy, young farm boy would shoot first and ask questions afterwards. I heard the cocking of a rifle as the guard shouted, "Jr bu," (halt). With my flashlight squarely shining on my face I showed I was the foreigner who lived right next to the bridge. "Hau" (good) he said," come on in. We talked briefly of the shots in the hills. He thought it might be some hunters looking for wild pigs. I was extremely relieved and happy to get home in one piece and readily headed to Yoyang the next day to deliver my precious cargo.

Spring in Linhsiang – 1949

Spring in Linhsiang was beautiful. We had fixed up our Quonset hut to make a unique and cozy home. We settled in excitedly though we knew our days of living there were undoubtedly numbered. Karen was a happy child and joyfully appreciated all the attention she received. For some time we had been calling our petite daughter "Dolly." To get out of this habit, we decided to name the cow Dolly, a very effective habit breaker. We had a young boy to take care of Dolly, so Karen got her name back. The cow thrived on the grass that we bought fresh daily from very enterprising young people. We acquired a nice dog of German Shepherd extraction named Kippy.

Barbara enjoyed walking in the market in the town, carrying Karen in a home-made sling instead of using the age-old method of carrying a baby on the back. One day on her walk she saw a donkey lying on its side on a table of sorts. The animal's throat had just been cut and several men were collecting the blood in their cups and drinking it. They said, "The blood makes you strong." Aghast, Barbara asked if that was why they had killed the donkey. "Oh no," was the reply, "the donkey was sick!" Culture shock never ends.

One event in early spring was frightening. During a very cold snap, "Dasifu", our cook, and Jyusheng, who slept in their room just back of the Quonset, were not up in the morning when I arose. That was really very unusual, as the cook was an early riser to start the kitchen stove for hot water. I went back to their room to see if they were OK. They did not answer the knock, so I opened the door to find Jyusheng groggily getting up. They had gone to bed with the charcoal brazier lit to provide warmth. The carbon monoxide had made them both sleepy and nauseated. Fortunately, with good fresh air and a day's rest, they recuperated fully. Chinese farm homes were always so loosely constructed the families never had any such problem.

It was pretty clear during that spring that the military situation was as precarious as the fiscal disaster. Missionaries from the provinces north of Hankow had flocked to the big city in order to find ways out of China. Accurate information about the situation came not from our American Consulate but from letters written by friends in North China who had sent information from inside Communist areas to other friends in the USA. Though the roundabout news was not entirely encouraging, it helped us to consider what our own role in the new China might be. It was clear to us that it was only a matter of time until the Communist army would take over the remainder of China. We were fast coming to the crisis decision point as Barbara's pregnancy progressed. She would not be able to leave China during the month of April. We really became very jittery, uncertain and quite confused as to what we ought to do. There were those who advised evacuation and those who kept us focused on our reason for being in China in the first place. We were pulled one way and the other, sometimes deciding we should leave and other times somehow knowing that we should remain at our post. You cannot imagine the tension and frustration in trying to come to a rational decision.

In our letters to our family we shared honestly the situation and our dilemma. They, naturally, were very anxious about us, even though we always tried to reassure them that we were safe. "Don't worry!" we wrote.

With the others in our Mission we agreed that it might be wise for some of us to go to HongKong so that there would be a sure point of contact. Two couples were indecisive. The Mission wanted the Daniels in HongKong, as Jane also was pregnant. Bill, her husband, decided to stay behind in Yuanling in order to see what he could do to help the church during transition. The Gregorys with two children decided it was time to leave.   We decided that we would move to Hankow, having been encouraged by the local church leaders to be in the big city rather than in the countryside. They definitely did not want to be responsible for foreigners when they were fearful of what the anti-church attitudes of the Communist authorities might be. We definitely did not want to put our church leaders and members in any jeopardy by our presence. As I was Mission treasurer, we felt we could be of some help to Christian institutions and the church as long as funds could be received from the US. How would we ever know unless we had the courage to try? It was hard, but Barbara was a strong supporter and encouraged this decision as being appropriate for us at this time. The decision made was such a relief that we went ahead in the certainty that we would be shown the next steps.

I took Barbara and Karen to Hankow sometime in March. We hated to leave our new home in Linhsiang after living there only there only three months, but fully expected that when the uncertainties "settled down" we could return. We took with us only clothing and essentials for Karen and the coming baby. We settled in the Lutheran Home, which had long served missionaries throughout central China as a good hotel and restaurant. In the interim, I seemed constantly to be on the road to Linhsiang, Yoyang, and Changsha as a very mobile Mission treasurer.

Continued Confusion

You can readily understand that the entire winter and spring of 1949 were lived in mental turbulence. From our vantage point in Hankow, we received daily reports from the interior where Chinese families had fled for their lives. There was also an influx of many "well to do" refugees whose economic status made them feel quite threatened by land reform and egalitarian measures. We still chuckle over our favorite political weather vane, Rev. Nesse, a Norwegian Lutheran, who was afraid for his bad heart and insisted that raw garlic kept him alive. We saw him nearly daily in the Lutheran Home with his constant refrain for all of us, "Things really look black today!" Both missionaries and Chinese intellectuals seemed to agree that it might take years for some sense of stability to return to China. The printing press money of the Chiang Kaishek regime had again reached an exchange rate of four million Yuan to one US dollar.

Even after we were settled in Hankow, events during those chaotic days revolved around making a decision one day only to reverse it the next. I met with Reynold Ziegler to say that Barbara and I might possibly follow them to Canton after the birth of our second child in April. A meeting the following week with Ward Hartman, our Mission president, reflected his feeling that he should be available to support all Mission personnel from some South China vantage point or HongKong since he also had a Mission checkbook. He assured me that he felt Barbara and I would be safe and useful to the Church in the new era. He clearly let us know that the way was open for us to stay in Hankow to continue the Mission treasurer's work to supply budgeted funds to schools, hospitals, and evangelistic work (salaries for pastors, evangelists, and colporteurs) if that became possible. Our feelings were constantly torn back and forth. We felt strongly God's call to step forward in faith.

I was still constantly on the go to Yoyang. As Barbara's due date of mid-April came closer, my trips became shorter in duration. It became quite obvious that we had made a clear decision to stay in Hankow. We decided to accept an invitation from the manager of the National City Bank to move from the Lutheran Home to his large penthouse apartment in the bank building on the Bund. These expensive properties fronted the Yangtze River, almost all owned by large corporations, housed offices and homes for high-ranking personnel. The bank's personnel had all returned to the US. The manager's thought was that if the apartment was left unoccupied, the Communist army would move their staff into it. We rented it for a nominal US$ 70 per month with the understanding that we could terminate the agreement at any time due to the situation. We lived there less than two months.

Sterling Christian Whitener — April 27, 1949

We made the move into completely furnished luxury, with huge living room, and bedrooms. The kitchen and dining room alone were almost as large as our Linhsiang Quonset home. The large refrigerator was eye popping!

We hired a young man to help us with food shopping, simple cooking, and laundry. Mr. Hall, the previous resident, did sell much of his equipment and family clothing rather than try to take it all with him. Barbara bought a Singer Featherweight sewing machine, which she enjoyed for many years before giving it to daughter Karen.

Earlier we had become friends with Doug and Fran Dalziel, United Church of Canada medical missionaries working at Union Hospital in Hankow. Doug, an obstetrician, agreed to take on Barbara's care. We most gratefully accepted their generous invitation to stay in their home until after the baby was born, so moved to the Union Hospital compound and for several days, Barbara took the castor oil treatment. The baby was two weeks overdue and we felt great urgency because of the political situation. Fran and Doug had several boys about Karen's age and she helped me take care of Karen. The castor oil didn't work, so she had a surgical induction and finally the delivery was under way. I was in the next hospital room watching through the door. I wasn't invited into the delivery room this time, but I did see Doug very deftly unwind something (the cord) and then heard a lusty cry. Our son, Sterling Christian (Chris), was born April 27, a husky eight pounds. After a wonderful week with Doug and Fran we felt ready to move back to our apartment on the river front deeply grateful for all of their help. We have remained good friends. Unfortunately, Doug died much too early in 1963. We still keep in touch with Fran in Canada.

In early May, I carried the May payroll to Yoyang to give to Ward Hartman. We were going to audit our Mission accounts before he left for HongKong, where he would take care of Mission and personnel needs from that side. As he was visiting Huayung, a small town across the lake where he and Mrs. Hartman had been living, I was waiting for him and working in his office on the night of May 6. I vividly remember wondering what would become of the work my mother and father had spent their lives undertaking. It seemed strange yet comforting to be seated at Dad's desk taking care of accounts for all personnel. I wrote Ward a letter and placed it in the basket for Mr. Dzung to mail the next day. I thought of the passion and devotion to the Church in China that had led my parents to return to rebuild churches destroyed by the Japanese war and wondered if Barbara and I could in some small way continue their hopes for a future independent and self-supporting church.

Working with a kerosene pressure lamp for light, I was completing the accounts when there was a knock at the door. I got up to find a young colonel bringing a message from the local area governor, General Wang Jianbo, an old friend of my father's. The message was a strong suggestion that I get back to Hankow as soon as possible the next day because the military forces would not be able to hold that city against the Communist army and would be evacuating in the next few days. I asked the young man to thank the general for his suggestion, his friendship to my father and our family, and to tell him I would catch the morning train. After spending most of the night writing a long report to Ward Hartman, I caught a "few winks" before going to the train station to make my way to Hankow via Linhsiang and our new Quonset home. All trains headed south toward Changsha were jammed with people hanging on the sides, as well as on the rooftops of the passenger cars. All freight trains were just packed with people and belongings. I have no idea how many fatalities might have occurred during this mass evacuation of major cities as people fled. The Chinese population was moving west and south for the second time in a generation, as the same thing had happened only ten to twelve years earlier when the Japanese army was moving across China.

My stop in Linhsiang was to pick up more clothing and suitcases full of other items I wanted to be sure we had in Hankow in case we did not get back in a short while. I spent an entire day and night packing what I could and then arranging transport from our home to the train station, two miles away. I had to make sure that the Mission servants knew what we were doing and assure them that we would be back in touch with them. I had enough funds with me to pay them three months' salary. The biggest problem was to make sure that Dolly, our good Guernsey cow, was milked and properly fed.

The weather was clear; otherwise, the five-hour ride to Wuchang sitting with suitcases and boxes on an open freight car would have been even more miserable. It was fairly easy to negotiate help in Wuchang to get everything across the river back to our apartment in Hankow, as I was traveling against the traffic of thousands fleeing south.

The next week was full of more worrisome uncertainty as the rumor mill had us being captured by the Communists daily. River ships left for upriver after discharging many people who were hoping to move farther west, but who were put ashore because tickets upriver had already been sold to evacuees from Hankow. We watched the movement of masses of people, equipment, and home furnishings across the river by barge so those with wealth and connections could secure train passage south and west. I was busy converting all paper money into silver, sometimes at usurious rates. The Nationalist banks began to move out, but we were told that some staff members were going to remain to see what they could do under the incoming regime. Then the army started moving out across the river to Wuchang by barge, ferry, and every kind of boat.

Liberation – May 16, 1949

It is impossible to describe the emotions and feelings we were having: uncertainty, anxiety, fear and real doubt that we had made the right decision. At the same time we had a clear sense of knowing that God was with us. We found great comfort and strength in the time of sharing and prayer with fellow missionaries who were remaining in Hankow. We awaited the fateful day of the Communist takeover of Hankow. We felt sure the many millions of ordinary citizens were also in a turmoil of emotions. They either were ready to welcome the newcomers or were unable to flee.

For two days and nights, the retreating Nationalist army had their engineers try to destroy all the floating docks that served riverboats. All commerce needed these docks to load and unload goods because the river fluctuated some 40 feet from winter to mid-summer. The explosions went on continuously. The wooden frame buildings on the docks burned furiously.

From our 4th floor penthouse on the Bund, we had a grandstand view. There was speculation that some of the engineers had been bought off and that some docks had been sunk partially into the shallower shore rather than destroyed completely because many were refloated very quickly.

May 16, 1949: the Liberation Army of the People came into a quiet Hankow. Almost everyone was indoors. Russian type Jeeps with Model A Ford engines came down the main streets followed by large army trucks loaded with soldiers. People who were standing around shouted welcome. We watched from the balcony of our apartment. Large contingents of veteran fighting troops clothed in clean but old uniforms walked in step. Some youth expressed joy and walked along at the edge of the large paved boulevard. It was an unexpectedly peaceful takeover.

A day or so after the takeover, hailed as "Liberation," I was out on the balcony when I heard the distant sound of airplane motors. Two planes were flying over the middle of the river at great height. I thought they must be looking the place over to see what was going on. I knew that the Communist army had no planes, but the Nationalist air force had quite a few left over from World War II. In the distance I heard a loud siren coming from the large customs building several blocks away. As I watched, the planes seemed to fly lower and as they did so, I saw small objects start to come down from them. I realized that they were bombs so I shouted to Barbara to stay away from the windows. She was inside nursing baby Chris and misunderstood me. Carrying the baby, she started to head for the windows when the bombs landed with a great explosion in the river opposite our building. Several of our windows were shattered, blessedly none in her immediate vicinity. At about the same time, we heard rapid firing of fairly large anti-aircraft guns from nearby buildings. I rushed to Barbara and led us all to a space in the basement where we were surrounded by heavy walls. There were several more explosions and continued anti-aircraft fire for several minutes. The planes departed and never returned. We surmised the air force pilots dropped their bombs in the middle of the river in order to protect their future status in those uncertain times. They may have been ordered to bomb the riverfront pontoon docks. In China that would have been dangerous to many common people, so my inference was that they took the ancient "Chinese" way of obeying orders but assuring no damage. "Make a loud noise, but do no harm." Later, when we went up on the roof of our building we found quite a number of metal fragments, either from the bombs themselves or from the anti-aircraft shells, several we still have as mementos of that harrowing experience.

One morning, shortly after Liberation, we heard a loud clamor on the street in front of our building. From the balcony we looked down on a horrifying accident. A large army truck had run over a woman who was carrying a baby. The woman lay on the street, mortally injured, blood pooling beneath her. A large crowd of bystanders gathered around her and someone took the apparently uninjured baby from her arms, but no one made any move to help the woman. We were terribly distressed and our immediate impulse was to run down to the street to do something – anything! There was no 911 to call and we were constrained for the same reason the local people stood back. If the woman died, anyone who had touched her could be held responsible. There was no Good Samaritan law to protect anyone. In addition, we were in a very tenuous situation. All foreigners had been instructed to remain indoors until we were registered by the new authorities. It was a terrible dilemma. The woman remained lying on the street almost that entire agonizing day. In anguish we watched from the balcony as she died with no one to help or comfort her. Finally, someone came and took her body away on a wooden wheelbarrow. Feelings of anger, frustration, sadness and guilt still remain within us today.

Celebrating Liberation

Parades and long lines of dancing the "yang ge," a kind of agricultural folk dance with constant motion of planting seeds and harvesting the crops performed while singing, kept up daily. This dance by the Communists represented their rural and agricultural foundations. At the same time different groups came by with effigies of Uncle Sam, Chiang Kaishek, and other enemies of the people. No youth thought of going to school when there was so much excitement downtown. We kept out of the way but were fascinated by our bird's eye view from our balcony of the continuous festivities.

The foreign affairs section of the new People's Government sent clear written instructions to all foreigners that we were to remain indoors until they were able to come by to register us. In a few days, a team of several young officials in uniform came to the apartment, looked around carefully, and then told us to fill out a series of forms. They stressed the last part of the form, which asked us to write all our connections with China, including all trips into and out of the country. All our communication was conducted in Chinese, though it was obvious that they knew English. They left, saying they would be back for the reports the next day.

Barbara and I decided that we would write down very factually our memory of events, travel dates, and all information that was requested. It is fortunate that we did so, as a few months later we were asked to repeat the performance. Although we did not keep copies, we did have pretty good memories in those days. Barbara's task was relatively easy since she had first arrived in China in the fall of 1946. My problem was a real effort because I had to record life from birth. My first travels from China to the USA were at age 3. After this first registration we received permission to travel freely in town during the daylight hours.

The Communists had learned much from the occupation of Peiping (Peking), now called Beijing. Banks were reopened and the infrastructure of government was soon established. It was interesting that the new money was soon made available. All of the populace was ordered to turn in all of their silver dollars. In just a few days we were able to cash our US checks in exchange for People's currency and open checking accounts. The trains started running, following schedules for the first time in many months. The telegraph and post office began operating as usual and we could communicate with family back in Salisbury, a great comfort to all of them.

The next few months were full because I spent much time reestablishing contact with our Mission Board in the USA, arranging bank credits to pay workers. Letters and communications were also reestablished with Ward Hartman in HongKong. Ward with wife Frieda, Jane Daniels with son Paul, and the Ziegler family were on Cheung Chau Island in HongKong awaiting developments. Bill Daniels, Mary Myers, and Karl Beck remained in the Yuanling area of West Hunan, which was not made a part of the New China until September.

In June I went regularly to the Foreign Affairs office to apply for approval to take the family to Kuling for the summer. Officials kept telling me that they were studying the application, which they did for a month before refusing permission. It was fortunate that we could spend the hot and humid summer in the comfortable bank penthouse with high ceilings and fans in each room.

Karen and Chris grew healthily. At age one and a half, Karen's favorite name for baby Chris was "goddie" for "doggie." So we adjusted to the new situation as family and as refugees. Fortunately, we were able to get together with the Dalziels frequently. There were very few western families in Hankow, but we did have opportunities to exchange visits with some of the families remaining.

In addition, by the end of the summer it was quite clear that we were not going to be permitted to return to Linhsiang or the work in Yoyang. Though there had been no real fighting between Hankow and Yoyang, the countryside had been pretty well devastated by the passage of two armies. We reestablished communication with our church, schools, and hospital but it quickly became evident that when their representatives could come to Hankow we were not in a suitable residence to welcome them.

I was able to transfer funds to them for operating expenses. The new government said they wanted all institutions to continue to serve the people. Only criminals and enemies of the people need fear harm. None of the Mission institutions had developed in the few years following World War II to a self-supporting stage, so the Mission Board honored the commitment to provide the budgeted amount for the year 1949. It was my task to inform all the church workers, physicians, and principals of schools that no one knew what a 1950 budget would bring. We decided to return to the Lutheran Home because it was a church-run institution and fully recognized as such. Other Missions were using it as their headquarters, so meetings with Chinese church leaders were a common and accepted practice. Our US Mission Board was able to promise most of our programs a final year of financial support in 1950. By that time the hospital and all schools had moved under government fiscal support and control.

We moved into a nice apartment on the top floor and quickly learned that our move had been appreciated by our colleagues in Yueyang who felt much more comfortable coming to the Lutheran Home. We received good support from the missionary community. We gathered for worship, for fellowship, and for discussion as to what our role might be in the new society. We were happy to become a part of the church life in Hankow. Barbara attended services at a Union church and also at the Lutheran Home. I was able to participate in the church life of Ge Fei Tang, the Griffith John Church, named for the London Missionary Society pioneer, where we asked the pastor to baptize Chris.

During the summer and early fall, the church welcomed the governmental directives that spoke of "freedom of religion." These same directives also spoke of "freedom to oppose religion." The Church of Christ in China, Hupei Synod, organized a series of meetings and conferences for Christians to relate to this issue. Speakers were invited from Beijing and Shanghai. My most vivid memory of one series was that of a dynamic preacher, Wang Mingdao, who, though conservative theologically, was dramatic in his sermons based on Biblical texts. His sermon on Daniel in the lion's den had all of the five hundred participants on the edge of their seats as we clearly heard his message that we all literally had to trust the Lord for protection in our new life each day. Only through faith in God and prayer would we be lifted from the lion's den. Another sermon vividly had us all in the "fiery furnace" with Shadrack, Mishak, and Abednego. As the Rev. Wang stretched his tall six-foot, six-inch frame and reached heavenward, he pulled God down to the people in a way that offered comfort and strength to all to hold fast to the faith.

The youth of China found their education turned around. They literally danced their summer away learning new folk dances that glorified the farmer and the working man. They studied the publications of New China. Mao's pamphlet on the "New Democracy" was one that we also studied. In fact, Dr. Wei, president of Huachung Christian University in Wuchang, which our Mission also supported, led a conference for missionaries on the Marxist dialectic as embraced by Mao Tzetung. His lectures on Mao's "New Democracy" were especially helpful as we tried to understand all that was being undertaken by the government.

An Interim Period

We kept a busy correspondence with our Mission folk in HongKong, where the Hartmans had moved into the Sailors and Soldiers Home and Jane awaited Bill at the Church Guest House. When Yuanling in far west Hunan was "liberated" on September 18, we were able to establish contact with Bill Daniels, Mary Myers, and Karl Beck. None of them were permitted to leave the city but from that date on I was able to forward funds to them directly from Hankow.

Since we had moved back to the Lutheran Home, Mom and Dad's cook, Fu Qunyong, came to help us, as his brother, our cook at Huping and Linhsiang, felt he was too old to begin again in Hankow. Unfortunately, Qunyong became ill after a few months. We got him to the hospital, but he had developed a tumor in his abdomen and died. We were very sad to lose this helper and friend and worked with his family to cover all expenses for his burial in the country on his farm. From that time on, Barbara did the cooking with the help of young Jyusheng from Linhsiang.

We had a tomcat who thought we were on the ground floor and at the call of a female friend decided to meet her in the garden. The loud cry we heard when he landed five stories below sounded like his death knell. When he was picked up, he smiled because his face was twisted. It took him a few weeks on a liquid diet before his jaw worked properly again. We decided that he had used all nine of his lives on that escapade.

Mr. Mei from Linhsiang came to tell of a clinic which would be opened there in our Quonset home as an outreach program. We were really happy that the Church had found such a good use for our home with the help of the Yoyang Hospital. He also told me about all the evangelists who had faced the new era in different ways: one ran off with a local girl; one went to bury his father (very biblical, Mei said); another came back after running away and was planting vegetables on the edge of town; and Mei Hauran was being accused of not keeping honest accounts. Very tough days but my co-secretary, Mei Shouchun, was glad to be able to pay them their salaries to keep up the spirits of the Christian community. In 1983, when Barbara and I returned to Yoyang, Rev. Meng having been ordained, was well respected and led 15 of us in worship in the church building that had been restored to the Christian community shortly before. He was the one who buried his father and was the one who I felt would "never make it." It makes one happy to be wrong at times.

In early September the head of the Hunan Synod, the Rev. Li Yungwu, came from Changsha to visit us to discuss developments in North Hunan. I respected him very much and appreciated his leadership. We had discussed several times in the past my sense that the Chinese Church would be required to stand alone. He came to ask me to move to Changsha to help with the finances of the church and the youth work. It was a challenge and probably would have been a wise move under different circumstances, but the timing was not appropriate. It had been made pretty clear to us that we were being tolerated by the authorities for the present and would not be permitted to make moves in China.

On October 1, 1949, the new government declared the founding of The People's Republic of China. The capital was to be Beijing, Mao Tzetung the President and leader, Chou Enlai the Premier, and Chu Te

Commander-in-Chief of the People's Army. There was a nationwide celebration on the order of the coronation of Queen Elizabeth II. We witnessed huge parades and thousands of people cheering. Without television, we saw this from our Lutheran Home fifth-floor windows, and I carefully sneaked my camera out to capture some of the dancing crowds.

I had gone repeatedly to the Foreign Affairs department to seek permission to return to Linhsiang and Yoyang. I was always told that it was "inconvenient" but it was obvious that they were not going to let me return. I then sought to get emergency permission to go back to Linhsiang for one or two days only, to bring our winter clothes to Hankow before the cold weather. When I came back for the answer, I was not surprised at the "No, you cannot go," but was really surprised by the follow-up. I was told to send someone to Linhsiang to pick up all our belongings. I suggested that it would be helpful if the "powers-that-be" would provide a simple note to the authorities granting permission to bring our things to Hankow. The young official at least four or five years younger than my 28 years, lost patience with me and said crossly I was not being "ke guan". That was a new Communist term to me, so I asked him please to explain it. He said loudly in English, "objective." I was obviously too prejudiced in my thinking. I then switched to English, but he immediately stopped me and said all communication would be in Chinese. He further stated that the government had no desire to confiscate any belongings of foreign guests. This was indeed a new wrinkle.

In my contacts with co-workers in Yoyang and Linhsiang, it had been necessary to conduct all communication in Chinese, so I had hired our former teacher-helper, Donald Cheng, as my Chinese secretary. He had kept up a large correspondence for me with Principal Liu of Huping School, Mr. Mei Shouchun, my co-worker in Linhsiang, and several others. When the authorities said I could send someone to pick up our things, I asked Donald if he would undertake the task. I must say I thought he had a lot of guts! He went to Linhsiang, telegraphing three days later that I should meet a certain freight train in Wuchang because he had leased an open boxcar and was bringing everything he could.

You can imagine my surprise when I met him, grimy with coal engine soot, smiling from ear to ear, and proudly displaying everything he could bring, including the kitchen stove and Dolly, the cow. Larger furniture and our Warm Morning room stove just wouldn't fit boxes he had loaded. As we were to move across the Yangtze River to Wuchang from Hankow, we found a place to store many things but had to find some way to house the cow. Fortunately, Huachung University had several milk cows and was glad to add Dolly to the college herd. They even had money to refund what we had paid for her. So we were blessed to be set with winter clothes and all my books, a real help for the next semester at the seminary, and extremely grateful to Donald for his incredible success.

Donald Cheng, the invaluable secretary, asked if he could have a short vacation. He wanted to return to Kuling to visit his family; his father was pastor of the Chinese church in Lushan. We were glad to grant his request but had a request in return. When we had departed Kuling in the summer of 1948 we had decided that we would not bring our treasured 1000 flower tea set, which we had bought in Kuling, back to Huping and then to Linhsiang. We felt we would like to use it the following summer when we returned to Kuling. We never received permission to go back to Kuling in 1949. We asked Donald to bring the tea set back to us in Wuchang when he returned. The only problem was that we had buried it under our house in a kerosene tin. I knew exactly where it was so drew a treasure map for Donald. He found it easily, and brought it to Wuchang. We used it there and brought it with us when we left. It is a well-crafted and very beautiful tea set made in Jingdezhen, the famous Jiangxi pottery center. It is now the proud possession of daughter Bonnie.

An important event during the fall was the visitation of a team of church leaders from Shanghai. Among them was Wu Yaotsung, a long-time leftist YMCA leader; Liu Liangmo, a YMCA youth secretary; Rev. Hui, the General Secretary of the Church of Christ in China; a leader of the American Methodist Chinese Church; and several Anglican/Episcopal priests. They were housed in the YMCA of Hankow, which was next door to the Lutheran Home. A problem in providing breakfast arose because the Y had no dining service. Some of the team came over to the Lutheran Home dining room, but most of them were eating at small food stalls out on the street. Barbara thought it might be special to invite them for an American breakfast one morning. Most of the team accepted. Wu Yaotsung declined because he said he had stomach trouble but more likely did not want to seem too friendly with foreigners. In any case, after an effusive blessing by one of the Episcopal priests, the group dived into the very tasty breakfast of eggs, bacon, and biscuits. Liu Liangmo said it was the best breakfast he had

had since his student days in France before WWII. Their meetings at many of the churches in Hankow and Wuchang were designed to interpret what Christians might expect from the Communist government in the coming months. Their predictions were certainly correct for a time, as the political system bypassed the issue of Communist atheism and "religion as an opiate" and granted the churches of China a brief respite period.

Move to Central China Theological Seminary in Wuchang

Sometime in the fall of 1949, I was asked to consider moving to Wuchang to teach a course at the Central China Theological School in the spring if we could secure permission to move. Our Mission had been a part of the seminary for many years, as Dr. Paul Keller was one of the founding faculty members in the 1920s. (Footnote – his son, Jean Keller, taught us at Kuling American School in the late 1930s, married our favorite teacher, Grace Eckvall, served as our scoutmaster and helped Headmaster Allgood close up the school in 1938. Grandson Paul visited the seminary in Wuchang in 2001 and helped us reorganize the Kuling American School Association in 2002/2005.)

We finally moved in March 1950 from the Lutheran Home to the seminary in Wuchang at Tan Hua Lin, a short distance from Huachung University. A duplex home was available. The move was complicated by the fact that the Yangtze River had to be crossed by ferry. It was hard enough to cross on the passenger ferry, but to get all our stuff over required using the freight ferry. Two British missionaries, Stewart Craig of the London Missionary Society and George Osborne of the English Methodist Mission, were living in one side of the duplex. They had families in England where their wives were caring for older children who needed proper British-style schooling. We moved into the vacant side of the duplex after Barbara Simpson moved to other quarters. This arrangement was a happy one for us, as we enjoyed very much the companionship of the older men and they really enjoyed our children. We were fortunate to have our Huping and Linhsiang cook, Dasifu, and Jyusheng join us. They were immeasurably helpful to us as we adjusted to a new situation.

Our months in the duplex were good ones. The children could play outside in the garden. We had a bicycle which I fitted with a double basket over the rear wheel which they loved to ride in. (I am now appalled that I put my two young children at such risk.) Other families with children lived on the nearby Huachung University campus and we enjoyed gatherings held there. Occasional social events across the river in Hankow as well, helped make our lives pleasant despite the pressures of the political situation.

Shortly after moving to the seminary campus we were invited by the Dalziels to spend the night with them at Union Hospital back across the river in Hankow. We happily accepted and made the ferry crossing to enjoy a few days with their family. Upon returning home to Wuchang, we were visited by two police officials in new uniforms. They were from the Foreign Affairs Office. They wanted to know what we were doing in Hankow overnight. The police had informed them that we had illegally spent the night away from home without gaining the required permission. Pleading ignorance of that requirement, we expressed contrition and promised that we would, in future, seek their permission should we wish to undertake any future visits. At the time we felt quite intimidated, as we had never received any instructions about the lack of freedom of movement. Needless to say, we did take precaution to assure our local police that we had intended no misdemeanor.

The seminary accepted candidates from a number of denominations: Church of Christ in China (a union of 25 denominations) and the Chinese Methodist Church (related to British, Australian, and New Zealand Methodist Churches). Our students had finished high school but were not going on to college or university. In fact, very few high school graduates were able to get into the universities because of the cost and the shortage of space, which created intense competition.

My assignment was to teach Christian ethics and to lead the students in a gardening/work program. The prevailing ethic was that farmers and workers were to be emulated. It was quite natural, therefore, that the students would want to ally themselves to the prevailing sentiment. Quite a number of the seminary students had themselves come from Christian farm families. They took to the gardens with great vigor, breaking the ground with mattocks to prepare for a wonderful harvest. My memory of learning to plant and fertilize from them has stood me in good stead for many ensuing years, as I have always loved to grow Chinese vegetables.

Each morning I worked with Donald Cheng to read a small book, in Chinese, written expressly for a Christian ethics course. It was nice to have a text, but I must frankly admit that it was nowhere near the complexity of my own seminary notes from Professor Richard Niebuhr. We did have a great deal of discussion of "right and wrong." In fact, one of my students told me some thirty years later that he enjoyed that class more than any other. I think he meant it was really easy, as he had actually made a career of serving in the maintenance department of the local Agricultural College for many years. Another student, who served the petrochemical industry as a scientist and had studied his specialty in Germany, was not nearly as effusive. He said, "It was an interesting time."

Adjacent to our seminary was a small city primary school. We often heard the students loudly reciting their lessons in the Chinese style of shouting their selections in unison at the tops of their voices. Our garden was almost touching their building wall. One day in May as we were laboriously chopping weeds and preparing to plant our summer vegetable seeds, we heard quite different sounds coming from the schoolyard next door. Men were talking and it sounded as though someone was commanding them to do something. We all looked carefully through cracks in the wall or over it only to discover a large group of soldiers in the primary school. The puzzling part was that we could not understand a single word they were speaking.

None of us could figure out who these new soldiers were. Some students thought that they were tribes-peoples from the western part of China who had a different dialect. None of the soldiers or their officers wore any insignia. Baffled, we kept careful watch. They seemed to stay for a few weeks and then an entirely new group would appear after a few days. We began to realize that the army had taken over the schoolrooms for a barracks and some form of training ground. When the normal school year ended and the army personnel still continued to come and go, we were really confused.

About July 1, we finally understood who these army personnel really were. North Korea attacked South Korea. Our students were glad to know that it was not the Chinese army that had started a war. We all realized why we had been unable to understand a word of the Korean they spoke. We still, unbelievably, had our radios and learned about the war from London broadcasts. No word of a buildup of forces was noted in any earlier broadcasts. We noted that even the ordinary man on the street knew the North had attacked the South and not the propaganda of the government which said the South had attacked first.

The realization that China had prepared Koreans to undertake the clearing of the Korean peninsula for the Communist north was a shock. It began to sink in that we would soon be the enemy of the people of China as the United Nations began to send help to South Korea. Many a gathering of missionaries in Wuhan was full of extensive discussion of what it might mean to families if, in fact, we became "the enemy." To go or not to go again became a decision we faced. We found that the seminary could provide the teaching needed and the Hunan Synod felt they could handle the transfer of funds as long as permitted. It became increasingly clear that there was no choice. We should leave.

In mid-July, I went to the Foreign Affairs Bureau to apply for an exit visa. The next month was a busy time. I packed my books in five-pound packages and mailed about five or six packs a day to HongKong to Ward Hartman to hold for me. I gathered all my photographs and negatives to mail to HongKong, as we had heard that pictures were being picked up at the border in case they showed too much of the country. In order to make sure that they were not all confiscated in one large package, I mailed them in small packets not knowing if they would make it to HongKong.

The summer of 1950 was extremely hot. The Yangtze valley is famous for its damp heat. For several generations, foreigners sent their families to mountain areas. Our beloved Kuling was a night and a day away but we were definitely confined to Wuhan. At night we slept on the living room floor on woven sisal mats under a ceiling fan in 100-degree temperature and 100 percent humidity. The western sun beat torridly on the side of our duplex. Ever the innovative builder, I devised a heavy cloth curtain which I had made at a shop on the street. The curtain was hung so it covered the entire west side of the house and helped a great deal to mitigate the intense heat.

During the spring and summer of 1950 the government had organized a big victory bond drive. All streets and institutions were assigned a certain number of bonds to buy. Our Tan Hua Lin street elders approached our seminary to ask if we could help them reach their quota. After much discussion by the foreign faculty we agreed to assist all we could. My victory bond was for about $10 US. I wish I could find it today as a trophy. As a part of this drive, there was an increase of peddlers coming to our door daily. Rich people in town were obviously targeted to buy bonds. They then sent family members or clever salespersons to sell whatever they could to foreigners who had some money. It was obvious that the pressure was on those who had any wealth at all to buy bonds or donate to the community. Almost daily, someone would come by our home to see if we would buy some art object that was for sale. Goodness knows, we were not "wealthy."

I always called to Barbara that there was someone at the door looking for a "sucker." She took this ribbing in good spirits, as she loved, as had my mother before her, to see the beautiful embroideries, dishes, scrolls, cloisonné, etc., that were being offered. We had pretty well exhausted our meager supply of ready cash on quite a number of smaller items, which we felt we could take back home to the US with us. But this time the salesman had some very unique items. One was an embroidered Ching dynasty royal gown that had not been cut out of its original, large piece of cloth. The gold threads and claws of the dragon indicated it had been a garment prepared for the royal dynastic family. We have donated this piece to the North Carolina Museum of History in Raleigh. They have established a collection of Chinese art materials collected by NC people.

In addition, we bought two very fine 12-foot-long scrolls of intricate embroidery. They obviously were real family heirlooms fit for the family ancestral hall. We admired them and said that we really could not buy anything. The man was distraught and said his family needed money desperately. What could we give? Offering our last $20 US, we have felt sad that the original owners had to give them up, and wish they could know how much we enjoy them.

We have since learned from the Freer Gallery in Philadelphia that the scrolls are genuine works of art and real museum pieces. In fact, when we were in Taiwan in 1985 and visited the National Museum in Taipei none of their embroidered scrolls were anywhere near the quality of our Wuhan scrolls.

New Developments

After we had made application to depart China we drafted the requisite advertisement for the Chinese newspapers. This required us to notify all persons interested that we had made application to leave the People's Republic of China and that if anyone had cause to object they should contact the Foreign Affairs Office. Also anyone to whom we owed any money should let that be known. Naturally, we had no idea if anyone would make any such representation. Our ads were to run for at least a week.

At this point we began to pack seriously for departure. Selling or giving away household items and clothing to our Hunan friends, we packed whatever we felt we could use in the USA as priority, along with the treasured Chinese objects of art we had. Our five trunks and boxes were minimal compared to the five huge crates we brought with us in 1946. We had made our final arrangements with our helpers to assure that they had funds for retirement and the means for their own future plans.

In six weeks, unexpectedly, since most foreigners had waited several months, we were informed that we could depart. We hurriedly made our train reservations for Canton and HongKong for September 2. Our packing done, we made our last round of visits to friends, some of whom were also getting ready to depart. School faculty and students arranged a farewell feast for us. We had no idea if we would ever see any of our colleagues and friends again.

Actual departure was not as easy as we might have expected. We were asked to accompany all our boxes, trunks, and baggage items to the train station known as the freight station, where the train was made up. Passengers were instructed to board the train at the main train station in Wuchang officially after all baggage had been inspected and loaded. It meant we needed to accompany our baggage very early to the freight station and then ride to the passenger station for actual departure from Wuchang. It would be a difficult task with two small children. We asked good friends Peggy Hawkings and Joyce Horner to bring Karen and Chris to the Wuchang station to meet our train. They never forgot that in the rickshaw to the station, Chris kept looking intently at the stars, obviously very impressed. There were several minutes of acute panic when our train arrived at the station and we saw hundreds of people pushing forward to board the train. We leaned out our compartment window searching frantically for Peggy and Joyce. They were equally anxious as they began to wonder what would happen if they could not find us! All ended well as they saw us waving from the first-class section. The crowds were so thick at the entranceways that our friends came right to the window and handed Karen and Chris to us with great joy. For years we heard from Peggy how honored she felt to be entrusted with our two precious little ones.

We were accustomed to the trains of China so had prepared well for the thirteen hour trip. Except for the two of us having been trampled unmercifully by two small children the trip was uneventful. We reached

Canton and transferred to the train to Lowu, the border crossing to HongKong. We arrived at the border to the British Crown Colony but could not cross the bridge to "freedom" until we had been cleared by one last customs inspection to assure the government that we were not smuggling anything out in our baggage. We were told that art treasures and photographs were definitely to be examined. Our baggage was removed to the customs area right beside the railroad tracks. We were asked to open several trunks and suitcases. Fortunately, we had placed our two scrolls right on top of everything in one trunk. The young customs agent asked if we had any art treasures. I told him I really did not know if our items were art objects or not but that he should examine the scrolls if he wished. He must have decided after seeing our rather ordinary clothes etc. that we would not have much anyway. Barbara is sure that the reason he did not search everywhere was because Karen and Chris were so exhausted after the long train trip that they were crying loudly and could not be quieted. Their crying was certainly nerve-wracking which may be the only reason we have our two beautiful embroidered palace scrolls today. On the other hand, as the customs official and I conversed about our past, he wanted to know what I had been doing, so I explained my teaching at HuaChung Theological School. He then told me he was a graduate of HuaChung University and he knew of the seminary. He waved us on and our baggage was transferred across the bridge. Our relief was inexpressible.

September 3, 1950 — we had made it! — three years and ten months after our first arrival as young missionaries to China and almost four years since leaving North Carolina! Our feelings on leaving China, however, were immensely mixed. We felt relief, great excitement, a real ending, a weight of sadness, yet full of anticipation of an unknown future.

Home to the USA – September 1950

The Hartmans arranged for us to stay at the Anglican Church Guest House. The first news we had from home was a telegram that Dad, Sterling Wilfong Whitener, had died of a stroke a few days earlier. This was shockingly grievous news as we had much counted on a reunion with him. We knew he had been unwell and was living in a Roman Catholic Nursing Home near High Point, NC under Don's supervision. Our Mission friends, the Hartmans, Jane Daniels and her young son, Paul, and a few others held a very comforting memorial service in the Guest House chapel. In sending on the news to Yueyang, we were confident his Chinese colleagues would honor his life even as we did. I had lost my father and mother within two years. They were both my role models and it was a stark realization that our children would never learn to know them. My father is buried in the small personal cemetery adjacent to Bethel Church in which he had grown up. Many of the extended family including his eldest brother share the quiet beauty.

We had planned to take the first passenger ship across the Pacific to hasten home but our colleagues wisely advised us to consider taking the longer way home via England to give us time to adjust to what lay ahead. Already, several of our missionary families had been reassigned to other locations. No one quite knew what the future would hold.

Learning that the cost of passage to the East Coast was no greater via England than crossing the Pacific and then the train trip across the continental US, we arranged passage to London on the SS "Carthage" leaving in October. Our Peninsular and Oriental Line ship was of ancient vintage. Without air conditioning we had metal scoops to place in the porthole to catch the breezes. We learned the meaning of "POSH" Port Out, Starboard Home, a favorite British term meaning expensive or especially nice! To catch the best air, be sure you have the POSH side

Our month long trip was by way of Singapore, Penang, Columbo, and Suez where we enjoyed those brief port calls. With a well supervised child's play room and excellent service, we arrived in England in dreary, cold November weather. We planned short visits with the Craigs and Osbornes, our Wuchang seminary colleagues' families. On entry to England we were issued ration cards which benefitted us all. Both families were most hospitable but in their homes we were so unused to unheated rooms we nearly froze. It was definitely post war England!

Our jaunt across the Atlantic was a real shake-up. The cheap tickets on the French liner "Liberté" placed us right in the stern of that huge ship. The only trouble was that the propellers immediately below us provided a constant shudder. Fortunately, the journey was not quite a week, so we arrived in New York excited to be so near home. We were met by Robert and Hermine, Barbara's brother and sister-in-law. That was helpful as they took us, after clearing customs, to their home in New Haven, Conn. He taught at Yale University Medical School in the subject area of pollution control and testing. We enjoyed a few days there before taking the train to North Carolina.

We had an interesting experience in the customs shed in New York. We had packed our crystal in an ammunition case, a solid wooden box that could be locked and easily take the strain of an ocean voyage, to say nothing of the rough handling while being transferred from train to truck and to boat in China and HongKong. In the New York customs shed, we opened the case to show that we had only crystal within when the customs officer frowned. It was obvious that something was wrong. Yes, we were return-ing missionaries, but we had no idea that the raw cotton we had packed our glasses and plates in was forbidden entry to the USA. After ponder-ing whether we should try to find alternate packing material and imme-diately repack the entire box, Barbara begged the official to let us pass if we promised to burn the offending cotton immediately after unpacking in Salisbury. He kindly did so and Barbara vehemently assured him that she would honor her promise. She really did burn the cotton in the parsonage furnace—absolutely all of it.

Our arrival in Salisbury on November 12 by train was a joyful reunion as Barbara's parents and family welcomed us into their parsonage home once again, this time with two new grandchildren. Time with her family whom she had missed so keenly in China was greatly treasured. The fol-lowing months with her family were also very therapeutic. There were nec-essary readjustments for us and our two little ones after our extraordinary China experience.

What to Do with an "Unknown Quantity"?

Correspondence with the Mission Board of International Missions of the Evangelical and Reformed Church in Philadelphia was disconcerting. The Asia secretary was the Rev. Gebhardt, a minister who had been a mem-ber of the Board but never a missionary. The treasurer was a good friend of my father's, the Rev. John Poorman. The executive secretary, a good friend of ours, Dr. Dobbs Ehlman, who had traveled with us on the "Marine Lynx" to China in 1946, was another non-missionary minister who had very little background in the study of Missions. It was clear that we would be given some furlough time, but very unclear as to what might be required of us in terms of deputation. That word was the term used to describe a program of itineration and speaking to churches whose leaders wanted to have a missionary help strengthen the total Mission program. As a result, I was asked to come to Philadelphia for a conference with Rev. Gebhardt.

My meeting with him was quite a shock. Barbara and I had agreed that it was important for Americans to realize some of the benefits that the common people had received from the new government, albeit Communist. For instance, the clear regulation of money, the Postal Service, railroads with real schedules, and the fact that our mission had been permitted to transfer funds for welfare and relief, even salaries, through hospitals and churches was a clear gift to the programs we had been supporting. We had experienced this as "guests" while still in China. Communist leaders were atheists and had temporarily bypassed dealing with the Chinese church which was seeking accommodation under the umbrella of Mao Tzetung's call for national unity and the policy of "religious freedom." There were signs that there was also a strongly implied "freedom to oppose religion," which meant that Christians would be walking a fine line. When I boldly proposed to Rev. Gebhardt that the good church people of the USA might be happy to learn of the trials, as well as the challenges and opportunities facing the church in China, I was quickly told that he could not permit me to speak to the churches of our denomination in these terms which would sound so positive about the Communists. "Did [I] not realize that we were in a very precarious position due to a senator named Joseph McCarthy?" That was the last thought in my mind, that the US Church was fearful of a politician. Obviously, I was quite out of tune and out of line. It was made very clear to me that I needed to find something to do that would not put the Board in jeopardy of facing the powerful McCarthy.

I remember how angry I was to be told that my own church leaders could and would not permit me to go to the churches to speak freely. The phrase "it is for your own good" reminded me of being offered castor oil when I was a child. I returned to Salisbury and the family knowing only that my confrontation was a real slap and put down. Though Gebhardt had suggested that I might find something else productive to do, such as some library study or a few courses at the Lancaster Seminary while living at the missionary furlough apartment in Lancaster, PA, I felt so let down and angry I hardly considered what an opportunity that was. When Barbara and I had talked the situation over and discussed the future with her parents, the idea of study began to appeal.

Thus, the "unknown quantity," missionary Sterling Whitener, became mobilized. I called my mentor at Yale Divinity School, Dr. Kenneth Scott Latourette, to share my feelings. His immediate and measured response was that this was a very real opportunity to prepare for further Mission work because the Chinese were everywhere in Southeast Asia and had taken their Churches with them. He suggested that I call Dean Liston Pope's office the next day after he had a chance to put in a good word for me. What a wonderful break for me! The time was short because the school was closing for the Christmas holidays and would reopen in mid-January for a new semester. I got on the ball right away and with Dr. Latourette's help was admitted to study Christian ethics. This was another break, as Dr. Richard Niebuhr accepted me as a candidate for the Master of Sacred Theology degree. It required negotiating a year and a half of furlough, but I think Rev. Gebhardt was so glad to get me off his back that he rejoiced in the solution.

Conclusions and Summary of the Situation in China

A quotation from our January 1951 letter to friends:

> *"It seems more and more evident that in exchange for financial stability and 'good' efficient (?) government, the people of China are learning the meaning of <u>thought control</u> and <u>rigid discipline</u>. After all, soldiers in the Chinese Army who get ten to fifteen hours a week of political training, soon learn what they are fighting for, albeit (from our point of view) the propaganda that country boys, Wu and Wang, get is all twisted up. It is amazing what a thorough job such a small proportion of the population can do. For nearly 90% of the population seem to be disillusioned and dissatisfied. Yet when we left, these same people would in no way wish to welcome back the old regime, with whom they were completely fed up.*
>
> *It is too soon yet for us to evaluate our experience in Red China, but these things we feel:*

1. *We were allowed to live there unmolested, though inconvenienced by restrictions in travel and official red tape.*
2. *We could perform most of our Christian work teaching and preaching, even though it was more and more embarrassing to our Chinese friends to be seen with us.*

3. *The common people regard themselves as friends of America and vice versa, all Communist propaganda to the contrary.*

4. *The students are generally very much absorbed in the 'New Democratic' movement.*

5. *The intelligentsia is paying lip service (in support of the present government) as are many others because there is no alternative. It would be impossible to measure the sincerity of the vast majority of the educated populace toward Communism because the Communists sold a 'New Democracy' (not Communism) to the Chinese and cleverly disguised their real motives.*

6. *We think the Church has been 'bypassed' so far and may now be due on the 'purge' list. There may even be Christian martyrs.*

7. *The Christians are faithful and will remain so! They deserve and need our* full *support, materially and spiritually. We* must *pray for them!*

Now that we are back in America much of our four years in China seems unreal at times. Never before have we felt so greatly the reality of God's goodness. Our happiness in China, the care and the guidance we received were all gifts of His love. Our hearts lift in song with the psalmist:

'Praise the Lord, O my soul,
and all that is within me, praise His Holy Name.
'Praise the Lord, O my soul,
and forget not all His benefits.'"

China (continued) 1946 – 1950

19. General and Mrs. Wong Yusan, Yueyang church leaders - Later the
general was martyred.
20. Baptismal service for the baby son of Teacher Hu and Mrs. Hu in the
Huping Chapel
21. All our young missionary colleagues vacationed on Lushan to study Chinese.

China – A Move to Linhsiang

22

23

24

25

26

22. Our Quonset hut in the village of Linhsiang
23. Mr. Mei, my coworker, in the Chapel at Christmas time
24. Smiling Donald Cheng, our language teacher, with Linhsiang Chapel at Christmas timemembers
25. In September of 1950 we departed China with our children, Karen and Chris.
26. Victoria Island and HongKong harbor

Chapter IV

Back in the US – Furlough and Study 1950 to 1952

New Haven – 1951 and 1952

Having made the decision to return to Yale Divinity School, Barbara and the two children stayed in Salisbury while I went to New Haven in January 1951 to confirm my study and locate a suitable home for the family. Our good fortune was that Barbara's brother, Robert Brown, with his wife, Hermine, and two young sons were there. I began the search for a house or apartment and found 360 Skiff St. in Hamden, near enough to the Divinity School that I could bike or catch the bus. One of our first purchases was a used lightweight, English-type bicycle, which served me well.

Although the Women of Catawba Regional Guild of Southern Synod Evangelical and Reformed Church had raised money in 1947 to buy a jeep for our work in China, the political situation never cleared enough to send one to Hunan. These devoted women of the NC churches decided to present us a check to purchase a vehicle to use while studying and then take with us to our next assignment. They knew we had no transportation, having returned to Salisbury from China in November 1950. They really had more faith in our future and the future of mission work than our Mission Board. Mrs. Hal Hoyle as well as Mrs. Omwake had been in correspondence with us for several years. They now asked what kind of vehicle might be best used in countries where we might be sent. We suggested a small British Austin would be economical to run and useful in HongKong or any other Asian city, though no decision to send us overseas had yet been made.

With that Christmas present, given to us in a special ceremony, we quickly bought a small, shiny, new, black Austin A 40 in New York. It proved to be a deeply appreciated lifesaver.

We were to share the Hamden house with Mr. Chenowith, the owner, who said he would be away most of the winter. Memories of cold and snowy days were mixed with some furnace heating problems. Grocery shopping was a chore for Barbara because she had two very small ones to manage. Fortunately, sister-in-law Hermine helped orient us to New Haven shopping, as well as to many other aspects of big city life. We were invited to their home for shared suppers and fun evenings for Karen and Chris. Of course, it was fun for me, too, as a hard game of chess with Robert was always in order. I was able to swim or work out in Yale's huge, modern Sterling Gymnasium with Robert. We would meet every afternoon to play handball.

Issues at the Divinity School, such as future degree choice, courses useful for Mission work, and study supervision were quickly resolved as my study adviser, Dr. Richard Niebuhr, agreed that I study for my STM (Master of Sacred Theology) degree under his direction. One bonus was an exciting Old Testament course dealing with history and the origins of the historical understanding of Genesis taught by new, young professor Davie Napier.

Dr. Niebuhr also suggested that my recent experiences in China under the Communists would help me if I undertook research in Christianity and Communism. It took us about three months to nail down a specific topic for my major thesis, finally selecting "The Christian Interpretation of History in the New China." This was later confirmed by the degree committee. I had been fortunate to have mailed all of my copies of "Tien Fong" (Heavenly Breeze or Wind from Heaven), the official news magazine of the Chinese Christian Church, out to HongKong before we left Hankow. Published in Shanghai each week, the reporting was very helpful when I was in central China and invaluable for my study purposes at Yale. In working through my several hundred issues of "Tien Fong" I found over eighty pages devoted to the Christian understanding of history. Most revealing was a small booklet put out by the YMCA in 1950 by a Chinese scholar-theologian, Jiang Wenhan. It was obvious by summer that I would need to translate those available documents in order to understand and write about the attitudes of the Chinese church in Communist China toward the new "historical" perspectives required of patriotic Chinese.

Summer of 1951

After the end of the stimulating spring semester we left New Haven, happy to be going back to North Carolina for the summer to rejoin Barbara's parents, Pastor and Mrs. P. D. Brown. Once again, the St. John's Lutheran Church parsonage provided a home for us. Two upstairs bedrooms were graciously turned over to our family. The generosity of the Browns was constantly evident, as they always took us in and cared for us. One favorite memory was the week we spent with them in the summer vacation home of one of St. John's parishioners in the mountains at Linville. I got to play golf with Barbara's father on the prestigious Linville course, a guest privilege. The time in the mountains with the Browns was very special, though we were concerned with P.D.'s shortness of breath. Karen and Chris were the life of the party and kept us all busy. Many an evening, P.D., "Pappy" to the children, would sit in a big easy chair with the children on his lap and would read to them and keep them fully entertained.

In July, I spent three weeks at the Johns River Valley church camp especially enjoying a strenuous week with senior high campers who were very interested in our China experiences.

After we returned to New Haven in the fall we learned that Barbara's father was diagnosed with lung cancer, so distressing to all of us.

Our Missionaries Released from Yuanling

Our fellow missionaries, Mary Myers and Bill Daniels, had been released from detention in Yuanling and had arrived in HongKong on March 20, 1951. Mary, a nurse, remained in HongKong to work with refugees as she could not communicate in Cantonese. Bill Daniels rejoined wife, Jane, and son, Paul, to make their way immediately to the USA by ship, the President Wilson. By May, Bill was advised to go to New Haven to seek enrollment in Yale Divinity School. That was easily arranged. We were happy for Bill and Jane that they did not need to go through the arguments with Rev. Gebhardt that had been our lot. We had paved the way. Consequently, we enjoyed fellowship with them during the following year in both Mission study groups and other occasions.

Karl Beck, our Church's remaining missionary in China, was treated as an enemy alien and brought to trial as a spy. His wife, Meta, stayed in California with her daughter. He was finally released in June 1952. We learned from him later that he had undergone a humiliating trial and had been accused as an imperialist by some church colleagues and former students. He said his solitary confinement in his home was not made uncomfortable, as he was permitted to keep a rather large collection of books. As with the rest of us who had remained in Communist China, he felt that the ordinary people seemed to have wide respect for the honesty of the government even though they had given up some freedoms in exchange. Karl was a loving person who devoted his life to serving Eastview School students, teaching English and Bible.

Land, the Mountain Cottage — Our Retreat and More

It was during this summer of 1951 that a project we had been considering for several years took shape. While we were in China my brother Don was serving as an obstetrician in the Army at Fort Leonard Wood in Arkansas. During World War II, he had been classified 4F in the draft because of his perforated eardrum. After he finished his residency he was drafted by the army to serve at US bases. He wrote our uncle, Dr. D.J. Whitener, who was head of the History Department at Appalachian State University in Boone, N.C., that he wanted a way to invest some money and hoped Uncle Jay could find him a small piece of mountain property. This was accomplished in 1949 when Don purchased the Ashley farm of 26 acres just off the highway between Blowing Rock and Boone. Don wrote us in China at that time, asking if we would like to share in his new venture. We were so involved with our situation and events in Communist China in those days that we could not respond. When we finally got to North Carolina in late 1950 we were hardly less busy, but Don renewed his offer. I decided to use some of my share of Dad's legacy to buy into Don's property and with him build a cabin.

By early summer of 1951 Don and I had some hand-drawn plans for a rough cabin in the woods: no plumbing, no electricity, nothing fancy, wonderful spring water, bunks around the wall, outside privy, and a fireplace. We were very enthusiastic when we presented this wonderful idea to Barbara. WOW! There was no equivocation, no discussion! Her decisive words were to this effect: "Go right ahead, fellows, but you can count the kids and me out! I have been there, done that with no electricity, no plumbing, and no running water in China. Have fun!"

After Don and I were instructed on the kind of "rustic cabin" we could build, we changed our strategy and drew up plans for a simple cottage with two bedrooms, kitchen, bath, and living room, an attic and full unfinished basement. We wisely secured the services of nearby mountain neighbor, Jay Shore, to help us build. He hired local workers when regular full-time work was not available. At the time Jay operated a grading machine for the county on an "as-needed basis." He planted potatoes and raised huge mountain cabbages at various locations. His father was a farmer who was also the Baptist preacher of the small Middle Fork Church just down the road. Aunt Chaney Ashley, who sold the farm pasture area of 26 acres to Don, was an aunt of Jay's. He secured his builder brother, Burmah, and a cousin, Perry Ashley to build the concrete block foundation and basement section, as well as the handsome fireplace. Perry was renowned for his fireplaces built with rare Grandfather Mountain granite. Jay found other unemployed neighbors who helped him cut large hemlocks on the hillside behind the house. He used his family mules to drag the logs out to transport to a mill. He tells me that those were the days when everything was done piece by piece. Using our father's legacy we were able to build the house for $7,500, which included the cost of paint and other materials that Don and I used to finish it up. We had to spackle the joints of plaster board, paint the entire interior, and then sand the oak floors so that we could stain them with the latest varnish. That the rustic-looking floors appear the same after over 60 years is a marvel in itself. That the walls need reworking is quite understandable

By the end of the summer, this was a place we could really call "home." I felt it was a real tribute to my parents who never owned a home of their own.

Don arranged financing through the Wautaga Savings and Loan and we picked up the $25 per month to begin paying our share. Little did we know that we would be paying such a high percentage of our salary for so many years, but after the little cottage, nestled next to a stream, was completed, it captured our hearts and has served as a repository for family possessions through the years. Ever since, it has really been our home in the USA, a rose-colored cottage with surrounding forsythia and native rhododendron. Karen (3) and Chris (2) were the first of our family to play in the small meandering stream, later named Sterling Creek, which flows past our cottage into the Middle Fork of the New River, then north to the Ohio before reaching the Mississippi. In those early days we wanted to come to the mountains any time we could get free during our furloughs from overseas.

The children fished the stream, made wooden block boats to sail and catch downstream, and found salamanders and crayfish. We walked the hills and rejoiced in the wildlife. With the family's love of the mountains of North Carolina, the Appalachian chain in particular, we began to be environmentalists.

Final Year at Yale Divinity School STM Program – September 1951 to June 1952

At the end of the summer of 1951 several decisions were made. My studies for the fall were defined, as I would take an independent study in Chinese translation with a teacher at the Language Institute, and we would find a more comfortable place to live. We were very fortunate in September to learn of a convenient apartment in Branford, about five miles from the Divinity School in the basement of Jerry & Ellen Kok's home. Jerry was the new director of the Yale Language Institute. We enjoyed our friendship with the Kok family. Their two small children and our two often played together and we exchanged some babysitting.

There was no time for a "social life" since my studies required a great many hours. Barbara had a full-time job taking care of all of us. It was good to have Walter Hald come for supper occasionally. We attended the Congregational Church in Branford.

Karen went to a daycare center for a time each week but she was not a happy child and easily upset. Chris was easy-going and learned very early how to "push Karen's buttons" resulting in our feeling the need to get help. Fortunately, we were able to take both of them to The Geselle Clinic for Child Development in New Haven. We learned that Karen's personality was "peripheral;" everything stimulated her. Chris, was "focal" and more laid back. It was very helpful to be aware of these differences as they developed.

We Are Assigned

Rev. Gebhardt was sure he could persuade me to agree to go to Central America where the Honduras Mission was requesting help. I felt strongly there were opportunities for service in Southeast Asia among the many Chinese communities in many countries. It seemed a time of testing. We had felt led to remain in China when most missionaries had withdrawn and we never doubted our decision. We also felt that we had been blessed in being offered this opportunity of further study but Honduras just did not seem to be a good fit for us to learn a new language and go to Latin America. We finally turned down the offer of a missionary assignment to Honduras. For a few months it appeared I would need to seek employment with another church board working with Chinese in Southeast Asia, a commercial firm, or other enterprise until such time as China reopened.

Fortunately for us, Ward Hartman, who was our own church representative in HongKong, decided that he was ready to retire. He made the suggestion that the Board send me to help with Hunanese refugees, who had been continuing to seek refuge and help in HongKong. Ward felt it was also time to begin the process of connecting to the Church in HongKong, which would require someone with the Cantonese dialect.

The Rev. John Ma, pastor of the China Congregational Church, suggested to Ward that his large Congregational Church would welcome a missionary colleague to participate in the youth work of his large congregation. The young people in HongKong were demanding a very high level of instruction and understanding of English. They really seemed to want an American. It began to appear before the end of winter that we would be going to HongKong to take over some of the work Ward Hartman and Mary Myers had undertaken in relief and rehabilitation. In April, we were notified by the Mission Board of our appointment to HongKong to continue representation for our Church. We acknowledged this by joyfully writing to our friends:

> "We feel it is a real privilege to be offered this opportunity to serve in one of the hot spots of the world. Knowing of the myriad problems which face the several hundred thousand refugee Chinese in HongKong, we hope that, somehow, we might be made instruments of God's will to bring comfort, relief, and assurance of His saving love."

In the meantime, life in New Haven was very busy. My study in a carrel in the Sterling Library kept my nose to the grindstone. I ended up translating (with the Language Institute teacher's invaluable assistance) over 100 pages of Chinese documents, quite an accomplishment for a "scholar" who could hardly write his name in Chinese characters. My sessions with the Missions group, as well as with Dr. Richard Niebuhr, were always meaningful and fruitful.

Particularly useful was the special course in "Christianity and Communism" offered once a week at Union Seminary in New York City.

Four of us shared the gas cost of the little Austin to drive the Merritt Parkway on Wednesdays to spend three hours with Reinhold Niebuhr (theologian brother of Richard), John Bennett, and Searle Bates (a former Presbyterian missionary in China). You can imagine the lively discussions among Hal Shorrock (Japan missionary and later World Council of Churches officer in Geneva), Masao Takenaka (future Dean and Professor at Doshisha University Divinity School in Japan), Bill Daniels (a future Association Minister for the UCC), and S. Whitener (car driver).

Upon learning of our appointment to HongKong we approached the Yale Language Institute to learn Cantonese, the dialect used in HongKong. Fortunately, they had a contract to teach a State Department language officer so we were able to join the "crash" course for the summer. Barbara and I spent at least four hours a day in class struggling to learn a new language. It was not a translation effort from the national language to Cantonese, but an entirely new beginning. The eleven tones (including those that changed) gave us fits, but we stuck with it. I was ever grateful for the three months' study as it facilitated entry into the Cantonese speaking Church in HongKong.

Once again, we turned to our good friends in New Haven, the Halds, with whom we had kept in contact. Walter had packed us up for China in 1946 and was always helpful when I needed advice about operating our car. We knew we would need it in HongKong so he helped me make arrangements for its shipment from a southern port. He also secured wooden boxes, smaller this time, from his warehouse for us to ship items we wished to take with us to HongKong. Again we were immensely grateful for all he did for us. Preparing for another move overseas was stressful as Barbara was pregnant with our third child due in January.

Early in the summer we learned that Barbara's father was failing fast. His radioactive gold treatments in Oak Ridge, Tennessee, may have slowed the lung cancer, but there was no cure. Barbara and the children went to Salisbury to be with her father and I followed later. He was hospitalized and died in August. His own implicit trust and triumphant faith along with his strong support of the cause of Missions was a great inspiration to us. Beloved by his congregation and family, he had served God all his 65 years and was deeply mourned by all. Barbara was very close to her father, affectionately calling him "Pappy." She felt greatly her loss and found it difficult to leave her mother. Knowing her sister, Lois, living in Salisbury, would be of great help and support to their mother, was a great comfort to us.

Don and I did find time to work on the cottage, though Barbara and the children could only visit the mountains briefly as she wished to be with her family during her father's last days. We had delayed plans to leave for HongKong, but secured passage by ship for November.

Chapter V

Return to Asia – Assignment HongKong 1952 to 1967

Sailing on the "President Wilson" to HongKong – November 1952

We were bound for the British Crown Colony of HongKong, returning to China though not YET China. That change from colony to nationhood would wait until 1997 according to treaty. It certainly could not be the China where I grew up and where Barbara and I had spent those momentous four years in Hunan and Hupei. We were familiar with HongKong as our entry port in 1946 to Hunan. Its population then of eight hundred thousand had swelled with refugees to over a million, yet it could still be called quaintly "old world" as it retained much of its special charm. We looked forward to a new and exciting life and work. We are quite unable to chronicle fully the incredible changes and events of that period; I must settle for highlights of the nearly fifteen years we worked there!

Our trans-Pacific crossing this time was on a new President Lines ship, "President Wilson." In any case, there was no comparison with our first trip on the troopship "Marine Lynx." In fact it was real luxury – comfortable cabin and too much food to eat. There was a social director, a good playroom for the children, and even mid-morning beef bouillon served on deck! Good company, good movies, and good competitions made for a comfortable crossing. One disturbing event happened to me during a deck quoits competition. I had played hard for quite a long time in the rather hot sun. I noticed I was becoming fatigued, but then I nearly fainted. I was taken to the ship's doctor, who checked me out but found nothing unusual. His only suggestion, "take it easy," was not easy to follow. I spent time reading and watching Karen (4) and Chris (3), as well as playing in a chess competition.

Because the Hartmans returned to the US before we arrived in HongKong, we were welcomed by YDS classmate, Harry Brunger and wife Grace and family, who had graciously arranged for us to stay with them for a short while. It was a happy reunion. Friends from New Haven days, Harry was working with the Chinese YMCA. The two children, about the same ages as ours, a wonderful amah and a small apartment on one of the upper floors in a row of buildings in Kowloon introduced us to HongKong family living.

We began an immediate search for a place nearby. We found an apartment on Carnarvon Road on the top floor of a new five-story building, terribly expensive due to the "key" money required (an accepted illegal charge just to get the key to the place). We did feel safe because all windows had steel bars along with peepholes in the doors and strong chains to prevent unexpected door entry. Karen and Chris found it great sport to toss shoes and toys out the windows between the bars, giving me the job of trudging down and up the stairs retrieving them – until we put a stop to the game. We got busy furnishing the apartment, and as soon as it was finished, just at Christmas time we hired our own helper and began to settle in. This was imperative with our baby due in January. Barbara had the task of shopping, climbing to the fifth floor, and struggling to communicate in our newly learned Cantonese.

I met with Presbyterian missionaries who introduced me to the various interdenominational committees assisting in relief and welfare work with refugees. Harry Brunger and other friends introduced me to YMCA and other groups. John Ma welcomed me to the Congregational Church of the Church of Christ in China, HongKong Council. Barbara joined Grace Brunger and family at the English-speaking Union Church in Kowloon. We were now under way in HongKong. I started immediately on language study, but Barbara had to see that the household was operating. She was later able to spend more time on common "kitchen" language so that she managed well in the marketplace.

Kim Whitener – January 19, 1953

On January 19, 1953, we welcomed our new daughter, Kim. Born in Kowloon Hospital, she was delivered by a nurse as the doctor had a broken arm. Kim was born with a piece of the amniotic membrane on top of her head and the British nurse told us an interesting bit of English folklore. Known as a "caul," it was highly prized by seamen. The caul was dried and then carried by sailors at sea to protect them from drowning. Kim was baptized by the Rev. Lee Ching Ming whom we learned to know as Pastor of Hop Yat Church, the oldest Church of Christ in China church in HongKong founded by the London Missionary Society.

Mission Service in HongKong: Our First Term – 1953 to 1957

Our little Austin A-40 car, freighted from the East Coast USA, arrived. My first task was to get a license for it. Unfortunately, it was an export model from England to the US and had a left-hand drive. All vehicles in Britain and HongKong were right-hand drive. A number of consultations with the police department ensued. I argued that because it was really British, they should grant me special permission to import it, which they did grudgingly. In those early days of very few cars, it was quite easy to drive vehicles in Kowloon and HongKong.

Finally, I was ready to undertake the many meaningful jobs ahead. We had helped prepare Christmas presents of rice, children's T-shirts, soaps & towels, apples, and suckers for over 1,200 refugee children, a gift from the Presbyterian Church in the USA. The Presbyterians also had some audio-visual equipment, so I helped several other younger missionaries begin an audiovisual group to provide programs for the Chinese Churches. That year I showed the classic King of Kings film to at least twenty church groups during the Christmas season.

I was asked to help organize a committee for the Rennie's Mill Church Clinic. This was the project begun by Nurse Mary Myers of our Mission several years earlier. She had regularly taken an hour-long ferry ride from HongKong Island to Junk Bay and set up a table to offer medicines to the refugees located there. The Rennie's Mill Refugee Camp was established in 1948 when a large group of 10,000 Guomindang army personnel crossed into the British Colony of HongKong as they were being pursued by the Communist army. The Chinese government did not invade the Colony but did demand that the army members being pursued be returned to them to be punished (clearly indicating they would be shot). The British had been accepting refugees for a few years so said they would turn the matter of refugee status over to the United Nations. The HongKong government, in a brilliant move, placed all of the soldiers and camp followers far from town on the hillside of beautiful Junk Bay in the New Territories. The camp was near an old dismantled residence of a man named Rennie who allegedly committed suicide when he became bankrupt after his flour mill failed. The hillside was known as Rennie's Mill Camp. The only access to it was a long walk over a mountain pass or a long launch ride from HongKong Island. It was a large sprawling tar paper shack village with very limited opportunity for decent jobs. Many relief organizations assisted by offering a variety of services. Our own Mission supported Mary Myers until she retired in 1951. Helen Wilson of the Church of Scotland took over Mary's work by moving to the camp. Our Mission offered support for the clinic itself, called the Rennie's Mill Church Clinic. This project remained a major focus for me for many years. I found the trip to the Clinic in Rennie's Mill Camp and later when we were building Haven of Hope T B Hospital very arduous. I would drive about 20 miles from town, hike down a steep path to Hang Hau, a small village opposite Junk Bay from Rennie's Mill and Haven of Hope. A woman who had a sampan would scull the heavy craft across the bay to my destination in about an hour and agree to return me in several hours. There was no easy way to get to that huge refugee camp.

The Church World Service program in which our E&R Church participated also required time, as the committee was planning housing for refugees. Due to recurrent fires in "squatter villages" on the steep hillsides, many homeless people needed assistance, relocation, and decent housing.

There were also many refugees camped illegally on all the hillsides of Kowloon wherever they could find space to build a shack. These were called "squatter villages." My friend Donald Cheng, who had been our helper and teacher in China, asked me to consider helping a group who had come from Hunan province in central China where we had lived and worked. They lived on a steep, bleak hillside called Grampian Village in many tar paper shacks. We started a number of projects there: a reading room also used as a chapel, and later a shack in which we could teach children who had no money to pay for schooling. Grace Liu, a graduate of nearby Bethel Seminary, developed that work over many years, a story that she has written in full.

Relocation for Health Reasons

During the late spring of 1953, I found climbing up the long flights of steps to our top-floor apartment increasingly tiring. To follow up on the episode of dizziness on the ship, I sought consultation with a physician. For about six months, no one could figure out why I was so chronically tired. I had become so discouraged by my physical fatigue that I felt as though my Mission service was really coming to an end. I recall feeling confused and depressed. Had I just brought my family so far to find that I was not up to the tasks and challenges ahead? I sought to clarify my sense of "call." What did God really want of me?

A very competent Chinese internist ordered a glucose tolerance test. The result was a diagnosis of hypoglycemia, low blood sugar. It was helpful to learn that trying protein intake six times a day would help alleviate the symptoms. A second series of tests in the fall confirmed the diagnosis and I learned how to manage with frequent "snacks." It was many years later that my pancreas slowed down so I did not need to monitor my intake so closely to maintain a stable sugar level.

Dr. Reginald Helfferich visited HongKong in July 1954. He was responsible for our E & R Church's Commission on World Service which funded the Rennie's Mill project, as well as the refugee hillside project in Kowloon. His enthusiasm, energy, and vision were astounding. He quickly discerned that I could hardly make it up to our 5th-floor apartment. When he discovered my ailment, he told us to find a place on the ground level and he would personally check with the Mission Board to see that it was OK. We spent most of the summer looking and finally located a two-story duplex house on Kadoorie Ave. We knew it was an area that was considered expensive, but we were able to offer Lucile Hartman a large room to live with us when she came back from furlough. We moved into our new home in late August 1953.

Someone suggested that since Kadoorie Ave. was a "posh" ("Port Out, Starboard Home," British term for "nice") neighborhood and often the target of thieves, we needed a dog. Our luck was an extremely useless black cocker spaniel who insisted on an inside toilet, refusing to use the miniscule front lawn. Jeff was completely "untrainable." Without a sound of protest from Jeff a thief used a long pole to steal my camera from my office desk. Then later in the morning Jeff raised "Holy Cain" with the arriving police. It was time to find a new home for Jeff. A few days later we were asked to accept a female German shepherd, who guarded us well and produced a litter of pups from which we selected one with floppy ears and sweet disposition. The kids named him "Flop" and cared for him as a long-time, beloved pet.

Back on the Job

An experienced Cantonese language instructor was introduced to us soon after our arrival. He had taught many missionaries and was a strong elder in his Castle Peak Church. Commuting every weekday the 25 miles by bus to Kowloon, Chan Yeung Kwong always arrived on time for my hour or more instruction. He patiently led me through the Bible passages and helped me try to sound "local" rather than as a transplanted Hunanese.

I must say, I would have preferred to have preached in my native national dialect but I did preach my first Cantonese sermon in the fall of 1954. I wrote out each word phonetically with the myriad tones. Fortunately, the members of the church were always patient and welcoming. By the time I left HongKong fifteen years later, I was often complimented on my ability to speak both dialects.

In those early years there was always something to do even though I was not officially connected to the Church of Christ in China, as I had been when we were in Hunan. My office was in our home. I worked on a visual aid program for the churches, particularly for John Ma's Congregational Church. There were many meetings among those of us who represented denominational church boards. We tried very hard to work together in a cooperative, ecumenical manner. I was also in charge of building a new stone clinic building for the Rennie's Mill Church Clinic, a project Dr. Helfferich had authorized on his visit. In spite of feeling tired and sometimes dispirited, there was so much to do that I kept right at it.

In the spring of 1954, I had the opportunity to teach a course on the Life of Christ to a section of freshmen students at Chung Chi College, newly organized and supported by many denominations. Six of us who had more recently come to HongKong were invited by Bishop R.O. Hall to participate in this effort to offer a section in the course titled Philosophy of Life, the first semester a survey of Jesus' ministry. Later in the year the college was officially organized with representation from all Mission societies who had contributed to the Christian Colleges in China. Funds for Chung Chi College came from the USA through the United Board for Christian

Colleges in Asia. I represented the Evangelical & Reformed Church on the new local management board.

Health Update

My doctor finally suggested that I could use some recreational diversion, so I checked into the idea of taking up the game of golf. Several American missionary friends were talking about it so I joined Herb Zimmerman (Lutheran), Loren Noren (Northern Baptist), and Charlie Long (Episcopal) for the one-hour drive out to Fanling, near the border to Communist China, to learn to play the honorable game at the Royal HongKong Golf Club. That I never could get my handicap down to less than 16 was quite immaterial because the half-day of walking the well-manicured courses and the banter with our Chinese caddies, plus an excellent meal at the clubhouse, was therapy in itself. In fact we had a saying, "it never rains in Fanling" because we often played in the gentle spring and summer rains. I did get to play in a pro-amateur match with an Australian great and even helped win one hole, a fluke, I assure you. When I left HongKong I was a "life-time" member and was able to play the course on a visit in 1974.

My most famous golf story was of the time we saw the usual Chinese "huang niu" ("yellow cows" always used for work) being tended by young boys to keep them from grazing in the middle of the fairways. The golf course was built on land purchased from the villages so one part of the compensation was the permit to graze their livestock but within limits. The youngsters always kept a close eye on the wandering cattle, keeping them on the edges during the hours when golfers were passing through. This day, I noticed a cow starting to head across the fairway a good thirty yards or so away, but I was confident that I would be lofting my ball far overhead. I took a mighty swing; the ball hit the cow in its withers just front of the hip. The next thing we knew the cow rolled its eyes, sank to the ground, and lay motionless. A small boy came running out of the woods, shrieking that we had "killed his cow." In consternation we walked up to the prone cow to find the little fellow with his arms around its head and crying loudly. Shortly after we arrived and while we debated what we should do, the cow suddenly opened her eyes, shook the boy off, stood up, and ran to join the herd. My partners never let me forget that episode always warning me if they saw any animals or impediments looming ahead.

Servicemen's Guides

The US Navy was using HongKong as a port of call for rest and recreation. Only the larger ships had chaplains aboard so a Maryknoll Catholic priest was assigned to see what he could do for the servicemen. It was soon clear that sailors and marines were at the mercy of Chinese touts, shady ladies, shady men, and conmen who grabbed them as soon as they landed and led the servicemen to dives, prostitutes, and stores where the guides received big rake offs. In addition, those Navy men who did not get liberty on Sunday had no services. I was called by Father Gilligan to help organize Protestant missionaries to undertake preaching services aboard ships in the harbor. It was clear that this process needed better organization, so we formed the Sevicemen's Guides Committee which over a few years did a tremendous job of serving both those aboard ship and those coming ashore. With the navy's concurrence we managed to secure Fenwick Pier in Wanchai (famous for Suzie Wong of the movies) as a point of entrance. Volunteers, mostly American women in HongKong with their husbands, provided accurate information and warning against theft and nefarious schemes to relieve the men of their money. Respectable stores, especially tailors, and restaurants were recommended. Eventually, both a Catholic and a Protestant chaplain were stationed at the pier. Our Mission Board provided the chaplain (Rev. Eccles) for several years and a good friend, Gordon DePree (Reformed Church Mission), later served a term. Our family was invited on several occasions to visit some of the ships in port, including a submarine and an aircraft carrier. These were big occasions for the children and parents.

Barbara worked as a volunteer at Fenwick Pier. She also found much to do at Kowloon Union Church, an English speaking interdenominational congregation. She helped with the Sunday School and also served as a member of the Council. She enjoyed teaching English Bible to a group of Swatow young people.

Family Life and Laan Tau Summers

No, we did not work twenty-four hours a day, seven days a week. As a family we regularly took time in afternoons to go to the beaches to give the children a chance to play in the sand and to enjoy the cooling waters when the day was hot. Our favorite beach was Silver Strand at the foot of quite a high embankment. A long flight of steps had been built to enable access to the beach from the parking area. One Sunday several young people from Barbara's Bible Class went with us. We were having a great time and lots of fun until we suddenly missed four year old Chris. We always kept the children in our sight, but somehow he had vanished. We all searched the entire beach front and the shallow waters and became increasingly frantic as we held hands searching in deeper water. In desperation we ran up the long flight of steps to the parking lot and found a very frightened Chris looking for us near our car. What immense relief was felt by all!

We visited friends, had meals out on occasion, and even went for overnight visits to the Portuguese colony of Macau several hours away by ferry. One of our favorite outings was to a small restaurant (He De Fu) where they made the best "jyaudz" dumplings (pot stickers). Fried or boiled, our family members could excel in putting them away.

We were fortunately able to take our summer vacation on the top of Laan Tau Island, an hour's ferry ride from HongKong. Our two-week vacation on the mountain the summer of 1953 was a real lifesaver. Laan Tau Camp became a very favorite spot for the family to get away from HongKong's summer heat. It is quite a trek up the 2800 foot elevation on a steep rocky path. Earlier missionaries had built stone huts atop the ridge, small but very secure with strong shutters for the typhoon (hurricane) winds. Windswept and treeless, this beautiful spot, with swimming pool and mess hut for communal meals and meetings was really a therapeutic respite for many of us. Often in the clouds, the mountain top took us away from all the pressing needs of refugees, political issues, and the hustle of the big city, offering a real vacation.

Laan Tau Camp was operated by the home- owners. Members took turns managing the dining hall and the orderly daily purchase of supplies from compradors in the city. The carrying of supplies and even of sedan chairs for those who could not walk up was the summer work of local farmers and residents from the village at the base.

By the end of 1954 our Mission agreed to purchase one of the small stone huts on the ridge at Laan Tau Camp. It was #13 and had belonged to the Shoops, whom we met when we first arrived in China. They were the couple in Canton who inspired Barbara to try to train a woman helper. The cottage was across from the mess hall and convenient to the pool. Nearly everyone came by so we often had visitors sitting on our steps and concrete slab. One of the first things I did was to study the water supply situation. We depended entirely on roof tanks and the rain to get our supply. I found it possible to run a pipe into a small stream that fed the swimming pool. The camp had a reservoir and a standpipe at the mess hall, as well as water to use in the kitchen. We discouraged the drinking of the pipe water. There was always a chance of contamination because the mountain served as the pasture for many farmers' cows, so we boiled the water to drink. The stone cabins were tiny with many bunks but they did have a septic tank. Maang Hau, a contractor based in the village of MuiWo at the base of the mountain, always arranged repairs for the houses as well as undertaking the swimming pool repairs. He agreed that he could install a galvanized pipe to bring water from the stream to our house. We soon had an outdoor shower attached to the pipe, which allowed the sun to warm the water on its way. On cloudy and misty days, however, it could be quite chilly. Actually, it wasn't long before several other houses decided to connect to the pipe system, too. As the children grew older the swimming pool was the center of daytime activities. Hiking to beautiful pools, named "Black Rock" and "Perfect," in streams down in the mountain valley increased. Wonderful memories centered on the evening programs and gatherings in the mess hall. No one will ever forget an elder London Missionary, Hedley Bunton, who was always asked to lead the children on a rousing romp snaking over chairs, out windows, and around the building to a snappy tune:

"One elephant went out to play, up on a spider's web one day.
He had such enormous fun; he called for another elephant to come.
'Another elephant!'" (Shouted loudly by everyone)
Thus, the line grew and grew as the shouts and laughter increased.

An Unexpected Blow

Our family was thriving; Karen, Chris, and Kim were all healthy youngsters. October of 1954, however, brought a sad disappointment. We had planned for our fourth child, but Barbara suffered the full-term stillbirth of a son. An autopsy did not reveal the cause of intrauterine death but it may have been due to pressure on the cord. It was a difficult time for us. We learned to appreciate the grief and disappointment of other families, but feel Barbara would have benefited greatly from the bereavement therapy offered today after infant death.

1955 – Increased HongKong Tasks

In January 1955, Grampian Village burned to the ground, leaving over one hundred and seventy-five families homeless. Our chapel reading room was destroyed. We had built a concrete roadway to replace a narrow dirt street the summer before, which was credited with saving many lives. During the cold weather we supplied funds to purchase blankets, tar-paper, and wooden materials so the people could erect sidewalk temporary living quarters. They were eventually resettled on a hillside in Chuk Yuen where our E&R Church helped provide 50 well-designed wooden structures. That area eventually housed over 10,000 people until it was replaced with multi-story buildings. Our Church of Christ in China, HongKong Council, built a Family Life Center at the top of the steep hill.

We received a big boost in the spring when Dr. Ehlman, our Mission Board Secretary, visited HongKong. Although I was sent to HongKong to work specifically with refugees from Hunan, the local district of the Church of Christ in China was in terrible disarray. At the time of his visit, the Church of Christ in China, HongKong Council, was undergoing reorganization. The local council badly needed renewal and improved leadership. The Rev. Dr. Peter Wong had just been able to enter HongKong from Canton where he had been the Executive Secretary of the Guangdong Synod of the Christian Church of China. He was a very logical choice to succeed an allegedly corrupt group who were constantly at odds with the major churches. Dr. Elhman met with the younger pastors, confirmed our Mission's historic role in Hunan province, and sought a welcome into the HongKong Church structure. The invitation to participate was extended and I was asked to become the social welfare secretary of the HongKong Council, Church of Christ in China.

Groundwork for the Rennie's Mill Church Clinic and future work with TB patients was laid. I spent long hours traveling to Junk Bay by car to Hang Hau, a small fishing village across Junk Bay from Rennie's Mill, and then by sampan across to the clinic. To get there by small ferry/launch from HongKong Island meant nearly a three-hour trek. I was able to help write materials and then get a journalist friend, Jack Shepherd, to produce the first of our annual reports with pictures, "Come Wind, Come Weather."

The work at Rennie's Mill Church Clinic proceeded apace. I do not need to document the history of that work since it is being researched by Dr. Lau, an associate professor at Chung Chi College who grew up in

Rennie's Mill Camp. Corinne Bergmann of our HongKong Mission also wrote a very accurate summary of the history of the Clinic Committee. In any case, Dr. Ehlman's presence provided us with a speaker for the dedication of a flat space on the edge of Junk Bay where we proposed to build a 100-bed tuberculosis sanatorium. This was named Haven of Hope.

To provide work for refugees in 1955, we hired men to dig decomposed granite from the hillside right at the sanatorium site. With three sand-brick machines that were turned by hand, the men pounded a damp mixture of the gravel, sandy soil and cement to produce the air-dried bricks for constructing all the buildings. We produced four wards for 100 beds using a unique design by a Christian architect, Y. O. Lee. It was not long before the patients were transferred from Rennie's Mill to Haven of Hope. Annie Skau, a Norwegian Holiness Mission nurse, was the matron. With a few nurses, Hanny Gronlund of her Mission, and Martha Boss of the Lutheran Church Missouri Synod, they began to train young Chinese women as nurse's aides and then as nurses. Annie was called a "gentle giantess" by Dr. Helfferich. She was also a very strong personality with a handshake to reshape your rings. Though undoubtedly a gifted administrator, she magnified her own role in the development of the work at Rennie's Mill and later at Haven of Hope Hospital.

Not long after the Haven of Hope was fully operational, I was taking Loren Noren to visit. We parked across the bay from the hospital and walked through the little village of HangHau. Beside the path on the way to the beach, we saw a farmer with three little piglets for sale. These white pigs were obviously from good "Kadoorie" stock. This stock was known throughout the colony because Mr. Kadoorie had made it his goal in life to upgrade the small Chinese pig raised for fat alone to a more marketable meat-producing pig. He had crossed numerous strains and had produced a very good white pig. I had an idea that the hospital could use its left-over food for a little pig. Carrying the squealing pig aboard a small sampan we were rowed across the bay to the hospital landing. Annie Skau was delighted and got the carpenters to build a suitable pen. A recovered TB patient was hired to care for the pig and be sure that the food from the patients was properly boiled and prepared. The pig venture was so successful that in a few years it expanded and became a very lucrative investment!

Chung Chi College: A Tale of Relationships

I wish I had known "R.O.," as Bishop Ronald Hall was always called in his younger days. He came to China with an Anglican group from England. It could have been one of the forerunners of the Moral Rearmament (Oxford Movement) or the Student Volunteer movement itself. In any case, a brilliant man, he learned Cantonese in Canton and worked largely with students in high schools and colleges. I know that he did work at Lingnam University, one of the twelve Christian colleges in China. All of the Christian colleges in China were supported by groups of Missions working together. In fact, most of them were unions of smaller colleges founded by different Christian Mission groups.

I learned to know R.O. in HongKong after we had arrived in 1952. He had been appointed Anglican Bishop of HongKong in 1946 following the Japanese war (WWII). He had single-handedly reopened Anglican churches and helped initiate the rehabilitation of the British Crown Colony by insisting that all people (Chinese and British) had rights. With the ear of the governor and the highest echelon of power circles, he was a formidable advocate for the ordinary man. Yet he was informal and even wore shorts in the summer.

In the fall of 1952, R.O. was busy trying to put together a successor college to Lingnam University. The University of HongKong was associated with London University and taught entirely in the English language. Bishop Hall insisted that HongKong needed a Christian University teaching in the Chinese language. The goal of a new successor college was to teach courses in Chinese to serve more of the common people. It was clear that only the very well-to-do could afford the high schools teaching only in English to prepare for HongKong University. Thus, most of those graduates came from and formed the elite of HongKong society. Practically no refugees had enough English to pass the very difficult HKU entry examinations.

It took more than a year to get our "Christian" college courses started because space was needed. There was a sense of urgency, as New Asia College was being opened by a Mencius scholar, and several other private colleges were rumored to be starting. None of them had the approval of the Colony educational authorities. R.O. was able to get some private approvals so started erecting a building to house classes next to his administrative offices on the Cathedral grounds. It was a clever use of funds, as he rented the rooms to our fledgling college to begin classes. We found a name for the college itself. "Chung Chi" pronounced "chung ji" – "Respect Christ" College opened its doors with the retired Dr. Lam, former president of Lingnam University as the new president. My role on the Board of Trustees was to report progress back to our Mission Board and to seek an increased level of financial support.

In those early days, I was quite an unknown to the founding board members of Chung Chi, which was composed of six or eight Chinese church leaders and about the same number of missionaries representing various Mission Boards. R.O. found it difficult to welcome Americans, as the British Colony had never before tolerated "foreigners" to work in their territory. Only after the Communist takeover of China did the wave of the 100 varieties of American denominationalism gain a foothold in HongKong. In those early days, R.O. saw me as a possible help to the new college and even asked if I would be willing to be President Lam's assistant. I respectfully declined, as I was in the middle of working with Helen Wilson to develop the clinic at Rennie's Mill Refugee Camp. I saw my chief function to work with refugees from Hunan and connect to the younger pastors of the HongKong Council, Church of Christ in China.

You can see that though I was an American, R.O. saw me as useful. I had several very good personal discussions with him at the "Bishop's House." I really thought we could get along pretty well. It seemed obvious to me, however, that R.O. considered Chung Chi College his personal "project" and he intended to be the prime organizer.

Chung Chi needed a new president. The elderly President Lam had died after only a year in office. It was the Bishop's plan that his friend and Board of Trustees chairman, Daniel Au (an Anglican businessman, owner of the Wing On Company), would take over, first as acting president and then eventually be elected as president. At the time this was about to take place, Dr. Walline was the Presbyterian Mission representative, I was Evangelical & Reformed representative, Loren Noren was newly arrived Northern Baptist representative, and several other Mission Board representatives were on furlough. Most of us thought the appointment of Daniel Au was a done deal. He was well-known, had only a BA degree, but was a strong supporter of the Bishop in the councils of the Anglican Church.

It was therefore a surprise when S.H. Pang, a Chung Chi College Board member and Executive Secretary of the Chinese YMCA, asked to meet with me regarding an urgent matter relating to the Chung Chi College Board of Trustees.

The issue of the presidency of Chung Chi College was of utmost importance to the churches in HongKong. I wondered what this special invitation from Mr. Pang was all about as we drank the customary "Tit Gwun Yum" (Steel Goddess of Mercy) tea at the Cantonese tea house where we were seated among several hundred chattering lunch guests. Unexpectedly, Mr. Pang strongly stated that Daniel Au was quite unacceptable to the HK Chinese Christian community. I was astounded, as Au was the Chung Chi Board chair duly elected by these same persons my friend Mr. Pang was representing in discussing this matter with me. I explained I was so new to HongKong, still studying Cantonese, that I was very unsure of all the implications and subtleties of which he spoke. He reassured me that what he and several members of the board required was someone who was not too involved in local church politics. I began to feel that I was being "set up." He pointed out that as a foreigner and as a newly arrived missionary, I could help resolve a very difficult situation by nominating an alternative to our esteemed present board chair. I had to know why!

"Daniel Au has a concubine," he said very carefully. In Christian circles I knew this to be quite unacceptable. In the Ching Dynasty the historic system of concubinage was an accepted court and national practice. The Christian churches, however, declared unequivocally that such a practice was not in the New Testament tradition. This meant that for many wealthy Chinese, the Christian religion did not fit Chinese mores. It was a very important issue in the church. But this was astounding news in 1955. Why was I being made privy to such information? S.H. Pang proceeded to outline why I was being courted. He asked me to place in nomination the name of a man who had his doctorate from Yale University and who was Hakka (a minority group in South China with a completely different dialect whose most famous member was Chiang Kaishek). Dr. D.Y. Lin was known as a competent teacher and a member of a small but well-known Hakka Christian Church.

I demurred in that as a relatively new arrival in the Colony, I really had no standing and very little background for this kind of effort. He assured me that no Chinese on the Board could make this nomination because the Bishop had ways to directly hinder projects in which a Board member might be involved. I was completely free because I had no such connections, was an unknown, and had no projects the Bishop could stop, manipulate, or alter.

Complimented? I think not! I was being offered up as a "sacrificial lamb" because I had no really important connections in this new career in this new place. As an unknown I had to decide whether to try to serve my Chinese colleagues who knew so much more than I did or just plain "duck out." As Mr. Pang explained the dilemma of our Chinese friends, I began to realize that in this moment of crisis or decision my loyalties lay with those who knew what the Church stood for and what appeared to be best for Chung Chi College. I opted to help out.

The official meeting of the College Board was held in R.O. Hall's office conference room. We were gathered around several large tables pushed together. I'll never forget how nervous I was at age 34 among three or four much older missionaries and seven or eight mature Chinese Christian board members. The chair of the Board, Daniel Au, excused himself as Bishop Hall assumed the chair for nominating the next president of Chung Chi College. A friend of the Bishop nominated the absent chair, and I immediately raised my hand to gain the floor. I was afraid that the nominations would be closed hastily. To the surprise of some, I nominated Dr. D.Y. Lin, stating that he was an academic, a sincere member of the Hakka Church, and one who could lead us to finding a college site in the New Territories. Quickly seconded by a Chinese businessman, it appeared to me that the surprised Bishop for the first time saw a threat to his plan to control the destiny of a college he had founded and named. The vote by secret ballot was called for. The ballots were opened by R.O. and placed in full view on the table. One pile quickly grew; the other had only two or three slips. R.O. Hall announced that the next president of Chung Chi College was Dr. D.Y. Lin. The Bishop's Chinese friends had deserted him. I never regretted my decision but was sad to lose my association with this very brilliant man. I was never again invited to Bishop's House to discuss any matters relating to the church or the college.

I had served as a founding member of Chung Chi College and continued on the Board for another ten years. As predicted, D.Y. Lin was energetic, capable, and able to persuade his fellow ethnic Hakka friends to sell an entire valley to the college. The village in that valley had for a number of generations been unable to produce sons. They had to bring in sons from other Hakka villages. The sale enabled them to relocate about 20 miles away to a very favorable business and farming area near Fanling. The college with the help of the Luce Foundation and funds from many church sources built a beautiful campus. By eliminating the wet rice fields, malaria and other severe health problems were eliminated. A train station was built by the rail authority. In ten years' time, the HongKong government agreed that a Chinese university should be created to serve the Chinese-speaking community. This meant that higher education in the Chinese language was assured. Two other colleges, United and New Asia, were placed together on the mountain site with Chung Chi. Each maintained a kind of separate identity but together formed the Chinese University of HongKong now financed by the HongKong government.

Much later, Chung Chi developed a solid Theological School financed by the Christian churches. A graduate School of Social Work now offers the MSW and the DSW degrees.

In the fall of 1955 Ray Whitehead, Don Mayer and Ralph Meyer, students at Elmhurst College, came to HongKong to work for three months as volunteers. We found them jobs in New Asia and United Colleges as well as several unregistered Chinese refugee colleges. They had paid for their travel, but were given a small living expense stipend by our E&R Mission Board. Our Mission group enjoyed their time with us. All three went on to Eden Seminary in Missouri. Ray earned his doctorate and with his wife Rhea joined our Mission in HongKong, and later worked many years with the United Church of Canada, Rhea in the Overseas Mission Service and Ray as a seminary professor.

1956 – Bonnie Joins Our Family

Barbara Brown, promptly known as Bonnie, was born February 9th. A real joy to all of us, she was a special consolation for Barbara following her earlier loss. Bonnie had a bubbly personality from the very beginning. Karen (9), Chris (7½), and Kim (3) were a great help with her. Our special friend, Rev. John Ma baptized Bonnie at a service in the China Congregational Church.

With the increasing size of family, we had to secure a larger vehicle. The Austin was retired to serve the HK Christian Council Audio Visual Committee. The family fit nicely in a Morris station wagon.

I had been nursing my knee injury from Huping days for some time. Once, while supervising the construction of the stone clinic in Rennie's

Mill, I jumped down an embankment and twisted it. By 1956 it had become so unstable that even a minimal twist caused collapse. The torn cartilage was removed surgically which resulted in full recovery.

After several years in HongKong we got right into the spirit of Chinese New Year, an annual spring festival in late January or early February when the entire population took off from work and literally enjoyed nearly a week of festivities, lighting firecrackers and sending a variety of rockets into the air in the evenings. Colorful paper gods were pasted on the front doors or lintels of houses. Sometimes even incense sticks were lit and placed in sandy pots or tins. Homes were swept and if people had small altars to the gods in their homes they made sure to smear honey or sugar water over the lips of the idols. As a part of the lunar calendar, the Communists renamed the New Year, "Spring Festival," because they felt that too many of the customs involved the local gods of past eras.

The markets were alive in the evenings, as everyone in HongKong wanted a plum blossom branch, paper whites, or other flowers for the big event. We often went to the New Year's market to see all the "goodies" for sale. The first time we went with the Brungers, all of our children in tow, we put them on our shoulders by turn so they could see what was going on. Once we were caught in a tight moving crowd and were frightened about keeping our footing. Sometimes we would stop to watch jugglers and stilt walkers perform. Then there were always people crowded around the "Punch & Judy" shows. Of course, they passed the hat for showing their skills. Delicious custard tarts were the best treat.

Our move from a 5th-storey walk-up in the business district to a quiet residential home was indeed a blessing for the whole family. The small yard was gated so the children could safely play with tricycle, wagon and dog Flop on the driveway. A busy hillside bordered the drive and here Kim found big fat caterpillars to lovingly caress. Conrad and Cassandra, children of a British physician neighbor family, were playmates. Conrad and Chris were chums even though Conrad liked to tell Chris that he had no germs because his father was a doctor. At our suggestion, Chris matched this bragging with proclaiming that he had no sins because his father was a minister! Only once did we have a huge firetruck come with sirens screaming to put out a frightening brush fire on our hillside which we could not extinguish. A chastened and very sobered Chris confessed that he and Conrad, playing with matches, had been the culprits.

We continued to take the family to one of the beaches often. These excursions were sometimes picnics. Karen and Chris would help with the two younger ones, so we all enjoyed the swimming, family time, and outdoor recreation.

We managed to learn the geography of the colony in order to visit new beaches or vistas on the hills surrounding Kowloon. This part of HongKong was on the mainland and was named Gau Lung (nine dragons) because of the nine peaks surrounding the harbor. Our trips were memorable because of the beautiful scenery itself. We did at times cross the harbor by car ferry and then drive around the island itself or take the tramway up to the famous "Peak," the highest point of the island.

Crossing the Dragon's Back

In 1954, when the planning for the building of Haven of Hope was moving forward in our Rennie's Mill Clinic Committee (very slowly, I might add), it became obvious that Rennie's Mill Camp was so inaccessible, staffing would become a very difficult problem. We noted that physicians were unwilling to spend a full half day in travel by launch from Shaukiwan or by rowboat from Hanghau across Junk Bay. I asked Dr. Helffrich, the executive of our Commission on World Service, if he could secure some refugee work funds in order to build an access road to Junk Bay. He said he would get the money if I could get HK government permission. With dollars promised, I went to Dennis Bray, the District Officer, who took the request to the District Commissioner, Mr. Barnett, who saw this as a way to open up another area of the New Territories.

We were told that we could use the existing Anderson's Road that was originally a Japanese mini-jeep (a 3-wheeled motorcycle) trail to anti-aircraft batteries high above Kun Tong during World War II. Abandoned, the roadway was being used by trucks to a stone quarry for about a mile and then it became a small walking/biking trail for villagers who lived adjacent to the gap through which we needed to cut in order to reach Rennie's Mill Camp. Our first action was to check with two villages on the route to secure permission to extend the road. This issue was easily resolved as the villagers sought to get their produce to market. In fact, part of Anderson's Road already open to several stone quarries was being used by Mr. Tong, who owned a used VW minibus to transport villagers and workers as far as the road was passable. He later became the primary bus service for Rennie's Mill Camp.

We started in late 1955 to recruit refugees from Rennie's Mill who did not have an opportunity for work because they lived so far from town. Two hundred refugees applied for our guaranteed ten days of work at the going rate for laborers, a very low wage. We told them that after everyone had completed their two weeks' effort, we would select forty or fifty workers to complete the road.

Maang Hau, the contractor with whom we worked on Laan Tau Island, walked the hillsides many times with me to find a feasible vehicle route. A foreman of some experience was selected. A former army officer, he was a canny and talented director of men. A young graduate of Chung Chi College, Peter Wen, was hired as a liaison person with Maang Hau to carry the weekly payroll and to keep time sheets and accounts.

Without any heavy equipment the men used picks and shovels, carried baskets of dirt with a bamboo pole, and used large tree trunks as levers. The workers literally moved huge boulders and dug the decomposed granite of the mountainside.

A British Army sergeant who was a friend of Dr. Harverson's Emmanuel Church was able to get his captain to give him permission to have a training exercise on blasting to take care of a very difficult stone ridge corner that formed a barrier for cars and lorries.

Negotiations with the village at the gap became serious when we learned that they considered the ridge the back of a dragon. Years earlier the villagers had made a walking trail across the dragon's back. They believed that act had angered the dragon so they had suffered for years a serious dearth of male children. They did not want any more misfortune so wanted assurances that we would properly propitiate all the spirits and the dragon itself. This we promised by offering to undertake appropriate ceremonies and feasts, as well as food supplies for the gods (read that as for all village elders). Maang Hau undertook negotiations and told Peter and me to stay away from any discussions with villagers. Peter was a northerner and I a foreigner so we obeyed. While negotiations took place, the workers from Rennie's Mill kept busy building the road around many bends and curves down the mountainside toward Junk Bay.

The negotiations concluded successfully with the approval of District Officer Bray who pointed out to the villagers the great economic advantage they would gain when they could ride into town and ship their produce to markets. Successful conclusion also included Taoist priests and their helpers who conducted a "crossing the dragon's back ceremony." All of us were properly respectful as long strings of firecrackers were fired, gongs beaten loudly, and flags or banners wildly waved. Chinese musical flutes and two-string violins screeched eerily as we told the dragon we were friendly and were borrowing his strong back to carry us from one side of the mountain to the other.

When Mr. Bray and I had carefully spaded some soil from the path of the proposed road, the marchers headed to the village for the feasts. The two of us were glad to escape at that point the revelry and drinking of rice wine and beer that was promised the villagers. I cannot remember the actual cost of this ceremony and meal, but was told that we really got off very reasonably — just the normal cost of doing business with a village.

The road was opened in November 1956 after the Haven of Hope was officially opened in 1955, but the workers who had faithfully built it were pleased with the extended work period. It seems to me that we spent somewhere in the neighborhood of US $15,000 to complete the job. It was a very rough road, a simple, single dirt track later named PO LAM Road. Helen Wilson, who was the actual founder of Rennie's Mill Church Clinic, had suggested that it be named after Barbara Whitener using her Chinese name, Po Lam "Precious Jade." Mr. Barnett, District Commissioner, officially opened the road dressed in white uniform, cocked hat, and long ceremonial sword – a fitting ceremony conducted in Chinese and English. Today it is a major four-lane highway linking Kun Tong and Junk Bay, serving more than 300,000 people, and still named Po Lam Road.

Riots, Typhoons and Hillside Fires

Early in the fall of 1957, HongKong was the scene of riots as anti-Communists and Communist factions battled each other. We kept indoors for a few days while the police quelled the looting mobs. Though the incident started over a flag of one group being pulled down by the other, it was obvious that the overcrowding, joblessness, high living costs, and the tension of feeling completely powerless prevailed.

HongKong had its annual typhoon (oriental hurricane) season. Almost every year at least one or two would hit the colony. Damage was extensive. Even large oceangoing vessels would be lifted up on the shore. Small craft would be crushed and tar-paper shacks would be devastated. For several years, we had to replace the asbestos type roofing on the wards of Haven of Hope. Fortunately, the good sand brick walls were sturdy enough to withstand the strong typhoon winds. In spite of such heavy rains during typhoons, the colony relied on reservoirs for water. If the rains were light, we faced water restrictions. In 1956, our water hours were cut for a period to three hours every other day. Survival for many depended on long lines at the public water taps because most of the squatter villages did not have any running water system.

One typhoon reminded us that no one was 100% safe from the damages a typhoon could inflict. The quarters for our amah/maid were directly behind our home. Very comfortably arranged, they were located near a rather tall wall that was built to protect the hillside due to the cut to a lower level where a large apartment building was being erected. The devastating rain softened the hillside behind the wall and collapsed part of the living quarters of our amah. It took quite some time for the hillside to be stabilized and the wall and building reconstructed.

In early 1955, the ShekKipMei hillside fire had alerted the world to the plight of refugees who had flocked to HongKong in the years following World War II and the 1949 takeover by the Chinese Communist Party of the government of China. The "Pearl of the Orient" was filled by former Chiang Kaishek army personnel, farmers' sons who were seeking their fortune and by job seekers from all over China. Crowded into tar-paper shack communities and perched precariously on unstable hillsides, these were concentrations of squalor. There were no sanitary facilities, no electricity except what they could steal by hanging wires from utility lines passing nearby and no organized drainage system for wastewater. Over the years following World War II, there had been a number of fires in these illegal hillside communities, but they had been relatively small.

ShekKipMei was different. Nearly 40,000 people lost their homes. With my 16 mm. camera I had just purchased, I was able to take movies of this catastrophic fire as well as the aftermath the next day. I filmed some of the devastation. This huge "squatter village" was completely destroyed. The film was used by our Mission Board to make a professional documentary film to use in fund raising projects for refugee work. The site of this first major fire at ShekKipMei was used by the HongKong government in

1957 to build the first of a series of seven storey buildings to resettle home-less refugees.

This major disaster created a response in the USA. Dr Helfferich sent us a cable he was sending $10,000 to match the Pope to rebuild housing for the refugees.

Katrina Enters Our Lives

Later a second fire broke out in an area called HoManTin. Not nearly as steep or as populous as other areas, it had also been filled with tar-paper and wooden shacks, the HongKong government Resettlement Department already had in place some plans to replace this area with small row houses as a temporary measure.

Church World Service was allotted space in HoManTin to build 25 small units for fire victims. Bulldozers cleared the land. Along with the housing were built public latrines; water and electricity provided. Each person was allocated 35 sq. ft. so families of four often crowded into rooms 10' x 12'. Whenever E&R Church visitors came from America, we always took them to visit the HoManTin project to see what our Church had helped build.

Thus, in 1956 we escorted the Secretary of our Mission Board, The Rev. William Shaffer and his wife, Katherine, to visit the work of resettlement as well as the other work the Church was undertaking in association with ecumenical bodies and the HongKong Council of the Church of Christ in China of which we were a part. As the Shaffers visited, they were greatly interested in the people being served. In Homantin we were followed by a lively group of children of school age. Mrs. Shaffer was surprised to learn that almost all schools operated on two shifts and that even the Government schools charged a tuition and book fee.

Mrs. Shaffer noticed a small girl of about eight years carrying a baby on her back. Intrigued by the way the child could keep smiling while carrying such a heavy load, Mrs. Shaffer asked me to talk with her. Kneeling down to speak with her, I learned that she lived in a nearby cottage space with a large family of grandmother, parents and children, the youngest the baby on her back. Mrs. Shaffer wrote after returning to the USA that she was haunted by the lovely face of the little girl who was not in school because she had to care for the baby of the family. She asked me to find out what could be done.

After receiving Mrs. Shaffer's heartfelt letter, I visited the family in Homantin with whom the child was living. The family's meager livelihood came from making small cones over a charcoal fire to supply street ice cream cone vendors. They were caring for FungKiu, "Sweet Phoenix," because she and her mother had been the family's neighbors in the burned out squatter village where they had been living. Later, when FungKiu's mother died, Kei Ma, the grandmother of the family, insisted on taking her in, but she would have to take care of the grandbaby to earn her keep. Since FungKiu was not blood-related, she could actually have been considered a "muy jai" (slave girl), a practice outlawed in the British Colony many years earlier. There was no money to send her to school. I told the family of our interest in finding a school for FungKiu. After negotiation with the grandmother's assistance, the figure of HongKong $1 per day (US$3.50 per month) was agreed upon as compensation for the loss of her labor. A missionary friend, Loren Noren, of the American Northern Baptist Mission helped enter FungKiu into their Swatow Church School in Homantin. Tuition, books, and uniform costs totaled about US$6.50 per month. Though difficult and quite a change for her, Fung Kiu studied hard and in two years made up a grade and was closer to her peers.

Life with Kei Ma's family, however, was very difficult. A new baby arrived every year, so the limited quarters became more crowded and more work was expected of her. It was at this point we went home on a year's furlough to North Carolina.

Mrs. Shaffer continued to send the grandmother, Kei Ma, US$10 each month for Katrina's schooling. After we returned to HongKong in 1959, Kei Ma came to visit me in my office for the first time. She was very distressed and had a difficult time telling me that all was not well in the family living situation. There was grumbling that FungKiu took up space and conflicts were not easy to resolve. The children were growing; the younger sons were now in their teens and FungKiu was only nine. She was not family. Then Kei Ma finally got to her point: she feared that FungKiu would be molested by the boys. She appealed to me to find some way to protect and care for the girl.

I went immediately to seek advice from a friend working in the HongKong Social Welfare Department, Ms. Dorothy Lee, a supervisor for Children's work. She kindly sent a caseworker right away to confirm the home situation. She reported to me the next day that FungKiu, having been born in the British Crown Colony, could become a "Ward of Queen Elizabeth of England." This made her eligible for care as an orphan. I told her that we had a sponsor, Mrs. Shaffer, in Philadelphia who was helping her at the present time. This could be continued if she was placed in Children's Garden, an excellent facility operated by the Christian Children's Fund. Ms. Lee made the arrangements immediately, so that the sponsor's $15 check was sent each month to the head office in the US.

Children's Garden was a lovely place, situated out of the city and reached by a small ferry. The children lived in small cottages as family units with housemothers. They helped with the cooking and housekeeping. They attended school and religious services and were permitted to visit in town on occasion. We were able to visit FungKiu a few times and she came to spend some time with us during her holiday periods. She mostly visited with Kei Ma, as there was a strong bond between them.

Katrina thrived at Children's Garden, excelling at academics and winning math and English awards. Her confidence grew, and in her junior and senior years she was class leader. She grew physically, mentally, and spiritually.

It was not until after our furlough of 1963-1965 that she spent more time with us in our home in Kowloon and also on Laan Tau, our vacation spot. As she matured she felt more at ease with our family, and we with her. She wanted an English name. It was hard to choose one that sounded like FungKiu, though the meaning, "Sweet Phoenix," was very special. Finally, we thought it meaningful to give her a name that was a variation of Katherine, the name of her wonderful benefactor, Katherine Shaffer. She liked "Katrina" best of the selection, and it was easily pronounced. She has been Katrina ever since.

Furlough - Salisbury, North Carolina 1957 – 1958

In preparing for this furlough, I knew that others could manage the farflung affairs of the refugee programs in which I had been involved. I also felt confident that being absent for a year would not be difficult for the HongKong Church of Christ in China. I looked forward to sharing with congregations of our new United Church of Christ the excitement of our work in HongKong.

I had just been selected to assist Dr. Peter Wong as Welfare Secretary. I did not know what that would involve but knew that my connections with the Colonial Government workers was one way the Churches were able to secure locations for schools, churches and social service centers.

We left HongKong for the USA in June 1957. For the first time in our transpacific crossings we traveled by plane, hopping from Hong Kong to Taiwan to Japan on to Kiska, Anchorage, Seattle, Chicago and on to Charlotte. It was a long flight on the prop plane, but our four children (2 ½ - 9) were good travelers. We had bulkhead seats so were able to bed the little ones down on the floor to sleep and the stewardesses were very helpful.

It was a blessing to have this furlough year back home in Salisbury where we were able to rent a large furnished house. Spending time with Barbara's mother, sister, Lois and family was most meaningful. We had frequent happy get-togethers, giving the children a chance to learn to know their cousins. We often grilled hamburgers, a new eating experience for us. Caring for our family without an amah's help was also a new and busy experience for Barbara.

After settling in at Salisbury, we spent the summer in our sparsely furnished Blowing Rock cabin and continued making various improvements. We had the jungle of rhododendrons in front and back of the cabin bulldozed out to create a real yard. The children loved the outdoor play, especially in the creek now accessible in the front yard, where they spent much time in the frigid water searching for crayfish and salamanders. For six weeks I commuted down steep Globe Road to our church's John's River Valley Camp to serve as Missions teacher.

In Salisbury Karen and Chris settled well into Frank B. John Elementary School, but had to be tutored at home in "pounds, shillings and pence" for returning to their British school in Hong Kong. Kim attended St. John's Lutheran Kindergarten. Barbara fitted in an evening course in Speedwriting at Salisbury Business College in order to help me when we returned to our Hong Kong office.

My furlough year was spent making Mission deputation visits all over the country. I helped lead three conferences, went to five synod meetings to present International Missions, preached fifteen times and showed slides of Hong Kong 14 times. I was proud to have had a part in recruiting Myles and Donna Walburn who served in Indonesia and Hong Kong. Later Myles held the position of treasurer of United Church Board for World Ministries.

In the fall I particularly enjoyed representing the Hong Kong Council of the Church of Christ in China at the founding of the United Church of

Christ by presenting a large scroll to the assembly in Cincinnati. Our new denomination was formed from the union of the Evangelical and Reformed Church and the Congregational Christian Church. We are very proud of our active and liberal denomination.

On a trip to Walla Walla, Washington I met another Sterling Whitener, possibly some distant cousin. His forbears had migrated from North Carolina to Missouri late in the 19th century, then later on west. The name, Sterling, seems to have come from the interconnection in western North Carolina with Scottish clans that originated in Sterlingshire, the Scottish lowlands. I have Scottish heritage, as my grandmother was a Kincaid.

We were so pleased to have a visit in Salisbury from our good Canadian friends, Doug and Fran Dalziel and family who had been so kind and helpful to us in Hankow at the time of Chris' birth and the Communist takeover.

Our furlough ended in August 1958, but we spent the first part of the summer in our mountain cabin. Rebekah Wang from Hong Kong stayed with us there during those weeks. She had come to North Carolina to enter Catawba College in the fall. We had a longstanding connection with the Wang family going back to Yoyang in China. Rebekah's grandfather was Wang Yo-san, the Nationalist general who was a leader in the church in 1946 when Barbara and I arrived in China. He was martyred by the Communists in 1950 because he was a landowner. Rebekah and her family escaped from Shanghai to Hong Kong and we knew the family there. Her father, Wang Kai, worked with me as bookkeeper at Haven of Hope and her mother Wu Yi became a teacher in a resettlement school. Rebekah, herself, became a research scientist. As our guest in the mountains that summer, she joined right in the wild strawberry and blackberry picking and it was a pleasure having her with us.

In 1958 we planted five acres of white pines in the mistaken belief that they would send our children to college. At the same time that the pine seedlings were planted I started a small Christmas tree farm with about 1,000 Fraser fir seedlings pulled from Roan Mountain. Each year, growers were invited to come for an annual pull for a very low price. There was a very great deal I did not know about such a venture but through the ensuing years my little farm provided a small harvest of about 30 beautiful trees every December. Each spring I enjoyed pruning them by hand. We sold the Christmas trees to interested friends or gave them to our Church or family members.

It was not easy for us in those days to keep paying that $25 per month for a home that we could use only very infrequently, so we rented the cottage when we were overseas. We had some good renters as well as some who were less desirable.

It had been a very happy and satisfying furlough and ended with an outstanding three week camping adventure. We left Salisbury in late July towing a Heil trailer, borrowed from Uncle Leonard, to camp across the country. Lois and Paul Carter and children, Scott and Kristen traveled with us with their own camping rig. We drove our 1953 Buick to the sound of Bonnie singing The Purple People-Eater - "Ooo Eee Ooo Ah Ah Ting Tang Walla Walla Bing Bang!" We had a great time camping at Mesa Verde, Grand Canyon, spending a night in Reno, and visiting more relatives in San Francisco. On the down side, Karen had broken her arm while we visited relatives in Missouri and was unhappily limited in some of the fun activities along the way. Lois and Paul towed our trailer back to Salisbury; we sold our Buick and flew from San Francisco to Hong Kong.

The work there was waiting, and this time I had a secretary who could sit on my lap. Barbara took up the job, but didn't have much time for office lap sitting.

Return to HongKong – 1958 to 1963

The era to be recounted here represents five years of our service in HongKong. On our return we became immersed again in HongKong life. I was asked by Peter Wong, the executive of the Church of Christ in China, HongKong Council, to work with government officials to secure land for the building of the new Morrison Center to house the church offices. We really had outgrown our rented facilities. We were able to build an auditorium as well as provide offices for all those who served educational, social welfare, and audiovisual work.

The Church also received funds from various mission boards to start an industrial project, so we began a Mechanics Training Program. A Canadian missionary and a Scots layman together developed an excellent program that later secured HongKong government funding to build a large industrial training school that included auto mechanics. The original class of mechanics really did well as Paul Chan, MongKok Church member became a teacher. He later immigrated to Colorado where he owns his own car repair business.

The Chuen Yuen Church in Tsuen Wan had grown along with the village. I was invited to be the advisory pastor assisting a new pastor. When we first came to HongKong the church was surrounded by fields and the village had a population of 15,000. Now five years later in a bustling industrial city, the church was struggling to meet many new needs. The young pastor, David Kao, asked me to perform his wedding ceremony. I must admit I was much more nervous than either bride or groom. It was my first wedding in Cantonese.

Our children were thriving in the British school system getting a thorough educational grounding. Barbara was involved in Kowloon Union Church. In handling our own Mission office, she efficiently wrote letters, kept up with reports and managed all the telephone calls.

In March 1959, Barbara was asked by International Social Service to escort five Chinese orphans to New York. The children aged eighteen months to fourteen years were welcomed by adoptive parents In Chicago and New York. Her free ride, rather "her challenging experience," also entitled her to ten days in NC with her family. She had a wonderful visit but it was a tough time for me. My urgent letter to Salisbury to Barbara: "Please hurry home! I'm just not cut out to be mommy, taxi driver, and alarm clock, nose-wiper, picker-upper and backer-upper!" Even more, added to my job description was "nurse" as Bonnie, age 3, managed to come down with the measles. I telephoned Barbara to hurry home from Tokyo where she had a layover. Needless to say, we all gave her an exuberant and rousing welcome back home.

It was obvious to me that paying high rent for a place to live was not an economic use of mission funds when it was possible to purchase a building with a lease extending until 1997. By a treaty of 1898, land in Kowloon was available only by Crown lease to run until it was returned to China in 1997. A building with four apartments, built by a Communist movie company in bankruptcy, became available at 11B Cambridge Road in Kowloon. I persuaded Church World Service and the US Methodist Women's Mission to join us to buy the residence. We bought the building to be held for us by the Church of Christ in China. It was directly under the Kai Tak Airport landing path. There were times when the roar of jet engines meant that all normal conversation ceased for a few minutes. The apartments were convenient to transportation for all, so we greatly enjoyed the move. We occupied a large ground floor apartment. The children enjoyed a center court for play. Later, I calculated that in the twenty years the Mission owned the two apartments, the savings ran to over $250,000. The building itself was donated to the Church of Christ in China in 1975, which meant a new school building or other facility could be funded when it was sold to developers.

On one occasion a refugee father came to us for help to care for his family, a son and a six-year-old daughter, while he searched for work. We found a place for the boy but took Siu Ling into our home for three weeks. It was a unique experience but a joyful one, too. We were proud of the way our children welcomed her and played with her. She went happily to a nearby Chinese school and loved being with our kids. She even enjoyed our Western food. She left, happy to be back with her brother and father when he had located a job on a farm in the New Territories.

Our good friend Helen Wilson was diagnosed with cancer in October 1959. We were crushed but Helen had the answer: "If we Christians really believe what we say we believe, what is there to be upset about?" Helen's leaving was a great blow to the Rennie's Mill Church Clinic as she had single-handedly operated the Clinic for a number of years. A big, retirement send-off was in order, as the refugees she had served insisted on many feasts and presents (which many of them could ill afford). Weeks later we learned with great relief that the diagnosis was mistaken and surgery corrected the problem. A miracle, it seemed, as she continued to serve her community in Aberdeen, Scotland, for a number of years.

Refugee Invasion

The early 1960s was an interesting time, as there were many refugee issues rising to the forefront. The HongKong government struggled to resettle one million refugees in just a few years. (Please note that one million was the total refugee population in Palestine which was never resettled.) The World Refugee Year did bring funds from the USA and Europe. Hundreds of seven-story H-style buildings were erected, each housing as many as 1,000 persons. The rooms were much too crowded and small for a family, allowing only 35 square feet per person. Even with communal bathrooms, located in the cross section of the H providing electricity and water faucets for each floor, conditions were extremely crowded. Children were able to go to primary classes on the rooftop schools. From 1960 to 1962, a series of events in China, including one of Mao's political purges, floods, some drought conditions, and crop failure, forced many thousands of ordinary farm workers and city dwellers in the southern provinces to try to enter HongKong to find jobs.

On a visit to our small Sheung Shui Church near the border to Communist China I found that a number of young people were being sheltered and fed there. Our woman evangelist must have assisted hundreds of refugees to make contact with relatives in town. In fact, the influx of refugees was so great on the border they had actually pushed over the chain link fence separating the colony from China. It was quite clear that people were hungry, so the Communist soldiers did not stop the fleeing multitudes. When they got across the border, however, the British army had the task of rounding them up and loading them in trucks to be returned. The colony was overflowing and could not cope with thousands more. One thing the government did first; they fed each person before return to the border. It was noted that many made the trip more than once because they were hungry. On one occasion even Chung Chi College students made regular trips to our church near the border to pick up college-age young people. They provided clothing (and even permanents for the austerely bobbed girls) and then escorted them en masse onto crowded trains so that identity cards were almost impossible to check. The HongKong government had a most difficult job because of the universal concern for the plight of the individual refugee. Many families were directly involved because relatives were among those detained and deported. Literally thousands of people made the 25-mile trip from HongKong and Kowloon out to the border area and tramped the hills, calling out names, hoping to make contact. When long-parted relatives did find each other, their joy was overwhelming. In one case it was just too much for one young British officer, on duty for hours, whose unhappy task it was to separate a reunited mother and daughter. A quick shove to the girl toward her mother and his turned back was dramatic demonstration of the compassion felt by many of those compelled to follow the orders of their government.

Among some boys hiding in the church was a young child Miss Lau, the evangelist said had a note to relatives in town. She asked me to take him with me in our car. It was a tough decision since I knew it was illegal. She made a strong case, including some scripture references, so I decided to take him to town through the police checkpoints. The Chinese policemen waved us right on through, smiling widely when they realized that even the Westerners were trying to help.

The 10-year-old had never seen water come out of a pipe, nor could he figure out what a bathtub was. In fact, he rolled his eyes when I ducked his head under water to get the soap out of his hair. I am sure he thought he had come all this way only to be drowned by a big foreigner in a lot of water. After the bath we delivered him to his relatives in a nearby resettlement area. They were very wary about acknowledging that he was their kin until they were assured that there was no charge for our bringing him to Kowloon. There had been many unscrupulous gangs who organized means to smuggle in escapees but charged monstrous sums for their services, capitalizing shamefully on family love and loyalty. In this case we assured the family that we were from the church so they opened their locked door and joyfully opened their arms. His father had died in some unknown place with the Communist army; his mother could no longer feed him so sent him to her brother in Hong Kong.

1960, World Refugee Year also brought funds to our Junk Bay Medical Relief Council. The Norwegian government sent US$50,000 for work with TB cases, which resulted in screening over 20,000 people with a mass X-ray program. This also helped build a Children's Preventorium, particularly for families with an adult infected with TB. These pioneer projects helped in the effort to eradicate tuberculosis in the colony. It was quite clear that church groups could initiate excellent social welfare projects, but the continuation often depended on sustained governmental assistance to meet maintenance costs.

About this same time the Junk Bay Medical and Relief Committee received funds from our United Church of Christ Mission Board to build a beautiful chapel on the small hillock next to Haven of Hope. It was designed with some typical Chinese architecture and became a center for meetings and gatherings for staff. For years it stood as a focal point for the entire Junk Bay area as there was no other auditorium. After the bay was filled in by moving the mountains into the sea, the Chapel lost some of its prominence. But it was not until tall 15-story buildings were erected in the 1980s for the Po Lam Estate that one had to search for the chapel surrounded by the forest of tall buildings.

Back to our story – We did celebrate the 10th anniversary of the founding of the Rennie's Mill Church Clinic.

Reinforcements

In January 1961 we were happy to welcome Dr. & Mrs. Ben Whitehill, Rev. & Mrs. Ray Whitehead, and Rev. Carl Smith. Carl Smith was to teach at the Church of Christ in China Theological Institute. Ben and Carolyn and two small girls were living at Haven of Hope in a Mission residence we had built earlier for the Schwerdts, Ben serving as physician at clinic and hospital. Ray and Rhea were scheduled to work in industrial evangelism for the church so included study of Cantonese in a busy day. With this large Mission contingent, we had many interesting and serious discussions as to the future of missionary work and life in general.

The World Council of Churches Meets in New Delhi

Of particular interest to me was my very special and personal report of my visit to the World Council of Churches meeting held in New Delhi, India, in November. I was able to be a "press representative" of the Church of Christ in China.

The sheer magnitude of the World Council really served to overawe most of us who were there. I recall especially the impressive speeches of the Rev. Thomas a leader in the very large and active Mar Thoma Church of South India. He challenged all Asian Churches to plan immediately for fiscal independence. His call to cast off a dependent role was a major challenge because the effects of wartime Japanese occupation and destruction had reinforced dependence on Western resources. The beauty and pageantry of the rainbow colors of church stoles and garments was overwhelming since the Orthodox prelates displayed their sartorial splendor without pause. It was a remarkable show!

Our new Mission Board executive of our United Church of Christ, Dr. David Stowe our neighbor in language school, joined me to visit the Taj Mahal. We were in luck that we found an interested group to share a taxi on a night with a full moon. No sight could match that experience. We both commented that if his wife, Virginia, and mine, Barbara, were with us the night would have been perfect! A visit since in daylight hours captured its beauty but under a full moon it is quite unforgettable.

I was so excited in New Delhi that I undertook to take slides of every nation's Christian representatives from Africa to Zanzibar. The only trouble was, on my return to HongKong, my Mission colleagues good-naturedly razzed my "enlightening" presentation of 200 color slides. You are right;

I have never lived it down! To this day at our subsequent reunions, I am reminded of the folly of trying to show so many BORING slides. A note: I did learn my lesson.

Following the World Council meeting, Bob Moss, future UCC president, and Don Dearborn, Catawba professor and future president of the college, were our guests in HongKong. We were so pleased to have them in our home and give them a glimpse of our work.

We Welcome Dana

On August 16th we welcomed Dana into the family delivered by Ben Whitehill our new Mission doctor. Chris threatened to call her "Crumbs" at first because she was another "crummy girl," not a brother for him. He had, however, a real knack for getting her to sleep when she had colic. He really enjoyed carrying her around. We asked our HongKong Council Church of Christ in China Executive Director, Dr. Peter Wong, to baptize Dana at our home.

Bonnie was an enthusiastic member of the True Light Kindergarten, the only blonde child among 30 Chinese preschoolers. She picked up Cantonese very quickly. Karen and Chris were always helpful with Dana, a very welcome fact for Barbara had taken over household duties of cooking, shopping and laundry. With having a washing machine, a weekly cleaning lady and the help of Karen and Chris, we got along fine

In HongKong our lives continued and we did still find time for relaxation. Barbara and I tried to take Friday afternoons off to go hiking or drive to a distant beach for a swim. Barbara took on more jobs at Kowloon Union Church, serving on the council and helping the committee with plans to build and furnish a new Sunday school building.

We also trekked to Laan Tau, treasuring our vacation there. One summer Peter Jenkins was burning paper in his trash pit when he saw a small snake. Intrepid Dr. Jenkins grabbed the tail, snapped it to stun it, and put it in a jar only to find that it rose straight up and opened its hood - a baby cobra. He killed it to make sure no one was harmed. Great excitement when the children took the jar to school!

New Help for Junk Bay Work – Don and Corinne Bergmann

Our requests for additional help for Haven of Hope Sanatorium and Rennie's Mill Church Clinic were answered by our Board in sending Don and Corinne Bergmann and family to HongKong in 1962. They were great sports, as they were to live in a small building perched on the hillside above Rennie's Mill Refugee Camp. This involved a daily trip into town on the winding Po Lam Road to get the children to school. Don was the business manager of the hospital, while nurse Corinne helped in clinic and everywhere else. If anyone would like to hear about the challenges of "missionary service" you should write to get some of Corinne's descriptive writings of those days when the rains literally brought floods of water through their living room!

For six months I was asked to serve as director of Church World Service when the director took a short leave. It was clearly a time of stress as Typhoon Wanda, a massive storm that destroyed the livelihood of many, hit the colony hard. Relief services were stretched to the utmost and the churches responded. Besides relief services, CWS had a number of special projects to manage. One was the knitting of sweaters and another was the making of neckties for sale back in the US. To my chagrin all the neckties had used Chinese silk which was banned for sale in the USA. It was a personal relief to have the director back by Chinese New Year of 1963. He came back in time for us to plan our furlough.

Furlough – 1963 to 1965

In preparing for this furlough, I had a great sense of anticipation. Since 1958 I had been immersed in work with refugees including the large number of new immigrants. Even our Chinese Churches were intimately engaged, as many new refugees were relatives of HongKong families. It was clear that changes were ahead. The Chinese Church had agreed that I should study so that we could more effectively communicate with the growing emphasis of the Colony on training young people to provide services which would be needed in the future. It was quite evident that it would not be sustainable in the world economy to continue to train young people to work in small factories making plastics and inexpensive clothing for world markets. HongKong labor had become more educated and skilled and other countries had begun to woo the making of plastic items as well as clothing.

In 1961 the first social worker with an MSW degree had been hired by the British Colony. He was a Canadian whose skill was immediately evident. I asked Peter Wong if he would support my securing a Social

Work degree to facilitate the interface between our Church and the HK Government Social Welfare Department. He considered the idea important enough to support my request to our Mission Board for an extension of furlough to complete the two year program. I had applied and been accepted at the University of North Carolina School of Social Work. I was excited about the future and the prospects for the Church to serve the people of HongKong with new insights and skills.

Heading to the USA, April 1963, and Camping through Europe

Earlier I had ordered a Volkswagen station wagon from Germany to be delivered in Naples. I had also written to Mr. Heil, a member of our E & R Church in San Francisco, who built trailers for everything. We had used the Heil lightweight camping trailer belonging to my Uncle Leonard to cross the USA in 1958. I asked Mr. Heil if we could buy a camping trailer from his company to take through Europe. He replied that as he had no agent in HongKong, he would appoint me as an agent, sell and send me a trailer at cost. What a break!

When the trailer arrived, we designed small, low folding chairs made to place around a table that we pulled out of the trailer from under the bed. Designing the cabinet spaces we would need was a skill Barbara must have learned from her mother, who specialized in intricate storage facilities! It was amazing how things fit together for daily living and for bedrolls, etc. We would sleep five of us in the foldout tent — naturally the driver and the cook got to sleep on the small spring mattress. All others had foam mattresses and sleeping bags; Karen, Chris and Dana on the floor of the tent. Kim and Bonnie were to sleep in the back of the Volkswagen station wagon we had ordered, where the back seat folded down. No space was wasted as we folded everything into the trailer. We demonstrated the system to the amazement of our missionary friends and Chinese church leaders, inviting them to come to "Open Tent Day" to make peanut butter sandwiches, as we would be doing through Europe. I should have taken them up on all the bets as they insisted we couldn't make it through Europe at all!

We sailed on the Asia, an Italian ship, to Naples in mid-April 1963 with stops along the way in Malaysia, India, and Africa. This story is told fully in a document Barbara penned, called "The Gypsy Travels of the Whitener Seven." We landed in Naples, managed to assemble our trailer, and operationalize the new Volkswagen Variant (small station wagon) to pull it to camping sites. That was almost a miracle in itself, as the Volkswagen Company had forgotten our trailer hitch order. I spent several days having a bumper hitch made by an Italian blacksmith living in a grape orchard. He knew no more English than I knew Italian. I often told him my ideas in Chinese because I was completely frustrated. His solution to the problem was to have me draw what I needed while repeatedly filling my glass from large pitchers of his own very delicious homemade wine. I am convinced that international relations conducted in this manner could be the solution to world problems!

Our visits to Pompeii, Rome, and Pisa, then north to Switzerland, were unforgettable. The family went into Switzerland from Italy on an express train while I rode with the car and camper on a freight train through the Alpine tunnels. Camping at Interlaken surrounded by the high mountains was awe-inspiring. We even took a day trip on the cog railway to the Jungfrau for breathtaking views from the glacier on top. We washed Dana's diapers at our campground facilities and spread them under the tarpaulin cover on top of the trailer if we were on the move. Many a neighbor-camper marveled at Barbara's organization of the family. We all had our duties. Barbara did the cooking on our little pressure stove; Chris and Karen set up our camp eating system by getting out the small stools and table. I had the task of getting the camper unhooked, leveled, and the tent unfolded. We all appreciated the excellent wash-room facilities we found in the Swiss campgrounds. Notably, Karen wore hair curlers most of the time. Chris managed to eat all his souvenirs rather than consider collecting anything. At Zofingen, near Zurich, we visited a distant cousin of my mother's. Luckily one member of the family spoke excellent English. The substitute tow-bar hitch, made by our genial Italian friend, was collapsing alarmingly but we made it to nearby Germany where a proper tow-bar was installed at a VW garage.

Our kids were suitably impressed with the Danish and Norwegian young people as we crossed the North Sea to Oslo. The girls joined the boys in bare-backed and bare-chested sunbathing, even in 1963. Our travel across Norway was somewhat cooler, as there was snow on the ground in some areas. We ended with a visit to Bergen and were impressed by the antiquity of their ancient wooden churches. The oldest stave church was called Urnes Church dating from 1150 AD.

We sailed from Bergen to Newcastle in England, and from there we visited our good friend Helen Wilson in Aberdeen, Scotland. After making our way to Liverpool, we sailed to Montreal before heading to New England. Our good friend Walter Hald came to meet us and took us to his home in New Haven for an enjoyable overnight visit with him and his sister before we made our way back to North Carolina. We did have an extraordinary adventure - and enough family togetherness to last a long time.

School of Social Work, Chapel Hill, NC – 1963 to 1965

There weren't any homes for rent in this university town for families our size. We had to buy one. Have you ever found that you needed a debt in order to get credit? We finally managed to get a credit card from Sears and bought something. With that we were able to find a comfortable small house in Carrboro and secure a home loan. We enclosed the attached garage to make additional bedrooms and a bathroom.

The younger children adjusted well but Karen had to learn how to cope with high school in America. There were some difficult struggles with our 16-year-old Karen as we all were indoctrinated into modern American teenage culture! We did survive letting her go on dates alone. We had early determined that both Karen and Chris would need to continue their schooling in the USA. They were sad to be leaving HongKong permanently. Karen would be entering Catawba College, but Chris would still be in High School when we returned to HongKong. We felt it would be helpful to send him to Mercersburg Academy in Pennsylvania while we were still in the US. He was unhappy there, apparently feeling he did not fit. No doubt it was linked to problems many missionary children have when readjusting to life in America. We appreciated the small United Church of Christ congregation in Chapel Hill, which helped our "foreign" family become part of the local scene.

This period turned out to be a momentous era in the USA. The tragic assassination of President Jack Kennedy rocked the nation! The beginnings of the civil rights struggle presented many challenges. We were glad for the brief opportunity to be engaged in the process of bringing justice to our society.

During my first year, I was sure that I had entered a "brainwashing" program, as I had to take the generic first year of casework studies, a mix of Rankian psychiatry and frustrated "old maid" professors. My younger brother Bob, a psychiatrist, helped me realize that fortitude and keeping my mouth shut might just win out. Fortunately, Dean Arthur Fink rescued me the second year by taking me under his wing in social work administration and permitting me to take six months of field work in community organization, the kind of courses I could use in HongKong. I found a placement with the North Carolina Fund, the predecessor of the national Anti-Poverty Program (The Economic Opportunity Act). The "casework ladies" all agreed that it would be OK if I promised not to practice social work in North Carolina, a vow I was happy to take at the time! The reasoning was that the Chapel Hill emphasis was on Casework and not Community Organization. Therefore, no graduate should be permitted to represent UNC School of Social Work who had not completed the full two years of Casework study.

Someone once asked, "If you had known what it was going to take, would you have entered the program?" My reply was always "yes" because I was confident that the profession of social work needed a boost in the eyes of the Church in HongKong. I did find this to be the case upon my return, but that is another part of this history-fable to be told later.

In 1964 - 65, my fieldwork involved the entire state of North Carolina, setting up six conferences so that counties could decide if they wanted to seek funding for Community Action. My travel was being paid per mile so I purchased a used VW bug, which worked admirably. The family used the VW station wagon. For three months of my field experience, I was assigned to Salisbury to organize a Community Action program for Rowan County. It was so successful, I was asked to take the job as director. This was definitely not in my planning, so I recruited Happy Lee who later ran off with his secretary, leaving the program very unhappy. I am not so sure about the significance of his name. I wanted to get back to HongKong.

My Masters of Social Work degree was awarded by UNC in June 1965. Karen graduated from Chapel Hill High School, a classmate of singer James Taylor. President Donald Dearborn asked me to preach the Baccalaureate sermon for commencement at Catawba College. At that time I was awarded the Doctor of Divinity degree.

Being in North Carolina again meant visits with our families. Several times we got together in our mountain home which was more and more a source of relaxation and joy. Each furlough, we had made some improvements. This time we had a new access road built. A wonderful mountaineer, Mr. Grider called "Bootblack", built the bridge. A self-educated engineer, he did it with a "doodle bug," a homemade mobile crane and tractor machine. With this he placed hemlock sleepers in the river and locust logs across the Middle Fork of the New River for our low-level bridge. Our new access road stood the test of flooding. We were really excited to see the slanting bridge still standing after a wall of water over three feet high had inundated the bottomland.

During this furlough the cottage served our growing family as a place the teenagers could stay while they worked in restaurants as waitresses, or worked in summer employment at tourist sites like Blowing Rock itself. We added two bedrooms and a bath in the basement. Barbara was with the family in the mountains while I commuted between Blowing Rock and Chapel Hill.

On August 26, 1965, we flew back to HongKong. After our full and varied two years in the US, it was with very mixed feelings that we returned to our Cambridge Road home in Kowloon without two children. We found it very hard to say goodbye to Karen and Chris.

Back in HongKong – Busy but Troubled Time

Our eldest, Karen, was now a freshman at Catawba College and finding her adjustment difficult at first, then making the Dean's list. Chris was living with my brother Bob and wife, Marion, in Greensboro attending Grimsley High School for which we were very grateful. His somewhat infrequent letters of that era revealed some of the stresses of being a teenager. He was adept at driving a car, won the State Safe Driving Championship for High School youth, and reached the national competition. In HongKong Kim and Bonnie settled well into 8th and 5th grades in King George V High School and Kowloon Junior School, while Dana enjoyed True Light Kindergarten as much as Bonnie had years earlier. Barbara settled back into activities in HongKong with more time because of the smaller family. She was again involved with Kowloon Union Church. Joining Mary Lou Allen, a long time good friend, she greatly enjoyed learning Ikebana Japanese flower arranging.

I had hoped to switch to social service planning upon my return to HongKong. Even though I got started on two new centers, I was asked to continue as planning officer for new church and school starts. This entailed helping Dr. Peter Wong, Executive Secretary, to draft background research studies for the development of a ten-year plan for the Church of Christ in China, HongKong Council. I put into action my "community organization" skills learned while working for the NC Fund. I organized a study group of young pastors, several lay church workers, and two Chung Chi College seniors. We met weekly at an inexpensive restaurant or at our home. I learned later that Peter Wong took a rather dim view of my using them as consultants. The document I finally shared with him was one that had much more grassroots input than had ever been given before. It was obvious that the HongKong Council, Church of Christ in China, faced some difficult decisions as to the kind of direction it might take in the future.

In April 1966 a series of riots disrupted the peaceful life of the colony. Similar to the pattern in other Asian countries, young people demonstrated when they found too few opportunities for livelihood, education, or self-expression. Miserably overcrowded living conditions and lack of meaningful employment boiled over as mostly teenagers took to the streets. It was a wake-up call to the colonial administration, but their response was to put more police and army units on the streets. It was about this time that great changes were taking place in China. The Cultural Revolution and Red Guard movement was under way as Mao assured the young people of China that he wanted them to take over all governmental infrastructures to root out corruption and laziness. The nearly ten years' convulsion and destruction that racked the institutional structures on the mainland obviously were reflected in the colony of HongKong.

In the 12 years since I had first arrived in HongKong, the Chinese church had become a more cohesive unit. No longer did the larger congregations ignore the problems of the smaller and more rural churches. There was a growing sense of unity and cooperation. At the same time, the methods of leadership development and selection seemed to be deteriorating. Young persons were not really encouraged to speak up in order to develop independent thinking, particularly about the future they would face in 1997 when the Colony returned to China. My growing interest was in developing integrated and cooperative projects rather than strictly denominational, self-centered, and self-serving roles. A case in point was the worldwide refugee year sponsored by the World Council of Churches. It aroused tremendous interest among philanthropic agencies. Lutheran World Service in the US sent US$10,000 to the HongKong Committee for the Refugee Year through the World Council, but when it arrived, the Lutherans claimed the funds as their right. This resulted in much bad feeling.

In our own Church of Christ in China (CCC), Dr. Peter Wong was a strong, brilliant, and charismatic leader who had really served the church by strengthening its infrastructure, its unity, and its standing in the community. He was no shrinking violet; he liked to make all of the major decisions. We did not always agree, but he always listened carefully to what I had to say. When he made a decision I accepted it and did my best to serve the Chinese church. He had agreed to my request for the study of social work since he knew we needed persons trained adequately to interface with the social welfare department of the Colony. Unfortunately, it became obvious to me that his perception of the needs of the vast population of underprivileged diverged from mine. We debated frequently on strategies for the future, particularly those facing us in 1997 when the colony returned to Chinese sovereignty.

He wanted me to take over the schools department rather than continue my deep concern for laboring people and the underemployed. I contended that I need not have spent two hard years of study for the job he wanted me to accept, but that I was not the one to make a final decision. When he made his decision, I had then to decide where I could fit in. During the fall, I had many discussions with Peter Wong. We had maintained a good relationship over the years since he was elected executive secretary of the HongKong Council, CCC. He had brought the church into the new era of growth and development.

We shared our differences in the privacy of his office. I assured him that once a decision was made I would honor it. It became clearer to me that he did not really want to develop a vibrant and leading social service program, although here was a chance to work for the era when the colonial period would definitely end. I felt I had just prepared myself to help the CCC look to the future, but Dr. Wong was turned more toward methods of the past.

The Chuen Yuen Church, previously mentioned, had continued a steady growth. Funds were raised to build a new building with a second-story sanctuary and a space on the ground floor for a youth center for industrial workers. The increasing demand for more space by the church made it essential to limit other programs. In addition, the government decision to take over all programs with industrial workers, forced a change which presaged the wave of the future. In China churches were designated to be responsible only for matters related to faith.

Opportunities to Use My Social Work Training

I remember that my greatest joy was not in securing half a dozen new sites for schools, but in finding that a new small social service center could develop a Neighborhood Youth Corps. In another area one center success-fully worked with delinquent 12 to16 year old boys in a work/study pro-gram. I found young Chung Chi College graduates who were excited to gather groups of young people in several rural Churches into study and service projects.

Opportunities were opening to share with youth of the Church my community organization skills. I also found to my great satisfaction that my two years of graduate study helped me serve a few missionary clients who had found the stress of adapting to a changing Oriental world very difficult. On several occasions I was asked by our Mission Board to help individuals from other Asian countries to find psychological and psychiat-ric professionals to help with problem areas, some related to health issues and some clearly the result of mental stress. There were very few such pro-fessionals available in HongKong, but they were helpful to some of my referrals. We found that the families with children were delighted to find our children as friends. In fact, our relationships have continued through many years.

The Crown Colony had definitely upgraded its efforts to provide qual-ity services for the people. I was glad to help prepare the materials for HongKong's report to an International Conference of Social Work. I was also asked to teach a course on community organization in the University Extension Service. It appeared to me that we needed to prepare along these lines for 1997 a short thirty years distant.

The Ending of an Era

It became clear to me that Dr. Peter Wong, the Executive Director of the HongKong Council Church of Christ In China, felt that my major work should be Education Director. This was a real blow as I had thought that the two years of new programs we had been able to initiate dem-onstrated the prospects for the future. Surely the Church might actively need to consider the longer range. A number of HongKong educators who were very familiar with the issues related to school management had been outstanding school principals. I simply could not reconcile my own call to social services with the tasks in education administration which Peter Wong was adamant I undertake.

In December 1966, after much soul-searching, Barbara and I agreed to write Peter Wong my letter of resignation. It was very difficult to know the right decision but I gave Peter the letter. He crumpled it up and told me to think it over. He did not accept my resignation. He was sure I was not serious. He certainly misread me.

In this decision to end our service of many years in HongKong, we were deeply saddened and disappointed but we felt led to return to the USA even though it had only been eighteen months since we had resettled in HongKong.

In a letter to friends we wrote in part:

> *"I have found that the Chinese Church is not fully ready for the kind of social work program to which I have become committed and for which I have received training. Thus it is for professional and personal reasons that I choose to leave the Mission field before the completion of this term. One of the personal reasons is my wholehearted support of the General Secretary of the Church of Christ in China who feels that the role of the missionary administrator needs radical reexamination. At my age I feel it wise to open this door to the Chinese Church while I can still find a job in my chosen field in the United States."*

My younger Chinese colleagues told me that I should stand up to Peter Wong and have a showdown in the HongKong Council, Church of Christ in China Executive Committee of which I was a member. I could not in good conscience publicly face a showdown with Peter Wong after years of pledging loyalty to the Church leadership. Many of the young pastors and workers I knew best later emigrated to Canada and the USA to serve the growing Chinese churches on this continent.

Jonathan Lau had been strong in my support. Earlier a student of mine at Chung Chi College, he became my highly respected colleague in the social work program. Also immigrating later to Canada, Jonathan earned a social work degree and worked in the state system with Asian immigrants. He and Cecelia continue to be our close friends.

It was a very sobering time for Barbara and me. There was no question but that the whole family, especially the teenaged Kim, felt very unhappy to leave HongKong after fourteen exciting and challenging years.

With no job certainty and with two in college we needed to consider our options. We thought that we would have only a few months of leave time. It was urgent to get some kind of employment because we would be responsible in addition for a share of our return travel expense. We eventually found an inexpensive route home through Russia. We left HongKong on the Russian ship "Baikal" to sail to Nakhodka near Vladivostok. As always we routed ourselves to see more of the world.

Travel to the USA via Russia – June 1967

The trip was exciting since it was our final trip home. We called it "The Gypsy Travels of the Whitener Five." Kim, at age 14, in her newfound maturity enjoyed the music entertainment on shipboard. Bonnie, 11, and Dana, 6, found other young people with whom to pal. Our experiences in Russia included learning to eat the simple fare, to learn that the Ussuri River border to China was not very peaceful, and to feel the warm friendship of the people with whom we traveled. We had a two day train trip from Nakhodka to Khabarovsk. The train attendant spoke very little English, so he and I conversed in Chinese. He told of the very real lack of friendship between China and Russia and the winter fighting of a few years previously.

From Khabarovsk we flew in a huge transport that had seats facing each other with a table between. Our tablemates included a family with several children the ages of Bonnie and Dana. Bonnie was enjoying playing with her favorite doll named "Skipper," dressing and changing clothes often. A little Russian girl could not keep her eyes off the doll. At one point, she tried to offer to trade her drab little doll to Bonnie for Skipper. Bonnie, who always wants to please others, was really torn, but we felt it was not right that she had to give up her favorite.

In Moscow we managed to see the usual sights. We even got tickets to the ballet *Swan Lake* at the Bolshoi. The circus was another treat. Aside from these special events, Russian life appeared extremely poor. The major department store, Gum, looked like a "run down bargain basement." From Moscow our inexpensive travel included an overnight train travel to Berlin. Our tickets included meals in the dining car with plenty of carrots, vegetable soup and cucumber salad. On the way we saw the countryside of Poland and as we traveled west the farming communities showed improvement. Notably the lack of vehicular traffic was a contrast to HongKong and the USA. When we arrived at the Polish border in the middle of the night, we felt the train being hoisted up on jacks as a new set of wheels was placed under each rail car because the track gauge was changed from Russia going into the rest of Europe.

Barbara and the three girls did manage to visit the tourist sites in Berlin, the wall, the ruins of the Reichstag, and other places. My train ride to the factory town was quite simple even though I passed through the checkpoints to get there. At the factory, German efficiency had me on my way driving to Berlin in a few hours. What a strange feeling to be driving on the right side of the road again after years on the left in HongKong. With passport stamped again, I arrived back in the hotel to prepare for our final driving trip through parts of Europe.

This time we had Kim, Bonnie, and Dana all seated in the back seat of our new VW. Each had a small suitcase designed to fit in the space behind the seat. Our tent, cooking supplies, and Barbara's and my travel case were in the "bonnet". Loaded and ready we took off for "Checkpoint Charlie" to cross into Eastern Germany. Having consulted more experienced travelers and our hotel people, we drove along the main roads for awhile before venturing into the smaller, less busy areas. We found campsites easily. Working our way down toward Czechoslovakia, we found a camp on the shores of the Prague River. I think the girls really enjoyed the camping, especially the canned goulash, but would have liked to have had more opportunity to interact with other young people.

In Prague, we had an opportunity to visit a Yale Divinity schoolmate of my STM days. Professor Stollar was teaching at the Calvin Theological School. He and his family were kind to us and helped us make our way around that ancient and beautiful city. We were particularly impressed with the old Jewish cemetery. We headed on to Austria to visit Salzburg, then into Bavaria. Our itinerary took us to Hitler's famous mountain retreat, the Eagle's Nest. Driving through the Black Forest and down the Rhine valley, we made our way to Luxembourg. All of us enjoyed the beauty of that small kingdom.

It was time for me to take the VW to a nearby port to join hundreds of other VWs for the trip to the USA. When I got back from this jaunt, we had only a day before getting on our Icelandic Airlines' "el cheapo" flight to New York, known as the "backpack" plane.

We had arranged with our friends Jesse and Mac McCoy to stay with them in their big house in Montclair, NJ. They met us, and welcomed us with open arms. The big question right away after setting up bed spaces alongside their kids was how we were going to get to North Carolina. We needed to get there right away and our VW was on the high seas. The McCoys were helpful to us as many decisions needed to be made. When we investigated the cost of train travel we faced reality. It was Mac who suggested buying a car since there was a panic to sell on the part of used car dealers whose vehicles were being vandalized. There was a general air of uneasiness because of the New Jersey riots of 1967. Sure enough, we located a sturdy, old Chevrolet station wagon that had suffered a knocked-out window only a few nights before. We bought the "white elephant" which was quickly repaired. We were then on our way to an unknown and uncertain future, but at least we were not sitting still, wringing our hands. Part of the sense of assurance was due to the full support of friends and family members.

Back to Asia in 1952,

27. Refugees flooding out of China lived in tar-paper
shacks on hillsides or on the streets.
28. The HongKong Government resettled a one million
refugees in seven-storey buildings.
29. Haven of Hope TB Sanatorium served refugees
living in Rennie's Mill Campe, 1956
30. Fast-forward to the year 2000 and note the Haven of Hope Chapel
dwarfed by new PoLum Housing Estate built on
land created by filling in beautiful Junk Bay.

HongKong (continued) to 1967

31. The Rev. Dr. Peter Wong, HongKong Council,
Church of Christ in China, my boss

32. Our Mission vacation house, part of Laan Tau Mountain Camp,
on an island near HongKong

33. Lei Fungkiu (Katrina) a refugee orphan, enters our lives.

34. With Dana's arrival we are seven. L to R — Chris,
Kim, Bonnie, Karen holding Dana

Chapter VI

New Challenge – College Teaching Years 1967 to 1987

Job Search and House Hunting – May 1967

It was a whirlwind time! Again Barbara's sister, Lois and husband, Paul Carter took us in, giving us a place to stay. A few weeks with them in Salisbury gave us the chance to be with Barbara's mother, meet with old friends and generally start adjusting to life in America. Our plan was to live at our Blowing Rock cottage until I had found a job and located a house. Then we could settle down in order to get the children in school in the fall.

I had telephoned Professor Morris Cohen at the University Of North Carolina School Of Social Work as soon as we reached the USA. I had quite a feeling of expectation that he would have some ideas of possible jobs for me. What excitement to think that I really might not have to join the ranks of the unemployed or pastor a small rural church without having had any such experience. Starting over at age 46 was a scary and daunting prospect.

Another encouraging possibility came from a friend, Dr. Paul Heckert. Paul, a former UCC missionary to Honduras and now chair of the Sociology Department at Catawba College asked about my plans for the future. He thought he might be able to offer a position teaching Social Work courses in his department. Another challenge and another uncertainty, but at the time everything was uncertain. One thing, however, was very sure. Settling in Salisbury, "back in the bosom of the family", had tremendous appeal to all of us.

I did interview for a position in Charlotte to which Professor Cohen had alerted me. The director of the Social Services Department with whom I would be working had decided he would operate a graduate Social Work program of his own. He had no intention of coordinating with the degree program at UNC Chapel Hill. It would be impossible for me to bridge the chasm so it was not the job for me.

In the meantime, Paul Heckert had been in contact with the president of Catawba College, Dr. Donald Dearborn, as well as the Z Smith Reynolds Foundation in Winston-Salem. It appeared that the Piedmont Consortium of NC Colleges had been funded by the Z Smith Reynolds Foundation to develop cooperative educational projects between black and white institutions. The events of the mid '60s, disturbing many cities as integration was being sought, brought pressures on higher education. President Dearborn of Catawba had been discussing with President Duncan of Livingstone ways to link the two colleges. The suggestion that a joint program in community development be considered in the sociology departments was taking shape. I was asked to meet with President Dearborn to discuss the position of associate professor to undertake this task.

The next day Dr. Dearborn outlined a program in which I would be working under the department chair, Dr. Heckert. I would initiate two courses: "Counseling" and "Community Work." Students from both colleges could sign up for the courses. One would be taught on the Livingstone campus and one on the Catawba campus. Students would be transported to class. The unique design called for credit for "field instruction," so I would be searching for internship opportunities in community service. After a thorough discussion with Barbara, we decided the opportunity to live in Salisbury was wonderful and the right place to begin my teaching career. I signed my first teaching contract with both Catawba and Livingstone Colleges in August 1967.

We left Salisbury to spend the summer in our Blowing Rock cottage, thinking ahead to plan for our coming year. At this time I learned that the United Church Board for World Ministries offered all retiring missionaries who had served "long term," or over ten years, a year of search time to relocate. This was not needed in my case, as I had been confident I could find some kind of job. In any case it did count as a very helpful year upon my subsequent retirement in 1987 because it enabled us to secure a health benefits package from the church for missionaries who had served 25 years.

A Job for Dad

What excitement ensued as the family began to realize that Dad had a job and that we would be settling down in Salisbury, our home town! Karen was now a junior at Catawba; Chris would start his freshman year there in the fall; and the younger girls were looking forward to being in an American school with their cousins.

The next challenge was finding a place to live that was suitable for our size family. We found quite quickly that there was nothing to rent or buy. It was clear that we needed to build a home so we bought a large lot on Grove Street from Paul Carter's brother, Sam. It was handily located half way between the two colleges, and provided wonderful garden space.

In planning to construct this new home, we searched hard for a style that would fit the neighborhood of rather small houses yet provided three bedrooms and baths. We found a "barn roof" style that gave us a very large top floor space for two daughters, two bedrooms on the next level, the kitchen/dining room and living room on the second level and a bedroom or den and workroom on the ground level. So the four or five feet between levels made for a compact and very presentable building, though one friend asked if we were building a "pagoda." Blinking only briefly, we borrowed the $28,000 and contracted for our home to be speedily constructed. We were happy with the design which would create the needed living space for everyone.

We could not get into our new home until after the first of the year so we rented an apartment in an old complex which would serve temporarily. It was not an easy time for the family that fall. It was necessary for all of us to adjust to life on a much faster and more stressful track. Living among our unpacked boxes from HongKong in that roach-ridden apartment while trying to housetrain an untrainable beagle pup named "Snoopy" made for rough family life. In the larger picture, we were supervising the building of our house with all the decisions and selections required by that process. It was overwhelming!

There were many stresses and strains faced by our family of active, growing children, increasingly aware of their multi-cultural background, and also fiercely independent. We had to deal with our own acceptance that life in the USA was different from what we had known previously. Perhaps, realizing that we had changed dramatically as a family in our expectations, this resulted in a magnified level of stress for each member. We deeply appreciated the wonderful support from family and friends. Having the mountain cottage as a getaway was a lifesaver.

Professor Whitener

My first job effort, upon learning what was in store for me in less than a month was to prepare two courses, a distinct challenge. No one had taught anything like it in Salisbury, so I called my mentor in Chapel Hill, Dr. Arthur Fink, who was Dean of the Graduate School of Social Work. Fortunately, he was living in his summer home near us in the mountains. His advice was to start with a generic course in social work much as they offered on the Chapel Hill campus. It was one I had taken my first year in Chapel Hill and was well developed by Dr. Fink himself. He was most helpful in offering support and advice. The department chairs at both colleges accepted the curriculum recommendation, resulting in most issues being solved rather easily. The transportation of students and the coordination of class scheduling hours between two colleges was a much more difficult problem. Fortunately, the department chairs and the deans handled that. Funding for the program was assured with the promise of a three-year grant, which included the purchase of a used stretch limousine to carry students between the two colleges for the two courses.

My teaching went well. I found my new professional career challenging and satisfying. By the beginning of the second semester, I was able to locate several agencies in the community where students could receive "on the job" social service training. Luckily, only a few requested field work that first year, so I learned along with them. I went to a training session on "Encounters" and was impressed with the dynamics of group process theory and practice so I undertook to incorporate some of this group process in my course on counseling. The sessions were very useful and successful because of the need to integrate the black and white students of both colleges. We even held several twenty-four-hour sessions. I will never forget a session on trust. We tested each other by standing in a circle with one member in the middle falling back with closed eyes, fully trusting the others to provide the "safety net." Imagine a 250-lb. football player reluctantly taking his turn but trying to make sure that his largest and strongest classmates were behind him. He finally closed his eyes and fell back to be caught securely. He said he had never in his life been so fearful even though he had grown up on the streets of Washington, DC. His younger brother had died of a drug overdose. He kept drugs off campus by bashing the heads of dealers he caught lurking around the dorm. No one ever accused him of assault, as he had witnesses to the drug dealing. The campus and the Salisbury police were supportive because he cleared the campus for four years. Larry Melton became a good friend and a very successful businessman in Charlotte.

At this same time, a regional educational project out of Atlanta was seeking to identify college programs desiring to undertake organization of courses to provide a new degree, the Bachelor of Social Work. In the interests of promoting integration of black students into the social service systems of the Southern states, the Southern Regional Education Board (SREB) sought a few faculty representatives to serve as interpreters. I was in the right place at the right time. It was quite obvious to them that I had entry into a black institution, Livingstone, and also into a white institution, Catawba. I was asked to be the North Carolina/Virginia interpreter for the SREB. That the foundation also paid a small stipend was particularly welcome, as college salaries were limited to nine months each year. Here I was, brand new to teaching social work and considered one who knew how to relate to college administrators. I learned that SREB had been completely unsuccessful in recruiting teachers at university graduate schools of social work. It could have been that those of us at the college level felt we were really on the "front lines" and the "cutting edge"!

I recall that academic year 1968-69 as very crucial for the future. The Catawba president, Dr. Dearborn, died of a heart attack at a football game in the fall. Dr. Duncan, president of Livingstone, also died of a heart attack the following spring. Both were well loved and superb presidents, so both colleges suffered immensely this loss of leadership.

Dr. Heckert, our joint department chair, and the prime mover of the "Joint Program," was busily raising funds from the Piedmont Educational Consortium to try to establish a completely joint Sociology department serving both Catawba and Livingstone colleges. This was such a new concept that the funding sources actually encouraged our two schools to try this experiment. This being the era of the civil rights movement, we all felt we were breaking new ground! A number of meetings were held, both in Salisbury and elsewhere, to discuss directions and possibilities.

It was quite clear to me that if we were going to develop a social service program for employment of college student graduates, we would need to fit into the national effort to upgrade the qualifications and recognition of social workers. This meant that we would need to offer the new Bachelor of Social Work degree. To do this we would require fully qualified and adequately trained faculty to offer the course work and the field instruction similar to the "practice teaching" process required of those who wished to become teachers in North Carolina. I turned, once again, to my colleagues at UNC School of Social Work in Chapel Hill, where I learned of several graduate students who would be looking for a job in June. At this point in history, there were really very few MSW graduates who were African-American (a term that came into use much later). One of my classmates back in 1965 was Howard Lee, an African-American who was subsequently elected mayor of Chapel Hill and later served in the North Carolina General Assembly. A telephone call to Howard was supportive and he said he would help us.

I felt it absolutely essential to recruit an African-American faculty member and was backed heartily by Dr. Heckert. By June 1969, William Lawrence Pollard, MSW graduate, was interviewed and agreed to become a member of the faculty of the Joint Department of Sociology at Catawba and Livingstone Colleges.

Bill was from Raleigh and had graduated from Shaw University. A real "live wire" speaker and natural leader, he won friends quickly on both campuses. In those days of militancy, as I look back on that era, I know we were most fortunate he had the personality that could tolerate some of the obnoxious attitudes of older faculty. His own maturity, aided by his beautiful and talented wife, Merriette, contributed much to the colleges and the social work program. Barbara and I were honored to be considered their personal friends. This was something new in relationships and really meant a very great deal to us.

Dr. Will Scott, of A & T State University in Greensboro, was working hard to establish a BSW degree program. He became a good friend of Livingstone College and over many years offered great encouragement and support to our efforts. For instance, he challenged Bill Pollard to think ahead to prepare for an advanced degree. In those early years, with only two of us teaching full time, we faced real challenges to prepare new courses for each semester and year. We found that the service agencies were looking forward to hiring our graduates who entered the professional field of social work with a real degree instead of the usual psychology, sociology, or English literature preparation. It was, however, many years before North

Carolina finally recognized that the professional social work degree was on the same level as the education (teaching) degree in the education departments of the colleges. At the same time our students were finding entry into graduate programs in social work facilitated by their BSW degrees.

The Council on Social Work Education (CSWE) was developing an undergraduate section to develop proposals for the accreditation of college departments and programs offering the BSW. My work with the Southern Regional Education Board gave me another head start, as I was invited to serve on a CSWE study committee. In those early years, I was often on the road to visit small colleges to share our experience and to help them understand the value of a working degree for their students. I remember going to Ferrum College in Virginia to find a single overworked African-American social worker trying her best to offer enough courses to meet some of the CSWE standards. It took that institution over seven years to raise its sights high enough to develop a good social work program.

Another small African-American institution, St. Paul's College in Virginia, found it absolutely impossible to consider raising the funds to develop a social work degree program. The visits I made to a number of small black institutions showed that it would be imperative for the federal system to finance social work programs if African-American social workers were to be available in sufficient numbers to make an impact on services in the south.

The Difficult Early 1970s

Bill Pollard and I were offering all the required social work courses in preparation for accreditation to offer the Bachelor of Social Work degree. We knew it would require a few years of experience working with students, faculty in other departments, and the agencies where our students were placed for their field work to develop the quality required. At the same time, as a member of the Council on Social Work Education, I was fortunate to learn that the council was preparing to recognize the Bachelor of Social Work as an entry degree to the profession. We began to look ahead. In my classes, I found that the bell curve for class grades was fairly consistent. It was true that the top students in class were equally divided between Livingstone and Catawba. There was usually a larger number of Livingstone students grouped at the lower end, but the middle was evenly split. This appeared to reflect the degree of preparation for college-level study in English particularly. Livingstone students were often the first member of their family to enter college.

It was disturbing to me that the administrators at Catawba were becoming very uneasy. The new president, Dr. Shotzberger brought in a new Dean, Dr. Turney. They saw our program as quickly developing into a new department. It was clear that would require an increase in expenditure as we sought faculty with DSW degrees. They often asked us if the Livingstone students were dragging down the quality of educational work. We noted that they began to seek some justification to end the joint program, even though it was receiving a very good subsidy from the Piedmont Consortium. The pioneering effort was really bringing recognition throughout the state and in eastern educational circles as a pilot effort. Dr. Will Scott in Greensboro was beginning negotiations to provide a cooperative program between A & T University and the University of North Carolina at Greensboro. That this close cooperation was finally mandated by the NC university system many years later is a different story. Our situation came to a head in 1970-71 when the administrators at Catawba decided to change from a semester system to quarter systems. This put the burden of two different term schedules squarely on our Joint Department of Sociology. We were forced to offer our final exams on the quarter schedule, an unfair burden on our Livingstone students. Our joint faculty protests fell on deaf ears.

In the spring of '71, the president of our Livingstone Social Work student club, Bill Gray, asked for a meeting with Dr. Shipman, president of Livingstone, and the academic dean, Dr. Turney, and president, Dr. Shotzberger, of Catawba. Dr. Heckert, Bill Pollard, and I were invited to attend also. I was proud of Bill Gray as he calmly identified the problems the students were having with the confusing structure. It was clear to the students that there could be no real "joint" program when one party was going its own way. He identified step by step the actions taken by Catawba and the efforts he had made to adjust. He and his fellow social work students had come to the conclusion that the acts of the Catawba administrators were clearly "racist" and then challenged the Catawba dean to explain why the need to change from the semester system had been necessary. The Dean was so red-faced he could not respond. It was clear that the Livingstone/Catawba Joint Program was over. It was never clear to any of us why this outstanding and thriving program with so much professional and financial support would be eliminated. I was very disappointed and feel that it was a significant academic loss to both colleges and community.

By the end of the semester, each faculty member was offered a choice to teach at one institution or the other. Dr. Paul Heckert, our Department chair, was so disappointed that he immediately started a job search and moved in the summer to a western branch of the University of Maryland. Bill Pollard and I were welcomed by Livingstone College to develop a Department of Social Work and continue to seek accreditation for the BSW degree. We worked hard with numerous visits by consultants and friends. The Council on Social Work Education granted Livingstone College full accreditation of the Bachelor of Social Work degree. Bill Gray graduated to go on to complete his MSW and later taught in a college in New Jersey.

Changes in Family Life – 1968 to 1974

Those early days also were a struggle financially for our family. Most College faculty members were contracted on the basis of nine months' teaching. Summer was supposed to be used for advanced study and vacations. The only way to budget with care was to live on a 12-month payment plan that was somewhat restricting. I needed to find summer work.

In the early 1950s the Evangelical and Reformed Church had established the Blowing Rock Assembly Grounds when the Hedrick and Shuford families donated a large summer manor house for summer conferences and retreats. It was well used by the Reformed Church/Evangelical & Reformed Churches. Later a cement block, motel structure was built to house youth conferences. Mr. and Mrs. Homer Bonds and family of Salisbury, NC, First UCC Church, had served the program as cooks, clean-up persons, secretary, and managers for nearly twenty years. They felt they could no longer continue. For two summers, 1970 and 1971, the Blowing Rock Assembly Grounds needed a manager to operate the summer program. With our plan to spend time in our mountain cottage, this job suited us well.

I was very fortunate to find a cook, Willie Clifton, from Concord, NC who helped me both summers. A student at Catawba looking for a summer job, Dolan Hubbard, was a lifesaver assistant, along with my whole family. Dolan must have received good training as he later earned his PhD, is Chair of the English Department at Morgan State University, and has published poetry and an Anthology. He serves on the Catawba College Board of Trustees. All of our daughters were also on the payroll helping out those two years at Blowing Rock Assembly Grounds.

These years were very busy and eventful on the family front. We had settled well into our new home and activities in Salisbury and the college community. We joined First Church, United Church of Christ, which we had previously attended. More conservative on social issues than we would have liked, we were still glad to be members there. Because there were relatively few teenagers, Dana eventually joined her cousins in the youth program at St. John's Lutheran Church. I sang in the choir in First Church and Barbara was active in the Women's Fellowship.

She also volunteered in various community service projects and especially enjoyed helping a couple of elderly women with shopping and some household chores. It was a new experience for her to join some art and craft classes as well as continuing her interest in Ikebana with a Japanese friend. Linking up with her sister, Lois's, Sewing/Bridge Club filled an empty social need. Being able to enjoy the company of her aging mother and assisting with her needs, which Lois had done for so long, was most satisfying. Life was good.

A new interest for me was gardening as our home had left a large area in back for plowing, tilling and having a private source of vegetables for the first time since my Dad had gardened way back in the 1940s. Barbara's brother, Robert, never did forgive me for drafting him to help secure a large load of fresh chicken manure to spread on the newly plowed garden. He said he had never had such a hard time getting his clothes clean again. Bonnie helped and was much more charitable. But the success of the garden was assured. Chinese vegetables were loved by the family so we grew them year round.

For several years I tried to develop two bee colonies. They did very well for awhile, but an early experience of a colony division was almost catastrophic. The old queen had left the hive with one half of all the worker bees and gathered in a tree behind our home but at least 15 feet off the ground. Thinking I could recover them easily, I drove our car into the yard under the bees. Placing my ladder against the car I carried a bucket up to get the swarm. Bees are gentle during this process. I retrieved the swarm and the queen but the ladder slipped and as my terrified family watched, I fell. Landing in the middle of the car roof safely clutching my bucket of bees, I placed them gently in an extra hive. Only my ego was injured, but I had to press our car roof back into shape!

This was the Jimmy Carter era with great emphasis on energy saving. Large tax credits were awarded for installing solar panels on the roof. Firmly believing, even then, in the need to care for the environment and to use alternative forms of energy, we had seven solar panels placed on our roof. These were some of the first in Salisbury and aroused much interest. We were very pleased that these panels provided our hot water from March until October, as well as boosting the efficiency of the heat pump all year round.

More Interest in the Environment

My brother Don and his wife, Ibby, were active in several Conservation projects. They introduced us to the Southern Appalachian Highlands Conservancy. This was a very active new program seeking to preserve Roan Mountain from a ski slope and many summer homes. I even served as Chair of the Board for several years. The success of the Conservancy was in purchasing land as well as securing land easements surrounding the mountain which assured its conservation.

During this time Barbara and I undertook a number of special hikes in the Blue Ridge Mountains along the North Carolina-Tennessee line. We hiked one weekend up Mt. Sterling to spend a windy, cold night camping at an ancient, but unfortunately locked, cabin.

We found a group planning to climb famous Mt. LeConte. It was a hard hike, but at least we had a ride to an appropriate takeoff point and a good pickup on the other side. The beautiful night in the rough cabins at the top was a welcome change from the hard ground.

As members of the Appalachian Trail, we felt obligated to do our part. We managed to cover 25 miles in three days from Roan Mountain top to Watauga Lake carrying 35 lb packs. We were proud of ourselves, and weary enough to think we had hiked the whole trail. On one of our later trips to New England we made a point of visiting Mt. Katahdin, Maine, the northern end of the Appalachian Trail.

Significant Developments in the Lives of Our Children

Catawba College granted the enormous benefit of free tuition, making it possible for all of our children to begin their college studies while still living at home.

Karen, after her initial difficult adjustment, enjoyed Catawba and graduated *cum laude*. In her senior year she was elected May Queen, the honor given her mother 25 years earlier. We were present at Karen's crowning and I was so proud that I could be the husband of a Queen and father of her daughter, also a Queen! We were glad to learn to know Steve Berry, Karen's classmate and to whom she was married in June 1969 after their graduation. (How could it be that "Dolly", our firstborn, was now married?) They moved to Maryland where Steve was a teacher in the Montgomery County school system.

Chris was unhappy at Catawba and decided to enlist in the Marine Corps. We could not dissuade him. We were very proud of his meritorious promotion out of basic training at Parris Island and the whole family attended his ceremony. We were heartsick that he was sent to Vietnam. He was trained as a heavy equipment operator, however, and spent his tour with 2nd Engineers burying fire-bases near the DMZ, and finally with Force Logistic Command in Da Nang. We were extremely grateful that he was never assigned to combat. He returned safely home in 1970 after attaining the rank of Sergeant. Using the GI bill, he attended NC State and then Appalachian State University in Boone where he graduated with a B.S. in Safety and Driver Education.

Kim was bored with her courses at Boyden High School and found her classmates cliquish, so applied for early entrance into Catawba College in the fall of 1970. She excelled, graduating *Summa cum Laude*. She had fallen in love with Bob Selby, son of the Religion Department professor. They were married in September 1972 on the lawn of our mountain cabin. They lived in our Salisbury home while we were overseas during the ensuing Fulbright year.

Like Kim, Bonnie (17) applied for early entrance into Catawba in 1972. She had completed one year when she took leave of absence to go with us for the first part of the Fulbright travels, returning midyear to reenter Catawba during the third quarter. After completing two years there, she transferred to the University of NC in Chapel Hill where she met Tom Mole.

Dana was 13, just completing Knox Middle School. She had enjoyed gymnastics. During the year she was accidentally knocked down and suffered a broken collar bone. Entry to high school was delayed a year so that she, too, could accompany us during the Fulbright year.

Katrina's Story Continues

In 1967 when we made the painful decision to return to the USA, Katrina asked to go with us. We wanted very much to take her, but there were several factors that made it impossible at that time. She had not finished high school and her English skills would not permit her to pass the TOEFL exam for entry into the US. She was still a "Ward of the Queen" and too young for adoption under HongKong law, but she was also over 14 and thus too old to be eligible for adoption under US law. We promised her that after she finished high school and had sufficient English we would bring her to the US on a student visa to study in college. During the several years after we left, Lucile Hartman, our good Mission friend, helped Katrina a great deal in finishing school and studying English. During this time of preparing for her new life in America, Katrina lived with Lucile for awhile and the two of them became good friends.

Finally, in February of 1970 we were able to bring Katrina to Salisbury from HongKong, a very important event for the family. She had passed the necessary English exam to get a student visa and Catawba College had accepted her to enter an English class. There were adjustments for all of us. Katrina's sweet nature and helpfulness were evident from the start, and she fit well into our family routines and was very grateful for the living arrangements we worked out for her. She shared a room with Bonnie on the top floor, Dana having made room for her by moving to a small room downstairs. Kim spent time with her educating her on life in America. Her English skills, however, were a frustration. Barbara finally gave up on the obviously unwanted practice sessions to improve her spoken English. Katrina audited some courses at Catawba College during the spring of 1971. In the fall she undertook full time studies for a year and managed the academic work satisfactorily.

Katrina wanted to be a social worker, so I was able to arrange her transfer to the accredited Bachelor of Social Work Department at East Carolina University. Because she was not registered as a citizen of North Carolina, she was required to pay out-of-state tuition which I felt was totally unjust since she was a *de facto* member of our family and our responsibility. Thus there ensued quite a "battle of wits" with the University treasurer. I carried my appeals through all levels of the University to the Chair of the Board of Trustees. At that time Robert Morgan, the NC Attorney General, was the Chair. I asked him for a solution to the problem in our favor. He intervened and told us of a new North Carolina law of "Adult Adoption by Mutual Consent." We acted immediately to become Katrina's legal parents. Our mutual adoption was made official at the Rowan County courthouse on December 21, 1972, when she became Katrina Whitener Lee.

Katrina received her BSW degree in 1974. She met husband-to-be Gerald Townsend at the University and upon their marriage, became a US citizen. Katrina wrote former Senator Robert Morgan in 2000 thanking him for what he did on her behalf and telling him about her family and her happiness. He very graciously responded and sent her a photograph of his family.

Through the years after leaving HongKong, Katrina continued to be in touch with Kei Ma, the old "grandmother" who had befriended her as a child in Homantin Village. She also sent Kei Ma financial gifts from time to time until her death. Katrina called her benefactor, Mrs. Shaffer, who lived in California, her "American Grandmother." The two of them remained close through correspondence and visits until Mrs. Shaffer's death.

A Fulbright Year – 1973-74

Our work days at Livingstone were full as we began to write our application for social work accreditation. At the same time, an opportunity was given me by President Shipman to apply for a Fulbright Fellowship. It was obvious that Livingstone College could not afford to give faculty sabbaticals. On the other hand, to win an opportunity to study and conduct research overseas was most attractive and seemed almost to be a form of reward. I quickly undertook to write to some friends overseas to find out what might be possible. I decided to undertake preparation of a new course in International Community Development by visiting the Schools of Social Work in Edinburgh, Scotland, HongKong and Taiwan, Bangkok, Thailand, and Pakistan. My contacts in HongKong were the easiest. I was promised assistance in all four places with the schedule of three months in HongKong and Taiwan, a month in Bangkok at the Thammasat School of Social Work, and about four months in Pakistan at the University of the Punjab School of Social Work in Lahore. I would stop in Edinburgh on the way. With the support of Livingstone College in granting a leave of absence for the academic year and the help of Bill Pollard who was willing to take over as Chair of the Department, I went to Washington to work out the details for the academic year 1973-74.

In order to finance a year away, a Fulbright Scholar receives generous awards in local currency as a living allowance and a travel ticket arranged by the State Department on US airlines, but nothing for accompanying family members to travel. To plan for Barbara, Bonnie, and Dana to accompany me, we were able to sell a few acres of land in the mountains, and I was able to work out inexpensive travel arrangements for them.

Scotland

I flew the required US airlines to Scotland a week early to visit the program developed under a new Scottish Social Service Act. My family arrived after a week so that we could do a little touring and visit some friends in the UK, and then I flew directly to Thailand. They were to leave London, cross the English Channel, take a train to Zurich from Paris and then a flight on to Bangkok bringing most of our luggage. I flew happily on quite unaware of the situation they faced: striking UK dockworkers, French intransigence, and altered train schedules which created most difficult travel for the family. The story of their trip was written by Barbara. You will understand how proud I was of their accomplishments. Without doubt their arrival in Bangkok was a most joyful reunion, as I praised them for overcoming a multitude of roadblocks. We proceeded to HongKong to begin the first three months of our Fulbright year, not really knowing what was ahead.

HongKong

It was wonderful to be in HongKong again. Peter Wong had been my HK Council, Church of Christ in China boss during my years of service with the Church. I had left HongKong feeling very disappointed in Peter's lack of interest in my desire to expand training in Social Services in the Church. When I learned about my Fulbright time in HongKong I wrote Peter of my project's interest in understanding what was being done for older persons. He asked me to help him to develop a plan to serve the elderly in the churches. I spent many hours writing a suggested work plan. I resisted writing a definitive plan, but rather a design to learn what the churches really wanted for their retired elderly and options for the church. He said he would take it to the Church administrative committee.

A comfortable apartment in the new Retreat Center called Morrison House at HK University was made available to us. The location of an apartment near the university was very pleasant and convenient. We had a beautiful view of the mountainside with a private "ting dz", or pavilion, facing us. From another aspect of the house we could overlook the university campus and a portion of the beautiful harbor itself. Barbara enjoyed her contacts with friends and took a course in Chinese "sumi" painting. We did not have a vehicle, but the public transportation system was so convenient we enjoyed many outings. Bonnie and Dana did a good bit of reading and study, but with their mother took the bus to old haunts and different places they wanted to visit. Karen and Steve came to visit us over their Christmas vacation. We had a chance to climb Laan Tau Mountain to our favorite vacation spot. Karen enjoyed showing Steve her school and other places of interest. Their visit and our holiday time together were very special.

Our Chinese friends were most welcoming, inviting us to a large number of dinners and events in the churches. It was as though we had not really abandoned them six years previously. I was invited to preach in my good friend Rev. John Ma's church. For years, I proudly wore the new suit of clothes they gave me.

I was able to interview a number of social workers, as well as faculty members of the Chinese University of HongKong who were working on development of a graduate school of social work to provide well-prepared new social workers. There was great enthusiasm among the younger workers as they faced the time when the colony would revert to China in 1997. Though a number of skilled faculty and managers of agencies and companies were seeking to emigrate to Canada, South America, and the USA, there was really no significant reduction of qualified persons to carry on. The agencies I visited helped me with curriculum options for my Fulbright project to prepare a course for the next year. It was soon time to move on to my next task.

Bangkok

Bangkok, Thailand, in 1974, was a completely different story. We arrived to find that only a few weeks earlier, a bloody revolution had taken place. Only the intervention by the king had prevented major bloodshed. It was indeed fortunate that the army obeyed the king. The students of several universities, led by students of Thammasat U, had become incensed at the corruption of the ruling government officers and attacked police stations and government offices. We learned that the engineering students had asked the social work students to organize a grass-roots process so that communication and planning could be coordinated. The engineers then provided the initial assault on the forces oppressing the country. The result was clearly evident. Many major buildings had been badly damaged by fire. I talked with many social work students who described the process of grass-roots organization and community development they had undertaken. It was exactly what I had come to study. My work was sponsored through the United Nations office, but the School of Social Work faculty and students were my contacts.

One project was particularly interesting. Many small boats that were obviously the living quarters of poor fishing families were now anchored and fastened semi-permanently to the mud banks in order to provide easy access for education of children and adults working ashore. A senior student led me over about twenty narrow and wobbly plank walkways through a network of canals in this floating shantytown. The poverty was astounding in a land of abundance where even the trees produced fruit for all. The people who lived there were not only cheerful but also optimistic. I learned how the students were involved to help families see themselves as part of a community, seeking the improvement of services such as electricity in their neighborhoods and even in their small boat living quarters. I was very impressed with the students and the faculty who were supervising their projects.

Barbara, Bonnie and Dana enjoyed the month visiting many of the fascinating temples and gardens in beautiful Bangkok. They learned a valuable lesson in the Temple of the Reclining Buddha. The three were sitting on the floor, resting in the area reserved for tourists facing the Buddha, Bonnie with her legs out in front of her. A Thai lady politely informed her that a foot pointed at the Buddha was very disrespectful. Chagrined that they unknowingly had offended Thai religion in this way, the girls profusely apologized.

We took a trip by train into the southern region of Thailand to visit friends Dick and Evelyn Bryant, refugee China missionaries who were in language school with us. It was a long trip to Trang, but we enjoyed the scenery on the way. Our friends were happy in their work with lepers and other projects. The leper project was an income resource for women who did a type of cross-stitch embroidery on beautiful fabric. We bought several pieces of the material and I really enjoyed the subsequent very handsome shirts Barbara made for me.

Nepal to New Delhi

It was now the end of January and our next stop was to be Pakistan via Nepal and India. To get there we found a reasonable flight on Burmese Airlines. They put us up overnight in Rangoon so we were able to visit a local market and look around even in that police state. The army was evident everywhere.

Next morning the flight to Kathmandu was a beautiful one, seemingly over the top of the world. We arrived on a sunny day, surprisingly warm for January. We were obviously neophytes in Nepalese customs as many young boys grabbed our bags to carry to a taxi. Although we had counted bags and tried to keep an eagle eye on things we failed. When we got to the hotel, we found two bags missing. Both Bonnie and Dana had lost bags containing not only much of their clothes but treasured gifts and items they had collected in HongKong. We all were very upset by the experience but determined that it would not happen again.

In exploring Kathmandu the ancient wooden structures of the old city were unique. We enjoyed learning how the people worshipped by twirling prayer wheels or going to shrines where they could spin larger wheels by hand. In each so called "prayer wheel" monks had written prayers on paper. These containers would spin around a central axis, usually a stick, so that the prayers were released to the gods. Busy people did not need to interrupt their discussions or work to let the gods know they were devout! We had time to visit a few popular temples often crowded with women, old and young. We were told that they came to touch the idols and symbols on the hillsides, as well as to turn large mounted prayer wheels inside and outside the temple grounds. The number of large lingams there were for women to come pray for children.

We got up in the dark very early one morning to take a 20-mile taxi ride before dawn to a lookout spot in order to view sunrise over Mt. Everest. Disappointingly, as is often the case, the entire range was in the clouds. We did get to see other beautiful ranges with their snowcaps on our return to the city. I was surprised at how much agriculture was being carried on even in that harsh climate.

New Delhi to Lahore, Pakistan

From the heights of Nepal to New Delhi was a total contrast. We stayed at the YMCA, planning only a few days in India to arrange travel to

Pakistan. To be so near, a day trip to the Taj Mahal and the Red Fort was a necessity. The Taj is definitely one of the wonders of the world and lived up to our family's expectations.

Learning that we could take an overnight train to Amritsar and then a short taxi ride to the border, we bought beautiful Indian wool blankets to keep warm for the train ride. It worked out OK, but we did have to walk farther than expected from one bleak police post in India to another one in Pakistan. Fortunately, we were able to engage carriers for our baggage. We made our way from the police post to Forman Christian College in Lahore by taxis. The college, founded by Presbyterian missionaries, was still operating in a difficult political and religious climate. Several American faculty members were in residence, so we were introduced to the life of the church.

We had earlier arranged to rent a small faculty dwelling through the president, Dr. Anwar Barkat, who had been introduced to us by some friends. The Barkats befriended us by helping arrange for a man to help us as cook and buyer. Mahboob (in English "lover") was a real jewel. He could make almost anything over a gas hotplate. We soon learned that he was particularly adept at making chapattis; a whole wheat wrap that served with small pieces of spicy meat and dahl was just delectable. He taught Barbara how to make the chapattis. He did the shopping at the markets for us. Milk was delivered at the house, ladled from a large brass pot, then boiled.

Barbara joined the Presbyterian women's Bible study group on campus. She also volunteered to help once a week in a small clinic, dispensing pills that she wrapped in pieces of paper. Transportation to the clinic was by pedicab, a harrowing ride through crowded streets with the Presbyterian missionary woman doctor.

Life in Muslim Pakistan was not simple. If you went to a restaurant you could order beer but it was served in a teapot since a bottle could not be displayed. We could purchase beer at certain shops to carry home, but generally alcoholic beverages were in short supply, though we learned that the populace found ways to avoid the strictures of their religion. We found that our girls were pinched even when they were walking with us. Barbara and the girls dressed modestly when they were in the markets but they did not shroud themselves because it was very hot. They had several unpleasant experiences as men attempted to pinch them or touch their breasts so they had to be very alert to avoid harassment.

My research at the University of the Punjab, School of Social Work, went well. I was offered office space and given opportunity to speak to several classes of graduate students. They were particularly interested in the Community Organization process in the US and also what I had observed in Thailand. In the land of Kim's cannon, prominently displayed in front of the university, it was quite evident that political tensions ran high. Fear of India was endemic, so Kashmir was a subject of great concern. The increasing gap between rich and poor was a matter of tension and study at the school. I often traveled with students on their field work assignments, learning how almost impossible it was for male social workers to serve families when no father or husband was at home. Many times I would be invited as a Westerner into a home when a female student was making a home visit. Without the presence of the husband and father, mother and daughters would come out only in burkas, a heavy garment that stretched from the top of the head to cover even the feet, but with a tiny area of criss-crossed stitched screen available for the wearer's vision.

Bonnie flew back to Salisbury in February in order to get back for the second quarter classes at Catawba College. She had opted to follow Kim's lead and gain early entry to college and was permitted to register for classes. Dana, 13, was enrolled in the Lahore American School, a small school for younger children of business people, consular families, and missionaries. Her biggest difficulty that spring turned out to be a broken arm. We took her to the Christian hospital near the college, where she was expertly placed in a cast. Also that spring, Barbara's routine exam raised some suspicions of cancer of the cervix. A biopsy was reported to be positive so it was worrisome. She found the hospital staff very caring and friends supportive but this health issue put a definite damper on Barbara's experience in Pakistan. (Upon return to Salisbury, the studies were inconclusive, so she underwent a total hysterectomy.)

Travel around town was quite a problem. I had to get to the university, but the bus transportation was virtually impossible. Old buses were slow and very overcrowded with men hanging onto the steps and occasionally on the roof. President Barkat's oldest son owned a Volkswagen van of rather questionable vintage. It required some mechanical repairs, but was available for rental. I questioned my ability to drive in the terrible traffic of carts, bikes, and crowds of people. Also there was a lack of reasonable road rules in Lahore, but I decided to give it a try. It really turned out to be quite a help getting to Dana's school events as well as carrying me to the university. On weekends, we took a few family outings, but most of the time, Barbara had little interest in getting out in public as she did not intend to wear a veil.

A Visit to Afghanistan

The weather during the spring really began to warm up. We decided to go to Kabul, Afghanistan, during the spring break. We took the long distance bus to Peshawar, the Pakistani city near the famed Khyber Pass. We had been informed at the hotel that visas to Kabul were available at the police post at the pass. What an adventure! We got to the border to find that there was no pass available to enter Afghanistan. The bus went on its way over the bleak, dusty, and dry mountains. We were stranded on the side of the road. Some local tribesmen with beards admired my beard, so we smiled a lot as we compared beards. We could not learn when the next bus would be coming through to take us back to Peshawar. We were fortunate, however, that in a short time a car with several French officials came through the checkpoint. Noticing our dejected looks as we stood beside the road, they asked if they could help us. After explaining our plight, they offered to take us back. A day later, with pictures taken and visas secured, we bought airline tickets for a flight to Kabul.

We really enjoyed our stay there, taking walks, visiting the many rug shops, and eating the local naan (flatbread). We often laugh about our experience in a restaurant when we ordered our meal to learn that they had sent out for naan, which would "be here in a moment." A little later we saw a boy ride up to the front door on his bicycle with a big batch of the two-foot long flatbread draped over the handle bars. Needless to say, we soon had a plateful set before us. Another eye-opener was the manner in which the rug merchants cleaned the rugs they were readying for sale. The rugs were spread out on the sidewalk in front of the shop for passersby to walk on. Then a young boy or a family member brought water, soap, and a long-handled stiff brush out to scrub the rug. Later it was hung up on a rope to dry and removed to a stack of new rugs in the shop. We suspect that as almost all the rugs were woven by hand in the tents of the nomadic tribespersons, the desert sand and dust, as well as the goat hair smell, needed to be removed. What better way than to have them well trampled and pounded by the feet of passersby! We bought a woven goat hair rug for our mountain cabin.

It was soon time to pack up for our trip home. We were to fly from Karachi to Paris to New York, then on to Charlotte. On our ill-fated trip to Khyber Pass, our French rescuers were very interested in what we were doing in that "Godforsaken" part of the world. They would not accept any payment for our special comfortable ride back to Peshawar. They did say they were leaving for Paris in a day or two and had ordered some tennis racquets made. One of them would not be ready when they left. They would be obliged if we would bring it to them. No problem, we thought. On our travel to Paris, we almost left the racquet on the plane at a transfer point. Horrors! Our French hosts said they would pick us up at our hotel, show us around, and get us to our flight for New York. On the morning after our Paris overnight, a chauffeur called for us, we turned over the tennis racquet, and then he gave us a brief tour of Paris, taking us to Montmartre. What fun we had, even to buying a small painting from a penniless painter in front of the famous church! Our error was in taking too much time, as we soon learned of the daily Paris traffic gridlock. We were getting nowhere; the hour of our flight to NY was approaching; our nerves were taut; we needed to find a bathroom! The driver was a sheer genius. He left the main roads, zigzagged through all kinds of districts, and got us to the airport with hardly a minute to spare. We were rushed aboard, exhausted but very happy to be on the last leg of our year-long journey. It was only then we began to wonder just what kind of contraband we might have carried into France in the handle of the tennis racquet! Since we were never challenged, we had blissfully enjoyed a most interesting glimpse of Paris!

This year for study, recognition of the many changes in Asia, and the opportunity for travel was indeed a real sabbatical for me. It was greatly enhanced because our two youngest girls were excellent travelers and serious students. They kept us closely tuned to reality in the various cultures! After the sabbatical I had time to write up a full report for the Fulbright Commission and also get my report published in a publication relating to overseas studies.

Livingstone Through the '70s & Early '80s

When we returned to Salisbury after my Fulbright Scholar's tour (1973 - 1974), I asked Bill Pollard to stay on as chair of our social work department.

He had done a good job combining the administrative duties with teaching and his busy engagement writing his dissertation. He had successfully completed his prelims at the University of Chicago. It was always exciting to talk with him about his study, his plans, and his family. His two sons, Frederick Douglass and William, were born during this period. As mentioned earlier, the department was able to secure accreditation by the Council on Social Work Education to offer the Bachelor of Social Work degree (1977). This had been the commitment of Livingstone president Dr. Shipman when the joint program with Catawba was ended. Our department was known on campus to be one of the "hard" majors, as we needed to be able to say to graduate schools that our BSW graduates could enter the second year of their Master's program. During the 1970s we always sought faculty who could challenge our students and encourage them to make career decisions to pursue further study and/or serve the social service agencies of our state. During the 1960s and later, Livingstone was fortunate in that students of the supporting denomination, African Methodist Episcopal Zion Church, were faithfully attending the college.

The department attracted serious students and had a good record of those who went on for their MSW degrees. In the early days of advanced standing where graduates of accredited BSW programs gained admission to the second year, we had several interesting experiences. A young woman who had graduated with very high standing decided to enter Columbia School of Social Work in New York. They would not accept her in advanced standing because they did not consider Livingstone very highly. Midway through the first semester, I had a call from their assistant dean requesting help in providing Ms. Smith's field evaluations, any special project papers, and materials that would help support their decision to place her in the second year program. We were happy to send them everything, plus a copy of her paper presented at the Southern Sociological Society. We learned that she went on to finish in one year, even graduating with honors. Several graduates subsequently earned their DSW or PhD degrees. It was truly gratifying when we were able to hire our own graduates to teach in the program.

During my teaching years at Livingstone, I often took the opportunity to take courses offered at other institutions. One very meaningful course, offered in Greensboro by NC State University, was taught by the famous professor Dr. Malcolm Knowles, a well-known thinker and pioneer in adult education. His theories of contract-teaching and student learning were very helpful to me, particularly in my teaching of adult students in our "off-campus" program. I also found time one summer to take courses in vocational rehabilitation so that I could offer a few courses to students wishing to enter that field. These were taken at Appalachian State University in Boone, NC. We spent the summer at our cottage between Boone and Blowing Rock.

It was during this summer that Karen, Steve and year old Michelle came to visit. Steve, an accomplished carpenter, designed a deck on the front of our cottage and directed all of us in its building.

In 1975, Dr. Shipman, president of Livingstone College, told me he had recommended to the division chairs and the Board of Trustees that I be made the recipient of the "Outstanding Teacher of 1975" award. This was an honor and a big surprise, as I was the only Caucasian so honored at Livingstone during my 20 years there.

Grant writing became important to our department to help provide additional faculty. In the 1970s the national objective was to help African-American institutions upgrade both facilities and programs. We took full opportunity to secure a variety of grants. As soon as we had become accredited by the Council on Social Work Education, we were able to secure a grant to offer courses to upgrade social work skills of workers in the state social service system. It was a great pleasure to see the large number of Caucasians who joined our regular Bachelor of Social Work candidates on graduation day!

Later the same process was used to offer a gerontology certificate off campus to employees of the State Area Agency on Aging. Over eighty persons in our area took advantage of this study. In my years at Livingstone, I was able to write and secure federal and state grants totaling $2,500,000.

Barbara, though still enjoying activities in Salisbury and helping Lois with their mother's needs, felt the need for a challenge. In 1976 she enrolled in the one year Licensed Practical Nurses training course at Rowan Technical Institute. She studied hard, her biology major in college standing her in good stead in the course work. She greatly enjoyed the nursing aspects of the training. She worked full time at Rowan Memorial Hospital for eight months to "set her skills". This was quite difficult, but also rewarding. For the next four years she worked on weekends in the Lutheran Home Nursing Center, especially enjoying working there with Sally Large, a good Salisbury friend.

Barbara's older sister, Janice (Sturkie) was her beloved mentor, and the two were always very close. She had bravely and successfully fought cancer through much of her life but finally developed liver cancer in 1978. She and Doug were active in the local Cancer Society, and just three months before her death on January 20, 1980, they were featured on Columbia's WISTV. They shared very personally their own experience with terminal cancer. Barbara, Lois and their mother went to Columbia to help her during the last couple of weeks and Barbara was deeply grateful for her nursing knowledge. It was a most grievous loss. After Doug died in 1995, Charme and Kin, their children, have been close to us and to Paul and Lois.

First Return to HongKong – 1980

It all started in 1980 when we received a surprise invitation from our good friend Rev. John Ma, pastor of China Congregational Church in HongKong on behalf of the HongKong Council, Church of Christ in China. Barbara and I were invited to attend a special week of celebrations of the 25th year of the reorganization of the HongKong Church. I had participated in this process, so it was very meaningful to have been included.

Airline tickets were sent to both of us and our stay was arranged at the European YMCA in Kowloon. Almost all of the missionaries who had served the Chinese Church from the 1950s had been invited as guests. It was a great reunion and a special treat to be included in the many special services and celebrations. I was asked to speak at John Ma's church, one of the largest Protestant congregations in HongKong. It was a joy to revisit the Haven of Hope Hospital and other projects in which we had been involved during the years of our service in HongKong. Not only was the invitation unexpected, but it represented the gratitude of the Christian community we had served for fifteen years. We were deeply touched by this celebration!

First Return to China Since Leaving in 1950

Some of the most significant events of the late 1970s and early 1980s were the opportunities opening to Westerners to return to China, which had been closed to foreigners during the Cultural Revolution 1966—1976. I had always hoped that one day I would be able to return to Kuling, my birthplace and to Yueyang where Barbara and I had served our first years as missionaries 31 years earlier. This was a strong feeling which grew as we heard of reports of friends who had been able to revisit their former homes in China.

The first such opportunity for me came in 1981. Early that year a letter from our good friend David Stowe of language school days and now Executive Secretary of the United Church Board for World Ministries, invited me to help with a United Church of Christ tour. It was unbeliev-able! I could hardly imagine that it would really happen. I even started thinking in Chinese to prepare myself.

The plan was that a United Church of Christ group of 270 members would travel to HongKong together and then divide into three groups to visit mainland Chinese churches. Paul Gregory, who had been in Yuanling when we were in Yueyang, would be teamed with me to direct one group of 90 Church members on this tour. What a wonderful opportunity! Paul was Asia Secretary of our Mission Board and had served very effectively in Japan. We worked well together. Our ability to speak Chinese and our past experiences in China were tremendously helpful. We arranged to meet Chinese Church leaders and visit Christian institutions such as schools and hospitals that had been nationalized.

In Shanghai we had a very meaningful gathering in the Community Church where I had worshipped as a senior in high school. Community Church was very near the Shanghai American School from which I gradu-ated in 1938. The Church had remained exactly the same since I had last seen it forty three years before. Memories of the service honoring Boy Scouts and my appointment as assistant scoutmaster swept over me. I always felt closely attached to the Church and to my time in school in Shanghai.

Pastor Yang who spoke excellent English told our group of 90 that only two churches in Shanghai had been returned to the Chinese Christian Council, but that many more would be reopened in a short time. He spoke of the tremendous interest in Christianity but that the many years of ina-bility to train ministers had caused serious problems, which meant that the "priesthood of believers" was a very real strength.

Our tourist visit was an eye-opener for all of us. The Cultural Revolution had ended in 1976, but tourism was still in its beginning stages follow-ing premier Deng Xiao-Ping's opening of China to the West. The foreign travel and hotel infrastructure was still being built. We were able to visit only a limited number of cities: Xian, Beijing, Nanjing, and Shanghai.

In Xian we attended our first service. The small church was so crowded there was not even any space on the front "guest" row. We were recognized by the pastor and welcomed warmly by the members. We were impressed by the many young people as several classrooms were filled by youth lis-tening to a loud speaker. Some of our group joined the crowded alleyway from the street as standees listening to the loud speakers. It was our first experience with the fact that few churches had been opened but that attendance was clearly very heavy.

In Beijing we attended the only church open at the time, held in a YMCA auditorium on the second floor. The service was so well attended that worshippers stood all around outside the church, listening to loud speakers.

Of great personal importance to me was the opportunity to meet in Beijing, my childhood playmate, Yuan Mei, wife of the Deputy Minister of Agriculture, Dr. Yang. They invited me to their home. Their daughter, Bai Xian, was very vocal with her parents in asking "Uncle" (meaning me) to help her arrange to visit the US to study. She felt cheated because the Cultural Revolution had prevented her from obtaining an advanced education. She had been a "red guard" for Mao Dz-dong and spent those years shouting political slogans from north to central China, walking all the way to the Yangtze River! I promised to consult with Barbara about a possible visit with us.

Dr Yang had himself been required as had most of the Communist leadership to renew his political dedication in the hysteria of the Cultural Revolution. He spent two years after the age of 70 working "in the countryside." He was assigned to a farm to clean out the horse stables and perform a number of vigorous exercises to show his loyalty. It was not until Deng XiaoPing became premier after Mao's death that he was reinstated as Deputy Minister of Agriculture.

Their son, Yuan Xing, was working for the China Association for Science and Technology. He asked me to bring my brothers and a group of medical personnel to China, saying he would arrange a lecture tour as well as be able to offer inexpensive travel and accommodation. He assured us that we would find such a trip both affordable and interesting as he could accommodate all of us to meet our interests.

Second Visit, China Association of Science and Technology Lecture Tour – 1981

When I got back to Salisbury, I immediately contacted my brothers, Don and Bob. With their contacts, we arranged a small group of physicians, a dentist, and spouses to go to China to lecture in the fall of 1981. I found an inexpensive "World Airways" special to HongKong and return because they were ferrying Vietnamese immigrants to the USA for resettlement.

The group was comprised of Bob Whitener, psychiatrist, and wife, Marion; Nelson Large, dentist, and wife, Sally; Don Whitener, obstetrician/gynecologist, paired with Ted Blount, pediatrician; Sterling, social worker/gerontologist, and Barbara.

Don and Ted lectured on some new findings and techniques in their practices. Bob spoke on the new drugs being used in psychiatric treatment. Nelson, brought slides of his dental practice that were well received. My topic was on the demographics of aging in the US as vital for planning. Unfortunately, not many in China understood the word "gerontology," but I did receive one invitation to speak to several hundred "barefoot doctors" in Changsha, Hunan. At the former Yale-in-China hospital, a resident physician who had been a member of our Yuanling Mission hospital team, Dr. Graham Wu, was my translator. I also used some Chinese which amazed the group. Dr. Wu had been a physician at our Abounding Grace Hospital in Yuanling where we met in 1947. I asked him if he would like any book I could mail to him. He replied that if I could find a used copy of Handel's "Messiah," there was a good chance such a copy would reach him and it did.

On this "exchange tour" we visited both Yueyang and Kuling (Lushan) as Yuan Xing, Dr. Yang's son, arranged our tour to suit our wishes. Our national guide was a friend of his, Dr. Huang Shan, whom we liked immensely, was a neurosurgeon who wanted to improve his English. He was to have an opportunity to study at Vanderbilt University in Nashville so needed practice in English. We met his family and are glad to know that he is working today in Nashville at Vanderbilt University School of Medicine.

This first visit to Yueyang was very exciting. When we first arrived at our hotel we could not believe our eyes! Standing there and smiling broadly was Li DzMing, who in earlier days was our water carrier and gardener. He had found out that we were coming to Yueyang and had the courage to meet us at the hotel. In those early days of welcoming American "imperialists," many persons were very careful in making contact fearing repercussions from the Party. We were glad to learn that he had been employed for years at a rice mill and was still the happy person he had been 35 years before.

The local Communist Party chief, Mr. Chang, certainly did a great job welcoming the three Whitener brothers, escorting us to some of the old residences where we had lived and also making sure we visited the old Hoy Memorial Hospital, now the modernized Red Cross Hospital. We have a wonderful picture standing with a portion of the original hospital building behind us and in the background, the famous Yueyang Tang Dynasty pagoda that so entranced me in my youth and inspired the title of this memoir.

Our host, the Party Chief, rode us around the city on streets that had been widened for vehicular traffic, proudly taking us to the newly renovated Yue Yang Lou, the ancient North Gate of the city where poets of early dynasties commemorated the DongTing Lake. We were escorted to a small building which served as an artists' workshop. Here the hosts had us watch a very talented young man who actually drew pictures of some of the famous fish of the lake, crabs, shrimp etc. using his fingernails for long delicate lines and the tips of his fingers for writing large characters – "Return Again to Your Former Home." These were given to us in the form of two scrolls.

One very memorable event was the "welcome meal" offered by our host, Mr. Chang, the party chief. Ten of us were seated at a large round table and served the insipid bottled orange drink. After appropriate words of welcome back and forth, the hot/spicy Hunan dishes started to arrive. One of the first was the Yueyang favorite, a large plate of fried Hunan red peppers. These pieces of dynamite looked exactly like the ones I had grown up eating with my amah 50 years earlier. Mr. Chang smilingly invited me as the leader of the delegation to take the first bite. I stated I did not deserve the honor. All were looking at me fully expecting a quick explosion, I was confident. I ate with enjoyment a reasonably small one, and told them the pepper was really delicious and reminded me of my childhood. Then I immediately urged them to join me. At that point, Mr. Chang pointed to his assistant. The poor man turned beet-red, gingerly found a very small pepper, and braved it down.

DzMing, who met us at the hotel, took us to the agency where Liu WenChu worked. He had been our bright young helper of many talents. He had worked hard to educate himself, had joined the Communist Party and had become a manager of the agency that contracted the cutting, collecting, and shipping of over 500,000 tons of the Dongting lakeside reeds to paper mills located down the Yangtze river. It was a joy to see him again.

Both DzMing and WenChu kindly arranged for us to visit our old Huping home, four miles out of town but now connected by a bumpy gravel road built on a long dike with a bridge adjacent to a temporary railway bridge being restored after the war. It was one we had used when we first came to China. We were quite appalled and saddened by the deteriorated condition of the buildings at Huping School even though the facility was being used to train Communist cadres for work in the rural countryside.

Our first visit to Kuling was also a special joy. We traveled downriver from Wuhan to Jiujiang overnight by river steamer and then up the mountain by small minibus for the first time on the narrow and winding vehicular road. Walking around the mountain with my childhood memories strong, I was amazed at the few changes since 1948. Barbara and I found the house we had owned, Lot 160.

We had received compensation for our house from the US government in the 1970s using Chinese assets held for twenty years in the US. Most Mission societies had donated all properties to the Church or to schools and hospitals before leaving in 1950. The mountain residences and roadways were being prepared for summer vacation visits by Chinese tourists, and our former Kuling American School was being used as a rehabilitation and rest hostel for Communist cadres.

We were hosted royally in Beijing by the Lecture Tour Association and by our good friends Dr. and Mrs. Yang. Barbara and I had our very first visit to the Great Wall and the Ming Tombs as well as all the other beautiful tourist sites as we never had the opportunity to travel extensively when we were living in China. We made tentative arrangements with the Yangs for BaiXian to come to Salisbury for study.

We were in touch with Principal Liu's son, Leonard, who had helped us so much when we first arrived at Huping. He had married a scientist who had once worked in the US. He had served the China Railway System as a Language officer. We were able to call him to arrange a time to meet with him. He suggested the famous Peking Hotel, but told us we would need to meet just outside first in order to take him inside the big hotel reserved for foreigners.

All actions by foreigners in 1981 were under careful observation by authorities, so we met Leonard out on the sidewalk down at the street level. He had brought his 16 year old daughter, Han Li. When we got safely inside, we decided to find a place in the large lobby to talk. Han Li was interested in elevators, saying she had never had the chance to ride one. Barbara offered to take her for a ride. They went up and down several times to Han Li's excitement. Renewal of our friendship after over 30 years was extremely welcome.

It is impossible to express how much these first trips back to China meant to us. There were few souvenirs available in those days, but we brought home many memories and photos. New viruses were abundant so most of us arrived home with raging colds! Having been to China, it seemed that we could hardly wait to go again.

Family Trip to China – 1983

From our previous trips in 1981 I had learned much about arranging tours and finding inexpensive ways to manage China itineraries. My tours always concentrated on the rural and "real China", assuring family and friends of very reasonable prices. It was amazing what we could save when we really knew how to find the bargains and the low cost Chinese, but clean, hotels. Admittedly, we had a few real bummers, but that just added to the interest!

Our 1983 trip was arranged especially for close family members and friends, all eager to "see China". Most of the friends were from Salisbury, a Social Work colleague, Hope Davis among them. We had arranged quite an ambitious itinerary for beginner China travelers and were very fortunate that our tour members were amazingly good sports. It was not a luxury tour!

Riding the train from HongKong and Guangzhou to Yueyang introduced the group to the rigors of Chinese "express" trains. I told them that unless they experienced what the ordinary person suffered, they would not experience real life in China. Rail service, though improved over that of 1946/50, was quite a shock, even to our well-traveled family members. All quickly learned to use trench-style Chinese toilets on a wildly swaying train.

In Yueyang, we visited Huping School. It was very meaningful for daughters Karen and Kim, in particular, to see where we had begun our life in China and the place that was Karen's first home. It was also special to see again our friends and former helpers, Liu WenChu and Li DzMing.

In the two years since we had visited Yueyang, it was quite evident that there was a clear change in government attitude toward the Christian religions. While religion was still called an "opiate," it was assured that if the strict laws of registration were followed, Christians and other believers would be permitted to follow their beliefs and meet regularly. This was most clearly seen in our Yueyang church in the funds available for planning a new church building. In 1981, at the time of my first visit, the church was in poor repair, still occupied by several dozen police families. It had been vacated by the authorities, returned to the church community and in 1983 some repairs made so we were able to meet in a newly whitewashed room for Sunday worship with Pastor Meng, now in his late eighties.

The Church was a part of the national Protestant Chinese Christian Church which had been formed by uniting all Protestant denominations. Only as members of the one Protestant Church or the Chinese Catholic Church are all Chinese Christians permitted to hold meetings. This meant that the single buildings in smaller towns and cities were forced to accommodate a great variety of theological and worship preferences. These very basic differences have continued to impede genuine union. All religions were permitted to reopen their temples and places of worship.

The tour included several marvelous scenic sites: Kweilin in GuangXi province for the unforgettable cruise down the Li River; the Stone Forest in Kunming: the incredible Terracotta Army in Xian and a shaking bus trip to DaZhu to see the grotto of fabulous Buddhist sculptures in a remote mountain area in Sichuan. Sleeping accommodations in the nearby village were pretty primitive, but our intrepid travelers chalked it up to part of being in China.

We love to relate a special happening when one of our buses broke down in the country-side between Changsha and Yueyang. A village was nearby as well as a small, family-run factory, belching black smoke from its chimney. Our guide telephoned immediately for a replacement bus which would take well over an hour to arrive. The delay was well used as we visited the small factory which was casting brake drums for trucks. It was clear that pollution controls were far in the future for China.

A few women from the village began to gather on the hillside near our bus so I asked if we might visit their village. They were friendly and welcomed us, interested in this group of stranded Americans. The women had a home industry going of making beautiful cross-stitched items for a company in Changsha. The visit was a great success as the women brought out their work and offered the items for sale. Our group purchased some things, but there was only one small tablecloth for sale and several of our women wanted it. I arbitrated by preparing straws to be drawn. The group agreed that the whole unplanned experience was uniquely special.

We subsequently organized or participated in China tours in 1986, 1988, 1989, 1992, 1996, 2000, 2007 and 2010.

Yang BaiXian Comes to Salisbury – 1983

Arrangements were finally completed for Yang BaiXian, the daughter of our old friends in Beijing, to come to Salisbury in the fall of 1983. The plan was to help her enter Catawba College so that she could earn a USA college degree, building on the meager education she had received in China much earlier. BaiXian was in her 30's and her extraordinary experience as a Red Guard during the Cultural Revolution had made her a very independent and headstrong young woman. She had the totally unrealistic idea that she could immediately enter a Master's program. Nothing that we tried to arrange was acceptable to her. Unfortunately, the same attitudes prevailed in our household. Suffice it to say, it was not a successful experience, and we were greatly relieved when she decided to go to Los Angeles where there was a Chinese community. She has lived there ever since, never continuing her education. She married an older man, a German, who has since died. She has one son, now an adult. BaiXian is a very smart woman and makes a living playing the stock market daily. She keeps in touch with us and is fond of me whom she calls "Uncle".

Taiwan Mission Service – 1984 to 1986

In 1983 I learned from Paul Gregory, Asia Secretary, that the United Church Board for World Ministries was making plans for the retirement of all who had served under the Board in the 1940s. We had completed total service in China and HongKong of nearly 23 years. We learned that we needed two additional years of service to meet the Board retirement criteria of 25 years' service for full pension and medical benefits. Following this news, Barbara and I were invited by Tainan Theological College president, Ching-fen Hsiao, through our United Church Board for World Ministries to teach in Taiwan for two years. The Mission Board would pay a missionary salary and travel expenses for this appointment.

Livingstone College did not have a school-sponsored plan of sabbatical leaves for faculty. If a teacher wished to take leave to study, it was usually easily granted but required a special grant, as I did in 1973-74 with the Fulbright Scholar's award, or find an institution willing to offer a living allowance for study. Taking sabbatical leave from Livingstone College meant that no college salary was paid during the leave period and that I would need to get special permission to take a second year of leave.

It was necessary to make an urgent decision to clarify the management of our Social Work Department in my absence. I had earlier recruited Dr. Pil J. Cho to join me after Bill Pollard was asked to chair the Social Work Department at Grambling University. Pil agreed to take over when I was granted a leave of absence to accept the Taiwan appointment.

Barbara had been working with her sister, Lois, to help in the care of their mother, who, in her nineties, was still living alone. Lois generously agreed that we should go to Taiwan.

Our preparations to go to Taiwan were onerous. We wished to rent our Salisbury house unfurnished. This meant, of course, packing up all our furniture and possessions and moving out. We managed to distribute our furniture among our family members up and down the east coast, and took some things to the mountains. Tools and such items we packed away in an attic-like storage space. One of our children used the car. It was all a huge undertaking! We rented to the family of a jeweler in town whom we hoped would take care of the house, giving them a list of dos and don'ts to which they agreed, and hoping for the best.

Mission Board Appointment – 1984 to 1986

Our "team appointment" by the Mission Board was to teach at Tainan Theological College, as well as offer a course or two at the Graduate School of Social Work at Tunghai University in Taichung. We were to join Board Missionaries Dr. Mark and Ginny Thelin. He was chair of the Department of Sociology at the Theological College as well as teaching Sociology at Tunghai University. I was charged to organize the Social Work program in Tainan to conform to the standards being used by the Council on Social Work Education in the US. I had brought my curriculum materials with me.

Barbara was appointed to teach an English section of the first-year class. Unfortunately, she was given no curriculum or materials of any kind. Presbyterian Missionaries, Tom and Eleanor McNair were the English department faculty and were invaluable help in getting Barbara started. They continued to work together with her during our two years.

We were assigned a small apartment in a faculty block on campus. We did all of our housework, shopping at local markets, and even had a washing machine, dubbed the "rope-maker." We enjoyed having student fellowship groups meet with us.

That year, I had purchased a portable (Televideo) computer, which weighed about 25 pounds. I marvel at its effectiveness even with its 5" by 7" screen, which certainly strained my eyesight. During the two years of teaching in Taiwan it helped me write out many a lecture, prepare weekly tests, and record over a hundred pages of a journal. It was a big help to Barbara also.

As my language skills in China had been clearly focused on theological teaching rather than social work, I was given a translator into Chinese national language ("gwoyu" formerly called "Mandarin") for my Taiwan lectures, even though the class was often able to speak clearly and simply enough for me to conduct discussions in Chinese. In fact, as the vocabulary became familiar, I often found my colleague, Miss Naomi Chen, telling the class that I had not really liked her first translation and then she would clarify what I meant. It was always because she would leave out some point I was trying to make so I would rephrase my statement. The students always got a big laugh out of the fact that I kept close watch on Naomi, who had her Master's degree in Sociology from a college in Texas. A lovely person, she taught several courses in our department and was a good sport.

I also insisted that the senior students become somewhat computer literate. We were able to secure gifts to purchase ten Apple E computers, which were being manufactured in Taiwan. We taught all of our students to program and write at least a very short paper in Basic language. It turned out to be one of the best things I was able to accomplish as our graduates found jobs in agencies much more easily when they explained their new skills.

The language in Taiwan was a dialect which had come from Fujian province in China. It was frustrating as it was quite different from the national language, understood by everyone. Our college was permitted to teach in Taiwanese because it was operated by the church, but the government had strict rules that all official meetings and classes were to be conducted in the official national language. This meant that all aboriginal tribespersons and persons originally from different parts of China communicated in "guoyu," the national language. The Government had decreed it must be used by all schools.

Barbara and I enjoyed Taiwan very much. Travel was easy by train or bus and we tried to visit as many of the beauty spots as possible. The names "Formosa" and "Taiwan" connoted beauty and we found this to be true.

From Kenting at the southern tip to Alishan, over 10,000 ft. high in the middle, to the rocky coast in the north and Taidung on the east coast, we tried to take it all in.

Barbara's Family Visit to Taiwan – 1985

We were fortunate that Robert Brown (Barbara's brother) and Hermine, Paul and Lois Carter (Barbara's sister), and Barbara's brother-in-law, Doug Sturkie, were able to visit us in Taiwan in the spring. We traveled the island to see the beauty spots. It was a first trip for the Browns and the Carters to the Orient. We were honored but were hard put to squeeze in the very best scenes for their short stay. Unfortunately however, several of them had some intestinal adjustments to make! One had raging diarrhea, another, a blockage. We took the latter to the emergency room for help. We howled with laughter at his account of the little Chinese nurse telling him to say "ah" as she inserted the enema nozzle!

Tainan Theological College - September 1985 to June 1986

We determined to spend our summers back in the USA so were able to find inexpensive airfare back to North Carolina, where we stayed with Barbara's mother and in our mountain cottage at Blowing Rock. This was necessary, as we had rented our Salisbury home when we left in 1984.

We returned to Tainan in September 1985 and continued to find our work pretty demanding but worthwhile. This second year, I was asked by President Hsiao to develop a ten-year plan for the seminary as he had prepared one a decade earlier. Once again I was faced with a decision. I felt it would be meaningless to write out "my concept of what the school ought to be in the future" so I told him I really could not do that. If, however, he wanted me to develop a process for planning and would give me the assistance of an interpreter, I would undertake the research. It was interesting that he took several weeks to decide whether he could trust the process I outlined of going to every presbytery of the Taiwan Presbyterian Church to meet with pastors, graduates, and interested lay-persons to discuss the future of the seminary. With the "go ahead" I was assigned a very talented recent graduate to help me with translation. We did travel the island in three months, meeting with pastors and church leaders. We asked for a commitment of at least two hours since we found that it always took an hour for everyone to tell us what was wrong with the school. A second hour was required to begin to learn what their hopes and expectations were.

I found that the ministers and laypeople of the church were interested and polite, sticking to "guoyu" at the beginning and then in their excitement switching to their "Taiwanese" dialect. Many a time, my helper stopped them to return to language I could understand. More than once I switched to Cantonese, of which they did not understand a word, so they began to get the drift of my problem. I returned home with my understanding of their concerns and suggestions and with my assistant, arranged the findings into categories. By putting these all on spreadsheets he would then translate everything into the Chinese written language. We printed off both for further study.

New Year's Trip – 1986

This was a visit to Bonnie and Tom in Thailand during our winter vacation at Tainan Theological College.

"Happy New Year!" - with sparklers, noisemakers, and some paper hats we welcomed 1986. No ordinary party this! The setting was quite strange. We were seated 10 ft. off the ground on a bamboo mat covering the rough teak floor of a Karen villager's house by a river in the Northern hills of Thailand. "Out of this world" aptly described our feeling. We had just completed the first leg of a 3 day trek to visit tribal villages close to the infamous "Golden Triangle" of poppy fields and bandits near Burma and Laos.

There were eight in our group - our daughter, Bonnie, her husband Tom and four other compatible trekkers and us. **After a ride in an open truck and then in a "long-tailed-boat," a flat-bottomed skiff powered by a car engine, we arrived at the village by 4 pm.** The skilled pilot knew his sand bars and rocks. In fact, I was the only one to get a soaking in the white water rapids just before arrival.

Yes, it really was New Year's Eve. Our guide had prepared a good Thai supper of vegetables, a little meat and plenty of steamed rice. It was served by the only light available, a single candle. We brought out the trappings with which to celebrate New Year, western style. It was only 7 pm. but we knew we could never stay awake till midnight. The children of the family delighted in the merrymaking and happily accepted the hats and noisemakers.

The Thai hosts asked everyone if they would like to try a short smoke of high-quality opium. They had plenty of paraphernalia so all partook. I struck out as the smell of the small bits of opium being lit turned my stomach. I had to go outside. The group had fun with the experiment, but I was anxious to get outside, as the odor was an extremely sharp reminder of our family trip on a small but crowded Japanese river steamer when I was about five or six.

All eight of us were preparing to bed down for the night on pallets on the floor of the main room of the house when we heard a loudspeaker presenting announcements in Thai as well as guitar music. This lured us to an outdoor community celebration of the coming New Year. A small wooden platform outside the Church held a pressure kerosene lantern. A car battery powered the public address system. Young people were singing around a guitar. The pastor came to organize the evening program. Children presented skits, sang songs they had learned in school, and provided a variety of entertainment as the villagers of some sixty homes gathered for the evening. At one point the pastor turned to Barbara and me and asked us to sing. He knew practically no English - we got the idea when he pointed to us and said "song". We sang, "O Come all ye Faithful" as we felt they would know it. The pastor had a tribal hymnal which was published in the 1970s by the Baptist press. The "amateur night" program continued long after we had returned to our house and "snuggled" down, fully clothed, on the hard floor wrapped in a couple of blankets against the chill. In the middle of the night we were awakened by rifle fire. No fear - just the local way to celebrate - 1986 had arrived!

The next morning we left on our elephants for another tribal village two or more hours ride away. Barbara describes the ride like being perched up on top of a rocking chair which rocked sideways. Each of us alone in the special seat watched a driver sit practically on the elephant's head. Barbara was very distressed that her driver kept whacking the poor animal on the skull to urge greater speed. The driver insisted it did not hurt the elephant at all!

I had stopped by the Church to listen to the preacher speak to his congregation of 40 adults and 15 children. Outside the Church a group of men led up a large pig to prepare the New Years feast. Huge cauldrons of water were set to boil. It appeared that the entire village must belong to the Church, or at least they were all happily anticipating the feast yet to come.

We felt warmed by the villagers friendliness, saddened that the foreign tourist trekking like ours was obviously changing their life style and customs, at the same time improving, at least a little, their very low standard of living. Our prayer for them was that in their own faith and understanding of God's will in their daily lives, they will be able to preserve what is best in their own culture.

Tainan Theological College and Seminary Board Meeting

The culmination of the process to define a ten-year plan for the seminary came in June 1986 when my son-in-law Adam Klein, Kim's husband, came to Tainan with Kim. He was a part-time faculty member at Harvard with his own consulting firm. He and Kim came with other family members on a tour so we were able to capitalize on his knowledge. Adam's ability to use process for decision-making helped the Tainan Theological College and Seminary Board work for an entire day setting priorities for the future. It was not a ten-year plan, but it did start a five-year church-wide discussion on the directions for the seminary and the eventual decision that all candidates for the MDiv (Master of Divinity) degree should first have a college degree. That it was a repeat of the history of most American denominations in early 1800, is a reminder that an educated society requires an educated clergy.

Family Travel to China

In addition to Kim and Adam, mentioned above, other family members – Mark and Dana, Gerald and Katrina also came with them to visit us in Taiwan. We all went together on a special mission to China to visit Katrina's half-brother, Li Qin, his wife, Huang LiZhen, and family in Wuhan. Her brother is retired on a good pension from the Communist army.

In the several years prior to the trip, Katrina had re-established contact with Li Qin, the son of her father's third wife and much older than Katrina, whom she had never really known. Katrina had recently shared with our family many details of her early life prior to being discovered by Mrs. Shaffer and me in 1956. Katrina's mother was from HongKong and met her father there, becoming his fourth wife. During the turbulent refugee years, the family lived in various hillside shacks in HongKong. When Katrina was only a few years old, they returned to Li Village in China. Because her mother had become sick and a "burden" to the Communist village, she and Katrina were allowed to return to HongKong. Her father was not permitted to go, however, and not long after they left, he died. After returning to HongKong, she and her mother were befriended by a former neighbor, Kei Ma, now living in Homantin, and brought into her home. Because of crowding, they were asked to leave, moving to the streets in Central, HongKong, and living that way for six months. Her mother became very ill and died in a hospital. Before dying, she told Katrina to go live with her uncle, her father's youngest brother. Katrina did so for a short month, living in terrible, crowded conditions with 20 other people. After several unsuccessful attempts by her relatives to locate her half-brother, they tried to place her elsewhere. Katrina finally ran away, and though only seven years old but a true survivalist, found her way across the harbor and city to her old friend Kei Ma in Homantin, who took her in. This was the point in time when Mrs. Shaffer and I happened upon her.

Thirty years later, in 1986 in Wuhan, it was a very emotional meeting, the first time Katrina and Li Qin had seen each other since Katrina was a tiny child. Her brother expressed much guilt that he had been unable to help Katrina and great appreciation to us that we had become her family. Katrina continues to keep in close touch with Li Qin and family.

Continuing on, our family group had great travels to Chungking and Dazu in Szechuan, and through the Three Gorges. Kuling, and Yueyang completed this familiarization tour for our small family group. Of special note in Yueyang was the planned destruction of our old Mission Church built in the early 1900s. The city used it from 1950 to 1981 for police family housing. It was returned to the Church members in 1983 and was scheduled for removal due to damage. The government paid the back rent on its use which the Chinese Christian Church used toward building a new church. During construction all the Christians in town were to use the former Episcopal Church. Rent was also paid for that Church and added to the rent for what I called "ours" to make the sum sufficient to begin construction of the new Church which seats over 1000 members for the use of all Protestants in the city.

During our time in Kuling, the Lushan administration held a big celebration for my 65th birthday. They provided a wonderful party! On this visit we met Frank Lu Ming who continues to be our friend and tour advisor par excellence.

Return to Salisbury – Summer 1986

We felt our work at Tainan Theological College was successful in that Barbara and I made good friends, worked with a group of wonderful young people, and were rewarded with experiences we will always treasure. We were able to tutor a young colleague, Jeanine Lin, who wanted to study in Canada, but was frustrated by her lack of preparation and language ability. Barbara helped her study of English; I helped with social work policy analysis. I personally knew several Social Work faculty members in HongKong who helped her become accepted into the graduate social work program at the Chinese University of HongKong, where she eventually earned both her MSW and DSW degrees. She is today the Chair of the Social Work department at Tainan College. She accomplished all this because her husband took care of two young daughters during her required semesters in HongKong. He was a connoisseur and grower of Chinese tea, especially the famous Wu Long tea grown on Mount Alishan. As noted on several occasions, we developed strong relationships with church ministers and leaders. All in all our two-year teaching stint was a very positive experience.

During our two years in Taiwan, I kept a running Journal of Notes. Over 100 pages were too much to include in this tome, so if you want to get a very brief glimpse of a few of our experiences, turn to the Addenda.

On our return from Taiwan, the first big task was collecting our possessions and moving back into our house. You guessed it! Our renters had not been as kind to the house as we had hoped. One "don't" we had agreed upon was "no dogs". Their poodle had piddled on our rugs so we had to replace them. Our bedrooms had hardwood floors on which the renters had glued carpeting so the floors had to be refinished. They had broken the locks on the storage space, used our tools and taken some of them. We weren't happy, either, with how they had pruned the shrubbery. It could have been worse, but we had, naively perhaps, hoped for better!

Last Year at Livingstone – 1986-87

A summer in the mountains of North Carolina was a wonderful rest before returning to Livingstone College for a final year of teaching. I had been able to recruit a former student, Carrie Hunter Bolton, from her social work position in Albemarle to come to Livingstone, offering her the chance to become Chair of the Social Work Department. As she was a very capable young woman, I hoped she would consider undertaking further study to stabilize her position as chair.

The year started with yet another new president for Livingstone College, as the Bishops for the AME Zion Church as Trustees seemed unwilling to challenge and/or pay enough to attract a top-notch educator to lead the college. Small colleges were all facing some difficult days due to inflation and to the cutting back of federal subsidies to assist black institutions.

Completing my twentieth year at Livingstone, I decided to teach the first introductory course, undertake some field supervision, and teach several advanced courses and one on aging. Rigorous coursework was always a good way to assure that the strongest students stuck to the social work major. We had maintained a good record at graduate schools, so we continued to hold our students to high standards, and worked hard to defeat "grade inflation." We were also one of the few departments utilizing computer tests, as well as demanding good writing skills. I really enjoyed my solid year of teaching and gladly turned over the task of Chair of the Social Work Department to Carrie Bolton during the second semester.

Dr. Greene saw as his agenda the need to reduce dependence on non-African-American faculty. Several professors from India, and also those of us who had been at Livingstone for a number of years, appeared to be targeted for "weeding out." Dean Olivia Spaulding told me in June, sadly, that I was to discontinue part-time contracts to very talented teachers and instead hire a full-time African-American faculty person. I was sorry that I would not be able to strengthen the connections with our state agencies which had been so successfully supportive of our program. It was obvious, however, that Livingstone was entering a new day of self-determination, a posture urgently needed in this new day.

It was a reminder of the last months of Barbara's and my time in HongKong when we realized in 1967 that many important changes had taken place. My 20 years at Livingstone College had also been very challenging as well as intellectually rewarding. Qualified faculty members were difficult to find even at premium salary rates because the social agencies were also vying for competent social workers. It was time to retire. As it had been for me in HongKong, I had always considered my tenure preparatory to turning leadership over to those who were ready to step up. I felt I had furthered much progress in that direction.

On the personal side I was ready to turn to a more relaxed schedule and new interests. With our increasing interest in overseas travel, retirement came happily for Barbara and me.

Teaching Years in Salisbury, North Carolina – 1967 to 1987

35

36

37

38

35. Chris served for two years 1969 – 70 in the US Marine Corps in Vietnam.
36. Barbi in their century-old log house reconstructed by Chris in the mountains
37. Bonnie in my big garden of Chinese vegetables
38. At Livingstone College Bill Pollard and I work for an accredited BA
in Social Work.

First China Visit and Taiwan Teaching

39. Yueyang 1981: Whitener brothers and childhood playmate Chen Lixien
    next to me with old Hoy Memorial Hospital and the Pagoda
40. Our Student Fellowship at Tainan Theological College 1984-86

Chapter VII

Retirement – Travel and More 1987 – 2011

True, I had retired from teaching at Livingstone College, but I was not at all ready for the proverbial "rocking chair!" During the year, I was invited by a friend to go to Raleigh to interview for a part-time position as a surveyor for a newly formed home care accreditation process. A group of agencies providing home health services felt that North Carolina needed to assure quality care because the federal health system was starting to reimburse Medicare and Medicaid patients, as well as other elders requiring care. I saw this as an opportunity to participate in a new venture and to use my social work skills.

NC Accreditation for Home Care – 1987

I undertook the two or three day surveys and found them very interesting, as well as income producing. In a few years, the agency became independent and was named the North Carolina Accreditation Commission for Home Care.

The policy of governmental systems was to find the means to keep the elderly in their own homes as long as possible. By offering good caregiver support in nursing, aides, homemaker help, and even offering remuneration to family members, the question of quality was extremely important. Our surveys were to assure participants of home care that the agencies contracted by their insurance programs were really qualified.

After one of my first surveys, I asked the committee for permission to make a home visit at each site to determine how the standards were actually working out at the grassroots level. On the other hand, nurses who were also surveyors felt that they could secure adequate information from other agency nurses. As a social worker, I insisted on seeing for myself. It was a fortuitous decision because I quickly determined a number of issues that could be resolved only after a home visit. This plan was adopted and subsequently used to advantage by our accreditation survey teams. After that, I was asked to help write up the standards, as well as the survey scoring system. In the ensuing fourteen years, I undertook three or four surveys each year, finally retiring from the commission in 2001.

Family Issues – Care of Barbara's Aging Mother

On reentry into life in Salisbury following our service (1984-1986) in Taiwan, Barbara resumed with her sister, Lois, care of their mother. Granna was still living independently in her own little home, but requiring much more assistance. She was still in amazingly good health and her mind was clear, but her sight was greatly affected by macular degeneration. She was an avid user of recorded material sent from the State program for the blind in Raleigh. Lois and/or Barbara visited her daily and coordinated shopping and other household tasks. It was a happy arrangement that all three enjoyed. It also meant that trips or other activities of the daughters could be arranged so that one of them was always on hand.

April 21, 1988 was a very auspicious day. It was Granna's 100th birthday and a huge celebration was held for her. Extended family came from far and near for the birthday dinner. One hundred red roses decorated the table and she successfully blew out 100 candles on her cake! The highlight of the occasion for the guests was the recitation by Granna of a poem about George Washington which she had memorized in grade school.

In the year following, however, Granna began to fail. She was not ill, but lost strength and then ability even to walk. It became clear that plans should be made for her future care. The family dynamics in this situation were very interesting. Granna had always had an inordinate dread of ending her life in a nursing home. Though we respected her feelings, it was still one of the options for her care. Robert, the elder son, had always been "Number One" and the rest of us felt that he would take the lead in planning and decision making. Instead, Robert's approach was "whatever Mother wants". He had always been supportive of what Lois and Barbara were doing for Granna, but he and Hermine lived in South Carolina and could have no part in daily care giving. I was the pragmatist, feeling that she would receive the best of care in the Lutheran Nursing Home in Salisbury. The difficulty for me was that I knew how torn Lois and Barbara were. They loved their mother and wished to do what she wanted. This led to setting up a small "nursing home" in Granna's home where she was bedfast for the next 18 months. Barbara and Lois took daytime shifts and supervised a fine team of women (our angels!) hired for nights and weekends. Again, Barbara was glad for the skills she had learned in her practical nursing program. Granna had funds to cover the costs. She was an appreciative and cooperative patient. It was a confining time for Barbara, but at the same time deeply meaningful to be able to be of service to her mother who had done so much through the years for our family. Florence Bodenhorn Brown died peacefully at age 102 on December 27, 1990 in her own home.

North Carolina National Association of Social Workers

I had been a member of the National Association of Social Workers following my graduation from the MSW program in Chapel Hill, NC, in 1965. I worked closely with the NASW, North Carolina Chapter, from the start of my teaching career in 1967 as I was seeking social work placements in community agencies with MSW supervisors. In 1988 I felt a responsibility to return some time and effort to the professional organization, so I stood for election as NC Chapter treasurer that year. My many visits to agencies surely paid off as I was easily elected. I found I had really bitten off more than I expected. The NC Chapter had a full-time executive director who was very talented but somewhat boxed in by circumstances beyond her control. With her, I assessed the entire financial prospects for the chapter. It was very obvious to me that the actual day-to-day operations were much too heavily loaded on her shoulders. I found that she had secretarial help for which we paid a full-time salary to the contractor, but that person was not caring appropriately for our financial concerns. After several months' study, I formed a finance committee to help prepare the annual budget for the following year even though it had always previously been a major task of the executive director. The Board was informed of the incongruities of our system and voted to dispense with the contract system and hire a full-time secretary who would be in the office helping to answer the many phone calls that had been fielded by our overworked director. I also insisted that we install an up-to-date computer system with new programs to cover our needs. I was not fired, fortunately. I served my two years and have been proud that the systems installed in 1988 have served us well ever since, as we have grown to almost twice the size. Here is a quote from the NC NASW Chapter executive director, Kathy Boyd, written 16 years later:

Raleigh, NC - February 2004
   "I can't tell you how much your note meant to me and how much I appreciated it. Yes, the Chapter is doing well. We have record high membership and therefore dues income. We are making a clear profit of $50,000 a year on our conferences, are putting on some innovative conferences that no one else does, and we just hired a 5th staff person (part time). What a change from our days in a rented office space with just me!!
   I will never forget what a significant role you played in helping to get us to where we are now. It really was your shove that got NASW-NC to move from a contracted service to hiring our own staff and getting our own equipment. And by the way, while I am probably still the least computer literate person in the office, we are darn well equipped and using technology very well for a small association. Sometimes it takes someone (and it was you) to just be the one to play hardball and move us all forward in the way we need to go. I do think we would have hired our own staff eventually but I think it may have taken another 2 years, and that would have been a real loss of time and resources and slowed our ability to move forward. So thank you for your note and thank you for the major role that you played in NASW-NC's history."
   Kathy (Chapter Director)

Missionary Emeriti UCBWM – 1988

In the fall of 1988, Barbara and I were surprised to be asked to attend a meeting of the United Church Board for World Ministries. We had served the Evangelical & Reformed Board of World Missions starting in 1945 when we were appointed to China and spent the first year in Chinese Language School at Yale. We returned to the USA after serving the church as missionaries for 22 years. I have documented the fact that we were to have had a year of readjustment after long service, but I was fortunate to have found the faculty position at Catawba and Livingstone Colleges in 1967.

The Board meeting was held in Raleigh, North Carolina, with several hundred Board Members and staff affiliates from all over the US, as well as a large contingent of North Carolina church members interested in Missions. During the proceedings Barbara and I were honored by being appointed to "Missionary Emeritus" status with full retirement benefits. We were each given a small medallion cast in remembrance of the first missionaries of the American Board who sailed to Hawaii. We are proud to wear this medallion on many occasions.

China Trips – 1988 and 1989

Before Barbara was so fully involved in her mother's final months, we were able to make two trips to China.

In 1988 Bonnie and Tom were living in Taipei where Tom was working with an export company. We decided to visit them there as well as make a trip south to Tainan Theological College to see the students we had taught two years previously before they graduated and dispersed. We had a splendid time in Taiwan, and then Bonnie went with us for a roving, vagabond, trip on the China mainland. Just the three of us, we had a variety of wonderful adventures, with me, the fearless Chinese-speaking guide. Our good friend, Frank Lu, had told us how to buy bus and train tickets.

We found that new developments in China included trying to make foreigners welcome. Once, in Jiujiang, when purchasing bus tickets, I started at the end of the long line of travelers in the bus station. Only one window was open for sale of tickets. I started asking the other patient standees the proper protocol to get to my destination. A buzz went up the line as they realized I could understand and speak Chinese. At that point they all began to wave me to the head of the line. I loudly demurred by saying, "I want to take my turn." They were not satisfied that this was proper etiquette as they discussed my intention. Suddenly, a second window was opened. No one moved to it, as the word came down the line that the new window was for foreign visitors. I tried to stay put, but was led by a farmer who escorted me to the ticket window where I purchased our ride to our destination. We all rode the same rickety bus that had only low wooden benches rather than proper seats in order to accommodate the numbers who wanted to travel. In 2007, nineteen years later, we rode from Jingdezhen to Kuling on a beautiful four lane highway in a comfortable modern tourist bus.

This was Bonnie's first opportunity to go to China so it was very special to her to visit both Yueyang and Kuling. We flew to Chungking and took the Yantgze River trip through the Three Gorges. We had a yen to visit Jingdezhen, the most famous pottery center in China, where all the royal ceramic pieces were made. From there we traveled to the beautiful southeast coast of Amoy and Shamen Island then leaving China through HongKong.

After a visit to the oldest walled city in China, we had a unique, unforgettable, overnight bus trip back to HongKong. In the early morning hours an accident stopped all traffic. One would expect word to filter back describing the situation, but drivers first started up the wrong side of the two-lane road. When that lane was completely blocked, traffic then moved up on the right shoulder until the road was gridlocked! After three or four hours of a completely clogged and immobile traffic snarl, we heard movement on the opposite shoulder. By jostling cars and trucks closer together, a stream of vehicles began to pass by us on that left highway shoulder. Next were cars and trucks moving forward in the line blocking the regular lane leading back where we originated. Finally, our bus inched steadily forward. We did notice several vehicles lying in the adjacent paddy fields where they had ventured too close to the edge. Daylight came and we were a long way from our destination, Shenzhen, but we finally made it, very sleepy and incredulous. Surely it had all been a bad dream!

In 1989 with Harry Allen, a Kuling schoolmate friend of many years, I organized a tour to Kuling as a special Kuling American School Reunion. We had each recruited alumni/ae schoolmates to make up a group of 65 to meet in Kuling on Mt. Lushan for a special reunion event in the summer of 1989. The Lushan Administration really treated us, who had grown up there, as old friends. We felt we had been welcomed home. They took us to all our favorite haunts and provided several banquets. It was clear to them that we had a real love for Kuling, and their welcome certainly increased our own attachment to China.

The group as a whole started out by going down the Three Gorges from Chungking on a well-equipped river tourist ship. Unfortunately, we had a national guide who was opinionated, uncooperative and downright surly. Because of his inefficiency we were not notified of the departure of the ferry that was to take us to see the ghost temple which would be submerged in the building of the huge Yangtze River dam.

The group divided into three after the special reunion event. The Allens took their group to Beijing and Shanghai. A small group of Fujian families went back "home" via the coast to visit the places they had formerly lived. Barbara and I led 15 trippers to Wuhan, Yueyang and Guilin (the Li River trip), and back to HongKong. Several of this group had been my classmates from 6th grade in 1931 to high school in 1936-37. The opportunity to renew these friendships was very meaningful.

Planning for Our Own Later Years

While at Livingstone College in the late 1970s and then in the 1980s I served as a social work consultant to several nursing homes as North Carolina tried to upgrade services to the elderly who were in need of institutional care. One of my contracts was with our United Church Retirement Home in Newton, NC. This led quickly to my own study of institutional care and end-of-life issues as a part of my interest and study of gerontology.

Over the years, I was able to write enough grants for our Social Work Department to assure summer employment. One summer I won a grant to study Aging at the University of Hawaii at Manoa. Barbara went with me and we had a happy stay with our good friend and former HongKong colleague, Grace Liu. The following year I was able to arrange a special program with Syracuse University to provide exchange of faculty for several weeks to strengthen our Gerontology Certificate Program at Livingstone. We also received funding from NC State agencies to train their workers by enrolling them in our program.

Serving as a social work consultant to long-term care facilities, teaching gerontology courses, developing the "Certificate Program in Aging" for our Social Work Department, prepared me personally for the planning of my own later years.

Our experiences with Barbara's mother in her later years, though essentially positive, convinced us that we wanted to plan our end of life eventualities differently. My own study of gerontology and my professional experience gave us new perspective. Several principles were clear to us:

1. We wanted our children to "care about us, not have to care for us". We wanted to remain independent of our children, financially and without relying on them for housing or daily care.
2. We wanted to live in an affordable retirement community, and enter it at a young enough age to handle the necessary decisions and adjustments. We wanted to be able to participate in activities and establish a new community of friends.
3. We wanted this community to be in a location convenient to traveling, including visits to and from our children.
4. We wanted this facility to have three levels of care – Independent Living, Assisted Living and Nursing Care as we intended to live there the rest of our lives.

Brother Bob and Marion were living in Greensboro, 35 miles from Salisbury, and had placed their names on the waiting list of Friends Home Retirement Community in Greensboro. We also signed up in 1984, thinking of entry in the mid '90's. The administrators, however, must have neglected their study of the demographics of our aging society as we were told in 1990 that it could be 10 or 15 years before our names came to the top of the list. Shortly after, we were notified that a new sister facility was being constructed close by, called Friends Homes West, and that we could obtain entry when the second phase was completed in 1994. We sent in our deposit immediately.

1992 Hoy Hospital Anniversary – Special Visit to Yueyang for the 90th Anniversary Celebration of the Red Cross Hospital

Our China trip in 1992 was integral to the 90th anniversary celebration of the founding of our Reformed Church Mission Hospital. The Yueyang Red Cross Hospital had adopted the founding date of their hospital as 1902, which was the starting date of the Pu Ji Yi Yuan (Hoy Hospital). A picture booklet from the celebration clearly noted that the Red Cross Hospital had accepted the Mission hospital as its forerunner. We managed to recruit over 45 persons for this trip. Corinne Bergmann wrote a splendid account of the celebration and the diverse group in attendance. Gary Hoff, an artist friend who served with wife Linda Petrucelli in Taiwan sketched a number of interesting drawings of events and people.

The Yueyang Red Cross Hospital provided entertainment for the event. On our part, Dr. Hsiao ChingFen, new Mission Board Secretary for Asia (formerly President of Tainan Theological College) was the main speaker, though several of us were also asked to say a few words. After the celebration, we spent two days visiting Huping and the famous North Gate, Yueyang Lou, where the ancient poets wrote their verses regarding the beauty and wonders of the Dongting Lake.

We went from Yueyang to Yuanling in Hunan. The purpose was to visit Wu Ling Yuan National Park in the Northwest corner of the province where the mountains are much like the karst formations of the Li river area. The mountains are what inspired so many famous Chinese paintings of precipitous hills and rushing streams with a lone tree clinging bravely to the hillside.

One exciting event included an afternoon walk of four or five miles on a pedestrian path from one hotel to another through this beautiful valley described above. The highway from one hotel to the other avoided the steep and treacherous mountains by going about 15 miles through other valleys. It was the role of the Chinese guide to make sure all members of the tour group were fully informed of the need to make a clear choice of whether they wished to walk or go by bus. My cousin, Bob Hegnauer wanted to walk with us but his wife, Martha, was not feeling too well so they decided to ride the bus. The guide forgot their decision and failed to check their room where they were waiting for the bus. By mid-afternoon we checked for everyone and found Bob and Martha missing. We also had a phone call from the original hotel so our guide hurried back in a car for them. All is well that ends well; they were happily reunited with the group.

Preparing for the Move to Friends Homes West in Greensboro – 1994

The time had come to make this big change in our lives and we were excited about it. We were moving into a newly completed building in the second phase of Friends Homes West and were able to choose the location of our apartment, a great advantage. We decided on a unit on the third floor that would require the most walking and stair climbing within the facility. We wanted to keep fit! Though only a one bedroom unit, the rooms were spacious with a very attractive layout, good closet space and a nice little kitchen.

We began to prepare by downsizing our Salisbury home's furnishings and the volume of accumulated belongings that would never fit into our new apartment. Barbara did a superb job of planning the process. The children all cooperated by coming on certain dates to make choices and carry away the spoils. A few useful items were moved to the mountain cottage. All of this took much time and effort, and we were very glad that we were doing it earlier in our aging than later.

We put our house up for sale and since we had overbuilt for the neighborhood, it took a few months to sell. A very nice Middle Eastern family bought it which really pleased us, as the neighborhood definitely needed some diversity.

Our move to Greensboro was accomplished smoothly in December 1994. We entered with a group of relatively the same age. We really were a very compatible group and became known as the "changers." We found that the earlier entrants to Friends Homes West were largely older, and had almost a generational difference of opinion as to why they had sought a retirement community. Some were there to find a good "rocking chair," while we were interested in networking and finding companions who wanted to do some of the same things we enjoyed.

We definitely had made a good choice. Friends Homes West has come up to our expectations as a satisfying place to live out our lives. Of course, we have our gripes. The meals are wholesome and generally very tasty even though the vegetables are over-cooked, southern style. When we crave stir-fried veggies and other Chinese favorites, Barbara enjoys producing them. The delectable aroma of ginger and garlic, however, is less appreciated by our neighbors.

I, along with others, wanted to improve the quality of life where we were living rather than sitting expectantly waiting for the administrators to decide for us just what we liked and what we wanted to do. Though Friends Homes, Inc has a reputation of managing their finances very soundly, some of us tend to push for more involvement in decisions that affect our daily lives. We know that with the three levels of care, we will have care in the future.

Greensboro was also a good choice. A beautiful city, it is progressive with many cultural activities, and an airport which has been invaluable to us with our many overseas travels. Two hours on the road gets us to our mountain cottage; one hour gets us to Salisbury.

Before joining a church, we spent the first year visiting a variety of churches throughout the city before deciding on Congregational, United Church of Christ. We found it to be a very friendly, welcoming congregation with much outreach and liberal views. We particularly liked the openness to all people. The young, vibrant woman minister, The Reverend Julie Peeples, with her excellent sermons was definitely for us a decision maker.

Our "Last" Visit to China – 1996

This was to be our last visit to Changsha, Yueyang, Wuhan, Xian, Luoyang, Beijing, Huangshan, Shanghai, and Kuling. Our daughter, Karen, went with us to help me as my assistant. We included two granddaughters, Michelle and Shawn as a graduation gift from both High School and College. Seven other family members, including nephews, cousins and their friends also thought they had better join us as a last chance to learn our stories. It was a very successful journey as we showed them all the major places we had lived as well as explained more than they ever wanted to know!

Particularly humorous were the looks cast by the Chinese on Michelle, Karen's six foot tall, blonde, beautiful daughter. On one occasion as we were admiring the scenery, a small elderly man approached and moved close to her. Michelle thought he wanted the space to look into the distance so she moved away. She noticed he followed her and again sidled against her. Feeling somewhat imposed upon, she called to her mother but then noticed an older woman standing nearby with a camera poised to take her picture. We all got in the act to help her pose with her new friend. Tall Michelle and very small Chinese friend made a beautiful picture in the lovely garden in Suzhou, a precious memory for all of us.

Our Mountains and Cottage

One of the great advantages of living in a retirement community is the ability to lock the door to the apartment, sign out at the desk and take off for as long as one pleases. We have done this for many summers. It is the time for family visits or just with a grandchild for a week.

During these retirement years our mountain cottage figured perhaps even more as a place we loved to go come spring, summer or fall. Forecast of snow ceased to be the signal to head for the frozen hills and walks in the snowy woods. We let the kids do that. We have enjoyed the hikes up the mountain through the rhododendron when the trees are leafed out and the wild flowers are blooming.

In 1990 Barbara and I embarked on a project of photographing the wild flowers we saw, identifying them and making an album. At first we thought we might find maybe thirty, but the more we scoured the hills and valleys of our acres and neighboring tracts, the more we found. We never uprooted plants. Either I photographed them on the spot, or we took a single blossom home. It was all such fun! Barbara spent hours poring over her wild flower books, identifying them by their common names. After several years we had at least 250 specimens in our album. Some very showy; some very tiny and drab; some varieties of one species, and some, sorry to say, are unwanted invasive species. Occasionally, though our hikes are now ambles, we still find a wild flower to add to our album.

Son, Chris and Barbi who live "just up the *holler*", keep an eye on the house in our absence which we really appreciate. It is still a very simple house with odds and ends of comfortable old furniture, and "decorated" with many souvenirs collected on our travels. It has a usable attic which has stored the junk of our children, as well as our own stuff. Our small granddaughter once commented, "No need to lock the doors. There's nothing in this house a robber would want anyway!"

Over the years we made some enhancing changes to the house. We built a deck of locust wood on the front; took out an inside wall to open up the living room, and much later had two beautiful large windows installed that look out on the woods and the birdfeeders. When our children had summer jobs we needed more space, so had two rooms and a bath put in the basement.

The cottage is the place for continuing special celebrations. In 1994 the children had a wonderful barbecue party for our 50th anniversary, inviting extended family and old friends. In 2003 the family feted Barbara on her 80th birthday, the highlights of which were a ride with Chris on his motorcycle and a beautiful ring with each child's birthstone especially treasured. Our family now with great-grandchildren has expanded beyond the little house's capacity for large gatherings, but we really love the one-on-one visits best anyway!

Back in the 1980's we deeded two acres of the land adjoining the tract the cottage is on to each of our children. For each child we held a "Seizin' Ceremony", an old fashioned transfer of property dating back to the days of freehold estates. In the ritual, the one who is giving the property presents the recipient with a clump of earth. In return, the recipient gives a green twig or leaf, thus sealing the transaction. We had a very happy time with this activity and even composed a song which was part of the ceremonies – with apologies to "This Land is Your Land".

This land is your land; this land is my land,
From the river valley to the pine tree forest
From the crystal springlet to Whitener Mountain
This land belongs to you and me.
We roam and ramble through the rhododendron,
Down leafy pathways, up rocky hillsides,
Through fragrant balsams and running cedar,
This land belongs to you and me.

In 1990, Barbara's sister, Lois, and husband, Paul Carter, built a vacation home on land we had sold them. We have enjoyed extended family reunions there each summer.

Harry and Mary Lou Allen, our friends from China days also bought a lot from us and built a summer home. We enjoyed happy times until they sold the house in order to move near their children in Seattle, Washington.

We have also participated annually in Whitener cousin gatherings at our United Church of Christ Conference Center outside of Blowing Rock.

In more recent years we have appreciated our summer church, High Country United Church of Christ, located outside of Boone. It is a new congregation, pastored by an innovative young woman, the Rev. Dr. Shelly Wilson, and full of enthusiastic young people. It has been a meaningful church experience.

We have spoken before of our environmental concerns which were the basis for our involvement in the Middle Fork Greenway Association, and its project to establish a walking and biking trail proposed to connect Boone and Blowing Rock along the Middle Fork of the New River. The Greenway would need access across the bottom land of our property, co-owned with brother Don and his wife Elizabeth (Ibby). We were able in 2005, together with Don and Ibby, to deed our entire bottom land (3.75 acres) to the Blue Ridge Rural Land Trust for the Greenway, and named the small park that it created "Sterling Creek Park." In subsequent years we have supported the

Greenway project as much as possible, but it is developing slowly. A very ambitious undertaking with funding a constant struggle, it will not be a full reality in our lifetime. We are hoping, however, soon to see the land we donated to be linked up with adjoining easements to form the first segment of this great endeavor.

All of our family members are aware of our personal interest and concern for ecological preservation of areas of beauty and have themselves developed a strong devotion to saving our little bit of mountain land. We have moved a distance from feeling that development is inevitable because someone will make "an offer we can't refuse." We want to save a portion of this beautiful treasure for other generations to enjoy as we have enjoyed it. We have moved from what our children said: "Whatever you want, Mom and Dad, the land belongs to you," to what together WE now say, "We are divesting, let's figure out together what to do to preserve this special place."

Catawba College Exemplary Life Service Honor – 2001

An unexpected invitation to be a part of a service of recognition honoring a number of Catawba College graduates was extended to me by Fred Corriher, President. The service, held in the Dearborn Chapel, was very moving, as tribute was paid to twelve persons in a variety of professions, but mostly ministers. We were robed in the proper regalia so the lineup on the first few rows was impressive. The chancel choir of the college performed beautifully and each of us was individually escorted to the chancel where the honor was read and a medallion presented.

Second "Last" Trip to China in 2000 with a Special Stopover with Grace Liu in Honolulu – A Private Trip with Gerald and Katrina

In 1996, our eighth trip to China we anticipated as being our last trip. After all, we were getting older and overseas travel was not getting easier. When a chance came to head for the Orient again, however, we were ready to pack our bags! So, in 2000 Barbara and I returned to China, having been away four years.

It came about because Grace Liu asked us to come to Honolulu for a month to help her polish up her autobiography. She proposed to fly us, feed and house us, as well as to take some time off to visit the sights. Grace, our colleague from HongKong days, we consider a true friend. We had grown to love each other while working together in refugee work for the church in

Grampian Village in Kowloon. We had tangled often over strategies, questions of faith and action, especially the interpretation of the theology of social service. Knowing her irascible nature, of insisting on having her own way, we countered early that we would be glad to help her with her book on several conditions. We would come for a two-week period first, take a trip to China from Honolulu and then return for about a week to finish up. This did not sit well with Grace, as she was convinced that nothing productive could be accomplished in so short a time. I suggested that we begin the process by having her send us her first chapter which we would work on and return to her for study. In the end, this is what we did.

Letters and a few faxes to Frank Lu in Guangzhou resulted in an itinerary for our China trip, which included HongKong, Yueyang, Sandouping (the Three Gorges Dam site), Wuhan, Lushan, and Shanghai.

In February, Grace sent us her first chapter, which I scanned into the computer. It was a difficult job. Kim helped by reading our efforts to keep Grace's unique style yet smooth out her short choppy sentences. "Too Chinese," Grace said, but approved the results so then I sent her the first hundred pages. In March Barbara and I had really completed editing the first half to take with us.

Arriving in Honolulu on April 4th, we were greeted by Grace, who had abandoned the idea that her hoped for editing could be accomplished, but welcomed us anyway. She had saved her upstairs apartment without renting it so we would have a place to stay. In her managerial style, she then decided it was "too hot" for us to live upstairs so had set us up in her living room. In that clash of wills we won! We got our privacy, but had to tote the double bed mattress up the outside stairway with Grace and Barbara hefting the front end. Got to hand it to her, she is a hard worker. She had bought eight pounds of carrots, knowing we liked vegetables, 400 "jyaudz" (frozen Chinese pot-stickers), had frozen 30 or forty portions of her own invented rice-bean mixture, and brought in a whole bunch of other food, enough to feed a family for ten weeks.

We quickly showed her that we meant business. It was too expensive to rent a larger computer. We decided to work with what we had (a small old Toshiba laptop) and buy an inexpensive printer. Barbara and I churned out the paper, revising, editing, and checking with Grace. We kept her busy in the kitchen (at her insistence though she is not much of a cook - Barbara is miles ahead!). We also made her laboriously read and review everything we wrote. When she got in the swing, she enjoyed editing and rewriting with Barbara.

The fact that we had a good printer was a great help. Our final draft of the entire document boiled down to 85 pages. Grace was left with the task of reviewing and writing the final chapter of recent history when we departed on April 15th.

On to Yueyang and Lushan

Following our visit with Grace in Honolulu we flew to HongKong to join our daughter, Katrina, Gerald and their children Eric and Emily. We all made a trip to visit Katrina's family home in Li Village near Guangzhou. It was very meaningful to observe the place of Katrina's family roots. When the kids went back home to college, the four of us took the train to Yueyang on the way to Wuhan and Lushan.

"Lau Jia" Retrospective

I interrupt the narrative of our travel to share my thoughts and feelings about again returning to my "old home." I was confident that this really was to be a "final visit"!

Easter Monday morning I had awakened on several occasions as our train stopped in the darkness at Hengyang and Changsha in my native province of Hunan. At early light, I stayed glued to the window to watch the rice fields flash by this "rice bowl" area surrounding the Dongting Lake. I couldn't help but wonder if this really was the "last" time I would view this land of my birth, youth and early missionary calling.

We drew ever closer to Yueyang, that city clinging to the shores of the important flood reservoir the Dongting Lake with its forty foot fluctuation in water level each year. Years earlier the city was much smaller and called Yochow when Don and I used to peer over our compound wall to marches, New Year's festivities, and even executions. There are now hundreds of acres of buildings housing a population of 600,000 or more stretching away from the lake. It is hard for old folks to come to grips with that kind of change in so short a lifetime.

We crossed one of the tributary rivers to the lake at Yungjiawan. I remembered how in my childhood our faithful messenger, Mr. Chung, would come rushing up to our house saying the train would be in Yochow in less than an hour for us to board enroute to Hankow. On Easter Monday,

2000, it was only fifteen minutes from there to the new train station. In my seven returns to my "lau jia" since 1981, I still felt a deep sense of satisfaction and comfort.

Later, as we walked the old familiar main street I knew so well, the fact that it was wider and could accommodate cars and trucks did not take away that feeling of permanence of the indomitable Chinese spirit. Tinsmiths still pounded their pots and buckets. Fruit vendors and meat stalls had the same wares they showed three quarters of a century earlier when Don and I would sneak out of the gate to wander near the ancient pagoda, still proudly standing with its crown of small bushes.

In the last 19 years, almost all remnants of the buildings of my early years have been removed and replaced. Only the old hospital gate was visible and it will be removed when the street is widened once again. The most permanent building stands opposite the Red Cross Hospital and very near the pagoda. It was the first clinic built for Dr. Beam in 1910. With the nearly obliterated whitewashed characters "Pu Ji Yi Yuan" (Universal Help Hospital) even the Red Guards over-wash could not wipe out this message.

On the other side of the street is the newly completed Yueyang Christian Church. From the sale of the old Episcopal Church in which we worshipped in 1992 and accumulated rentals of the former Reformed Church which was returned to the small congregation in 1983, a Church seating over 1000 worshippers has been erected. Unfortunately, the debt on the building is very large.

I am overjoyed that the Christian Community has a place of worship as well as a large number of house meeting places, all officially registered. No doubt there is theological tension as the remains of denominational baggage weighs down the joy and promise of real unity in Christ. In our talk with a retired "Bible Woman" and her daughter who had lunch with us at the Hotel, we learned that they felt the situation was improving between the young pastor and older members. Pictures of the Easter and Christmas celebrations where over 2000 mostly young people were gathered for worship provide hope.

Going out to Huping School site, where Barbara and I began our missionary efforts, was a nostalgic visit to a decaying infrastructure, a past that is no more. The new day is different. The impact is clear and severe. We rejoice in a country which has been able to move ahead. We are humbled that we had a small part in the lives of a few students and Christian friends. Yet our greatest impact may have been on a young boy who served us well as 'houseboy" performing a multitude of daily tasks. As an ardent communist party member he also served his country well by collecting the lake reeds for the paper mills of China. In his retirement he welcomed us and paid us the great compliment of saying, "You treated your workers as equals." We deeply appreciate this friendship.

Leaving Yueyang after this short but meaningful visit was not hard. We left by a small river boat, traveling second class, but comfortably. Pulling away from shore opposite Yueyang Lou, the famous Tang Dynasty North Gate pavilion, reminded me of my own life's many leavings – Yueyang, Kuling, Wuhan, HongKong and Salisbury. As we departed we remembered our life in China with great fondness, and we prepare for the next day, the next year, the next stage.

Second Last Trip (continued)

Katrina, Gerald, Barbara and I went on to Wuhan to visit Katrina's half brother. We then took a bus to visit the site of the largest dam in the world, which was being built on the Yangtze River at Sandouping, near Ichang, still a very controversial project.

Returning to Wuhan, we boarded a hydrofoil to get downriver from Wuhan to Jiujiang in three hours for another visit to Lushan (Kuling). We were there several days during the annual Chinese May Festival tourist inundation. We were allocated space in a famous "Luxurious Villa" which was scheduled for repair and remodeling. The night was cold and rainy; the window in Katrina and Gerald's room was broken which admitted the storm winds to chill the apartment. We were finally moved to the hotel next door. The accommodations were much better even though a leak in the closet got their clothes all wet. Much needed to be done to prepare for future foreign guests.

Kuling was different for me because we were retracing my childhood and ancient footsteps. There was a sense of vitality in the week-long May Day vacation visit of the thousands of visitors to our lovely Lushan Mountain. Now not ours, yet still ours in memory. It is comforting to know that this beautiful and meaningful spot can be shared by so many. As we met hundreds of visitor/hikers coming from the Three Trees (ancient ones rivaling the giant sequoias of California), I could not help being reminded of the enthusiasm and vitality of the people vacationing. Car drivers were extraordinarily cautious. The fact that everyone walked unconcernedly across busy traffic, knowing that the first person to get to a space has right of way, blew our minds.

While we relaxed in the serenity of the historic Botanical Gardens in the Forestry and Flower Research Center near Lion's Leap to the east, we also could enjoy the frenetic energy of hundreds of young and old walking on the rather narrow paths to the Cave of the Immortals overlooking the steep cliffs of the western side of the Lushan range. We did not have the energy of my youthful days of running all over the mountain.

We did revisit our old house, # 160 (not very attractive on that visit so we preferred to remember it as it was in 1948), and then the old KAS buildings. The refurbished main building was beautiful as a hotel for youth visitors. The staff member who spoke with me asked for some pictures of the old School so that they could use them in a history room. They want to invite international youth conferences to come visit. Our old recreation field holds a large hotel building which is a youth hostel, called a mountain retreat for hikers and visitors.

After our visit to the White Deer Grotto and other sites at the base of the mountain, I felt satisfied that the home of my early school days was in good hands. It was fitting to say "good bye" and to keep the memories alive with my school family in our reunions!

From Lushan we flew to Shanghai before heading back to HongKong and home.

The Continuing Care Community Residents of North Carolina (CCCRofNC)

In 1998 I was challenged to organize a chapter of the Continuing Care Community Residents of North Carolina (CCCRofNC) in Friends Homes West. This 3000+ member organization is dedicated to raising issues of concern with the NC legislature and with the organization for administrators of North Carolina communities. I did organize a chapter and within two years we had 200 of our independent living residents signed up. At $5 a year, it was easy. Our chapter organized the annual meeting to be held in our FHW living room in 1999. It was a big order, but over 60 members dug in and did a great job for over 200 attendees from other communities.

The founder of the organization, Harry Groves, was our speaker. As a former dean of a law school, he had single-handedly started CCCRofNC in 1988 because a friend of his was not permitted to come home from the hospital to his community nursing center for a period of rehabilitation because the insurance company would pay only a very small part of the cost. The organization (CCCRofNC) mounted a campaign for a "right to return home" law. This was very successful and the organization has grown to nearly 4000 members by 2011 with representatives and members at over 40 of the 53 retirement communities in North Carolina.

Next on the agenda was a request to serve as secretary for CCCRofNC for two years. I found it a difficult task because it was a period of transition as we sought to clarify the goals of our association for the next five years. Unfortunately, several other jobs came with the secretary's role. Meetings with the Administrators of NC Retirement Communities' leadership group followed, as well as appointment by the Department of Insurance on the Advisory Committee for the state. It has been quite evident that our CCCRofNC is useful because some administrators have, in the past, been reluctant to work with the residents of their communities creating issues that needed resolution. The North Carolina law regulating retirement communities is supportive of residents as well as good management. Evidence is growing that administrators are paying much closer attention to the requests and desires of residents as the market becomes tighter.

As of 2004 it became increasingly evident that government policy of supporting the effort to keep people in their own homes combined with a generational fear of "rest homes" and "nursing homes" until desperately needed, had an impact on admissions to retirement communities. We find that a greater number of frail elderly are being admitted to NC continuing care communities creating a direct effect on the kind of leadership available to keep everyone active and involved. Frail people who are deeply involved in their own real health problems are less able to accept volunteer responsibilities of any kind. The next era of how the Baby Boomers handle retirement will be interesting to note. I expect that many will not have saved enough to do what our generation has been able to afford. This will mean that retirement will be redefined and restructured and that many present facilities will need to redesign their space to take care of the influx of people who can no longer stay in their own homes despite home care. They may also be unable to live independently in these communities.

The result of the Bush recession brought about by the unnecessary and unsupportable war in Iraq has caused many widows to face low monthly income from their husbands' retirement investments. This has resulted in a new reality. Former very solvent persons are forced increasingly to face the need to seek federal support through the Medicaid process. All communities are wrestling with this development. In the current climate where both the States and the Federal Government are in economic crisis and recession, these issues are even more critical.

My Yen for Travel

Uncle Leonard Hegnauer, my mother's beloved brother who encouraged his younger sister to go to China at the age of 19, was always in a hurry. Though he was a dedicated and wonderful pastor, I believe he would have joined the China Mission if he could have. He loved to travel and I'm sure I inherited his yen for it. My middle name is Hegnauer, well chosen because I always liked to get on the way and find new places to explore. Barbara has always been ready to join me. I have related many travel experiences shared by our children through work-related furloughs and teaching trips. They have often been part of our subsequent China tours. Only Chris as an adult has not traveled with us. He says he saw enough of Asia during his service in Vietnam as a Marine. The rest of our children, however, have as keen a yen for the adventure of travel as we do.

We joined several very good tours, but mainly preferred to plan and navigate our own touring so we could go where we pleased. This way our travels often gave us the happy opportunity to see friends or family members living all over the world.

Most of our travel experiences, aside from the China trips, took place during these retirement years at Friends Homes West. We were often greeted by our friends here with "Well, where are you going next?" We were usually ready with a planned destination.

Our ten trips to China are chronicled throughout the body of the book, as they were all of such personal meaning to our family and us. In the Addenda is a list of our other trips with a short explanation or description of special interest or significance.

We do have documented photograph albums which Barbara has put together after each trip and which are a joy to review occasionally. We cordially invite you to come for a cup of tea to look at our albums and hear endless tales of our travel adventures!

Visiting Washington DC with David

One unforgettable travel idea I had was to take our grandson David to Washington to see the sights and visit some of the very important museums. David has autism but as a teenager is very bright and interested in all areas of art and science. We rode north by train which was a new experience for him. I had arranged an overnight in a Red Roof Inn in Springfield because cousin Jack Whitener said he would meet the train and take us there near the subway into town.

David definitely wanted to start with Museums after we had walked most of the mall. He climbed at least part of the Washington monument while I enjoyed the breezes. I soon realized I was going to have to find ways to let him wander on his own in museums and arrange meeting times. That did work for awhile, but when he stood me up at an easily distinguished site, I began to recalculate what to do. After I had waited nearby for thirty or forty minutes without a sign of him it occurred to me that he might eventually head for the large lunch room since it was past our lunch hour. There he was looking for me. He said he thought the cafeteria was where we had agreed we would go for lunch. We covered the other museums by writing down carefully where he would find me on a chair and he viewed more exhibits than I have seen in many years.

Back at the Inn, I could not figure out what was so engrossing in the cowboy book Barbara and I had found in the "giveaway quick read paperbacks" of Friends Homes West for him to read on the train. He spent the train ride to Washington and time at our inn carefully studying the story of "The Trail Riders." When he had finished it, I asked to see it. Aghast, I found it highly spiced with the steamiest sexual descriptions I had ever read. No wonder teenage David loved it! What had I, his grandfather done? When David asked if he could have the book, I had to tell him it was going to his Mom! David survived this unique educational experience and Barbara and I have had a hilarious time regaling our friends with the story.

Activity and Health

We never quite anticipated that we would be so busy in Friends Homes West. We quickly learned that there were all kinds of volunteer jobs just waiting for eager retirees. Gardening, health care committee, programs and activities planned for all independent living folk were plentiful. I had a

Troy-built tiller which I donated to our gardening group here at Friends Homes West. It has performed nobly ever since. So I still had a garden plot to plant some flowers and some tomatoes during the growing season. I have now aged out of big gardens, particularly as we are away in Blowing Rock during the summer vegetable growing season.

We have been active in our church, serving on the Council and as Deacons. We have enjoyed some volunteering in the community; delivering Mobile Meals, collecting food for Urban Ministry and helping to provide lunch once a month at a center for HIV/AIDs victims.

No different from other inmates (as some children refer to us), both of us have had health issues. Actually, we consider ourselves in pretty good shape with immense help received from modern surgery. In bionic manner I set off all airport systems with one full and one partial knee replacement, both very successful. For more than thirty years I have travelled almost annually to Baltimore for the National Longitudinal Study of Aging, a research project at John's Hopkins Medical Center. I am very pleased to be a continuing participant in this study as it not only benefits research on aging, but also gives me a top notch physical exam each year. Now that I am 90 years old they are also anxious to continue this participation so pay my ticket by Amtrak.

In 2007 I had forty radiation treatments for prostate cancer and continue to check out totally free of any recurrence. I guess they call it "in remission."

Barbara had a very successful corneal transplant, greatly enhancing her vision loss from corneal dystrophy. A fall, resulting in a pelvic fracture, slowed her down the summer of 2011, but we both continue daily walking. We have been fortunate in our health, convinced that keeping physically active and mentally involved are very important steps in keeping on the go. Barbara insists that an important part of her good state of health is the cup of hot tea with milk and sugar that I bring to wake her up every morning.

We have completed our 18th year here at Friends Homes West and have not a doubt about having made the right choice of where we wish to live out our years. Barbara and I have been married 68 years. Having passed my 90th birthday, June 27, 2011, celebrated with an outstanding week at the beach – a gift from our children – I'm ready to continue life at a slower pace.

Friends

A major focus of our personal lives, besides our family, is our friends, both those around us and those far flung. We have enjoyed the new friends we have made here at Friends Homes West. I mention one couple to whom we have felt particularly close – DeWitt and Becky Barnett. Not surprisingly, their ties to China were an immediate bonding factor. Both were born in China in the same era as I so their appreciation of and love for China are like my own. We have had many Happy Hours with stories and opinions to share. Very sadly, DeWitt has died and we miss him keenly, but are still close to Becky.

Neighbors on our hall who moved into Friends West when we did are Betsy and Bruce Stafford with whom we have also kept in close contact.

We have mentioned our friends, Mary Lou and Harry Allen who built a beautiful home on an acre opposite our mountain cottage. For many years we continued to keep in touch with them after their move to Seattle , and with Mary Lou following Harry's death in 2012.

As many folks do, we keep in touch with friends around the world with a yearly newsletter of our activities, trying not to dwell on how exceptional our grand- and great-grandchildren are. Always welcome are the letters that come in reply, especially those from friends who have also had China experiences.

An especially meaningful contact has been with three other couples with whom we worked in HongKong: Corinne and Don Bergmann, Ben and Carolyn Whitehall, Ray and Rhea Whitehead. Having three couples in our Mission with names beginning with "White" was quite a challenge to our Chinese coworkers. After we had all retired, we decided to have a reunion of the "BeWhites", as we called our group of four couples. That was such a nice experience we planned to have a reunion every two or three years, alternating places: Bergmanns in Pasadena, CA, Whitehills in Santa Fe, NM, Whiteheads in Toronto, and Whiteners in Blowing Rock. Great losses to our group have been Corinne and Rhea, both from cancer. The rest of us will continue these special gatherings as long as we are able.

Losses

The older we get, the more we should expect that our older friends and loved ones will leave us at some point, but it never gets easier. It is especially grievous when we lose those closest to us. In 1999 Barbara's older brother and wife, Robert and Hermine Brown both died in an auto accident, made all the more tragic because they had unknowingly driven off of a country road not far from their home in South Carolina into a deep ravine. Despite all searches and efforts to locate them, they were not discovered for almost three weeks, an inexpressibly difficult time for our family. The coroner's report that they had died instantly was an enormous comfort. Now Barbara and Lois are the only surviving siblings. They call each other frequently and visit when they can.

Less than two years later our oldest daughter died in her sleep in the early hours of Father's Day June 17, 2001. What timing could be more cruel? Karen, age 53, healthy, with no history of illness, was taken from us. Autopsy blood studies found nothing to have caused her sudden death. We can only surmise that a totally unexplained arrhythmia brought on cardiac arrest. There is no way to express the shock and pain of the family in the loss of our first born, beloved Karen. We all gathered in the mountains to scatter her ashes on the two acres we had given to her, and laid a stone there inscribed – "Forever in our hearts". The Chinese custom would call for firecrackers, but we all felt it more fitting to light sparklers for our girl whose life had sparkled for us. We keep a supply of dried rose petals to scatter around her marker when her sisters or we climb the mountain to that lovely glade.

Several years later Barbara's niece, Kristen Carter, Lois and Paul's daughter who was close in age to Karen died. These losses of our children as such young adults have been hard to understand and accept.

My much-loved, the "gentle" brother, Don, died after a long illness. He was in an Obstetrics and Gynecology Practice in Winston Salem. His friends filled the Presbyterian Church where we were told he had delivered over five thousand babies and was much appreciated. He and his wife, Ibby, had just lost their oldest daughter, Ellen, who was a Dean of the Business School at the University of Virginia. The younger daughter, Beth, and her two grandchildren have been a great comfort as well as assistance to Ibby.

Now Bob and I are the survivors. Bob and his wife, Marion, who now sadly has advanced Alzheimers, also live at Friends Homes West, so we see them often. Bob is Marion's exemplary caregiver. I admire him greatly.

The Kuling American School Alumni Association & KASA International nfp

The Kuling American School Alumni Association was organized in New York in 1938. There is no known record, however, of any meetings between that time and 1978 when a joint reunion was held with all schools which had formerly helped educate the children of American citizens living in China. At this meeting in Hershey, Pennsylvania we who had attended KAS in our youth reestablished ourselves to organize continued occasional meetings on the east coast and as groups on the west coast. Harry Allen was elected our new president.

The Association had been able to meet sporadically in various locations over the years, finding each gathering a happy reunion with our former schoolmates. In 1989, as I have previously recounted, the KAS Association held a reunion in Kuling. For some years, however, as we all aged, fewer and fewer members were able to attend such events. Reluctantly, the decision was made to end the meetings. Our very last gathering was planned to take place in the low mountains of Helen, Georgia in 2002. Principal Allgood's daughters, Rita and Elsa, and I were responsible for the agenda for this, our last KAS Alumni meeting. We had early determined that we would accept the responsibility for the ending of our reunions. We notified all KAS members of our intention and urged everyone to attend and bring or send their children to the big FINAL gathering. The response was very good with over fifty attendees, quite a few of them in the second generation.

The main item on the agenda was the planning of a special closing event to mark the termination of the Association. Instead, to everyone's great surprise, a brilliant proposal, originating with Jim Day, Paul Keller, Peter Burt Lauridsen and Kim Whitener, and supported by Rita and Elsa, was presented to the gathering: a "take-over" by the Second Generation. The deliberations and suggestions that followed were positively received, and a new Kuling American School Association, nfp (not for profit) was formed. Jim Day was elected as Chair and Kim Whitener as Vice-Chair and Secretary-Treasurer. It is difficult to express the appreciation we felt for our children's close sense of our history and purpose, and their desire to carry on the intimate connection with our past. The "take-over" was enthusiastically embraced!

In 2005, the new KASA nfp held a reunion in Ivoryton, Connecticut at a beautiful Episcopal Church camp, the Incarnation Center, with a larger number of second generation members attending. One focus was a visit to the Day Missions Library project at Yale Divinity School in New Haven to learn how our families' China papers can be saved for future scholars. A large bequest from Dr. Kenneth Scott Latourette has provided a location and a scientific process for preservation and cataloguing the writings of mission personnel of our generation.

Jim Day, our Chair, had invited Mr. Mu Dehua from the Lushan Administration to be our main speaker. He was warmly received and spoke interestingly of his work with artists and foreign guests to Lushan. After the meeting Mr. Mu visited several of the Association members on the east coast, including Barbara and me in Greensboro. We enjoyed the fuller opportunity to learn to know him.

Very important on the agenda of this 2005 meeting of the KASA nfp was the decision to have a big reunion in China in Kuling on Mt. Lushan in 2007. Throughout the years at every gathering, there were yearnings expressed related to how our old school building might be restored or utilized for a memorial purpose. We recognized that this reunion in 2007 could offer the Second Generation the opportunity to realize our love for Kuling and our old school. Mu DeHua was quite supportive of our plans for this meeting.

Our Third "Last" Trip to China – May 2007

When the new KASA npf decided at their meeting in 2005 to have a grand reunion in Kuling in 2007, it was the signal to Barbara and me to plan for our Third Last Trip to China. The fact that we had lost all credibility among our friends on this Last Trip subject bothered us not at all. Of course, we wanted to attend the KASA meeting, but, in addition, we wished to travel in China with whoever of our family was also interested. We especially wanted to show Erin, our granddaughter, what we could in two short weeks, in association with the Lushan meeting. We rejoiced in her anticipation of seeing the places she had heard so much about. We were delighted that Dana, Erin's mom and Kim went with us on the first leg of the trip, including the reunion in Kuling. Katrina and Gerald joined us for the last week.

It has been our custom each time we return to China to go to our "lau jia" to see our old friends. In addition we always travel to at least one of the cities, or places of wonder which we have never before visited. We followed our plan on this trip also.

First Stop – HongKong

Our few days in HongKong were a true nostalgia trip filled a great mixture of reactions and feelings. It was fun to cross the harbor on the Star Ferry. We took the Tram up to Victoria Peak and were dismayed that smog obscured Lion Rock and the Nine Dragon hills of Kowloon. We looked down incredulously on the huge high-rise buildings everywhere and tried to imagine a population of six million people. HongKong is a fabulous place, but Barbara and I are very happy that we once knew it as a quiet, scenic little colony of less than one million people. Of course, I also remember it as a place teeming with refugees from China, and my work among them, in the 1950's and '60's.

The highlight of our HongKong stay for Barbara and the girls was a pilgrimage to our familiar haunts in Kowloon. They reported that the taxi driver was very amenable and seemed to enjoy the junket. They found our first apartment location in Tsimshatsui, where Kim was a baby, now replaced by a bank. 103 Kadoorie Ave. where all the kids except for Dana lived was unchanged, still lovely. 11B Cambridge Rd. has been replaced by a handsome five-story apartment building. Kowloon Junior School and Union Church were much the same, though the school has since been rebuilt. Kowloon City and the big produce market were much like the old days.

The time in HongKong was too short, but some day one or more of the girls will return and climb Laan Tau and show Erin where we spent our wonderful summers.

On to Yueyang

Our good friend, Frank Lu, helped us immensely with our travel and accommodation plans within China. Our well-laid plan was to travel by bus on the modern highway from Kowloon to Guangzhou (Canton), have a delicious dinner at a hotel, board the train and sleep all the way into Central China. Not to be! An earlier accident on the highway enroute to Guangzhou delayed us for hours. We barely had time to grab a bite at "Kungfu" fast foods in the dirty Canton RR station before our train left. Actually the food was quite tasty, but Erin, the neophyte, made a bad choice from the menu – soup. One never knows what might be immersed in soup, and her first spoonful brought up a chicken foot. Her expression was priceless! It was hilarious! Her comment: "It wouldn't be so bad if I didn't know what chickens walk in!"

Boarding the train was a terrible hassle with rushing hordes of people, multiple steps up and down, no escalators or elevators. Our girls and a friendly worker who was sweeping helped Barbara and me with our bags. Then there was a big to-do over one of our tickets that seemed to be missing. We finally collapsed in our compartments. Poor Erin, overwhelmed by the rigors of traveling in China had a quiet little weep. After that she was a real trooper all the way.

As we arrived in Yueyang, I was again struck with a sense of homecoming when I saw the centuries' old Tang dynasty pagoda, still standing tall on the shore of DongTing Lake. On that day in May 2007 the ancient tower looked weary, afflicted by small trees and bushes growing out of dusty cracks. One could only wonder if it felt that its guardianship of the small town and fisher folk of the early 20th century was now complete in 2007 as Yueyang continued to grow to nearly 600,000 and was clearly taking care of it.

What joy we felt on being greeted once again at the Yueyang station by Liu Yunchu who had worked for us in 1946-50. In western greeting style, Barbara and I both embraced him. We were so happy to introduce him to our daughters, Kim and Dana and granddaughter, Erin. We had arranged for a local guide and a car so that we could visit our familiar places in Yueyang, and YunChu accompanied us. It meant so much to us to take Erin to see Huping School and the big house where Barbara and I had lived, now divided into apartments for parents of students. The school is being used by a local school and there has been little restoration. Some of the buildings, including the chapel are gone. The site on the shore of the lake was as beautiful as ever and we were struck by the luxuriant growth of the trees, so many of which had been cut down by the Japanese.

There is little to see of the mission compound in the city, but we visited the new Protestant Church. The young woman pastor, Rev. Chen, took us on a tour of the large building and we were happy to hear that the congregation now numbers more than 2000 with many homes registered to hold weekly services. In stark contrast with the Southern Baptist Church, our United Church of Christ has supported only the National Protestant

Church – The Church of Christ in China. I wrote earlier of my father's participation in the founding of that Church in 1935.

A visit to the ancient Yueyang Lou was also a must for Erin. I remember in my youth that it was a revered, but quite dilapidated, pavilion erected long ago over the North Gate to the Lake and a favorite spot for the famous poet Li Bo to write his poems. Now, beautifully restored, it is an outstanding historic site with its unique helmet-shaped roof.

Our friend, Yunchu, invited us to his apartment for lunch which his wife, who is almost blind, and their daughter had prepared. It was a delicious home-cooked meal which several other members of the family enjoyed with us. We had a wonderful time taking lots of photos of our families and the generations represented. When we said goodbye to these special friends, we knew the usual "dzaijyan" (see you again) of the Chinese goodbye was only a wish, for this truly would be the last trip to China for Barbara and me. Jason, Yunchu's grandson and a college graduate, does keep occasional correspondence going for us with Yunchu via email. We were sad to learn that his wife has died and are glad that he has his children to care for him.

On to Beijing

We had a rather harrowing van ride to Wuhan to catch our flight to Beijing the next morning. There was much to see and do in Beijing with only four days to do it with a new James Bond as our tour guide! Again, convenient arrangements had been made previously by our friend Frank Lu. James was an engaging young Chinese, self-named, training to be a guide. He had pretty good English, was eager to please but somewhat clueless - and loved Kungfu. I think we taught him a lot about being a tour guide. We had as our driver an older man, Mr. Yue, very kind and helpful to us and to James. With the two of them we had a splendid time doing the sights of Beijing: the Great Wall, the Temple of the Bells museum with its enormous Yongle Bell, The Summer Palace, Tienanmen, and the Forbidden City.

On the tours when we went with James to a restaurant we had a hard time convincing him that what we really wanted were just a few wonderful vegetables, stir-fried as only Chinese chefs can do it! As we traveled the modern streets of Beijing and saw the rebuilding of that great city, we mourned the vanished "hutungs," the small lanes with houses where families had lived for generations. Only a few are left as historic examples. In stark contrast were the fantastic, one-of-a-kind structures being created for the coming Olympics. James told us much about all the preparations being made for that huge event.

One afternoon while the girls went shopping, Mr. Yue drove Barbara and me across the city to visit Leonard Liu and his wife Lydia. Leonard, son of Principal Liu at Huping, was our good friend and coworker in our time of teaching English there. I have written previously about the time he and his daughter visited us at our hotel on an early visit to Peking, and Hanli's having her first elevator ride. Leonard had a stroke years ago and is able to communicate only with his eyes and the movement of one hand, yet his mind is clear. We, with Lydia, visited Leonard in the very nice nursing home where he is loved and cared for. It was a poignant visit, for Leonard recognized us and we were so glad we were able to see him one last time.

On to Shanghai

The five of us flew to Shanghai to join the KASA Reunion group. All were happy for the chance to experience a couple of days in this eye-popping city. For us who had visited Shanghai in earlier days the growth and development were truly incredible. For everyone, the resulting air pollution was a tragedy. Nevertheless, we made the most of our visit with seeing a fantastic acrobatics performance, shopping in the Old Market, relaxing in a wonderful Chinese garden in the middle of crowded shops. Some of us went to see the Jade Buddha; others went up the Pearl Tower on the Bund. It was also a time to begin to get acquainted with the other members of the Reunion group whom we had not met.

Reunion in Kuling and Meeting with the Lushan
Administration - 2007

Forty-five members of the new Kuling American School Association joined this special reunion in Kuling. Only four of the group were of the generation who attended the school in their youth. Others were Second Generation or interested friends. I was one of the four alumni attending and I was very pleased that our family was well represented. This was Erin's first trip to China and our high school/college graduation gift to her. It was a very special chance to share with our granddaughter many places and experiences from our past that had meant so much to us.

The Reunion itself had begun with several exciting days in Shanghai, then a flight to Jingdezhen, the famous pottery center. Traveling on in two busses to Kuling, our group arrived at the Kuling American School, itself, to be enveloped in the most incredible celebration imaginable!

Greeting us with an overwhelming welcome were a row of smiling officials of the Lushan Administration, several groups of children, brightly dressed and waving colorful plastic flower bouquets, a large uniformed drum corps, a group of women dressed in red, dancing and beating small drums, and more! Photographers were everywhere. We were stunned, and moved to tears. We gathered at the foot of the steps for a welcoming ceremony on the landing featuring the four original alumni: Don Libby, Rita Allgood, Marit Allgood and I. Speeches were made. Jim Day responded for the Association and I gave a brief expression of appreciation in Chinese. It was all truly unforgettable.

Many of Kuling's old stone residences, now called villas, have been renovated and are used to accommodate visitors. We were housed in the rebuilt Hoy house, now a small hotel. Barbara and I had summered here with Dad in 1947. At the back was a large deck where our whole group ate our meals together, had Happy Hour and brief meetings. Right next door, beautifully restored, was the little house that we had owned. Many memories crowded us!

Kuling seemed unchanged as the old image was firmly held in my memory. So much is the same as in the "old days", yet much modernization has occurred. The Administration is trying very hard to retain the special scenic beauty of this mountain resort, yet make the changes necessary to attract tourists. Hordes of them do come to enjoy the wonderful coolness and visit the age old temples and other revered sites on the mountain. It is wonderful that the enjoyment of Kuling is now available to all people, not a selected few. The schedule of our group also included many of these scenic visits. Our daughter, Kim, did a masterful job of organizing them as well as other activities of the Reunion.

The Administration continued to extend a lavish welcome with a big banquet at a fancy hotel. There was a 12-course dinner, including hamburgers, fried potatoes and corn on the cob, a gracious gesture to make us feel entirely at home. There were more speeches. A handsome bronze plaque was presented by Jim Day from KASA to the Lushan officials in appreciation of all that they were doing to preserve the history of the school. The four special alumni/ae sang the school song; Don with his usual exuberance, Marit impishly raising her sweet voice and dancing in joy. Rita was most expressive for us all as she shared her deep emotions on returning to the mountains where she grew up. More restrained, I made a few remarks in Chinese. More pictures were taken by the photographers who followed us everywhere throughout the entire time.

The days were very full as we visited all the scenic places and historic sites we could work in: the Three Ancient Trees, Cave of the Immortals, Heavenly Bridge, Botanical Gardens, the mansion of Mao Tzetung, now an interesting museum. We especially enjoyed our visit to a small tea plantation and seeing how Kuling's famous "Cloud and Fog" tea is grown and processed. Of course, we all shopped in the "Gap", Kuling's small market center with many things to attract the tourist.

Very special was spending some time with our friend, Mu Dehua, and meeting Jupiter, his 18-year-old daughter who speaks excellent English. We were glad that she and Erin had the chance to become acquainted.

A few of the group appreciated attending the small local church on Sunday to join in the singing and a brief time of fellowship. It was quite touching to feel the warmth of welcome and friendship as I spoke briefly and prayed in Chinese.

The Administration of Lushan was very interested in utilizing the Kuling American School building in a viable, lucrative way and definitely wanted to work with our Association to make this a reality. The highlight of the Kuling visit was an invitation to the entire group to a meeting in the government building. A banner saying "Friendly Meeting Between Lushan and KASA" stretched across one wall of the large meeting room. Tables and chairs were arranged in circles with the Administration officials, the KASA board members, Don, Rita, Marit and I seated in the inner circle. The rest of the large group and others attending sat in the circles behind. There were flowers, fruit, snacks and bottles of water at every place. It was impressive! There were various speeches of welcome. Then Jim Day presented what was the real heart of the meeting: his vision of the school building's use as a joint operation by Lushan and KASA to teach English and Chinese, and be a center for arts and culture. It was such an exciting possibility, though a huge undertaking. We had real hopes that with Jim's amazing leadership his vision would materialize and a fitting use for our beloved school, long yearned for, would be realized.

At the final meeting of the Reunion, Jim and Kim were presented with beautiful scrolls in appreciation for their excellent direction of the entire Reunion. The hotel management had asked for the signatures of everyone present on a document to be framed and hung in the entrance. There was unanimous agreement that the Reunion had been most memorable in all ways.

Before leaving, our busses drove once more by the school, and there, awaiting us, were officials and another drum corps to bid us farewell. We all left the busses and made our farewells to our gracious hosts. Several photographic exhibitions set up inside the front door of the old school building was a clear review of the few days we had spent on Lushan Mountain.

Following the Reunion, Kim, Dana and Erin returned to the USA. We treasure that adventure together with our girls, having indulged in each opportunity to share the personal pieces of our life in China with them, as well as delighting in their enjoyment of the whole experience.

On to Wuhan and Yunnan

Barbara and I went by bus to Wuhan where we had arranged to meet Katrina and Gerald. They very generously put us up in a Four Star hotel, the Shangrila, for two nights. The name was very appropriate since we were soon actually to be in China's new city, named Shangrila! We had a lovely visit with Katrina's family who took us to a restaurant for a sumptuous meal. They told us that they had seen me on TV being interviewed at the meeting in Lushan. Imagine being on China's national television!

We also were able to contact a very old friend Zhang Zexiang. He is quite frail, but still going. We appreciated his coming to the hotel where we hosted him at the buffet lunch. It was wonderful to have that chance for a visit.

The four of us then flew on to Yunnan, the southwestern province of China. Our destination was the northwest area where four great rivers, the Irrawaddy, Salween, Mekong and Yangtze come down from Tibet, but only three flow parallel before diverging to far corners of Asia. This is where the Yangtze makes a sharp bend before rushing through Tiger Leaping Gorge on its way through the heartland of China. This is the land of Jade Dragon Snow Mountain that "hovers over Lijiang like a great mythical beast". This is the land of cultural diversity, home to 25 of China's ethnic minorities. This is the land of Shangrila!

We flew into Lijiang where we met our guide, A Dong, We had signed up with a small tour company named Hai Wei Trails (Highway Trails). A Dong was a treasure, an excellent guide in every way. He knew some English so with my Chinese, we communicated well. A native of Yunnan and a member of the Naxi tribe, A Dong was a natural to introduce us to the people, their customs and culture, as well as take us to some of the places of extraordinary interest and beauty in this area of China.

We drove several hours north to Yuhu, a Naxi village, to spend the night at a family home. On arrival we rested and walked slowly through the village as we adjusted to the 7,000 foot altitude. The evening meal was simple, cooked by the friendly wife, a rosy-cheeked older woman. We relaxed in the small courtyard, awed by Jade Dragon Snow Mountain glimmering through the clouds above the tiled rooftops of our little compound.

The city of Lijiang is historically the capital of the Naxi minority; part of the Tibetan Empire from 600 to 900 and known as Baisha. We visited a beautiful old temple on the outskirts of the city. A very large Old Town in the center is well preserved with traditional courtyard houses, cobbled street, small canals and arched bridges. Now full of shops, restaurants and hotels, it has been appropriately modernized.

We drove on south through pretty farming country with snow-capped mountains on the horizon. There were precisely planted vegetable gardens and vast fields of wheat. It was harvest time and the roads were lined with farmers and their families strewing the cut wheat on the road for passing traffic to do the threshing process. The grain and straw were raked up, the grain to be winnowed by the wind, and the straw saved for fuel. All of it was a fascinating process.

We had another very enjoyable overnight with a family in Shaxi, the only surviving market town on the Southern Silk Road linking Tibet with SE Asia. The Swiss have a plan to encourage eco-tourism here to raise living standards for the villagers without commercializing the cultural aspects of this unique place.

Then we headed north to "Shangrila." Zhongdian County was a little known corner of Northwest Yunnan. All that changed when permission was given in 2001 to change the name to "Shangrila", the mythical paradise created by James Hilton. Many people there believe the story to be true. One village head claimed to have a piece of the crashed plane which his grandfather had passed on to him! The people are largely ethnic minorities with Tibetans being the largest single group. Our guide, A Dong, was a very careful driver, but on a straight stretch he was pulled for speeding by a cop just waiting for him. Can you imagine a speedtrap in Shangrila!

The small city of Zhongdian is on a 10,000 foot plateau and has the largest Tibetan monastery in the area, named Songzanlin. Our hotel with the same name was located right next to it. It was quite an experience to visit this active monastery of 800 monks chanting from their scriptures. It was quite amusing, however, to see the small boys in training sitting on the back row squirming and poking each other and acting like – little boys!

We were so pleased that A Dong took us to two more homes in outlying villages. We had a delicious lunch at one of them, seated on a low bench behind the open fire in a unique stove; served yak butter tea made in a churn of bamboo, fried flat bread, yak cheese and yogurt. We learned how to make a barley ball from barley mixed with yak butter tea and melted cheese. Mixed with the hands, it is eaten uncooked. We all ate heartily – and all of us stayed well!

Obviously, we have given the briefest of accounts of our wonderful travel experiences in this magnificent area of China, so different from any we have had before. We enjoyed so much our time on this trip to Yunnan with Katrina and Gerald. They are great travel companions, very open to new experiences, and we appreciated so much their generosity and helpfulness throughout the trip.

We flew from Kunming to HongKong to head home, profoundly grateful for:

A fantastic Third Really Last Trip to China -

For traveling with some of our children all the way;

For seeing Chinese friends and old homes one more time;

For experiencing China again in old and new places;

For participation in the KASA Reunion and meeting more of the Second Generation;

For surviving the rigors of the trip and returning safely home.

My Fourth "VERY LAST" Trip to China – To My Birthplace, Lushan, for One Week!

In the late spring of 2010, while we were making our usual plans to enjoy the summer in our mountain cottage, we began to consider a trip to Korea to visit our daughter, Bonnie, and husband, Tom, who were teaching

English in Andong. At the same time our granddaughter, Erin, a student at the University of Georgia, was preparing to go with a college study group to China for two months to join with the University of Nanking on a project researching the DNA of invasive plants. When her research travels were completed, she had a three-week vacation and chose to return to Lushan which she had visited in 2007, knowing it is the place where I was born. My decision was immediate! This was a great opportunity for me to go back one last time to my birthplace, Lushan, Jiangxi province, China. I was filled with joyful anticipation as I thought about joining her to show her all the favorite places of my youthful days. Fully understanding, Kim and Barbara set off for their wonderful two weeks in Korea with Bonnie and Tom and I for my return to Lushan.

Our friend, Mr. Mu Dehua, who worked in the local Lushan government as Director of Art and Art Studies, and had stayed with us in 2005, invited Erin and me to stay with his family in their home. Living with the hospitable Mu family was a real blessing. Erin especially enjoyed Jupiter, their daughter, a university graduate with excellent English, but the family used Chinese only to strengthen Erin's one year of language study at the University. I was really impressed with the progress she made. We reveled in their home-cooked Chinese food and Mrs. Mu taught Erin some good recipes. We could not have had a warmer and more meaningful experience than our stay with the Mu family. There was a major challenge, however, in traversing the 75 steep stone steps to the Mu home. I was very glad for Erin's presence by my side up and down those steps.

The purpose of my trip was to share with Erin my boyhood experiences in those beautiful familiar places, amazingly unchanged. As part of his work, Mr. Mu was able to drive us around the base of the mountain to the scenic sites which were so familiar to me: Three Falls, Horsetail Falls, Goddess of Mercy Bridge and the famous Confucian Study Institute which was founded in the Sung Dynasty around 500 AD. It meant a great deal to me that Erin was truly interested in my stories and the many other things we talked about concerning my life in China.

On this very special and very last trip to China, I learned the real meaning of "guanxi," a special term for "relationship." In an earlier chapter I have written about Yuan Mei, my childhood playmate, the daughter of the pastor of the church in Yueyang, and how we kept in touch with Yuan Mei and her husband through the years until their deaths. We visited them in

Beijing on our first return trips to China. At that time we arranged for their daughter, Baixian, to come to stay with us in Salisbury to study for a college degree. Though her stay with us was short, she has continued to keep in contact with me whom she calls "Uncle", calling on special occasions or just to talk.

She had often asked me to go back to China with her, so when I asked her to find a way for me to get from Beijing to Lushan in 2010, she took over and arranged everything. Her brother put me up at a Beijing hotel to get a night's rest after 14 hours on the plane, fed me a big dinner, and then got me to the airport to fly to Lushan the next morning. He bought tickets both directions so when I left, all arrangements had been made and paid for. It was all because of "guanxi" as the family felt obligated to us for caring for the younger sister, Baixian.

In addition to this tremendous break, my host Mr. Mu did the same thing because of "guanxi." He had stayed in our home for about 5 days in 2005. He would not accept any remuneration for Erin's two week stay and my one week stay with them in 2010, a valuable learning experience. The feeling of obligation is much stronger in Chinese culture than our own culture's feeling of reciprocation and responsibility for reciprocity. The "guanxi" relationship is so important one must accept with grace or never ask for help.

KASA International nfp, Nanjing University, and the Lushan Administration – Plan the Lushan Institute, 2007 to 2011

The Lushan Institute is a reality!

It has been an amazing journey – in 2012 we celebrate ten years since its inception in 2002, when the new leadership of KASA, under Jim Day's visionary direction, took the association on a new course toward the founding of the **Lushan International Language and Culture Institute**. With Steve Harnsberger's vigorously picking up the torch in 2010 and forging the relationships with the Lushan Administration and Nanjing University, the first session of the Lushan Institute took place for four weeks, beginning July 4, 2011!

The ten students who attended the pilot program hailed from Australia, Switzerland, South Africa, and the USA, including two great-grandchildren of the 1930's Kuling American School Principal Roy Allgood – a very meaningful full circle. The language professors came from Nanjing University, which is renowned for its Chinese language and culture programs for international students. In addition to providing dormitory and classroom facilities, the Lushan Administration delivered a supporting cast of a dozen middle school volunteers who helped students learn their tones and improve their Chinese speaking ability. Visiting Lushan at the same time were forest artists from Germany, Italy, France, Japan and China who created natural art along the Yellow Dragon trail. Completing the international team was a talented Philippine band that played songs from Paul Simon and the Beatles in the town square, as many cultures returned to the mountain to join in true cultural exchange. There were smiles everywhere and laughter in the corridors as the Institute sprang forth in international friendship.

The Lushan Institute website www.lushaninstitute.com includes information and history about Kuling American School, features information about the Institute program and registration, Lushan and environs, and many materials from the KAS years – photos and reminiscences.

That today this story has become a reality is due to several factors. There was a visionary, Jim Day, four years earlier, whose extraordinary vision captured our attention. Even though no one was confident of the ways things are done in the New China, he pursued a process he felt was appropriate to the task. A Memorandum of Understanding was signed with the Lushan Administration. Translation of the vision into such a different culture, language, and process in Lushan was very difficult. When the new culture demanded a change of direction and a new leader, the vision still persisted. A new KASA member, Steve Harnsberger, was able to accept the task to carry the vision forward to stunning reality. A new partnership was officially formed by three entities: The Kuling American School International Association, nfp; The Lushan Scenic and Historic Interest Administration; and the Nanjing University Department of International Studies. A one-month pilot program was opened in Lushan on July 4, 2011 by the new Lushan International Language and Culture Institute.

Approaching age 90, four years was a long time for me to wait through an Institute's birth pangs. I knew from the first day, however, one cannot rush Chinese officials. I have known since my father's era and my own experiences that, in China, sometimes it takes a generation to get things done. Thus, when I was asked by a KAS friend if I expected we would ever see the fruition of our efforts, I responded that I was sure it would take a great deal of negotiation and patience.

I felt it was wonderful that our two cultures, Chinese and Western, as well as political ideologies could work together so rapidly to reach a common goal. It was wonderful that the vision originated with the Second Generation, that our children, including our daughter Kim, carried it through to completion. Wonderful is the feeling of having a part in this process along with Elsa Allgood Porter as advisors, accepted for our generation's collective wisdom having grown up in China. Wonderful is the feeling of happiness I remember of my schooling at KAS that merges with the feelings of joy in the reality of the Lushan Institute.

Feed your soul on Lushan.
Clear your mind.
Seek the source of the spring.
Listen to its water rushing down the mountain
below the Yellow Dragon Temple.
Breathe in qi.
Breathe out li.
Meditate on Chinese traditions.
Walk in the footsteps of Zhu Xi and Pearl Buck.
Relish the cultural blend.
Find your path on historical, mystical, inspiring Lushan.
You can.

Myrla Magness
(Lushan Institute Student in 2011)

A Special Ending - 2011

Having realized a final trip to Lushan, my birthplace and having seen the Lushan Institute become a reality, I was eagerly anticipating another major event in my life – my 90th birthday. It is a strange phenomenon that hesitancy at one point in life to reveal one's age, turns to bragging when age 90 nears.

The kids began early in the year 2011 to plan a gala family celebratory gathering in my honor on Topsail Island on the North Carolina Coast. In August they rented a spacious house for the nineteen of us who were able to come for parts of the week of beautiful weather.

The highlight for me was my birthday dinner, a festive celebration. Our daughters, all of them talented cooks of Chinese cuisine, prepared a feast of my favorite dishes! Watching them vie for the garlic, ginger, and special spices was part of the fun. Best of all were the large servings of Chinese vegetables which I loved.

At the end they brought out gifts of pressed Chinese tea, Korean Andong Soju and some of Scotland's famed Glenlivet. Fortunately, I was ordered to take these specials home to savor over time.

You can readily understand that this family has much to keep Barbara and me very happy. We are immensely grateful for our children. We love them dearly and are very proud of them. There were times, as in every family, when circumstances were difficult for them and also for our relationship with them. Perfect parents we are not, but mutual, lasting love and respect continues. In our older years, knowing they care about us and will support us in any way they can is deeply reassuring.

In Retirement

41. Six siblings in Salisbury – Clockwise : Karen, Katrina,
Bonnie, Kim, Chris, Dana
42. Mountain House, Blowing Rock, NC with Sterling Creek in foreground
43. Our children feted us with a 50th anniversary
celebration at the Mountain House.
July 1, 1994

In Retirement

44

45

46

44. We entered Friends Homes West in Greensboro, NC on December 16, 1994.
45. Our daughter Karen 1948 – 2001
46 Three brothers – Bob, Don, Sterling

Third LAST Trip to China, 2007

47. Kuling American School Association Reunion in Kuling on Lushan. Four
KAS students from the 1930s are in the front row.
Others are Second Generation or friends.
48. Our good friend and former helper, Liu Yunchu,
now in his 80s, and his wife.
49. Kim, granddaughter Erin and Dana on the roof of the new Yueyang
Church with an Elder and Pastor Chen. The ancient pagoda still prevails.

Family Celebration

50

50. August 2011, Bonnie, Katrina, Dana and Kim organize a gala family
week on Topsail Island, NC to celebrate my 90th birthday.

51

51. 2012, Happy Year of the Dragon – "Gongxi fa cai" (May you ever prosper!)

Chapter VIII

Family Update

1973 into the New Millennium

How do I write my memoirs, really my life history, without including Barbara's and my children? They have been a major focus in our lives, but the focus changes as children grow older and leave home. They cut certain ties and continue to create their own history, so it becomes impossible to record all the events that make up their ongoing lives even though we have always been in close contact.

This update brings our children's history to the year 2012.

Karen and Steve Berry living in Maryland presented us with our first grandchild, Michelle Marie, on September 14, 1974. After eight years the marriage dissolved, but Karen continued to live in the Washington, DC area, working at the National Institute of Health. She was a skilled electron microscope technician and co-authored a publication of her research. Later she went into the private sector as a biomedical sales representative for leading companies in that field. She was among the first women to be selected for the Baltimore Longitudinal Study of Aging and later invited me to join her in the study.

Years later Karen reconnected with a former admirer, Milton Ganyard, and moved to Durham, North Carolina. It was so good to have her closer to us. After their marriage, Milton and Karen, both biologists, developed an educational farm for field trips for school children, most of whom had never seen a cotton boll or explored a corn maze. The highlight of the field trip was the selection by each student of a pumpkin from the field to take home. Karen created large colorful signs around the farm which illustrated how bees function and other interesting facts related to nature. She also put together a similar pamphlet to give to the children.

It must be included that Karen was a talented Chinese cook. Her Peking Duck, a very difficult delicacy to create, rivaled that of professional Chinese chefs. Her feasts were a delight for all the family.

Karen, at age 53, inexplicably died in her sleep early on Father's Day, June 17, 2001. It was a crushing loss which left a gaping hole in our family. Her daughter, Michelle, was married to Tim Kaps, her high school sweetheart in 1997. It is deeply saddening that their two girls were not born until after Karen's death: Samantha Marie in 2003 and Alexandra Nicole in 2005.

Chris – We have forever been thankful that after serving his country as a Marine in Vietnam, he returned safely home in 1970. He met Barbi Bolmer at Appalachian State University and following Chris's graduation they were married in the summer of 1973. They have set the record for the longest marriage of our children, now over 38 years!

Chris and Barbi took on an amazing project in 1975. They found an authentic 175-year old log cabin in a cow pasture near Mooresville, Barbi's hometown, then dismantled, transported and reassembled it on an acre of property we had given them near our mountain cottage to make a rustic, attractive home. They later built on to the original log cabin to accommodate the arrival of their three girls - Heather, Megan and Anna, all now adults.

Chris taught Driver Education at Watauga High School for 11 years. Then, in 1989, with all the girls in school, Chris worked with Barbi to establish and operate for twenty years a successful gift/novelty shop called "G.Whillikers" in downtown Blowing Rock. Megan was Barbi's artistic assistant. Chris works with a large business outsourcing company where he is currently a compliance officer.

Heather, after owning and operating a coffee shop and taxi service, returned to school at the University of NC in Wilmington, very successfully graduating with a degree in Geography and Spanish. Megan manages a health foods store in Boone and also receives commissions to paint murals in private homes. Anna is an outdoors person and works in landscaping. All three have longtime significant others.

Kim completed her Catawba College BA in English with distinction (*summa cum laude*) in the spring of 1974. At the end of her sophomore year she had married Bob Selby whom she met at Catawba, and on December 9, 1974 they gave us our second granddaughter, Shawn. While they lived in Salisbury over the next two years, Kim was most valuable help in my office at Livingstone when the department secretary, Vicky Hyman, had to resign for health reasons. Kim was super efficient and well liked by the students. The family soon moved to Providence, RI where Bob found a job as a cartoonist/illustrator for the Providence newspaper. They separated in 1978 and Kim moved to Boston where she became engaged in editorial work. Several years later Kim married Adam Klein, a South African who was teaching at the Harvard Business School. They enjoyed many world travels, including visits to Adam's family in South Africa and two family trips with Barbara and me to China. During this time Kim earned an MA in International Relations at the Fletcher School of Law and Diplomacy at Tufts University. Kim also became involved in volunteer work with the American Repertory Theater in Cambridge. This experience of working closely with the management and fundraising side of a major contemporary theater was life changing. She plunged into this new career in 1988, thriving on learning the business from soup to nuts in a variety of venues. Her marriage to Adam had dissolved; Shawn was in McGill University, so Kim left Boston for Philadelphia and New York to pursue theatrical management work in the professional world. She became Managing Director of the prestigious experimental theater company, "The Wooster Group" in 1997. After four years she founded her independent producing/consulting company, KiWi Productions, working as an executive producer with contemporary theater and dance theater companies for six years. In 2007 Kim joined the downtown Manhattan venue, HERE Arts Center as Producing Director where she now commissions, develops, and produces full theatrical works in multi-disciplinary forms.

After a 14-year relationship with composer/musician, Don Dinicola ended in 2005, she has been independent and thoroughly enjoying her time with her daughter and her grandchildren, Miles (6) and Zoe, (3½)

Shawn's children in her marriage to Shawn Hainsworth. The family lives in western Massachusetts, and Shawn, a talented RN, is volunteering in a local hospice.

Bonnie completed two years at Catawba College. In the summer between her freshman and sophomore years she and her best friend worked at a posh restaurant in Berne, Switzerland. They had a wonderful time and were able to visit Paris and the French Riviera.

In 1976 she transferred to UNC Chapel Hill and thoroughly enjoyed the intellectual challenge of her International Studies major as well as campus life. She met Tom Mole, a fellow travel enthusiast, who had graduated four years earlier with the same major. It was not surprising that when Bonnie graduated in 1978, Tom invited her to join him on a grand vagabond tour that included Europe and India. It was difficult for us to accept our unmarried couple's traveling together, but we sent Bonnie off to join Tom with our blessings.

Tom earned an MBA in 1984 at Thunderbird, an international business school. A dedicated couple, Tom and Bonnie were married in our home on June 7 to be sure that Bonnie received benefits from Tom's new employer, Exxon, on their first assignment, Malaysia. We have joked that Exxon was the "shotgun" that finally got them married. Having no children, they have spent many years working overseas. While in Singapore, Bonnie earned an MA in English Language at the National University of Singapore in 1992. She then taught for almost three years at Tomasek Polytechnic there.

In 1995 Bonnie and Tom returned to the USA. They lived in Mexico studying tile-making with artisans, and then settled near Wilmington. They started their own home accessory business specializing in coastal theme designs on tiles which they made themselves. Their most popular products were large mirrors decorated with colorful tiles of fishes. They were on the road a lot, not only to Mexico, but also up and down the entire Atlantic coast selling to interior decorators and high-end gift shops. They also entered juried art shows. Though this was a successful business, they were ready to head overseas again. In early 2008 they went to Vietnam and earned certificates in teaching English as a second language from a Cambridge University program. They taught in Danang, Vietnam for the remainder of that year and have now been teaching English in public schools in Andong, South Korea for the past three years.

I definitely passed on my passion for travel and adventure to Bonnie. As a consequence, Barbara and I have enjoyed traveling with Bonnie and Tom in widespread locations around the world: Thailand, Taiwan, China, Singapore, Bali, England and Mexico. Most recently, in 2010, Barbara and Kim had a wonderful two weeks with them in Korea while I went to China.

Dana, at age 17, followed her sisters' lead to do something different for her senior year in high school. She won an exchange opportunity to study in Siegen, Germany. Unfortunately, her host family was not compatible so her exchange year was not a great success from our point of view. She did have some pretty wild experiences, like going to Pamplona, Spain with some cronies at the time of the running of the bulls! She learned German amazingly well and later in the year was befriended by a very kind family. We visited her there in 1978. Barbara and I then went on to spend a delightful week meandering around the south of Ireland.

When Dana returned to North Carolina she entered UNC at Chapel Hill. Her immaturity led her into an unhappy relationship. She came home to Salisbury for a while and attended Catawba College, thus completing the Whitener tradition. She transferred to NC State University in Raleigh and graduated *summa cum laude* in Animal Science. After working for a year, she turned to nursing. She won the Johnston Scholarship at UNC, Chapel Hill and completed with honors her BS in nursing. She met Mark Froetschel in Raleigh while he was completing his PhD in Ruminant Nutrition at NC State. They were married in 1987 in the Little White Church in the mountains. Mark joined the University of Georgia and is now a full professor in the Department of Animal and Dairy Sciences. Dana has thoroughly enjoyed her career as an RN, having worked in a neonatal intensive care unit, a pediatric cardiology group, and the University Health Center.

Dana and Mark have three children: Erin (23), David (22) and Joey (15). Erin graduated with a BS in Ecology at the University of Georgia. She has had the wonderful experience of traveling in China with us, and has inherited my love of Lushan. She is studying Chinese and spent a summer of research with her university ecology group in China. David was diagnosed with Autism as a young child and has overcome many obstacles. He is now a 3rd year student at the U. of Georgia working on a BA in Art with an emphasis on drawing and lives independently. Joey is a freshman in high school with plans to be an engineer.

Katrina met Gerald Townsend at East Carolina University in Greenville, NC. Both graduated in 1974, with Katrina earning a degree in Social Work. They were married on the front lawn of our mountain cottage in 1975. Katrina worked as a house parent in the Methodist Children's Home and then as a Housing Counselor for the city of Raleigh. Gerald earned his certification as a CPA. Later they established a very successful financial planning firm. Katrina's amazing achievement in education, work, marriage and family is attributable to her strength of character, her determination and her generous spirit.

Katrina has remained very close to her friends from Children's Garden; they get together often in HongKong, Canada and the US. They have formed The Children's Garden Foundation to help orphans around the world, especially in China.

They have two children: Eric (32) and Emily (29).

Eric is married to Megan Carpenter. They are parents of Madeleine (4) and Violet (2½). Eric has been working with Townsend Asset Management for six years as a Financial Advisor. Megan has received her PhD in Education Research and Policy Analysis at NC State University.

Emily is married to John Luisana and they are parents of Maxton (2½). They are now expecting their second child. Emily graduated from NC State's School of Veterinary Medicine and is now a licensed veterinarian at the Cary Animal Hospital. Cary is a suburb of our State Capitol, Raleigh. John is in the computer gaming business.

Chapter IX

Reflections

One of my social work teachers had a favorite maxim for all students: "Beginnings are hard and endings are often even harder!"

I thought I was fully familiar with this concept and had often used this phrase in my own teaching, accepting its premise. I was, however, reminded of this truth when I was asked to reexamine carefully my own life experience while revising this story. Only then did I realize that having to abandon my dream of following my parents in a lifetime of missionary service to the Chinese Church and China had a profound effect on me. What I had never fully accepted was that in leaving Central China, though followed by 15 years of very meaningful work with Chinese refugees in HongKong, I harbored many of the feelings of the refugees with whom I had spent so many years. Feelings of abandonment, frustration with uncontrollable and rapid change, loss of self confidence, and loss of a sense of my own roots, all flooded through me at various times.

I also found it difficult to express clearly, succinctly, and accurately how difficult it was for me to adjust to the many cultural changes in the USA upon return from the Orient. What I sense now is that this change of life career was so dramatic and forceful I repressed my feelings of deep sadness in being forced into a new career at age 46.

I clearly saw the difficulties these changes caused members of my family. That they have surmounted cultural obstacles and found meaningful lives is a matter of joy and thanksgiving. Transitions in my personal life and work as well as the cultural changes for our family could be described by a Chinese expression, "wei ji", translated as dangerous, critical opportunity or crisis.

It is hard to analyze with much accuracy what my life has meant. Karen Anderson writes, "as soon as the earliest humans clearly left the trees, they sought meaning in life through art and architecture. They sought meaning in beliefs, in faith and a supreme being (God)." So I also have sought meaning.

2011 – Valentine's Day

Valentines Day is a fitting time to write of the daily gift from my loving partner. Life could not have been the same without Barbara. Through all our shared experiences, frightening and joyful, painful and happy, serious and frivolous, noisy and meditative, Barbara has always been a partner and team player. When we had to make the decision whether or not to leave China in 1948, she said she would not leave with our two small children by herself; we would stay as a family or leave together. She was always known for her competence and empathy.

Barbara did change the course of my life with her integrity and sound judgment. Those who know me as strong willed might also agree with my seminary roommate who said, "It was a great day when Barbara decided definitely to throw your lot in with hers!"

My father, Sterling Wilfong from North Carolina, sought my mother, Marie Anna living in Missouri. He courted her long-distance by mail. I, Sterling Hegnauer, was fortunate to be on site and in sight of Barbara but life-long deep love and respect was shared in both marriages.

Serving China and the Church

In the year 2000, Barbara and I discussed our journey together. Barbara has felt that my call by God was to serve China as much as it was a call to be a minister. I am sure she is right for the two always seemed to go together. Yet there were times when my sense of God's call and closeness to God, my faith, was particularly strong. When the aged woman in Niehjyasz was being considered for Church membership, she did well repeating the Lord's Prayer. When it came to the intricacies of the creed, she was distressed to find that the difficult words escaped her lack of even a rural education. In desperation she turned to me, though I was not the inquisitor, and said,

"Young minister, I just can't say all the words that they tried to teach me, but this one thing I know, Jesus died for me and has saved me!" This was a confirmation of my own faith and provided me with a strengthening of my reason for being there. There was no question of her acceptance into the fellowship of believers of that small church community.

In 1949 we finally made our decision to move to Hankow from Linhsiang and there to await momentous change and face a new unknown, "liberation" by the Communist army. It was a difficult struggle as we tried to sort out conflicting feelings and responsibilities. I knew I could be helpful as Mission treasurer to arrange transition support for all Mission workers, missionaries, hospital staff, teachers in schools, and church workers. We also needed the assurance of contact with our homeland. We really had faith that we were led always by God's grace and the comforting assurance of God's love and care.

Though we may not have understood it at the time we did experience successions of confident faith which could follow. One clear example was shown when we returned to Yueyang in 1983 and found that a small remnant of the church had survived. The chaotic situation in China caused by the Japanese invasion; the political divisions which grew between Nationalist and Communist; and, the massive, pervasive, and grinding poverty in China had clearly called for new approaches. My learning had been led by my mentor at Yale Divinity, Dr. Kenneth Scott Latourette. It was evident to me dramatically through the following event.

On this trip, 13 Christians, including Barbara and me, met in a small room in the church that had just recently been returned by the city police department to the local congregation after 32 years as a police barracks. Rev. Meng, nearly eighty, had been the one evangelist I had worked with in 1948-49 who I was confident lacked the ability to reach ordination. The fact that he was the only one of the six evangelists I had worked with and still living was significant. He had been ordained by the Hunan Church and was obviously undertaking a very difficult rehabilitation task.

He was expressively glad to see Barbara and me among the small group attending worship that morning. We were seated in a circle and he insisted on holding my hand while he preached. He told the simple story of Nehemiah returning from exile to a destroyed Jerusalem. He explained how this small group of Yueyang Christians had the task of gathering the faithful and restoring the church building to its original purpose. I felt a mighty sense of power entering the group, evidence of the Spirit working in the midst of change and offering hope for the future. The physically tiny Rev. Meng was a man of faith who shared it with us that Sunday. We all received strength.

The woman who had walked for an entire day to attend this service spoke of how much it meant to be in a real worship service after so many years. I thought back to how I had encouraged Mr. Meng in 1948 to read and study for we knew then we would be leaving China before long. The message was his to share, ours to trust and to pray.

As I witness the growth of the Church of Christ in China today I feel that the roots were planted by the faith of those hardy and persistent early missionaries and then the message carried on by the faithful. In spite of all mistakes, both theirs, and ours the Holy Spirit has touched the lives of millions of Chinese people.

Living Through Turbulent/Chaotic Times

That era I grew up in was one of revolution and chaos and had little to do with day to day studies, but we students did learn that conditions were unstable and dangerous as was evident in the number of evacuations and times when we were real refugees, faced with great uncertainty.

Betty Jean Elder, the daughter of a missionary colleague in Hunan province, has written a beautiful book of her childhood, *The Oriole's Song, An American Girlhood in Wartime China*. She captures the sense of being caught in impermanence.

"Back at SAS (Shanghai American School), all was hurried as we disposed of the things we couldn't take, said our goodbyes, washed our hair, and packed late into the night. I was in a daze from excitement and fever from the shots, and I have no clear memory of our last hours at SAS. The next morning we departed for the ship on a bus with the others.

I said goodbye to SAS almost without thinking. Perhaps I could afford to do so because I took with me, at last, a sense of permanent belonging. In Changsha and Yuanling I had felt I belonged, but I had also known it wasn't permanent – I would always be a foreigner. In the States, although I had learned how to fit in, I was always something of a visitor – an outsider. But at SAS I was neither foreigner nor outsider. I was with others like me, whose traditions and worldview were a combination of the country we lived in and the very different country from which our parents came, and yet not totally of either. From the common experience of partial belonging and our intensely shared lives at SAS, we created a heritage unique to us – a third culture from the precincts of which we would gaze out at the rest of the world. Wherever we were, our point of view would always be slightly outside the norm for that place. But within this third culture we were the norm. Within this third culture we had forged bonds that held across time and space and change and race so that when we came together again, we did not have to grope for understanding. At reunions in later years we picked up where we'd left off forty, then fifty years before, and although we were delighted to find out what had become of each other, we were not surprised. What we had from SAS was our home country, the place of our full belonging. At last I had found a group that shared my origins. No longer suspended between two worlds, at SAS I fell into place." (p 194)

She captures the sense of feeling she belonged as she left China in haste. I too felt "suspended between two worlds." Growing up, I can remember wanting desperately to know what American boys were doing and thinking in the USA. Brother Don and I would pore over the Montgomery Ward catalogues to find something for our local tailor to copy, sometimes with quite disastrous results. At the same time, as I lived and learned at Kuling American School, I knew that I was living in two worlds for I was studying to go in the future to college in America when my Chinese peers were studying to fit into life in a chaotic, changing China.

Learning to milk cows electrically and taking part in ice-cream suppers at the country church in Missouri that summer of 1938 was an unanticipated cultural shock and change which helped me begin to learn my biological roots. When my Kuling American School friends gather, we have a unique sense of connection which I do not find with other friends. I always look forward to seeing them and learning the unexpected.

Chaos Theory

Approaching the time when my story ends, I have become more impressed with "chaos theory" which includes "new evidence for an early origin of modern human behavior" ...as well as "the interconnection between art and meaning in belief, faith and a supreme being." (Michael Crichton, *The Lost World*)

Crichton notes that the rapidity of change is connected to urgent and unrelieved stress which results in chaos or near chaos. As polarization of opposing viewpoints hardens, behavior becomes unpredictable and results in chaotic conditions. I sense that I have lived through and continue in quite a period of unpredictability and chaos. Quite clear to me is the fact of chaos in our lives to which Barbara and I can bear witness. I can most easily identify five periods of chaos, uncertainty and change in my life:

1. The 1927 Revolution when Sun Yat-sen and Chiang Kaishek led the Kuomingtang party to victory.
   Early memories recall that many discussions by my parents with all the other adults in Yochow often centered on "bandits." Ho Lung, a bandit and later a Communist general, was sometimes conjured up by our faithful Amah to get us to do something which we were required to do like getting into bed. Our evacuations from our mission station in those years to Hankow and Shanghai and once to the USA were the result of chaotic political and economic times.
2. The 1930 Yangtze River flood.
   The immensity of the Yangtze River flood in 1930 overawed my nine-year-old mind. I remember being in Kuling (Lushan) that summer and looking out over Jiujiang and the surrounding countryside as far as the eye could see. Where the river had been, there was only an ocean. I wondered if all the farm people had been washed away. Such disruption occurred that we actually moved to Shanghai to wait out the chaotic situation everywhere in the Yangtze valley.
3. Japanese invasion of Northeast China in 1931 through World War II, 1945.
   I have already documented my experience with the Japanese army in 1938. That I spent the last half of my senior year of high school at Shanghai American School was an indication of the upheaval of that era. In China at the time, we could not understand why the US was letting Japan have its own way, especially after the rape of Nanking.

4. 1946 through 1950 when Barbara and I were serving as missionaries in Yueyang, Hunan.
   Beginning our work amid the devastation and destruction left by the
   Japanese army in Hunan in 1946, Barbara and I were appalled that
   even all trees had been cut down. The churches had been destroyed
   and the population was living in makeshift homes. Clearly the long
   years of war had devastated the land. Yet the chaos only intensified
   because of the collapse of the Chinese currency twice and the war
   between the Nationalists and the Communists. We returned to the
   USA after fifteen months living under the new Communist government. The fighting had ended but the times were very stressful.
5. Return to the US from HongKong in 1967, ending our missionary service and facing US cultural changes with a young growing
   family.
   Our life of work with the HongKong Church of Christ in China
   and Rennie's Mill refugees was able to survive destructive typhoons,
   the refugee invasion and workers riots. It did not survive a lack of
   change in the Church structure itself. An older style of Chinese
   administration kept able younger social work leadership and
   younger ministers under strict control. With this policy I could
   not continue to develop young leadership as many felt that their
   opportunities in HongKong were being limited and that emigra-
   tion to Canada and the USA was their only solution. My determination not to intervene in that development certainly created for
   us the termination of our mission years. We did arrive back in the
   US during turbulent times of social change. Many attitudes and
   mores we grew up with were changing. Alcohol abuse and sexual
   freedoms were often openly displayed. We felt our family was living in a period of chaotic times.

My work in HongKong relating to the housing of refugees had introduced me, unwittingly, to "chaos theory." I had worked with the refugees
who were being crowded into seven-story buildings at 35 square feet per
individual. Ten years later in Chapel Hill, I learned from an epidemiologist
friend that there was a valid research design which in crowded USA cities
had shown that such overcrowding resulted in a breakdown of family values and increase in crime of preying on the weak and elderly. Today large

segments of our global society live on the edge of insolvency and fear. With hopelessness and despair, we may see increasing chaos in our world. What will the lack of strong and wise global leadership produce for the young people in North Africa who seek freedom today?

Pierre Tielhard de Chardin suggests in *Letters from a Traveler* that "the most unexpected is not necessarily the most unlikely (in China)." I sense this in the children of my Chinese colleagues of yesteryear, some of whom are here in the US to stay and others who have already made their way back home to China.

A Few Final Words?

Loren Mead in his book *Meltdown of the Mainline* presents a compelling analysis of how the mainline churches are facing the same issues that the major US corporations face: an urgent necessity to change their old approaches. Some will restructure their infrastructure, i.e., cutting jobs, cutting pensions, trying to restore fiscal balance as evident at the time of this story closing, 2011.

Mead suggests that with the death of the older generation in the church, the tithe givers have largely departed. This necessitates drastic rethinking of what we can do by uniting our efforts and operating on reduced budgets. He calls for a completely renewed spiritual dimension to meet this crisis that is facing all churches.

Tom Brokaw wrote *The Greatest Generation* to honor a group of Americans who grew up in the Great Depression years, fought the 2nd World War and then came home to rebuild their lives and serve their communities. We were also a very fortunate generation. We had learned the meaning of saving, having grown up carefully using every penny. Our large post WWI generation which lived through the great Depression was the first to begin early to plan for years of retirement as the life span increased and we learned better health habits.

We oldsters have not learned enough, however, as our own sons fought in Korea or in an unpopular war in Vietnam and now the grandsons are fighting in an unfunded war in Iraq and Afghanistan. As a generation we have not learned justice and peace. We have learned to be world travelers and seen the global economy develop, explode and in many ways fail as greed overtook the management of money in our economy. Technology is far ahead of most of us, but we have seen and lived with change.

It has been an exciting era; we have passed the baton to the next generation in the race! What glorious challenges now face today's young people! The optimists among us are hopeful, our pessimists are fearful of the inability of all with varying opinions to learn consensus building and to work together in cooperation. We cannot make choices for others, but we do have hope and expectations for the future, particularly for our brightest young people and the experienced veterans of Iraq and Afghanistan who have training and discipline to be a new, "great generation" of leaders for our nation!

This Record Ends

The optimists among us are hopeful; our pessimists are fearful of the inability of those with varying opinions to learn consensus building and to work together in cooperation. We cannot make choices for others, but we do have hope and expectations for the future, particularly for our brightest young people and the experienced veterans of Iraq and Afghanistan who have training and discipline to be a new, "great generation" of leaders for our nation!

My personal journey, begun in the Land of the Pagoda, has been so meaningful and rewarding because it started in Lushan where I received blessing and so many beautiful memories. This record of my journey is ending, as I contemplate the realization of dreams:

- A Yueyang minister in his 80s ready to rebuild a wounded church and trusting in God's guidance;

- A group of HongKong young people seeking God's plan for ways to rebuild the leadership of their Church to serve all people;

- Livingstone College Social Work students learning new roles to build communities to serve their people in spite of calls to riot;

- The call of our United Church of Christ to seek justice and peace for all peoples in the world; and,

- Finally a Lushan Institute that many of our KAS second-generation children have helped to develop, to share the cultures we own.

May our pagodas always cast their shadows not only on us but also to inspire the dreams of our children and grandchildren!

Addenda

Addendum A

NOTES FROM TWO TEACHING YEARS IN TAIWAN – 1984 to 1986

We arrived in Tainan to start teaching in September 1984. Here are a few notes from my journal that give a sense of what we were doing and experiencing:

December 14, 1984

Friday: For the first time, I felt that the Community Work class got worked up sufficiently to speak up and argue with me. It came about because I had worded a question in a test somewhat ambiguously, according to the two poorest students. It was surely a minority position, but it gave me a marvelous opportunity to discuss community theory (the subject for the day). The concept of pulling a community together requires consensus. I tried to get some sense of unanimity and when that failed, suggested that they needed to do it the Chinese way of speaking to their class representative who would tell me the sense of the entire class. But the discussion was good, heated at times, feelings were high but non-threatening. All semester, I have hoped that they would climb out of their polite, quiet, and reserved selves.

Our first Christmas present arrived - from the Halds. They spent a fortune on airmail, but it was a thrill to open a package. The pecans are very precious because there aren't any to be purchased here. The other little goodies will be appreciated. Today we received a check for NT$1400 (US $46) as a Christmas present from the Women's Work Committee of the General Assembly of the Taiwan Presbyterian Church. The nice note said they wanted to share their offering of their World Day of Prayer service with all missionaries serving the Church. What a meaningful expression of appreciation!

Sunday was a day with the Mountain Church (Aborigines) group. It started at 10am with the Church service, followed by about 25 young people sitting in the grass in the shade of the classroom building to play games while eating a tangerine, candy and some wafers. They are good at these informal games some of them using Chinese words for lion and mouse similar to the use of bear and hare in telling a story which demands a slap or something for one or the other expression. The group was composed mostly of high school students who are here because there are no senior highs in the mountains. They live in dorms and do not get to go home very often. They are from a variety of tribes. At the service on Sunday the various readings were in tribal dialects, some of them sounding quite like Japanese. We were told that many of the tribes had to borrow words from Japanese as the tribe moved into the 20th century because they did not have the expressions in their own language.

Lunch was a small box of rice, vegetables, some pickles and a piece of chicken. All this comes in a plastic dinner box with a pair of chopsticks. A soup made in the campus kitchen was delicious and provided the liquid.

December 30, 1984, Sunday:

What a different four days! We left early Wednesday morning for our senior class trek (<u>Nan Heng Lyu You</u>, southern route excursion). This winter tour was a hiking and scenic bus trip across the island from Tainan up above 10,000 ft then down to Taitung on the east coast. Five faculty members were invited and foolhardy enough to accept @ NT$1,200 each (US $30). We had been preparing for weeks by buying camping equipment like knapsacks, inflatable pillows, plastic ponchos for rain and even some thin foam pads (which we gave away as being useless for our hip bones on hard wooden floors! - one of the students wanted them so carried them out). The trip was a fascinating combination of new sights, sounds, tastes, smells as well as feelings. First, the smells - DUST, DUST, & DUST. All of it tasting about the same, but with most of the road unpaved gravel, the weather perfect, and the busses full of cracks, etc; we really had a full dose of it. Our wash today showed that we carried quite a bit of it back home with us. The smells of the high mountains will remain with us for awhile as we were reminded of Blowing Rock as we wound our way through some beautiful forests and then farther east where it was more moist, groves of fern and tropical plants like poinsettias growing wild, both white and deep red. Makes us want to escape regularly from the polluted, plastic burning, and smokestack belching plains. The smell of sulfur at the hot spring was welcome when we had a most wonderful HOT bath after three days of hiking and spot washing in mountain ice water. We gloried in the sights of the blue, blue sky and the brilliant sun, the clouds below us when we were up at the 9,000-foot level for the first night and Thursday morning, a soaring hawk, rushing mountain streams. Even during this dry weather some of the waterfalls were beautiful, and ice where one small stream splattered an area of the bank on the roadside where the sun didn't reach. We marveled at the sea of clouds below us when we were at the upper level mountain youth hostel. Marveled even more at the village which lives in perpetual mist and drizzle during a long winter. What contrasts and beauty all around as we walked some six miles along a steep gorge with a very beautiful small river below winding its way toward the sea.

The mountains themselves with evidence of numberless avalanche slides are quite unstable; even the ridge tops seem ready to crash down the steep valleys. The road is single tracked, carved into the side of the mountain with evidence of being buried often. Sounds? The wind whistling in the hills, the waterfalls, the call of large crows and other birds, as well as a glorious silence. We had the most moving experience listening to the sounds of mountain people singing in their eight-tone scale in an almost "plainsong" manner their mountain tunes and hymns, imagine each person choosing his or her own notes, but they were in harmony with at least four or five different tones making up a series of moving chords. It was fantastic. Feelings? The closeness of living and traveling with our students was heartwarming. They are generous, funny and full of vitality. As future leaders in the Church and laypersons one can feel confident in their depth of faith and their convictions. Some surprises - the open display of affection which was not very typical in the past. They spoke mostly Taiwanese so had to translate into Mandarin or English for us. Also, I can now tell you how funny and exciting it is to be mistaken for a Chinese (The lady photographer who asked for my picture was clearly nearsighted)! Let's start over from Wednesday morning.

We were up at 5am to get our breakfast before a 6:15am gathering at the Library. We wound through the villages and fertile fields of western Taiwan. It isn't really very far to the mountains, we soon saw them rising in the distance. Then we began the process of winding up the valleys where rice paddies gave way to fruit trees of all kinds: coconuts, lichee, orange, and mango and at the higher elevations, pear and apple. A rest stop at a small town gave us a chance to taste a local specialty - taro candy and taro filled hot biscuits (we passed up the taro ice-cream). We followed ridges with very steep hillsides. Sometimes we wondered if the small bus would make the sharp turns required as we looked down precipitous slopes. Our destination Tien Chr was the village we had chosen to start hiking. As we got closer, we realized that the better part of wisdom would be to take the bus half-way to the next stop where we were to spend the night. The first discovery was that these villages consisted of only a police station or a highway work office. Anyway, at noon we arrived at the end of the Tainan bus line and the jumping off place for a 14-kilometer hike. The Taitung bus was to arrive at 2pm so four of us (McNairs and Whiteners) waited to ride it at least half-way while the rest started walking after a short lunch break. It was interesting to see what each person brought for lunch. Some had "dzung-dzes" (rice with meat or beans wrapped in palm leaves) others had brought plastic containers of rice, meat, egg and pickle - called "byan dang." We brought cheese sandwiches, some tomatoes and fruit. I guess they thought we were as strange in our tastes as we considered theirs. We took pictures and bid them "goodbye" but later passed them on the upgrade. One of the girls hailed the bus as she was going ahead to assure our reservations. She also managed to take several of the girls' packs which helped some. We determined to carry our own since we were only going to carry them for about six kilometers (about four miles). The day was perfect. We got off below the tree line and started walking on up the road waiting for the student group to catch up.

At the very top was the tunnel through the mountain - 2,731 meters high - (9.100 ft.). About a hundred feet below this, we came to the Yakou Youth Hostel. Along with the police station it was the only building in the town (if you can call it that). Anyway, it was a welcome sight. We found raised platforms separated by movable partitions, but we had one room to ourselves. Men and women had separate rooms and that is how they thought we would like it, but we really preferred to be by ourselves (McNairs and Whiteners each had one). There were cotton pads for the mattress and "bei-wohs" (cotton padded quilts) for covering so we had plenty for warmth even in the cold. A nice Chinese supper really tasted good. We were above the clouds so the evening sky was starry bright and very crisp. I went to the police station to get some boiling water for tea and coffee after supper only to find that the local mountain policeman was deep in his cups. He could hardly stand up, but had courteously invited the young people to come up to heat water on his wood stove so that they could take baths. The girls were anxious to do so but when they saw his condition, they asked me to get a couple of fellows to come up to stand guard. Our first night was not an unqualified success, sleeping on the floor really was uncomfortable because we did not use all the pads available. B. put an extra one down in the middle of the night and found that it made a great deal of difference, except that she ended up with a huge allergy attack from the dusty, musty bedding. I tossed and turned all night and ended up with stiff muscles and sore hips from the hard floor. The next morning, after a Chinese breakfast of rice gruel and small dishes of peanuts, "dou fu," peppers etc. the young people hiked up to the top of the mountain, several hundred feet, straight up. B & I decided we needed to gather strength for the next day, so we walked a couple of kilometers on the level, looking at a waterfall and taking some pictures. The hostel, so beautifully nestled above the clouds, was a peaceful place. We hated to leave at 2:30 when the bus came by.

Our next stop was Li Dao, a small mountain village of some 400 persons of the Bunin aboriginal tribe. The people were smaller and had a Polynesian appearance. Unfortunately, the mountain tribes are very much 2nd class citizens. The village had a small primary school but for junior and senior high, the kids had to travel by bus for an hour each way down the mountain. Not many of them bother to complete more than primary or junior high and are consequently at a great disadvantage when they seek employment in the larger cities on the plains. Coming into the village, some half-mile from where the bus let us off, we saw a church spire. One of the students suggested it was a Catholic Church. I said that it was probably St. Johns, another was sure it said Presbyterian. We had a great time guessing only to find out that the characters said "Gospel Church'" We found out later that it really was a Taiwan Presbyterian Church of the Bunin presbytery. The minister, Rev. Wu, has a family on the other side of the mountain at his home village so he commutes. He has been at the church for seven years, though the Church itself was built six years ago. It seats about a hundred, even has an electronic organ which can only be played by a student of the Yushan seminary near HuaLien (some three or four hours away). The student comes on Saturday and helps out with Sunday School and worship as a part of field work, just as our students here also work in Churches on Sundays as a part of their training. Rev. Wu earns $100 a month, not enough to live on, so he is given some space in the village fields to plant corn and vegetables. Corn is a cash crop and was being harvested at this time. The village is in the mist and drizzle during the winter so everything grows like crazy. It never freezes and there is plenty of water for irrigation.

Unfortunately, the villagers are at the mercy of middlemen who take great advantage of the mountain people who have a quite different set of values. Alcoholism is rampant and young people leave the mountains at an increasing rate. They never really find good employment because they are not adequately educated. The plains people take advantage of them. This is evident here in Tainan too among the youth whom we have met in the Mountain Church here on campus. They speak the national language as that is what is taught in school, as well as their mountain dialects, but few of them are completely fluent in Taiwanese dialect.

Soon after arrival at the village we ordered a big pot of noodles because our lunch had given out - it was great. We also visited the Church and talked with the pastor and arranged that after supper at the Li Dao Youth hostel we would come for a 7:30 evening worship service which they had planned. The church was full - it has about 80 adult members with about 100 children in Sunday school. The service was most meaningful as Rev. Chen of our Social Work faculty was asked to preach. He talked about the Family and its importance. He quoted some startling statistics - that 40,000 mountain girls have been sold into prostitution in Taiwan cities. He also urged the families to prepare their youth for the difficult days ahead. He used the prodigal son as a reference that young people can be given the basic Christian faith to be able to come back when the times are too rough. He also urged that the village consider ways to strengthen communal life in the beautiful mountains so that young people will not be enticed away. I am not sure that he offered much in the practical sense, but they did appreciate hearing him. It appears to me that the Church will require a much more sophisticated leadership. Rev. Wu trained in Japanese and not a very dynamic person told us that most young ministers will only stay for a year or so. I am sure that it will be the Church which can provide the leadership for a better life, but this will take more leadership than presently available. Rev. Chen spoke in Mandarin, was translated into Bunin. At the end, I was asked to say a few words too, which I did in Mandarin. Tom McNair spoke in English which Rev. Chen translated into Mandarin which was then translated into Bunin, the tribal language. The singing, as mentioned earlier was inspiring and so different in sound and tone. After the service we talked with an elderly man (84) who could not speak mandarin, because he had learned Japanese long ago. He had a long white beard so we stood together for our picture. After we had returned to the hostel, the evening ended for us at a small restaurant where we had a famous Taiwanese dish - wine chicken. This was a whole chicken for 7 people cooked in rice wine only, along with some ginger and other flavors. It was really delicious. You should have seen the seminary students acting as though the alcohol had not evaporated. They kept going to the mirror to see who had the reddest face. They forgot that they were in a warm room with hot, spicey food and that they were all overdressed. It was great sport!

Let me comment about the mountain village and its people. In 1967 and 1974, Mark Thelin conducted a research project on the Bunin people. He says that it was before the road was put in and took all day for a strenuous hike up mountain trails to reach the village which had a population of 40 families. Today, with the road and the influx of retired soldiers who have been granted government land, the population is over 400 persons. The houses are of wood but are neatly placed at one end of the area which is flat enough to grow crops. The church is at the very end of the valley away from the entry road. A bus comes down into the village as a terminal point twice a day and another two buses can be boarded about a kilometer away (uphill) where the village road connects to the cross-island highway. The economy of the area has changed because the mountain people have access to markets for their cash crops. They also have ready access to alcohol and machinery. We saw a number of motorcycles in front of homes as well as some new small four-wheel drive trucks which obviously carried wood, farm supplies and other supplies wherever needed.

That night went much better as we had learned by then to pile up five or six heavy comforters under us. At 8:30 on Friday morning, after another rice gruel breakfast, we hefted our packs for a 9.3 kilometer (nearly six miles) hike down to the next village where we caught the bus into Taitung. The walk was spectacular - along a ridge which was above a beautiful river. We followed a gorge which had interesting springs which obviously carried mineral salts so were hot springs. This land is volcanic in origin and there are many hot springs throughout the mountains. B & I along with two girls kept a steady pace, arriving at Wu Li in two and a half hours. The next group was a whole hour behind us. We just couldn't stroll. The four of us ordered a hot bowl of noodles at 11:30 and really enjoyed them along with "mountain coffee" a seed which when roasted has a coffee taste. They boil it with some sweet herbs so no sugar is added even though it tastes really sweet. The 2:45 bus got us to Taitung by 5pm. There we were met by another senior student who had made arrangements for our stay there - at his home of all places. First he took us out to a hot springs hotel resort where we had a most wonderful HOT bath. What luxury, to get really clean and then to get into the hot springs pool. We had our swimming suits although some Japanese merely took towels to get into the water and politely fold the towel on the side of the pool. We could go into a warm pool, and then climb into a hot pool and then jump into the cold pool. Even B. got into the act of making the circuit - great for the pores, I'm sure. We then drove the eight or ten miles back to town, all 15 of us in a Toyota van which belonged to the Church Kindergarten, to the Huang family residence for supper. It was a good dinner with fried noodles and plenty of meat and vegetables. The house has three stories with three generations under the one roof (at least seven grandchildren left for school the next morning). We were given the bedroom of a daughter who is working in Kaohsiung, some four hours away by bus, and who comes home only on some weekends. We were very comfortable indeed.

This was the end of our trek. The next morning, Saturday, the group headed different directions. The McNairs were going to a Church program in the area, some students were heading home, and others headed back on early busses to be sure to get to their weekend Church assignments. We decided to take a later bus so we could look around Taitung. We were taken to a Church which was designed by a Roman Catholic priest for the local presbytery some 16 years ago. It was an interesting and unique building with particularly interesting marble designs outside representing the poor, the prisoner and the dispossessed. We enjoyed coffee with the young pastor and his wife and baby, visited the kindergarten (130 kids) and then went several blocks away to the Hwa Tung Mountain Center where we learned more of the Co-op efforts for mountain people and the LanYu Island fishermen. The former efforts are cooperative stores and buying; the latter a business to develop sales of tropical fish, deep diving to get them and a long process of caring for them until they are sold. The job is a long range effort; not one that can be done quickly when one considers that the training of mountain people for this effort starts from scratch. Their mores, for example, suggest that if one needs to borrow money from a relative or a friend, then one really does not need to repay the loan. That makes it hard to get across the idea of the capitalist system. No wonder they get taken for a ride!

At 10:30am we went to the bus station. Because we were thirsty we ordered some warm chocolate milk. What an experience, for we have always been very careful of what we ate and drank. The guy took a pot, rinsed it out in a bucket of who knows what water, put in on the fire and dumped the bottles of chocolate milk in it, stirred it with a dirty spoon and then used a dirty funnel to pour it all back in the bottles. With two non-descript plastic straws we drank the poisoned brew and waited to get stomach cramps. Guess what? We didn't even get the runs. We caught the bus for a 20-min. ride along the coast to a "small wild area", a park on the rugged seashore where the Pacific surged against coral encrusted rocks, and where we could see Green Island - the penal colony for political prisoners. We enjoyed walking around, had a papaya and while B. went to get some small pebbles for her ikebana arrangements, I sat on a park bench. A Chinese tour group (sponsored officially by the Defense Ministry for broadcasters) appeared; we nodded and smiled. One of the last of the men said to his companion that Santa Claus, "lau gung gung," was sitting there. I immediately responded by saying I wasn't "Santa". They had a great laugh that I had understood them. A young woman who had heard all this came back up and waved to me asking if I would come down to the beach because she wanted to take my picture. I told her I would be glad to. Just then Barbara came up. The girl became very embarrassed and asked if I was a foreigner, apologizing like crazy. She was sure, she said that I was an elderly Chinese gentleman - the best compliment I've had yet. I told her she surely could have told by my western accent. She took a couple of pictures, she said she was entering in a photo contest, but then I'll never know. By coincidence, their bus driver recognized me because he had driven us up the mountain from Tainan to Tien Chr. We got back into town by 1pm so decided to check out the bus for home. One was being loaded, and even though we both needed to check out the "johns" we were able to get on. What an ordeal! First the bus driver ignored the first rest stop because the road was being repaired and he didn't want to take the time. Next, the road repairs were so rough, I was sure there was going to be a puddle under my seat any minute. After two-and-a-half grueling hours we did stop, thank heaven. The scenery along the east coast was really very spectacular. Barbara must have been in better shape than I was because she reports on details I obviously missed while looking at the nice bushes I could have used if only the guy had slowed down!

We returned from our extended excursion with the impression that pollution in Taiwan was "out of control". We had seen tons of plastic dumped on beautiful mountain hillsides, small towns with factories belching unhealthy smoke, and streets poorly swept. We tried consistently to educate our students to be more environmentally aware and active in cleanup.

January 1985

Yesterday, the 2nd, we attended our first Taiwan Christian wedding. Shu-mei, a second year Church and Community student member of our Wed. fellowship, married a final year theological student. The groom had arranged to hire a bus from the Chang Rung High School, a Church girls' high school nearby. We piled in at 8:15 am for the one hour trip to the country village of "Ox Yoke", a real farming village with a nice Church and small kindergarten. The Christmas decorations were still up, a manger scene outside and streamers inside. New character phrases had been pasted on the wall for the wedding and a large 1 + 1 = 1 on the curtain behind the pulpit along with congratulatory characters such as "double happiness" used at weddings. I was surprised that these were in white as weddings traditionally use only red colors - white being the color of death. That seems to be changing in Taiwan now because of the influence of the west. Almost all wedding gowns now are fluffy white things, so our bride came to her wedding all in white. The groom in a black suit with large bow tie, both of them made up to the hilt with rouge and lipstick. The officiant was Ted Ellis, teacher at the Seminary, so things moved along quite quickly. The young pastor of the Church had another wedding at 11:30 so was quite anxious, especially afterwards when picture taking took so long. We actually kept the other bride and groom waiting in their car for 15 minutes.

The thing that bothered us about the ceremony was that the photographers seemed to have right of way over everything. The man videotaping the wedding stood between the pastor (who was up on the pulpit centered raised platform) and the bride with the camera poked a foot from her face as she spoke her vows. The service had many meaningful moments of sharing for the couple. After their vows, they stood facing any group who sang or brought congratulations. The hour must have been tiring for them for they were on their feet the entire time. Different classmates' groups sang appropriate hymns or songs. The families spoke to couple and guests, and then the couple bowed to everyone, their families, the officiating ministers and themselves. An amusing incident was when the groom rolled up the bride's veil after they had been pronounced husband and wife, he bent down to give her a kiss, but she ducked to one side. We learned that this "kissing" is a relatively new import and that many just don't want to show such affection in public.

The picture taking was endless. Each family group, each church which was represented, and each of the Seminary class groups had to have a separate picture with the bride and groom. They had set up some benches outside the Church so that is why we were blocking the preparations for the next wedding. We got into three pictures by being part of different groups. There were about 200 people there to participate, some fifteen or twenty came from a Church where the groom had done his field work last year when they had no pastor. The new pastor (more about him later) came with them, leaving Kaohsiung at 5:40 in the morning in order to get to the village in time. One of the formalities of the past was preserved. As one entered the Church you signed a large embroidered silk piece which will be framed. At the same time you leave your present or red envelope containing money. Gifts of money are counted on to help defray the cost of the wedding feast. We gave NT$500 each a total of US$25. No one has to do this but it is appreciated, of course. And also, there were a few firecrackers, nothing like the non-Christian explosion needed to scare all the devils and spirits away!

The feast was pretty big for a country town, seemed like there were hundreds of people there, relatives and all out of town guests and village elders. We were sitting with students eating watermelon seeds when the head of the groom's family, the eldest uncle, came to get Rev. Ellis and us to go in the house to sit with the bride and groom. We refused as being happy to sit where we were, but 15 minutes later he came to insist as the feast was about to be served. We learned that the problem was one of protocol and seating. If we hadn't changed, they would have had trouble deciding which family members would be invited to sit at this head table. The food was not spectacular as Taiwanese food is not as spicy as Hunanese food, nor is it as well flavored as Cantonese. There were large prawns (cold, served with very sweet mayonnaise), snails (rubbery), a roast pork and pickled bamboo dish, shell fish soup, fish tripe and Chinese chives (B liked it best), fish ball soup to end up with as well as sweet almond soup and a small round wedding cake (sponge) for each table. Served with gallons of strawberry cream soda, we could hardly make it back to the bus. The traditional Chinese wine as well as Taiwan beer was available, but we noted that most of the students and the family abstained. We hope it saved them a lot of money, because most wedding feasts are very expensive because of the amount of wine people consume.

We got home by 3:30 though a number of us stood up in the bus most of the way back to Tainan. We brought the Kaohsiung church group along back to town so they would not have to take so long to get back home. I had a chance to talk with the young Pastor, Jeremy Chao who spent some 3 months in prison at the time of the Kaohsiung incident when Dr. Kao was given his prison sentence. Chao was let off with probation, having served the 3 months prior to trial. He had been involved, somehow, in transporting Mr. Shih from one hiding place to another. He is still under surveillance by the Security police, but as in the case of Dr. Kao, he says he welcomes them into his Church and hopes that all Christians will be a witness to them. He worked for the Bible Society for awhile before a Church was ready to accept him as pastor. It probably takes some courage for most congregations to fly in the face of governmental pressure.

February 19, 1986 - Wednesday

First class of my new course – Gerontology: It was real fun. It is a two hour lecture course, meeting once a week. Timothy Chen is translating and is superb. He doesn't just translate, he interprets concepts and illustrations into meaningful local equivalents. I prepared 25 outlines thinking that as this was an elective course, there would not be that many enrolled. We had to change classrooms when 61 showed up. I found out some had skipped a required English class, so will have to drop them out somehow.

The high spot of the semester were the lectures on "Sex and the Elderly." I had gone over the subject, written out the lecture, and Timothy really did a masterful job translating. Even the students were very respectfully attentive.

Addendum B

LUSHAN INTERNATIONAL LANGUAGE AND CULTURE INSTITUTE
A Program of Nanjing University, The Lushan Scenic Bureau, and The Kuling American School Association

Lushan (Mt. Lu), Jiangxi Province, is one of China's ancient, sacred mountains, shrouded in mist and cooled by soft breezes during the blazing summer months. Rising abruptly 5,000 feet above the Yangtze River in northern Jiangxi Province between Nanjing and Wuhan, Lushan, has for centuries been a place of refuge and learning for mystics and, poets, artists and scholars, monks and missionaries. In the early 20th Century it became a summer retreat called "Kuling" for western missionaries and the summer capital of President Generalissimo Chiang Kaishek. Pearl Buck's family was among the very first foreigners who summered here to escape the blazing heat of the river valley; people from many countries still consider Lushan to be their home in China.

The Kuling American School offered a western education to students year-round on the sacred mount Lu starting in 1916. In the Mao era, the Chairman held several highly important political meetings on Lushan and enjoyed its exceptional climate and natural beauty. Today, Lushan stands unique amongst China's mountains, a blend of Western and Eastern history.

Now designated a UNESCO World Cultural Heritage site, Lushan draws visitors from around the world to view its misty peaks, waterfalls, bamboo forests, scenic lakes and majestic waterfalls. It is home to mainland China's first botanical garden and its oldest academy, a place where multiple religions and peoples of the world gather together. More than 400 unique stone villas remain as lasting reminder of the shared history and deep emotional connections between Westerners and Chinese families, who lived there together in the early 1900's.

The Lushan Language and Culture Institute, located in the mountain village of Kuling, provides an ideal place to study Mandarin and Chinese culture and to explore the historic mountain's history. Escape the blistering heat and the crowds of the big cities and study Chinese in a National Park rich in scenic history. The Lushan Institute is operated by Nanjing University as a joint program of the Lushan Scenic Bureau and the Kuling American School Association.

For full information go to: www.LushanInstitute.com.

Addendum C

BRIEF NOTES ON WHITENER TRAVELS

Australia and New Zealand

After ten days of a self-guided tour of the two islands of scenic New Zealand we had a wonderful visit in the Bay of Islands with Peggy Hawkings, our friend from China days. Her father had carried a sour gooseberry plant from Kuling in China to New Zealand, cultivating it there to become the kiwi fruit. In Sydney we enjoyed seeing Hedley, Peggy and Rosalie Bunton, friends and former coworkers in HongKong.

Nova Scotia

At our B&B at Mahone Bay we chatted with a couple, Alf and Marie Bell, from Canada. We discovered that Alf's parents had been missionaries in China and Alf had attended the Chefoo school in Kuling 1948-49. Incredibly, he actually lived in our house there after we were unable to return to Kuling. He and Marie joined us on our next tour to China.

Mexico:
Copper Canyon

After a few days on Baja with Bob and Marion we had an exciting four-day trip on the narrow gauge railroad which wound along awesome canyons from Las Moches to Chihuahua.

San Miguel d'Allende

Here we visited our daughter, Bonnie, and Tom who were working with local artisans in a tile-making venture. Christmas festivities were special. Outstanding was our trip to Rosario, the largest Monarch butterfly sanctuary.

Cuba – Church Seminar

Lead by Ted Braun, a retired UCC pastor and Cuba expert, this trip was a wonderfully diverse experience, a great help in understanding exotic Cuba, politically and culturally.

Turkey

With a personable, knowledgeable young woman as our guide, our 17-day, 1,500 mile bus tour was a memorable study of ancient and modern Turkey. We bought a 6 X 9-ft, woven rug made by nomads near Mt. Ararat. The symbols on the rug mean mountains, running water, fertility and the four directions – perfect for our mountain house.

Ecuador

Our first Elderhostel in Quito and Banos was also our first visit to South America. In Quito we also visited Eugene and Helen Braun, also former UCC missionaries, who have retired in Quito. Following the excellent Elderhostel, Barbara and I flew to the east coast for a few days. Here in Manta we had another first experience – and the only one of this kind we have ever had in all of our travels. We were mugged on a traveled street by three young men who came from behind, knocked us flat and jerked our cameras from around our necks. When I resisted, one pulled a knife. That and Barbara's screams convinced me to let the camera go. Escaping with only scrapes and bruises, but badly shocked, we were grateful for the very kind attention given us by our Chinese hotel owner who was most distressed. He prepared a special Chinese meal for us and took us in his pickup the next day to the special desert national park we had planned to visit. He called the police regarding the cameras, but we never retrieved them.

Cruises:

The Panama Canal

Our ship went into the Canal - such an interesting procedure - as far as the Lake in the center, and then returned to the Caribbean to make several port calls. including Costa Rica and Cozumel on the tip of Mexico.

Alaska

Joining a church group from Greensboro, we had a delightful cruise up the Inland Waterway from Vancouver to Anchorage. We traveled by train to the marvelous Denali National Park, returning home by air from Fairbanks.

Home Exchange in England – Summer of 1997

We found Ray and Marie Therese Alston through the World Wide Exchange Club. They were quite interested in spending two weeks in our mountain cottage and we were very excited about living in their large home in Crouch End/Hornsey, a suburb of London. We alternated strenuous days of "doing London" with breathers at home on Mount View Road, enjoying the pleasant little garden. The exchange included the use of the car so we made day trips to places like Oxford and Cambridge. We invited Lois, Barbara's sister and her husband, Paul to join us for a grand week. Squeezing into the Alston's little Renault, we meandered to Land's End and Stonehenge. Of interest to Paul was a visit to the location of his WWII Air Force base.

We visited the extraordinarily beautiful Coventry Cathedral the very day of the tragic death of Princess Diana and attended the impressive Sunday service in the Cathedral the next day. Much of the service was interwoven with a most moving remembrance of this beloved young woman. In the following week we made a visit to Buckingham and St. James Palaces and were amazed at the crowds of mourners and mountains of flowers and other tributes.

After the Alston's return, we spent a very pleasant week with them. Both are accomplished musicians. We have kept in touch and have seen them several times on their trips back to the USA.

Sardinia

Our two-week stay in a little villa on the island of Sardinia was another kind of house exchange. Barbara's cousin in California married a Sardinian and though they no longer live there, they have kept their little house in an olive grove as a vacationing place near the family. We happily accepted their offer to stay there and learn about this beautiful island west of Naples and south of Corsica. Their villa is located outside the coastal town of Alghero, an attractive bustling little metropolis. Kim, our daughter, and her partner, Don went with us and we had a wonderful time housekeeping, shopping, and exploring locally.

We had the use of a little Fiat Panda and made frequent trips to the winery of Santa Maria la Palma a co-op where grapes grown locally were brought by the growers. We took our own plastic liter bottles and lined up in front of six pumps; three for white wine (Bianca) and three for red

(Rossa). Tasting is permitted. The bottles are then filled with your choice just as gas is pumped into your car. We really enjoyed the fresh wine with no preservatives – good flavor and very light and only about $3.00 a gallon. Our wine forays were a highlight of our stay.

Our excursions in the little Fiat to places along the scenic coast were experiences out of a travel brochure. All in all it was a very successful adventure.

Italy

At the end of the two weeks, Barbara and I went on to Italy for a week to visit Florence and Venice, fabulous places we had not seen in our earlier travels with the family.

Portugal and Spain in 2009

We call this trip "The Trip to End All Trips"! It was First Class all the way, a striking contrast to our usual "on a shoe string" mode. Barbara's niece, Charme Davidson and husband, Chris, invited us to join them, all expenses paid, on an 18 day marvelous tour - "Paradores and Pousadas of Portugal and Spain". Since the emphasis of the trip was on the special and often historic nature of the lodgings we enjoyed, we list them.

With Charme and Chris - great travel companions, a very congenial tour group, a young Portuguese woman as a gem of a tour guide, and a pleasant and skillful bus driver we had a marvelous trip.

Beginning the tour in Lisbon, we stayed in the Tivoli, a fine hotel where having five pieces of laundry done cost more than the original price of the garments. In Lisbon we were introduced to the gorgeous azulejo (tiles) of Portugal and Spain, and the most delicious custard cream tarts ever!

Traveling on to Evora, we stayed in Pousada dos Loios, a restored 14th century convent. Charming and comfortable, our room number was Cell 02. The city of Evora, now a UNESCO World Heritage Site, was established in Roman times, and right beside our pousada are the ruins of a Roman temple.

Regretfully leaving Portugal, we traveled on into Spain to Carmona where we were lodged in an impressive castle/fortress converted into a beautiful hotel. From Carmona we made trips to Seville seeing the fabulous Alcazar and to Cordoba with its huge Mosque.

Ronda is a charming, unspoiled town with breathtaking views from the edge of the El Tajo Gorge where our parador was located in the restored medieval city hall.

In Granada we toured the magnificent Alhambra and then had an overnight in a former nobleman's enormous home in Ubeda.

En route to Toledo, the capital of medieval Spain, we saw Spain's Happy Pigs. The smoked ham of the region is so good, we were told, because the pigs are free range. They are bathed and fed before being gently euthanized to become an acclaimed delicacy! Toledo's Gothic cathedral was, in our eyes, the most beautiful of all that we saw.

On to Madrid where our parador was the splendid Wellington Hotel. Highlight of the Madrid stay was our afternoon in the marvelous Prado. The actual tour ended here and there was a lovely Farewell Dinner for the tour group.

Charme, Chris and we flew on to Barcelona for a four-night add-on visit. Gaudi's famous unfinished cathedral and other of his creations were highlights. A trip to the Montserrat Monastery on a mountain outside of Barcelona was a grand finale to an incredibly generous gift.

USA & Canada

Though our aim in our travels within our own country, the USA, was not purposely to go to each state, we have almost done that through the years on various trips, too numerous to even list. Up and down the east coast; across the country to California; out to the northwest, Oregon and Washington; deep into the south to New Orleans; out to New Mexico and fabulous Canyon Country. While some of the trips were made for meetings of various sorts, many represent time with family or friends – traveling with them or to them which multiplies the pleasures of the travels. We have crossed the border into Canada – Toronto, Calgary, Regina, the Canadian Rockies, Victoria, and Vancouver. We have been richly blessed with all of these opportunities throughout the years. Observing so many of our Chinese friends seeking opportunity to come to the US, and increasingly appreciative of our own marvelous country and the wonderful diversity of people, we are grateful to be citizens of the United States of America.